UNDERSTANDING PUBLIC RELATIONS

'Edwards thinks deeply about the world we live in, delivering thoughtful, accessible prose on PR's role in society. Ideal for PR students, scholars and practitioners.'

Clea Bourne, Goldsmiths, University of London

'A must-read for any serious PR student or scholar, Edwards' socio-cultural approach presents an important and timely challenge to the dominance of functionalism in the field of public relations.'

Dennis Mumby, The University of North Carolina at Chapel Hill

'Pushes the genre of the public relations text into new territory. Edwards looks beyond organizational boundaries to vividly illustrate and explore the public relations occupation as a social and cultural practice.'

Øyvind Ihlen, University of Oslo

UNDERSTANDING PUBLIC RELATIONS

THEORY, CULTURE AND SOCIETY

LEE EDWARDS

$SAGE

Los Angeles | London | New Delhi
Singapore | Washington DC | Melbourne

SAGE

Los Angeles | London | New Delhi
Singapore | Washington DC | Melbourne

SAGE Publications Ltd
1 Oliver's Yard
55 City Road
London EC1Y 1SP

SAGE Publications Inc.
2455 Teller Road
Thousand Oaks, California 91320

SAGE Publications India Pvt Ltd
B 1/I 1 Mohan Cooperative Industrial Area
Mathura Road
New Delhi 110 044

SAGE Publications Asia-Pacific Pte Ltd
3 Church Street
#10-04 Samsung Hub
Singapore 049483

Editor: Michael Ainsley
Assistant editor: John Nightingale
Production editor: Imogen Roome
Marketing manager: Lucia Sweet
Cover design: Jen Crisp
Typeset by: C&M Digitals (P) Ltd, Chennai, India
Printed in the UK

© Lee Edwards 2018

First published 2018

Apart from any fair dealing for the purposes of research or private study, or criticism or review, as permitted under the Copyright, Designs and Patents Act, 1988, this publication may be reproduced, stored or transmitted in any form, or by any means, only with the prior permission in writing of the publishers, or in the case of reprographic reproduction, in accordance with the terms of licences issued by the Copyright Licensing Agency. Enquiries concerning reproduction outside those terms should be sent to the publishers.

Library of Congress Control Number: 2017955724

British Library Cataloguing in Publication data

A catalogue record for this book is available from the British Library

ISBN 978-1-4739-1309-7
ISBN 978-1-4739-1310-3 (pbk)

At SAGE we take sustainability seriously. Most of our products are printed in the UK using responsibly sourced papers and boards. When we print overseas we ensure sustainable papers are used as measured by the PREPS grading system. We undertake an annual audit to monitor our sustainability.

TABLE OF CONTENTS

Acknowledgements   vi

1 Starting Points: Defining socio-cultural research in public relations   1

2 Public Relations as Promotion: The production and circulation of meaning   23

3 Public Relations, Discourse and Power   45

4 A Political Economy of Public Relations   65

5 Deliberative Democracy and Public Relations   85

6 Public Relations and the Public Sphere   103

7 Public Relations and Globalisation   121

8 Public Relations as an Occupational Field: The professional project   141

9 Race and Class in/and Public Relations   161

10 Feminist Public Relations: Performativity, black feminism, postfeminism   179

11 Ethics, Public Relations and Society   197

12 Conclusion: Public relations beyond the organisation   217

References   225
Index   271

ACKNOWLEDGEMENTS

The majority of this book was written while at the University of Leeds where, in the course of many enlightening conversations with colleagues, students and friends at the School of Media and Communication, I was able to explore how my work might be positioned within a wider community of scholars. I owe a debt of gratitude to the many students and colleagues who helped me develop my thinking along the way, both there and elsewhere. Particular thanks go to the anonymous reviewers of chapters, whose generous comments helped me refine my arguments. I have benefited from the inspiring insights of too many academics to name, but they can be found in Stirling and Edinburgh, Auckland and Waikato, Perth, Melbourne and Sydney, Texas, New York and Georgia, Gothenburg, Oslo, Leeds, Leicester, Sheffield, Lancaster and London. Bob, Marisa, Matthew and Sally have made this book worth writing. Mitsu, Mia and Aunty Greta have helped me understand why it matters.

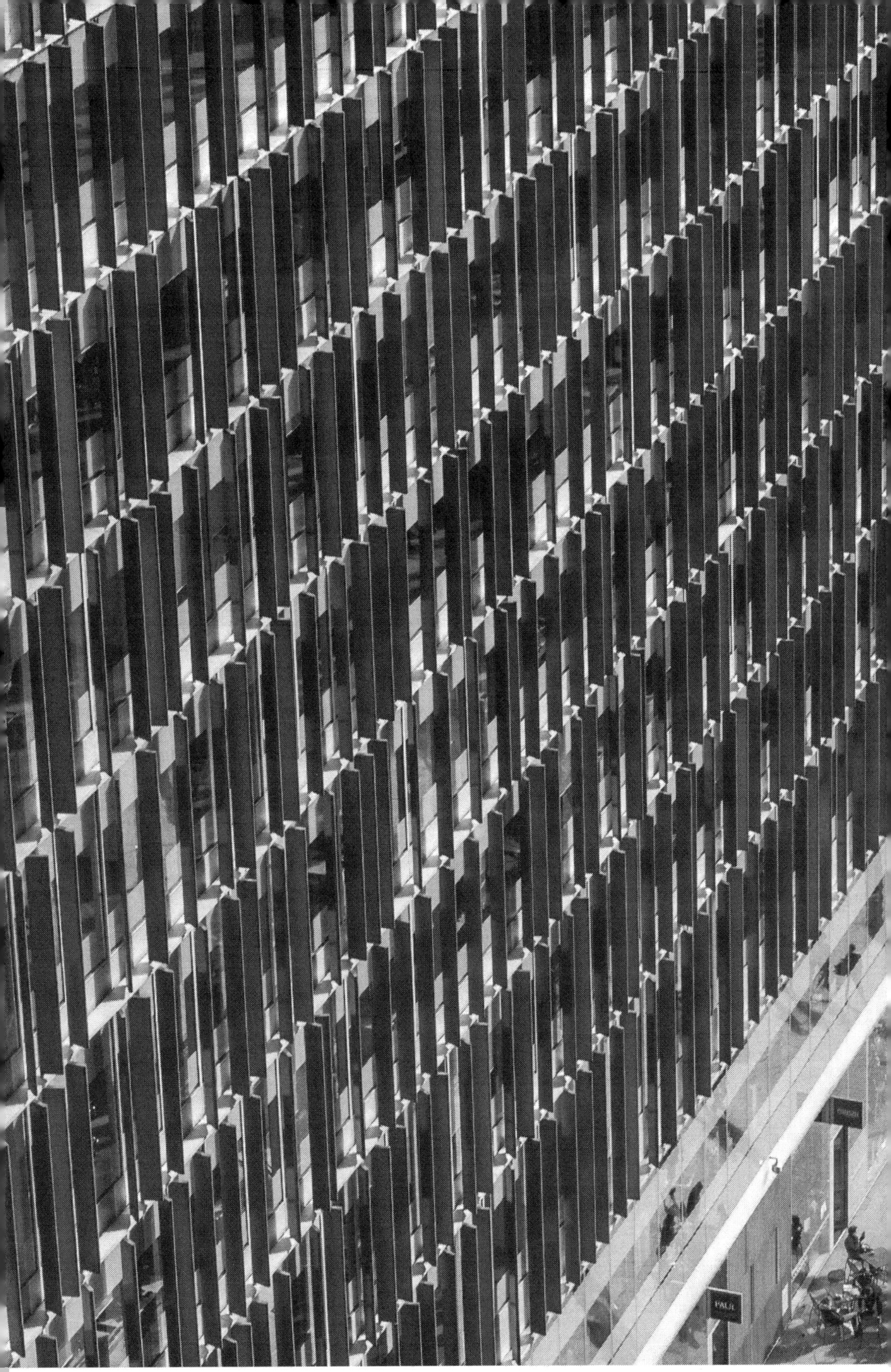
PAUL

CHAPTER 1

STARTING POINTS

DEFINING SOCIO-CULTURAL RESEARCH IN PUBLIC RELATIONS

INTRODUCTION

In the course of the past century, public relations has become a normal part of the promotional environment that surrounds us on a day-to-day basis. It has been integrated into the activities of all kinds of organisations; taken up by individuals to promote narratives of themselves and the world they know through online and digital media; used by high-profile celebrities to manage their public profile; and deployed by governments and terrorist organisations alike to manage public opinion and build alliances. In contrast to the 'hidden persuaders' of the past, public relations work is often very visible: new technologies mean that campaigns make use of private as well as public spaces, engage us in 'conversation', promote 'relationships' with organisations and co-opt our loyalty to maximise their persuasive power. The ubiquity of public relations means that it now has an inescapable influence on us, as part of the resources we draw on both individually and collectively, when we navigate our way through life.

In this book, I argue that understanding the importance and influence of public relations in the contemporary world is best achieved by examining its effects on society and culture. I consciously depart from the functional approach to studying public relations, which tends to focus on its role within organisations. Very little of that approach is reflected in the following pages. Instead, the discussions in each chapter have their roots in the edited collection *Public Relations, Society and Culture* (Edwards and Hodges, 2011), in which we argued that the body of work adopting a socio-cultural approach in public relations was both burgeoning and important. Then, as now, the point was made that organisational analyses of public relations are essential to understanding what practitioners do, how their work fits within organisational structures and how they contribute to organisational survival. However, organisations are not the only places where public relations techniques have been used, nor do organisational boundaries constitute the limits of public relations' effects. While contemporary forms of public relations have developed in the context of modernity, the growth of capitalism, the spread of democracy, globalisation and networked societies, they have their roots in a much longer and more variable history of persuasive communication. Institutions and individuals, from churches, emperors and kings to scientists, politicians, army generals, merchants and slaves, have long used public relations-style tactics, even if they were not formally labelled as such. These histories of public relations remind us that it can take many forms and is used for a wide range of purposes, by formally and informally constituted groups as well as individuals. It may be institutionalised and formalised in modern organisations, but its tools and techniques are much more widespread (L'Etang and Pieczka, 1996).

Given the scale and reach of public relations work, there remains a need for more comprehensive analyses of the occupation as a social and cultural practice in its own right. This is not to say that organisations are unimportant. On the contrary, organisations of all kinds play an enormously significant role as an institutional force that influences our lives.

Yet, studies of public relations focused on its role within organisations do not generally acknowledge this dimension of their existence. Instead, they tend to examine organisations in isolation from their social, cultural and political contexts, and organisational objectives as unproblematic ends. Public relations is understood as a tool to support organisational survival – and the environment is a factor that must be managed along the way.

Adopting a socio-cultural approach redresses this balance somewhat. It complements the detailed understanding we have of practitioners as organisational functionaries, with a broader and more critical lens focused on the implications of their work beyond organisational boundaries (L'Etang, 2008; McKie and Xifra, 2016). It opens up extensive new territory for public relations research, and there has been a socio-cultural 'turn' in public relations scholarship (Edwards and Hodges, 2011), producing creative and interesting work.[1] In the following pages, I bring together a number of different areas of interest for scholars adopting a socio-cultural perspective in their analyses of public relations. It is by no means exhaustive and should be viewed as a set of starting points, a springboard for new work that will continue to develop the field.

In this chapter I set out in detail what is meant by a socio-cultural perspective of public relations, to provide readers with a reference point for the arguments made in the rest of the book. I then consider what aspects of contemporary society and culture underpin the socio-cultural research we might do. These themes reappear throughout the book, and I discuss them here as a reference point for readers to use as they delve into other topics in more detail. Finally, I introduce the structure of the book and provide a brief summary of each chapter.

WHAT IS A SOCIO-CULTURAL APPROACH TO PUBLIC RELATIONS AND WHY IS IT NECESSARY?

What does it mean to explore public relations 'beyond organisational boundaries'? Does such an idea make sense, given that public relations is most often executed by practitioners working on behalf of organisations? It is important to note that socio-cultural research on public relations does not ignore organisations; on the contrary, the point is to interrogate the kinds of influence that organisations have on the way we live our lives. As functional research powerfully illustrates, public relations is a tool through which organisations try to exercise that influence with particular outcomes in mind, but it is also a practice that has agency beyond organisational objectives. It generates change in ways that organisations rarely foresee or plan for, because it has embedded itself deeply in the fabric of our social and cultural practices.

What forms does this embeddedness take? First, public relations draws its tools and techniques from the ways we habitually connect with, communicate with and inform each other about the world around us. Practitioners are encouraged to be in touch with social trends, technologies, communication channels and cultural phenomena, which they use to enhance the relevance and circulation of organisational messages to target audiences. They piggyback off the latest movie or pop sensation, calendar events (Valentine's day, Mother's day, Gay Pride parades, other national days of celebration) or the latest news stories to weave topical themes into their campaigns. They follow audience information-seeking behaviour and place stories where they are most likely to be seen – on Twitter or Instagram, via a blogger or vlogger, via mainstream news sites or in offline spaces. Alternatively, they will adjust their communication around cultural norms to make it more powerful (for example, by challenging norms in a dramatic way) or acceptable (by aligning with norms to make a message more easily understandable). For example, Proctor and Gamble's 'Touch the Pickle' campaign aimed to break taboos around menstruation in India (AFAQS, 2017), while in the UK, TV broadcaster Channel 4's ongoing 'Superhumans' campaign for the Paralympics challenges stereotypes about people with a disability (Channel 4, 2016). In the process of doing all these things, practitioners disembed socio-cultural norms and practices from their original context, relocate them into new environments, and repurpose them in communication that serves specific ends. In this way, public relations both intervenes in and instrumentalises different aspects of society and culture.

Second, the pervasiveness of promotional practices means that public relations-style tools and techniques have themselves become woven into our assumptions about the ways we can and should relate to and engage with others. In an 'attention economy' (Davenport and Beck, 2002), we expect organisations to communicate with us, explain their actions and persuade us to support them. While we may be sceptical and even cynical about their communication, we are likely to be disappointed if they do not respond to our complaints, or critical if they are unable to deal effectively with a crisis. In our relationships with other individuals, we often adopt techniques of self-promotion in our interactions, working with an implicit understanding that to be successful our identities need to be appealing, to stand out, to act as a 'brand' that can generate social and economic benefits – better jobs, greater popularity, more income, greater purpose in life (Lair et al., 2005; Hearn, 2008). We also use brands as resources to build narratives of our own identities – to show our values to others (for example, when we shop for fair trade products, or animal-friendly cosmetics) (Harrison et al., 2005; Arvidsson, 2006; Aronczyk, 2013a).

The integration of promotional thinking into daily life has become so ubiquitous and matter-of-fact that we may not even be aware of it. Nonetheless, it constitutes fertile terrain for public relations to influence the ways in which society and culture are organised, and is the basis for the case that socio-cultural research on public relations is warranted. However, while the idea of a socio-cultural 'turn' in public relations is frequently cited, it is often deployed without further explanation. For the sake of clarity, it is worth considering what is meant in more detail. A precise definition of a 'socio-cultural turn' is not possible (the potential terrain for research – society and culture – is huge and varied) or desirable (definitions have a tendency to produce 'habits of mind' (Margolis, 1993) that can limit the scope of thinking and research). However, the following assumptions about public relations provide a good starting point for understanding the foundations of socio-cultural research and allow us to differentiate it from functional work:[2]

1. Standpoints for understanding public relations are many and varied.
2. Public relations is shaped by the cultures and societies in which it operates.
3. Public relations has agency; it intervenes in society beyond the organisational context, and generates some kind of change.
4. The effects of public relations work must be measured in social and cultural terms, as well as in terms of organisational interests.
5. Public relations is value-driven rather than value-neutral; it has the potential to engender both power and resistance.

Characteristics of research based on these assumptions are variable, but there are some commonalities across most studies. First, the focus of empirical investigations is on revealing public relations as a 'contingent, cultural activity that forms part of the communicative process by which society constructs its symbolic and material "reality"' (Edwards and Hodges, 2011: 3). The changes it generates will be intentional (built into the public relations strategy) as well as unintentional (unforeseen effects of campaigns on the way we think about the world, our place within it, and our relationships with others). Analyses go beyond whether or not organisational objectives have been met, to reveal the wider social, cultural and political consequences that those objectives might have instigated.

Second, the relationship between public relations and society is mutually transformative. Public relations is shaped by its social and cultural context and is 'a locus of transactions that produce emergent social and cultural meanings' (Edwards and Hodges, 2011: 4), where transactions are events that happen 'across actors who are aspects of a relationally integrated whole ... the actors *are* the continuously emerging meaning in a trans-action' (Simpson, 2009: 1334) In other words, because public relations stimulates transactions between societal actors, it also contributes to their meaning in relation to each other and over time. The changes to the fabric of society and culture that result are, in turn, integrated back into public relations identities, processes and practices.

Third, research tends to complicate the identity and outcomes of public relations by rejecting simplistic explanations of cause and effect and instead searching for complexity in context and practice. As Caroline Hodges and I have noted, '[t]he messiness of day to day practice, with its contradictions and inconsistencies, should not be regarded as a "difficulty" of public relations, but part of its ontology, of the continuous flow of transactions that is public relations reality, simultaneously producing, enacting and feeding back into, social and cultural norms' (Edwards and Hodges, 2011: 8). Fluidity and change are often at the forefront of analyses, with rigid categorisations less common. Persistent continuities in social and cultural hierarchies remain crucial to explanations of public relations' impact on society, but they are rarely framed as absolute.

Fourth, socio-cultural analyses of public relations engage in various ways with questions of power. They may focus on the way public relations affects the distribution of power between groups in specific contexts or across society, its capacity to empower or disempower different audiences, its use as a tool for securing or resisting power by different organisations, the ways in which different identities, behaviours and values are represented as more or less powerful in public relations discourse, or the way power operates within the profession. The focus on power is crucial because it reveals how public relations work plays into the struggles between dominant and subordinated groups that mark all societies.

Finally, socio-cultural work on public relations is concerned with how public relations is experienced and understood in people's day-to-day lives. It 'shifts the ontological and epistemological focus of the field towards the socially constructed nature of practice, process and outcomes' (Edwards and Hodges, 2011: 3). Research is most often guided by an interpretive epistemology and qualitative methodologies; questions of meaning, representation and lived experience all take priority over measurement and quantification, although the latter may serve a useful purpose in some studies.

If these are the characteristics of the socio-cultural turn in public relations research, then what kinds of questions do researchers adopting this approach actually grapple with? The short answer is that they address public relations' role in many of the long-standing analytical challenges that arise when we try to understand how societies and cultures operate. Below, I explore some of these questions in more detail. The discussion here is necessarily brief: many books have been written on each of the areas I discuss, and many different theories ventured. This is not the place to review them all in great depth. However, it is important to introduce them because they are relevant to many of the chapters that follow, and the debates about them reappear in the pages of this book in different ways.

HOW ARE SOCIETIES STRUCTURED AND ORGANISED?

Social structures are institutionalised ideological and material systems that provide the parameters for the ways we live our lives and organise ourselves into groups within society (Swingewood, 2000). They are grounded in different aspects of identity, such as our gender, class, caste, disability, 'race' or religion, which are constructed as more or less valuable in society (Hall, 1997a).[3] In the case of gender, for example, women tend to be normatively viewed as subordinate to men; in the case of 'race' and ethnicity, people who are white tend to be privileged over people of colour; for class, higher levels of education, wealth and white-collar employment tend to attract higher status; and LGBT identities tend to be subordinated to heterosexuality and cisgender.[4] These categorisations play a role in determining what kinds of opportunities are available to us – for example, employment, healthcare or housing. Consequently, social hierarchies are reproduced through institutional structures such as the education system, the labour market and the housing market (Bourdieu, 2005).

Structures matter because the social hierarchies that emerge from them translate into systemic, institutionalised (dis)advantage (Ridgeway and Correll, 2004; Reskin, 2012): if we have better access to material resources such as education, housing, healthcare and employment, and to symbolic resources such as status and worth, then we are likely to enjoy a life that is marked by greater wealth, privilege and choice about our life course. Good schools and housing, for example, tend to be concentrated in wealthy areas and are therefore more accessible to upper-class groups; access to good healthcare can also be determined by income and housing; senior positions in organisations tend to be occupied by white men, rather than people of colour or women. We also pass on privilege to our children, both through inherited wealth and through the norms, values and attitudes that we communicate to them in their formative years (Bourdieu, 1984). The opposite is true for those whose social position is disadvantageous: their access to material, social and cultural resources that might support social mobility for future generations is likely to be much more limited.

For socio-cultural research on public relations, the importance of structures raises questions about the degree to which public relations plays into the perpetuation of structural inequalities. On the one hand, it may reinforce social hierarchies by presenting them as taken-for-granted realities rather than socially constructed categories. It may also reinforce the legitimacy of material structures – the segregation of education, employment or healthcare by wealth, gender or age, for example – as ideal or appropriate ways of achieving social goals. On the other hand, it may be used to challenge these same things, when marginalised groups use it to object to the categorisation of their identities, or when new groups and organisations attempt to change the institutional status quo.

HOW DO INDIVIDUALS MAKE CHOICES ABOUT THEIR LIVES?

How our identities are defined by society and how resources are allocated are, of course, related, but the causal link between them is complicated by the normativity of structure: that is, we often regard structural norms as common sense, integrate them into the ways we conduct our lives, and use them to make sense of the world (Giddens, 1984). We take our privilege and our disadvantage for granted, and thereby perpetuate structures that constrain the lives of some while facilitating progress for others. In other words, structures are an important and relatively stable source of social inequality. They do not fully determine our lives; people can and do 'break out' of social hierarchies, achieving social mobility and other forms of change that counter prescribed pathways. Our capacity to confound the deterministic power of structures is a matter of agency, or the degree to which we can make choices about our lives that are independent of structural norms.

Most theorists agree that complete independence from structure is not possible because structures provide the context for action (Haugaard, 2002). In our relationships with others, we therefore inevitably reproduce structure because we draw on its characteristics and resources (Giddens, 1979: 88). Nonetheless, the reality that we do make choices that sometimes go against structural norms needs an explanation, and this is most often found in framings of structure and agency as a duality rather than totally independent entities, as well as in our human ability to reflect on our lives. As reflexive beings, we have the capacity to step back from situations, understand them from a perspective external to ourselves, use new information that comes our way to inform our opinions, and make choices that incorporate the insights derived from distancing ourselves in this way (Giddens, 1991).

The pragmatist philosopher George Herbert Mead, for example, places reflexivity at the heart of human agency, proposing an interpretation of selfhood that is grounded in sociality, or 'the situatedness of actors in multiple temporally evolving relational contexts' (Emirbayer and Mische, 1998: 969). Mead conceptualises agency as the development of reflexive capabilities to make choices about action, based on a notion of self that incorporates both the individual and the social in the form of the 'me' and the 'I' (Mead, 1934). The 'me' arises in relation to the 'generalised other', 'the organized community or social group which gives to the individual his unity of self' (Mead, 1934: 154). The 'me' reflects on the self from the point of view of this generalised other. Inextricably linked with the 'me' is the 'I', an aspect of the self that reflects independently of the generalised other, and is a source of innovation and change. The actions of the 'I' are ultimately incorporated into the 'me' that, in turn, engages with and may alter the social environment. Building on Mead, Emirbayer and Mische (1998) argue that agency must account for temporality and context, since

> [t]he ways in which people understand their own relationship to the past, future, and present make a difference to their actions; changing conceptions of agentic possibility in relation to structural contexts profoundly influence how actors in different periods and places see their worlds as more or less responsive to human imagination, purpose, and effort. (Emirbayer and Mische, 1998: 974)

They suggest agency is best understood as a three-dimensional, temporal and relational engagement with structure involving reflections on past, stable patterns of thought and action; imagining future possibilities for action; and choosing actions from a range of options available in the present (1998: 970). These three dimensions of agency co-exist in any situation, but their relative dominance will vary.

The degree to which structural power is subject to what Giddens (1984) termed a 'dialectic of control' is a matter of intense debate. Skeggs et al. (2008), for example, demonstrate that reflexivity is a resource stratified by class, rather than being universally available to all. Indeed, if the ability to choose how to use structural resources (our gender, age, education, for example) in our interactions with others and reflect on those choices were common, one would expect a more variable distribution of resources over time along with corresponding changes in social status (Stewart, 2001). In reality, social mobility is remarkably slow to evolve (Social Mobility Commission, 2017). Moreover, our choices are not independent of history – our past informs how we see ourselves and the possibilities available to us, as well as determining how others see us (Hall, 1990; Ahmed, 2006). In the digital age, the online world both constrains and facilitates agency, offering enormous possibilities for empowerment, but also opening up individuals to judgement and ostracisation. Given the impossibility of stepping outside our social context, perhaps a more appropriate understanding of agency is that it takes different forms and is expressed differently, depending on the aspects of identity (race, class, gender, and other forms of status) that come into play in a particular context (see, for example, Hulko, 2009; Rampersad, 2014; Blum-Ross and Livingstone, 2017; Vivienne, 2017).

When focused on agency, socio-cultural research on public relations engages with the ways in which the interplay between structure and agency is shaped by public relations activities. Some campaigns may facilitate choice and reflexivity, for example, by bringing new information to light and revealing new possibilities for action, or by making visible the lives of 'others' and prompting us to reflect differently on our own privilege or disadvantage. Others may simply reinforce structural norms by reiterating and normalising historical relations, reinforcing what we understand as our 'place' in society, and reduce our capacity to consider alternatives. The specific circumstances of particular campaigns – the country, target audience, organisations involved and the wider political, economic, social and cultural environment – will also affect the impact they have on agency, and so analysing agency in socio-cultural research would place public relations work in these contexts in order to fully understand its effects. It would also recognise that our capacity to act in relation to others can vary greatly, depending on the structural parameters we are faced with.

HOW IS IDENTITY CONSTRUCTED AND REPRESENTED IN THE CONTEXT OF A COMMUNITY?

Questions of how we make sense of our identity and communicate it to others are closely related to the ideas about the self that underpin agency, and link the idea of an intrinsic self to the social context. Identity is generally understood to be socially constructed; that is, it develops through our interactions and involves choices about how we want to be understood, positioned or seen by both ourselves and others. The changing conditions of modernity have included an increase in the need for individuals to take personal responsibility for those choices, including decisions about how we construct our identities symbolically (for example, by associating ourselves with different brands), physically (for example, by wearing particular clothes, hairstyles, tattoos, jewellery) and cognitively (by understanding and communicating our identities to ourselves and others via face-to-face or online channels such as social media) (Beck et al., 1994).

Giddens (1991: 75) suggests that '[t]he self is seen as a reflexive project, for which the individual is responsible …. We are not what we are, but what we make of ourselves'. Reifying reflexivity to this extent would assume that all our choices are rationally and consciously made, with the individual a free-floating subject, disconnected from structural constraints. Even for those people for whom reflexivity is a ready skill, this is an unrealistic assumption. And yet it is true that contemporary popular culture is awash with models and techniques for self-management (Banet-Weiser, 2012; Blum-Ross and Livingstone, 2017; Hearn, 2017). The different modes of selfhood they suggest introduce opportunity as well as the risk that our choices turn out to be suboptimal or have unintended consequences. From this perspective, '[s]elf-actualisation is … a balance between opportunity and risk' (Giddens, 1991: 78).

History plays an important role in how identity emerges: we make choices not only in the present and as a function of our ambitions for the future, but also based on what we know about ourselves and others from the past. The physical body plays an important role here as 'the signifier of the condensation of subjectivities in the individual' over time (Hall, 1996: 11), a basis for stereotyping our identities. Stereotypes attributed to us produce preconceptions about our abilities and our right to belong in certain locations and groups, acting as 'conditions of arrival' that accompany us into different locations. In predetermining who we 'are' for others, these (incomplete) discourses of identity generate subject positions which others orient towards, shaping our experience in different ways, marginalising some, while welcoming others (Puwar, 2004; Ahmed, 2006). In our individual responses to these subjectivities, we may partially or fully conform to or resist them, reinterpret or reject them. Correspondingly, identity should never be understood as complete or final, but rather as something that emerges continuously in a fluid, ongoing process as we encounter new environments and subject positions to which we must react. As Hall (1990: 222) notes, '[w]ho speaks, and the subject who is spoken of, are never identical, never exactly in the same place. Identity is not as transparent or unproblematic as we think. … [W]e should think, instead, of identity as a "production", always a process, and always constituted within not outside, representation'.

Questions of how identity is formed, maintained and represented are central to socio-cultural research on public relations. The call for practitioners to 'connect' and manage 'relationships' with audiences inevitably entails appealing to us as individuals with personal hopes and aspirations. The latter provide the material for constructing public relations discourses that offer a pathway to realising those aspirations, by associating ourselves with different kinds of products, services, causes or political identities in ways that allow us to be, and be seen as, particular 'types' of people (ethical, 'cool', technologically savvy, connected, professional). Public relations campaigns also draw on stereotypical identities that can act as a 'shortcut' for us to interpret the messages that are being communicated (for example, associating women with the family, the domestic sphere and 'emotional' work, associating men with professional status, physical work outside the home). Socio-cultural research on public relations interrogates both the use of identity in campaigns as well as the ways identity 'cues' and stereotypes are taken up or challenged by audiences. Identities also play into social hierarchies, and critical research would investigate how the power of certain groups is perpetuated by the protection and reification of their identities in campaigns, as well as how others might assert their identities from the margins, in order to achieve greater visibility and recognition.

HOW DO WE MANAGE TO LIVE HARMONIOUSLY TOGETHER?

In any society, there is an inevitable tension between the need for individuals to compromise with others in order to sustain a peaceful co-existence and the desire to serve one's own personal interests. Reaching agreement about how to manage these tensions is an important social process, and analysing how it is achieved helps us to understand how societies come to establish the norms and values of community life, as well as how that life should be governed. That said, the tension between collective and individual interests is permanent, and makes it impossible to have a situation where agreement is constant. Consequently, the focus of many theorists working in this area has been on how disagreement and conflict might play out.

Debates revolve around the pre-conditions for debate and disagreement to be managed in a positive way, and have attracted detailed theoretical investigations of the role of conflict in social life. The quality of deliberation between individuals and groups is crucial. Jürgen Habermas, for example, has argued for the pursuit of the public sphere, an ideal discursive space where members of society engage in discussion about matters of public interest and challenge decisions made by those who govern society (Habermas, 1989, 1996). For Habermas, deliberation in the public sphere should be based on equal status between participants, inclusivity of all those affected by an issue, rational argument and a focus on pursuing agreement about the common good, rather than the realisation of individual interests (Garnham, 1992; Lunt and Livingstone, 2013; see Chapter 6). Critics have challenged some of Habermas's assumptions, arguing that multiple public spheres exist, focused on different issues and group interests (Fraser, 1990), or that deliberation plays out across a range of different locations and in a range of forms (Dryzek, 2000). The interconnectedness of societies across time and space in the context of globalisation has led to the suggestion that public spheres should be transnational, focused on challenging international regulatory bodies that have much greater power over how we live than national governments (Fraser, 2007; Nash, 2014). Others argue that the emphasis on reaching agreement is misplaced, because disagreement is inherent to social life; instead, the focus should be on engaging with those who disagree with us respectfully, as antagonists rather than adversaries (Mouffe, 1999; see Chapters 5 and 6 later).

Another way of looking at the problem of living harmoniously together is by examining how we actually reach agreement about things once we are engaged in debate. Luc Boltanski and his colleagues have argued that we do this through a dialectical process of justification and critique, where different principles for organising social life are drawn on during debates. The disconnect between them is overcome only when a higher principle of agreement is identified that all parties to the discussion can accept. These situations are always temporary, however, because 'ordinary people … never stop suspecting, wondering and submitting the world to tests' (Boltanski and Thévenot, 2006 [1991]: 37). Moreover, the inherent plurality of a globalised world means that new information is constantly circulating and alternative 'readings' of a situation always come into play, prompting a renewed cycle of justification and critique (Boltanski and Thévenot, 2006 [1991]; see also Edwards, 2018).

How do these insights inform socio-cultural research into public relations? Like media theorists, who have asked difficult questions about the ways that media industries influence our engagement with political debates both positively (by making information available to us) and negatively (by marginalising some voices), public relations theorists need to ask questions about how the promotional work carried out by practitioners on behalf of different groups contributes to the quality, scope and inclusivity of discussions about matters of public concern and interest. Just as the role of the media is complex and context-dependent, the role of public relations needs to be understood as fluid, sometimes contradictory, but always important. The ubiquity and relative cheapness of public relations techniques, particularly in the digital age, where messages circulate more freely and rapidly than ever before, means it will be used by all kinds of groups wishing to make their voices heard. In public relations texts, we see forms of justification and critique, the different principles that people draw on for their positions, and the ways in which those positions might converge over time. Detailed empirical work focused on this complex role is a mainstay of socio-cultural approaches to public relations.

HOW IS SOCIETY CHANGING?

Persistent questions of structure and agency, identity and harmonious living are all inflected by contemporary social conditions, and so understanding how society is changing is fundamental to how we answer each of the previous challenges. In recent years, the rise of neoliberalism, the digital age and the emergence of networked societies have all resulted in deep shifts in the fabric of society and culture, and are particularly important to understanding public relations today.

THE RISE OF NEOLIBERALISM

Neoliberal ideology is grounded in a belief in the fundamental importance of individual freedoms to the management of society and the pursuit of capital (Harvey, 2005). Manifest in economic and political arrangements, it leads to the prioritisation of private property, individual choice and free market systems over public ownership, collective welfare and state interventions. Its popularity began during the global financial crisis of the 1970s, when the collapse of Keynesian economics led to worldwide recession and a renewed and strategic interest among elites in the preservation of their wealth. Neoliberalism promised a path to reducing state management of their assets, opening up new opportunities for capital accumulation and limiting the power of troublesome institutions such as unions and activist movements. Thus, it has always been a mechanism for constructing and maintaining inequality, rather than overcoming it (Harvey, 2005).

The proactive promotion of neoliberal principles during the 1970s, through think-tanks, economic advisors and global institutions such as the International Monetary Fund and the World Bank, eventually led to governments worldwide adopting neoliberal policies that position the market as the main mechanism for managing all sorts of social arrangements. This normalisation of neoliberalism as a rationale for action in a wide range of contexts (Couldry, 2010) has reified markets as the ultimate mechanism for exchanging public and private goods, deregulation and competition as the parameters for exchange, and the consumer as a figure to which producers must orient themselves. These forms of market logic now affect sectors not formerly thought of in market terms, such as education, healthcare, public transport and the media, because they generate public rather than private goods.

Once markets become the primary mechanism for the distribution of resources and wealth, the language of markets becomes more visible in sectors where it was previously unknown, and organisations begin to act in accordance with market principles (see, for example, Sanders, 2012; Cronin, 2016). At the same time, other ideas and priorities relating to public life, collective welfare and the common good become neglected, are often absent from public and organisational discourse, and the language to frame them as a viable alternative to markets becomes less practised and easier to dismiss with hegemonic, market-based arguments. Consumption is now used to describe our use of anything from toilet paper to university education; we are designated consumers and customers in the process; and organisations focus on measuring satisfaction, value for money, appropriate pricing and good service in the process of establishing their legitimacy (Du Gay and Salaman, 1992).

Understanding the environment as a market also means that organisations must recognise the competition they face from other institutions and sectors, and correspondingly prioritise promotional activities in order to be visible and manage their reputation. Branding, for example, thrives under neoliberalism, while the public relations industry has grown exponentially as the ideology has extended its global reach (see Chapters 4 and 7). The power of promotional work can seem unassailable in the context of the hegemonic rationality of markets for organising our collective lives. For organisations, promotional logic is now indispensable and drives many decisions about production, as well as being a mechanism for managing stakeholder engagement, reputation and consumption (see Chapter 2). The power of marketisation and promotional logic to regulate even our own personal identity management has become enormous. We are encouraged to think of ourselves as a 'brand', something to shape, adapt, instrumentalise and ultimately use in our pursuit of a better life (Lair et al., 2005; Hearn, 2008, 2012; Thumim, 2012). Public relations plays into these dynamics in an important way: it benefits from them as an industry; it perpetuates the normalisation of promotional logic; and it provides the tools for individuals and organisations to compete with others in the way that market logic prescribes. On the other hand, it can also give voice and visibility to alternative ideologies that might challenge neoliberalism, and be used to reassert the importance of collective welfare and the public good (Thörn, 2007; Taylor, 2010; Sommerfeldt, 2013; Edwards, 2016b).

THE DIGITAL AGE

The expansion of digital technologies since the last decades of the twentieth century has produced a world where digital modes of connection and communication pervade every aspect of our lives. Digital technologies are fundamental to the processes of time–space distanciation and disembedding that Giddens describes: relationships are no longer bound by geography, but can be conducted in a shared digital space that persists regardless of geographical or temporal constraints (Giddens, 1990). Our means of communication, connection and community-building have been transformed. The digital age is also characterised by datafication, or a world where quantification and numbers carry enormous power, and the 'desire for numbers' drives action among organisations and individuals, including the normalisation of data mining processes that deliver big data. This desire for numbers is accompanied by a desire for more: more likes, more shares, more hits, more followers – all evidenced numerically and demonstrating sociability, connectedness and status for organisations and individuals as digital participants (Kennedy, 2016).

Digital technologies have transformed the conditions for public relations work. In organisations, the variety, speed and reach of communication allow messages to be carried further and faster than before, and generate the capacity to create connections between them and their desired audiences across the globe (Zerfass et al., 2017). In the media, new outlets for public relations work have emerged as platform innovations, while enhanced engagement with audiences means that eye-witness footage, bloggers, citizen journalists and alternative news sources now compete with dominant news producers – who in turn have consolidated their online presence (Jenkins, 2006). In civic life online connections have the capacity to take small-scale activism and political engagement to a wider, potentially international public (Castells, 2012). By communicating via the internet and social media platforms, social movements can raise their profile and prompt action among widely dispersed audiences, while politicians and their parties can instantaneously adjust messages based on feedback from citizens, to appeal more convincingly to voters (Dahlberg, 2001; Strömbäck and Kiousis, 2011; Coleman and Price, 2012; Gerbaudo, 2012).

These extensive connections also characterise the way we conduct personal relationships in the digital age, using all sorts of digital platforms to tell people about our lives, stay connected with friends and family, build our networks, access information and otherwise self-promote in ways that would have been unthinkable in the pre-digital age. Digital communication has become deeply embedded in the ways we present ourselves, our activities and our relationships; the personal narratives that populate social media appear authentic: 'open and honest and close to a "true self"' (Lüders, 2008: 697; Senft and Baym, 2015). Digital self-representations can also be a route to speaking politically for or as others, delivering 'authentic accounts of individual "ordinary people" in the context of power-laden social relations' (Thumim, 2012: 4) and potentially contesting existing patterns of discursive and material authority. The public relations industry can take advantage of our use of these very visible connections and platforms in order to both normalise and personalise its persuasive work.

However, there are significant downsides to the digital age, which are marked by tensions that arise from the openness of digital technologies, the ease with which they can be used and the connectedness they offer. These advantages simultaneously generate opportunities for surveillance, control and manipulation of communication and relationships. For organisations, information that previously stayed behind closed doors is now often discoverable online or may be leaked and circulated rapidly and widely, while the openness of digital media threatens the ability to control communication, particularly in crisis situations. In the case of the media, the openness of digital platforms, the ease with which anyone can create content, and increasing competition between popular news sites to attract large audiences and ensure stories travel by audiences liking and sharing them, mean that the line between truth and entertainment can become blurred. This leaves us vulnerable to the circulation of fake and manipulated news on a worrying scale, with the potential to affect the shape of civic and political life (Allcott and Gentzkow, 2017; Levin, 2017).

Even the potential for civic life that digital technologies offer aside from our engagement with media is limited: online activism may not be sustainable in the long term and could undermine more traditional forms of protest (Harlow and Guo, 2014), while the 'echo chamber' effect of the internet, where we tend to search for or hear about events and individuals that we agree with, is exacerbated by the algorithms used in search engine and social media platforms that point us towards content based on our online history and preferences (Barberá et al., 2015; Birchall and Coleman, 2015). This diminishes the opportunities we have to encounter and engage with 'others', or with new perspectives, arguments and information, and thereby prevents the development of an expansive online public sphere.

On a personal level, digital technologies act as a ritualised system of mediated routines (Schroeder and Ling, 2014), and constrain the potential for solidarity with others by prioritising and facilitating some norms of communicative practice over others. As Thumim (2012) notes, self-representations in the digital world are always mediated by their form and function; Facebook, Twitter, Instagram and Snapchat all constrain as well as facilitate what we say, promoting certain types of self-representation over others and pre-empting the connections we make through the algorithms that deliver our information feeds.

From a commercial perspective, the more we use digital platforms, the more we enable the monitoring, analysis and commercialisation of our communication because the habits of our daily life are revealed with every key we press or screen we swipe. For those who want to understand or control our activities, the data they obtain from our engagement with social media, online shopping, web browsing and information searching provide a goldmine of information that allows them to 'know' us through our online activity, often without our knowledge (Turow, 2011; Hearn, 2017). Organisations monitor and monetise our connections and community-building activities, pushing commerce into previously private spaces and targeting us on our phones, laptops, gaming machines and other devices (Andrejevic, 2002). State surveillance is also on the increase, justified by a 'war on terror' where the online world is presented as a location for radicalisation and a source of dangerous connections rather than of community life (Amoore, 2009).

In the context of socio-cultural research on public relations, the digital age raises questions about the role played by the occupation both in facilitating the advantages of digital technologies for individuals, groups and organisations, and in perpetuating more problematic aspects of the digital age, including datafication, surveillance and the instrumentalisation and marketisation of the private sphere. Included in the contemporary arsenal of public relations are tactics that encourage us to share, like, create or promote content on behalf of clients, integrate data analytics and search engine optimisation, and manipulate algorithms. When these activities are done unreflexively, without concern for our subjugation to data, our vulnerability to surveillance and abuse, or the 'free labour' we offer in the process of engaging online (Terranova, 2000), public relations contributes directly to the disadvantages of the digital age even as it benefits from the community and connectivity it offers. How and why this happens is critical to understanding public relations' effects on local and global inequalities in contemporary society and culture.

NETWORKED SOCIETIES

Understandings of societies as networks have developed in opposition to theories based on structure and agency, and are a response to the changes in society that have emerged as a result of globalisation, technological change, digitisation and the rise of information economies (Castells, 2000; Benkler, 2006). Network theories focus on the web of interactions between many different kinds of human and non-human social actors (technologies, material resources, channels of communication, discourse and people) that define and direct activities in all aspects of our day-to-day lives (Callon, 1986). For example, networks of actors emerge on a global scale to constitute the global finance industry, the global development industry, the global advertising industry and, of course, the public relations industry. Networks also emerge on a much smaller, local scale – for example, around local schools, community groups, or in work contexts. Networks are fluid and constantly evolving, extending over space and time, but also shrinking time because of the speed of digital technologies that facilitate them (Castells, 2000).

Social and organisational networks are bound together by 'communication networks that process knowledge and thoughts to make and unmake trust, the decisive source of power' (Castells, 2009: 16). Actors program communication networks to ensure they contribute to the 'ideas, visions, projects and frames' (Castells, 2009: 46) that are the principles on which the network is based. Different communication networks expand and compete with others for communicative dominance, and as they intersect, the points of contact generate constant change and opportunities for new connections. Thus, networks evolve through a process 'by which conscious social actors of multiple origins bring their resources and beliefs to others, expecting in return to receive the same, and even more: the sharing of a diverse world, thus ending the ancestral fear of the other' (Castells, 2009: 38).

By definition, networks are contingent and emerging because all actors are constantly engaged in some form of action that influences the network. Agency is relational, and structure (conceptualised as the organisation and logic of the network) continually evolves; networked power is therefore diffuse and fluid. Actors can only become powerful by co-opting other actors in a network, but such situations cannot last because of the constant activity that characterises networks (Latour, 2005). Nonetheless, two nodal positions are particularly important in networks: programmers, which define the internal purpose and parameters of the network, and switchers, which facilitate communication between networks by sharing resources and promoting strategic co-operation. Programmers and switchers can be any actor that facilitates action: an individual, organisation, technology, culture, or even another network (Castells, 2009). In addition, some network actors serve as 'centres of calculation', or locations for the accumulation and distribution of information in a stable form (for example, in the world of higher education, degree programmes, textbooks and highly cited scholars might serve this function). As this 'inscribed' information circulates and becomes embedded in the network, it transforms into knowledge that eventually becomes 'black-boxed' – normative and taken for granted as fact (Latour, 2005).

The optimistic view of networked societies is that they create opportunities for social connection and a greater capacity for social change (Benkler, 2006). Network analyses certainly reveal spaces where individuals and groups come together to resist the deterministic power of structural norms and work with others to pursue change. While these activities can scale up to be important social movements (for example, the Indignados movement, or the anti-globalisation movement that has emerged from protests at the 1999 World Trade Organization Ministerial Conference in Seattle: see Juris, 2005; Anduiza et al., 2014), there are questions about how they can generate lasting changes in governance (Couldry, 2012). Networks may be always 'underway', but they are also constructed from pre-existing hierarchies, where some actors have more power than others to occupy powerful nodal positions – large corporations, for example, are more likely to be able to act as programmers than small companies (Castells, 2009). Challenging this kind of institutionalised power is an ongoing struggle. As Benkler (2006) notes, the potential for networked societies to offer liberation ultimately depends on the choices we make about how to implement and control the new technologies that underpin so much of our networked interactions.

Networked analyses of communication and of society as a whole broaden the scope of public relations theory significantly, because they require us to take a step back from traditional approaches analysing what practitioners or organisations do, to explore *why* they are able to do what they do. How public relations works and the effects it has are reconceived as a result of the associations between all kinds of different actors, always contingent on the specific circumstances in which they emerge. Audiences, practitioners and organisations can be understood as complex clusters of actors rather than single entities, including not only people, but also the technologies, capabilities and networks those people access as well as the knowledge they have about relevant issues and the resources they draw on to act. Network analyses also reveal the important roles practitioners can play as programmers and switchers and help to explain why public relations discourses disperse across society in unpredictable ways (Somerville, 1999). Public relations may be understood as an attempt to program networks by framing communication in particular ways, but practitioners may also be switchers, creating connections between networks as they communicate with different audiences. Network analyses are also helpful in illustrating the way that the public relations industry, with its clusters of practitioners, technologies, social networks and media access, can be a centre of calculation in a network (Schölzel and Nothhaft, 2016), normalising particular forms of knowledge that become black-boxed and exert a powerful influence on network logic.

STRUCTURE OF THE BOOK

Structure, agency, identity, collective living and social change all provide ways of understanding the environmental conditions in which the five assumptions of socio-cultural research on public relations are realised. Treating them as separate entities is somewhat misleading, in so far as our experience of them is not parcelled up into separate moments. They are deeply entwined in our day-to-day lives, articulating differently in different social, cultural, political and economic circumstances, and their influence is composite rather than discrete. Correspondingly, there are no definitive answers to questions about the relationship that public relations has with each of them. Their complexity inevitably generates multiple avenues for exploring the mutual influence between them and the public relations industry, its practices and practitioners. They provide an ongoing challenge for public relations researchers interested in socio-cultural analyses and offer many different starting points for theoretical and empirical work, some of which are explored in the course of this book.

In each chapter I address a dimension of social and cultural life that has attracted some attention from public relations scholars, but is under-researched. The aim is to reflect on what is known about public relations in these areas, but also to provide new analyses that will generate an impetus for innovative research in the field. I begin by focusing in Chapter 2 on promotional cultures, carving out an understanding of the role that public relations has in the promotional practices that permeate all our lives. Chapter 3 focuses on the discursive dimensions of social life, and the inherent nature of public relations as a politically significant communicative intervention in social and cultural arrangements. In Chapter 4, I draw on political economic theory to explore how the distribution of power and wealth across the globe both shapes and is shaped by public relations. The complex reality of public relations work in deliberative democracy is the focus of Chapters 5 and 6, which engage with deliberative systems and the public sphere to explore how we might imagine public relations as a productive (though not always positive) democratic force.

Globalisation is addressed in Chapter 7, where I consider how public relations contributes to both the hegemonic dynamics of globalisation and to pockets of resistance, opportunity and change. In Chapter 8, the focus moves on to an examination of the occupational field and its narratives, structures and cultures, to consider how the imperative to survive shapes the ways that public relations is framed and legitimised both to its own practitioners and to the clients and audiences that it serves. The inequalities of race, class and gender that haunt public relations are the focus in Chapters 9 and 10, which provide a critical analysis of their connection to deeper social stratifications that mark many different areas of life, as well as new ways of understanding their effects. Finally, the vexed question of ethics is tackled in Chapter 11, with a new approach to a topic that continues to challenge public relations despite decades of scholarly engagement.

In concluding, I bring together in Chapter 12 some of the insights from the previous chapters to consider the opportunities and challenges for scholars working in this area. The beauty, and the difficulty, of socio-cultural research on public relations is that it is always a project underway, with many more questions to ask than can be answered. I reflect on the potential breadth and depth that this kind of scholarship can achieve; pursued at scale, by enough researchers, socio-cultural work in public relations has the capacity to transform the current academic field.

NOTES

1. The idea of a socio-cultural 'turn' suggests that socio-cultural analyses of public relations are relatively new, but in fact, since the earliest days of public relations scholarship there has been work on the relationship between public relations and its social context, including studies on gender, race, rhetorical and communitarian analyses and critical studies (see Edwards, 2016a, for a longer discussion of the history of critical public relations research, which covers some of this development). While functional and quantitative work still proliferates in the contemporary field, alternative perspectives are now well established, driving public relations research in many new directions. It is this more balanced pattern of scholarship that Caroline Hodges and I designated the socio-cultural 'turn' and has given rise to this book.
2. See Edwards (2012a: 16–20) for a discussion of assumptions 1, 2, 4 and 5.
3. I use scare quotes around the word 'race' to indicate that it is a fluid, socially constructed category, rather than an objective term or an absolute reality. This is the understanding of race that applied throughout the book.
4. 'Cisgender' describes people whose gender identity is the same as their sex at birth.

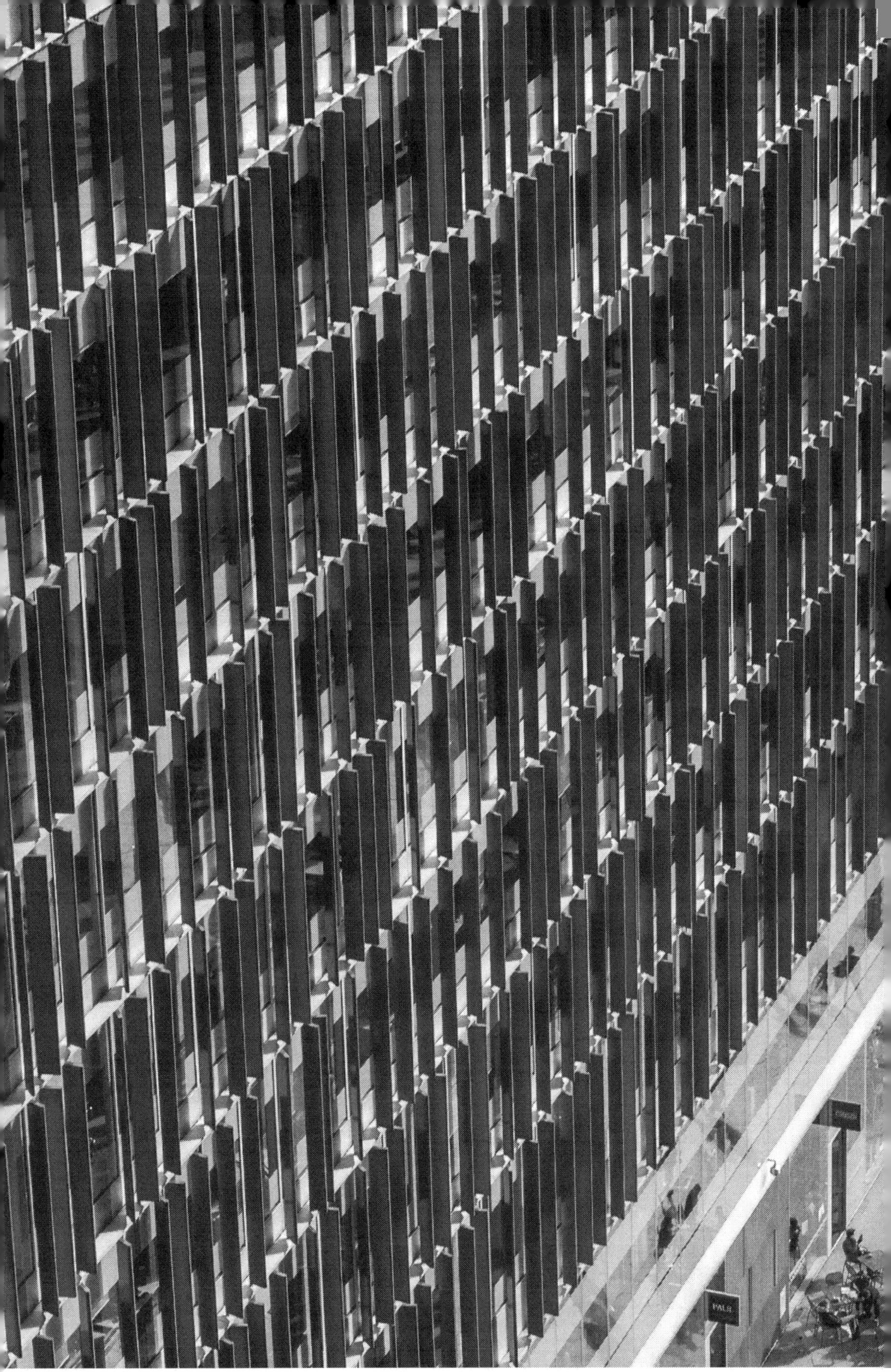

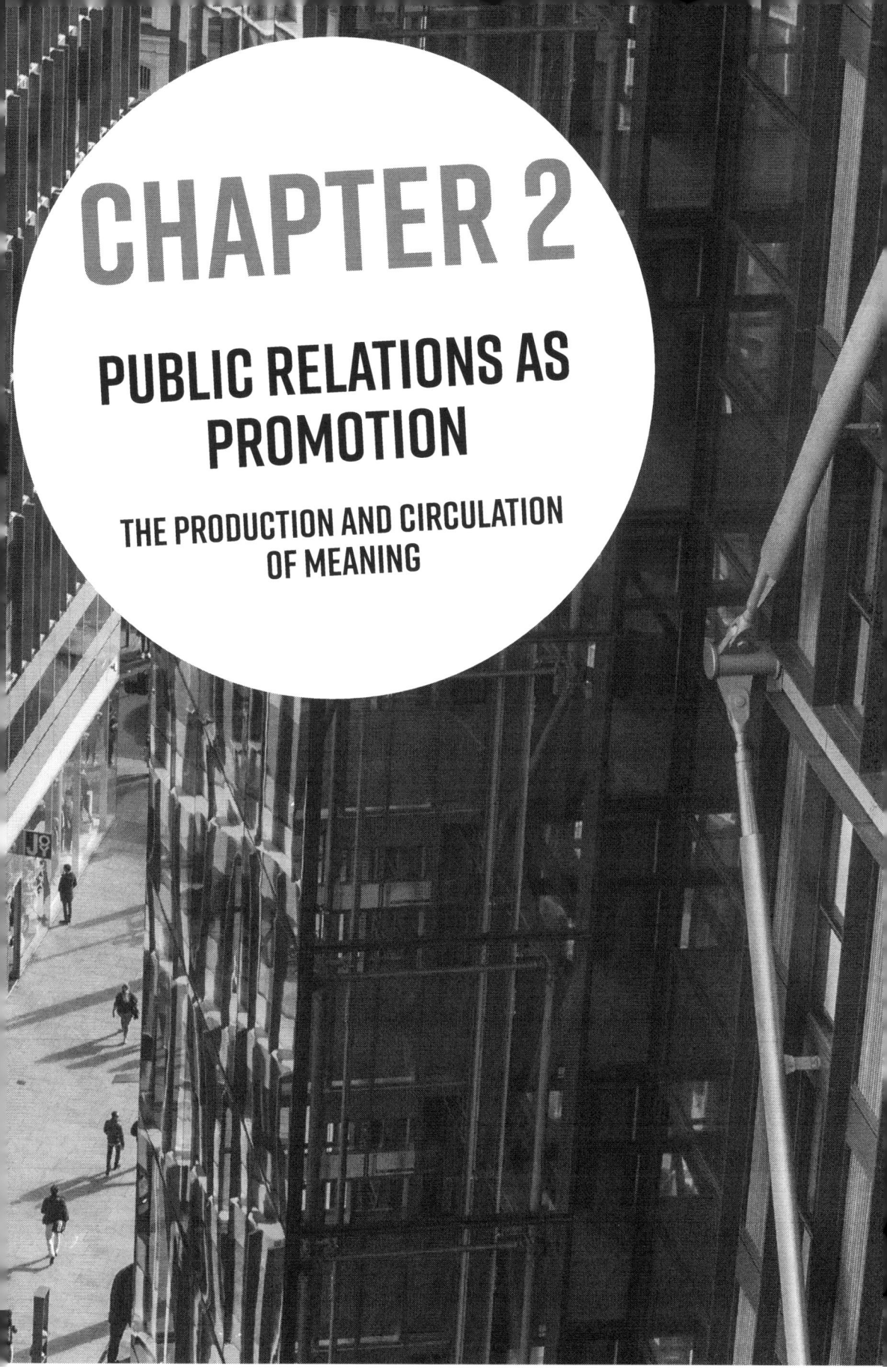

CHAPTER 2
PUBLIC RELATIONS AS PROMOTION
THE PRODUCTION AND CIRCULATION OF MEANING

INTRODUCTION

Public relations is perhaps most readily identifiable as a promotional industry yet, perhaps surprisingly, relatively little research has been carried out to critically explore the ways in which the promotional nature of public relations fundamentally shapes its activities. While a good deal of work has been done to find out how public relations is practised, and how to improve its persuasive potential on behalf of organisations, scholars have remained largely silent about how this activity fits in the wider promotional environment or with other promotional industries, particularly branding and advertising. Few scholars have problematised the fact that public relations makes a significant contribution to the volume of promotion to which we are subjected on a daily basis, and is a prolific source of meaning in the 'promotional cultures' that characterise many societies today (Edwards and Hodges, 2011; Davis, 2013). Nonetheless, the scale of public relations as a promotional presence deserves attention because it has significant effects on the possibilities that we perceive for ourselves, the choices available to us for building our identity in a fast-changing society, our knowledge of 'others', our ability to be reflexive and, more generally, the choices we make about how we live our lives.

Promotional practices are more widespread, more systemic and more absorbed into our day-to-day culture than ever before (Davis, 2013). They are also more complex: digital technologies mean that both individuals and organisations act as producers of promotion, while organisations can be targets for promotional campaigns, just as individuals are, and commodification extends well beyond products and services to the values, beliefs and attitudes that define our way of life (Jackall and Hirota, 2000; Ilmonen, 2004). Promotion publicises the attributes of artefacts (e.g. facts, figures, look and feel), but in a crowded marketplace a set of attributes is rarely enough to induce audience loyalty. Consequently, alongside factual communication, promotional techniques invariably associate different meanings with promoted objects. These meanings draw on social and cultural norms and may invoke politics too; in the process they provide an argument for audience loyalty that appeals to identity, aspirations, social status and political leanings. Such arguments engage with emotion as well as rationality, and are arguably more powerful as a result (Wernick, 1991).

In this chapter, I explore the nature of public relations as a promotional industry, a prolific source of meaning and a crucial circulatory mechanism in promotional cultures. First, I consider the insights into the social and cultural role of promotional industries from sociologists and media scholars. I then outline the characteristics of the core promotional industries of advertising, branding and public relations, and the differences between them. The heart of the chapter focuses on public relations as a value-laden circulatory mechanism for promotion, drawing on the theoretical framework of the circuit of culture (Curtin and Gaither, 2007), and the conceptualisation of practitioners as promotional intermediaries, working on both meaning-making and circulation. I conclude by considering further avenues for research that might provide a more detailed understanding of public relations' identity as a promotional industry (Aronczyk et al., 2017).

PROMOTIONAL INDUSTRIES, SOCIETY AND CULTURE

Histories of promotional industries demonstrate that they are engaged in competitive struggles over the ways that meaning is created and circulates across society, and are entwined with complex changes in social, economic and political landscapes, media systems, and cultural beliefs and norms.[1] Organisations are deeply invested in such struggles because finding an association that their audiences relate to, or that captures a zeitgeist that makes a product or idea seem 'of its time', can deliver material and symbolic advantages (investment, innovation, people, status) that are then less available to competitors (Bourdieu, 1991; Mosco, 2009; Edwards, 2011). Promotional industries use a wide range of channels, from advertisements and town hall meetings to films and documentaries, media relations and sponsorship, in order to promote corporate and government interests, construct national values and identities that resonate with audiences, and lead them to consume more, vote more, or support organisations in other ways.

From a positive perspective, promotional industries have helped to develop healthy markets and economies by facilitating the movements of goods and services, monitoring consumer 'needs' and ensuring corporations are recognised for their social contribution (Kotler et al., 2012). They deliver economic growth, individual wealth, social development, and healthy government where public opinion is integrated into the policy formation process and debate and discussion thrives (see, for example, Lees-Marshment, 2001; Institute of Education Sciences, 2009; Leach, 2009; Kent, 2013). Public relations and advertising arguably also help sustain a financially viable, independent media sector by providing funds and information that reduce the reliance of news outlets on the state.

In contrast, critics of the promotional industries point out that they use unethical techniques, including telling lies and partial truths, and manipulate the public and the news agenda for dubious ends (Michie, 1998; Mickey, 2002; Miller and Dinan, 2007). Indeed, the continued use of ideas from mass psychology in public relations to play on emotions, prejudices, fears and instincts, as well as the prevalence of audience surveillance and monitoring to develop promotional strategies, provides ample support for such claims (see, for example, Barber, 2007; Andrejevic, 2009; Turow, 2011; Andrews et al., 2013). Critics also note that the influence of promotional work on the news agenda reduces the quality of public debate and can lead to populist, 'lowest common denominator' arguments that cater to social prejudice. In contemporary information environments, this effect is exacerbated by the prevalence of 'fake news' on social media (Einstein, 2016) as well as the mediatisation of politics, where communicative imperatives, audience research and narrow segmentation are as important as ideology in shaping policy[2] (Bennett and Manheim, 2006; Esser and Strömbäck, 2014).

These critiques notwithstanding, promotion is not a one-way street and it would be wrong to suggest that organisations dictate the ways we live our lives through their use of promotion. Indeed, it is notoriously difficult to isolate and measure the effects of promotional work, and its influence on social change may be over-emphasised (Cronin, 2004; Watson and Noble, 2007). While audiences are not immune to promotion, nor are they duped by it; the fact that promotional work is now an established part of many cultures means that organisations are addressing 'knowing' audiences that easily see through and reject efforts to manipulate them and demand 'authentic' communication rather than instrumental sales talk (Powell, 2013a). History is littered with examples of unsuccessful promotion, where audiences subvert promotional rhetoric and distort its symbols (for example, by distributing doctored logos to substitute for the real thing). Consequently, organisations and industries must engage with promotion in part to legitimise their existence, for example by constructing campaigns that appeal to civic values focused on a 'greater good', including national identity, social trust, citizenship or democratic participation (Goldman and Papson, 1996: 228; Jackall and Hirota, 2000; Stole, 2013). Contemporary promotional work is framed in terms of building relationships, engagement and dialogue across multiple platforms, respecting audiences rather than addressing them as a means of achieving organisational goals (Arthur W. Page Society, 2007; Powell, 2013a).

As the neoliberal tenets of marketisation, consumption, individualism and choice have become more widespread, corporates and governments have become the most prolific sources of promotion as they try to persuade audiences to co-create value, contribute to production through co-operation and engagement, and make political, economic and social choices that support the continued existence of organisations, institutions and markets (Zwick et al., 2008). Promotion has become institutionalised within capitalist economies, a cultural norm for the management not only of markets, but also of behaviours, attitudes, values and identities (Williams, 1980; Jhally, 1990; Wernick, 1991: 25). For individuals, it has become a route to navigating contemporary society, building individual biographies by identifying with promotional messages, and a way of understanding the risks associated with the choices we make (Giddens, 1991). As Williamson (1978: 13) puts it in the context of advertisements, 'in providing us with a structure in which we, and those goods, are interchangeable, they are selling us ourselves'. One effect of this has been to reify corporations as social institutions, while also creating a strong association between consumption and progress towards a modern, civilised society (Ewen, 1976; Marchand, 1998). At the same time, the hegemonic power of corporations has bred resistance, and promotional industries have also supported groups contesting dominant views and challenging policy priorities (Meijer, 1998; Coombs and Holladay, 2012; Demetrious, 2013; Curtin, 2016). Thus, promotion lends itself to civic as well as commercial objectives and can support citizenship, both when civic values are the object of promotion (as in third-sector or grassroots public relations campaigns) as well as when it is exercised in the context of markets (for example, in the context of ethical consumption).

Online communication has emerged in recent years as a crucial promotional vehicle for the development of existing and new markets. Connectivity and cybernetic commodities, or 'the information or feedback created from [consumers'] actions and interactions online' (Cohen, 2013: 179), have together delivered much greater knowledge about consumers and their potential to be persuaded. Digital channels are often praised by industry players as a way of building genuine relationships, getting to know customers and ensuring companies better deliver to their needs. Because they bypass existing gatekeepers, they also present a powerful form of leverage, the 'relationships' that all organisations wish to 'own' and 'manage', by communicating directly with audiences (Zwick et al., 2008; Turow, 2011; Cohen, 2013; van Dijck, 2013). However, there are important ethical challenges in using digital communication for promotion, because it commodifies our human desire to engage and connect with others (van Dijck, 2013; see Chapter 11 later). Promotional industries actively manipulate algorithms, technological infrastructure and user engagement by, for example, search engine optimisation, using big data to target individuals and groups with tailored messages, encouraging word-of-mouth recommendations, and creating content that will 'go viral' (Collister, 2016). In the process, they instrumentalise our sociability as a form of 'free labour' and use our desire to identify and share with others as a way of lending credibility to content and making meaning travel further (Terranova, 2000; Zwick et al., 2008; Banet-Weiser, 2012; Hearn, 2012).

On a global scale, promotional industries help organisations to reach and come to 'know' audiences on different parts of the planet (for example, through global product launch campaigns by multinational companies, or public relations work for international non-governmental organisations (INGOs); see Chapter 7), while promotional industries and practitioners themselves evolve and develop through their contact with regional markets (Weaver, 2011; Kim and Cheng, 2013). Aronczyk (2013b) argues that promotional workers in global corporations can be defined as part of a 'transnational promotional class' (TPC), whose work contributes to the global mediascapes and ideoscapes that people and organisations use to construct 'imaginary worlds' and through which resources are mobilised to perpetuate global capitalism (Appadurai, 1990; Edwards, 2011). More often than not, the TPC supports hegemonic power structures; however, in some contexts it can resist hegemony. In the face of globalised problems such as trade inequalities, environmental degradation and migration, none of which governments can resolve at a national level, promotional industries have supported campaigns that co-opt consumption for civic purposes – for example, by imposing socially responsible behaviour on corporations (Simon, 2011). Positive outcomes include legislation to protect consumers, changes in voluntary regulation within companies and across industries, the emergence of new ethical consumption norms, and occasionally changes in the distribution of political power (Klein, 2000; Kozinets and Handelman, 2004; Harrison et al., 2005; Gerbaudo, 2012).

One critique of promotional industries that is vital to socio-cultural analyses of public relations is the suggestion that they undermine the quality of civic life and collective welfare. Promotion, and especially the highly targeted, niche promotion of the digital era, is by nature divisive, since it targets only audiences that are likely to respond or are instrumental to a particular objective; other groups are ignored and valuable information may circulate far less widely than it should (Marchand, 1998; Hallahan, 2000; Munshi and Kurian, 2005; Bennett and Manheim, 2006; Collister, 2016). Products (and policies) are matched with appropriately classified consumers, and 'something is provided for all, so that none may escape' (Horkheimer and Adorno, 2002: 97). Davis (2013) uses the term 'mediatised capitalist democracy' to indicate the ways in which promotion directs behaviour towards servicing markets and individual values rather than towards community and collective welfare, even when it is used as a means of resistance and protest. When activist voices are strong, they run the risk of being co-opted as a 'market opportunity' rather than a challenge: many corporations have incorporated social action into their identities, using promotion to instrumentalise and transform political struggles into marketable commodities.

While corporate activism might generate visibility for a cause, when protest is constructed as part of a corporate brand its political significance is always reduced because it blurs the distinction between markets and politics, public and private interests, and consumer and citizen identities (Barber, 2007; Mukherjee and Banet-Weiser, 2012; Aronczyk, 2013a). It masks the vested interests behind the promotion, while truncating the options for popular resistance because it constructs consumption as a normative form of protest en route to an individual lifestyle and identity, and thereby weakens the social and civic significance of collective action (Goldman and Papson, 1996; Binkley, 2008; Ruskin and Schor, 2009). Individualised consumer activism may *appear* to be an option for collective action outside the market, but rather than protecting the political sphere from the influence of commerce and private interests, it positions the market *at the centre* of politics and civil society – the activist consumer is still a consumer (Richey and Ponte, 2011).[3] As Aronczyk (2013a: 2) notes:

> When corporations act like social movements or non-governmental organizations, taking political stances on issues of global social and environmental concern, appealing to consumers via the ethical or moral rightness of an issue, the notions typically associated with these forms of collective action – protest, activism, resistance, radical politics, struggle – are made flexible, weak and contingent.

These critiques deal with the macro-level effects of promotional industries on the fabric of society, and provide the context for analyses of public relations as a promotional industry (as well as some critiques that can be exercised directly at public relations). However, scholarship on promotional industries can often obscure the detailed practices of promotion in favour of broader criticisms. The remainder of this chapter attempts to remedy this by first considering the differences between the core promotional industries, and then exploring in more detail the specifics of public relations as a circulatory mechanism in promotional culture.

PROMOTIONAL INDUSTRIES: ADVERTISING, BRANDING AND PUBLIC RELATIONS

The term 'promotional industry' describes those sections of the economy engaged in the symbolic practices that transform the use value of products into exchange value (Powell, 2013b) – a process that involves collaboration, rather than persuasion, in the contemporary context, in order to maximise the benefit to be had from 'the consumer's charmed transformation from a passive recipient of messages and commodities to an active interpreter and maker of both' (Zwick et al., 2008: 167). The three most powerful promotional industries are advertising, branding and public relations, each of which is firmly embedded in the global economy and comprises a significant portion of the revenues of the transnational promotional industries (see Chapter 7). They are often discussed as a homogenous group in promotional scholarship, but there are significant differences between them. Space precludes a full discussion, but here I offer a brief summary of each one in order to put the subsequent discussion of public relations in context.

In functional terms, branding helps organisations develop an identity that can distinguish them and their offerings from their competitors (Kotler and Keller, 2009). A brand is a signifier – a constellation of tools (name, logo, design, slogan) that are managed in ways that actively communicate and construct a unique association with a product, service or organisation (Keller, 2013). Brands are an important form of promotional capital: they allow organisations to communicate identity and quality, and to preserve and grow economic value by actively managing, investing in and protecting the brand as a form of competitive advantage (Keller, 2013). From a sociological perspective, however, a brand is an essentially rhetorical device, a 'platform for the patterning of activity, a mode of organising activities in time and space' (Lury, 2004: 1). By disseminating information, brands promise *possibilities* to audiences, ways of being that are realised through consumption of the brand in its material forms (Lury, 2004; Arvidsson, 2006; Simon, 2011). Brands are talked about; the associations they construct are reflected upon and circulate through self-reflexive discourse, a form of 'consumption labour' in which sociability and loyalty are instrumentalised in order to increase the value of the brand (Ilmonen, 2004; Arvidsson, 2005; Aronczyk, 2013a). At the same time, brands are inherently mobile – they transcend specific objects and so travel across time and space, fitting neatly into the de-territorialised nature of globalised markets (Moor, 2007) and encroaching on private and public spaces in ways that normalise promotional logic in all aspects of our lives (Klein, 2000).

Advertising relates to paid forms of communication in various types of media (Jobber, 2010). Advertisers sell products, services, ideas, wars, ways of life, political arguments and cultural norms and use visual, audio and written forms of communication to persuade audiences that buying (and buying into) products and services, companies, lifestyles, behaviours, political principles or national identities will make their lives better (Ewen, 1976; Schudson, 1993; Fletcher, 2008). Advertisements are ubiquitous, inserted into spaces and screens, programmes and publications, online and offline, as advertisers search for ways to ensure audiences engage, and combat technologies that offer routes for bypassing marketing and promotion material (Turow, 2006, 2011). In the act of selling, advertisers simultaneously create what Thompson (2004) has called 'marketplace mythologies', or constructions that relate not only to individual products, but also to understandings of the market and society itself. They draw on social structures, hierarchies and trends to communicate (and sometimes challenge) how the object of our attention, whether an iPhone, a washing machine, a car or a right-wing political party, can help us signify our belonging in a certain social location or group (Frank, 1997). Advertising is recognised as a 'creative industry' (Department for Culture, Media and Sport, 2001; Hesmondhalgh, 2013) and has a history of providing work to artists and writers trying to make a living (including Salman Rushdie, George Orwell, Toulouse-Lautrec, David Hockney and many others). Successful adverts can become collectable items (we might buy them and hang them on our walls) and are also valuable historical artefacts, because they reflect social and cultural change (consider the images, tag lines and jingles that we grow up with and absorb as part of the fabric of our daily lives), and allow us to track social and cultural norms as they evolve over time (Schudson, 1993; Fletcher, 2008).

In contrast to both branding and advertising, public relations deals with more discursive forms of communication in order to persuade. Practitioners tap into popular culture, socio-cultural and political trends, and prevailing climates of fear or positivity that affect an organisation's work in order to create communication that audiences readily relate to. They focus on managing relationships with audiences by engaging them through ongoing 'conversations' built on messages and discourses that support their cause. Influencers (journalists, analysts, vloggers, bloggers, celebrities, chat show hosts) and sponsorships are used to generate third-party advocacy, where respected, trusted, successful or popular intermediaries are used to enhance the promotional message. Stunts, events, viral campaigns, media relations and sponsorship all form part of the arsenal of tools that public relations practitioners use to create, stimulate and manage communication. Public relations is also in the business of keeping some communication out of the public eye: not everything about an organisation is up for discussion, despite claims that transparency is desirable (Christensen and Langer, 2009), and crisis management, focused on damage limitation through the control of information flows, is an important occupational specialism.

Public relations is the only promotional profession that engages in behind-the-scenes work to 'coach' organisations into appropriate communication. Media training, spokesperson coaching, stakeholder management, audience surveillance and analysis, and media monitoring are all used to help ensure the people who speak on behalf of organisations are adequately prepared for a public conversation (Bourne, 2016). This background management of communication might include steering senior executives away from acts that will induce public anger, or pre-empting unpopular actions by communicating in a way that can ameliorate their effects. Such work is complemented by practitioners' active management of interactions between organisations and their audiences on an ongoing basis (for example, as a gatekeeper for journalists or as a point of contact for the public).

The core promotional industries exist in relation to each other and are combined in a range of ways to deliver marketing and communication campaigns. For example, branding can provide the context for advertising and public relations, because it sets the framework for the ways in which an organisation is allowed to communicate its identity (colours, typeface, tone, look and feel of materials, but also relationships and identities associated with the brand). As rhetorical devices, brands are disconnected from specific places and times, and their abstraction and mobility differ from the context-dependency of public relations and advertising (you have to advertise or communicate *about something*, while a brand is created and circulates in both abstract and material forms). A brand may be advertised, but an advertisement has to work with the brand that is already in place in order to maintain a consistent identity that audiences recognise. Advertising differs from public relations in so far as it produces 'above-the-line' artefacts where it is obvious that organisations are paying for the publicity, and because of its focus on selling over and above longer-term, relationship-oriented communication. The construction of proactive public relations campaigns will reflect brand values and its timings may coincide with an advertising campaign, or other marketing initiatives, to maximise persuasive impact. On the other hand, public relations may adopt a less overt approach to persuasion through third-party endorsements of various kinds or advertorials, or take on a behind-the-scenes role to ensure organisational alignment with advertising messages and the prevention, rather than circulation, of undesirable communication.

PUBLIC RELATIONS AS A CIRCULATORY MECHANISM

One important aspect of public relations' role as a promotional industry is as a vehicle for the circulation of meaning. While critical attention has been paid to the ways in which public relations creates meaning in its discourses (see Chapter 3), those meanings are powerless unless they circulate within and beyond target audiences. Aronczyk (2013b) has noted the need to interrogate the strategies and mechanisms of circulation that facilitate promotion given that, as Lee and LiPuma (2002: 192) note, 'circulation is a cultural process with its own forms of abstraction, evaluation, and constraint, which are created by the interactions between specific types of circulating forms and the interpretive communities built around them'. Network theories (see Chapter 1) also suggest that examining the systems and actors that facilitate the movement of meaning is indispensable to understanding the power of promotional work. Yet in promotional scholarship generally and public relations research more specifically, the processes and practices that make up circulation are all too often left unexamined.

Arguing that circulation processes deserve critical attention challenges the representation of public relations as a channel for communication that simply carries, rather than shapes, meaning. For example, when public relations consultancies present reputation management, risk and trust as concrete realities that they are able to enhance, mitigate or protect through the apparently neutral process of engaging in conversation and dialogue (Edwards, 2014b; Bourne, 2015), they avoid any suggestion that they are actively mediating value and instead explain their role in terms of 'objectivity and rationality' (Aronczyk, 2013b: 160). However, the argument being made here is that the choices practitioners make, not only about message formulation but also about how those messages are distributed, are ideological and therefore play into the power that public relations exerts as a promotional industry.

Public relations deploys a wide range of technologies of circulation – defined here as the tools and tactics used in campaigns to disseminate messages. All are motivated by the need to achieve certain outcomes for organisations, and therefore reflect particular ideological interests. They are also heavily inflected by the use of networks – of people, organisations, discourses and technologies – to ensure circulation happens. For example, using third-party advocates engages powerful, networked actors to mask the instrumental nature of public relations work and increase its persuasive power. Practitioners' gatekeeping role between organisations and audiences is designed to intervene in communication networks by managing the flow of information from organisations to other parties, while acting as a boundary spanner (Leichty and Springston, 1996) ensures that relevant information flows into the organisation in order to improve its communication. On the other hand, crisis and issues management strategies often focus on avoiding promotion, actively *interrupting* the circulation of messages across networks; the use of silence has the same effect (Dimitrov, 2015). In contrast, choosing social media and online channels for communication taps into the advantages of digital networks to secure rapid and widespread circulation among (digitally and socially) 'connected' audiences. Behind the scenes, coaching spokespeople and working on presentation techniques are designed to increase the chances of communication being impactful enough to be picked up and transmitted further by audiences via social media and other online channels.

CASE STUDY 2.1

UNPACKING PUBLIC RELATIONS: AUTHENTIC PROMOTION ON YOUTUBE

The use of vloggers as influencers in promotional work, including public relations, has become a mainstay of digital promotion. Vloggers communicate with their audiences in ways that suggest peer connection, friendship and fellowship in consumption. Their speech is direct, they invite responses from their viewers, and they use various presentational mechanisms to emphasise their 'ordinariness' – such as filming in their own homes, shooting close-up rather than at a distance, or providing 'behind the scenes' perspectives of their lives (Tolson, 2010). Beauty vlogging has become one of the most prolific areas of vlogging on YouTube, with some vloggers attracting millions of subscribers to their channels. They deliver beauty tutorials and review products, presenting these as a way of helping their viewers to become beautiful themselves, and generating an intimate setting for their product demonstrations (they reveal themselves without any make-up on, they share anecdotes from their lives). The result is a conversation more akin to a chat between trusted friends than a sales pitch. This commodification of intimacy (Berryman and Kavka, 2017) creates what marketers call 'moments of truth' for viewers, that create an impression about the brand grounded in word-of-mouth recommendation that is all the more powerful because of the vloggers' apparent ordinariness, and because of its potential to be further disseminated via follower conversations as well as across platforms (Moran et al., 2014).

The maintenance of a beauty vlogger's identity as 'someone like me' for their followers has to be maintained in order to retain their promotional power, and this is done through different ways of taking their followers 'behind the scenes'. A recent trend is to present videos that 'unpack' the gifts they have received from public relations agencies. Tati, a beauty vlogger with 3 million subscribers, calls her unboxing videos 'Free stuff beauty gurus get: Unboxing PR packages', and opens her first one by inviting subscribers to join her, saying 'I have been saving these packages to sit down and share everything that's inside of these packages with you … new launches from companies and PR stuff … so we're just gonna dig in' (see https://www.youtube.com/watch?v=3LcirPO7seo). She then reveals her promotional identity 'value' by 'admitting' that she loves opening packages, enjoys receiving PR. However, she simultaneously minimises the instrumentalism this implies by denying that she has any kind of special status (she is not the only one to

(Continued)

> receive such packages) and reasserting her commitment to honesty with her subscribers (companies have got used to her honesty in reviews – 'I really pro and con things' – and this is why her opinion is valuable). In this way, she distances herself from 'PR' by positioning herself as a target (just like her subscribers) rather than a part of the industry. She also demystifies public relations (and thereby disempowers its critics) by including subscribers in the process of opening packages (although the actual selection of what to show and review is done in advance). These techniques of masking her promotional role help retain her subscribers' loyalty and her own celebrity status, through which brands can access and expand lucrative word-of-mouth recommendations.

Decisions about how to structure and use communication channels are part and parcel of campaign planning (Gregory, 2015) and may be seen as deceptively straightforward, based on simple realities of which audiences are being targeted and how best to reach them. Yet none of these choices are without consequence. On the contrary, they reflect ideological beliefs about the right messages, audiences and forms of communication underpinning all this work. Communicating digitally, for example, privileges younger audiences, those who have access to technology and richer populations in the global North and West. Using third-party advocates may limit the circulation of a message and neglect audiences that are affected by an organisation but have little influence over its operations (for example, an oil company may use analysts to endorse its investment strategy, but this ignores the channels through which local populations, directly affected by new extraction activities, might learn about plans for their future). Interrogating these ideological underpinnings is an important but under-researched area of public relations research.

CIRCULATION AND THE CIRCUIT OF CULTURE

The circuit of culture (Du Gay et al., 1997) has the capacity to extend our understanding of the ways in which public relations contributes to the circulatory mechanisms on which promotion depends. It has been used as the basis for the cultural-economic model of public relations developed by Curtin and Gaither (2007), which starts from the principle that 'PR is predicated on communicative relationships and culture is a constitutive part of any communicative enterprise' (2007: 206). Culture is defined as 'the process by which meaning is produced, circulated, consumed, modified, and endlessly reproduced and negotiated in society' (2007: 35) – and consequently, public relations is fundamental to the changing nature of culture over time. Following the arguments above, I pay particular attention here to the place of circulation in the circuit of culture, and the implications of this for our understanding of public relations as promotion.

Circulation processes are at the heart of the circuit of culture, because the circuit itself is sustained through the articulations of five different moments: production, regulation, consumption, representation and identity (Curtin et al., 2016). Meaning emerges through the processes invoked at all these locations, but is never static because each moment continuously articulates with the others. Thus, '[m]eaning-making processes operating in any one site are always partially dependent upon the meaning-making processes and practices operating in other sites for their effect' (Du Gay et al., 1997: 10) and can only be made sense of in these terms. Public relations work is present in all five moments as a locus of meaning creation, but also prompts their articulation because of its focus on the dissemination of meaning, and is therefore fundamental to the circulatory processes that ensure meaning remains fluid, contested and temporary.

CASE STUDY 2.2

FUR OUT! CULTURE, COMMERCE AND PUBLIC RELATIONS IN JAPAN

Award-winning campaigns often provide examples of public relations' circulatory prowess and its role in the different moments of the circuit of culture. The Fur Out! Campaign, run by Dentsu Public Relations and commissioned by Akita Inu Tourism in 2016, is a case in point. The campaign was designed to boost international tourist numbers in the Akita region of Japan, which was little known as compared to more high-profile destinations such as Tokyo and Kyoto, although its name has global recognition as a popular dog breed. Market research suggested the campaign should target the Taiwanese market, where Japanese culture, and particularly girl pop groups, are popular. The campaign combined these two cultural factors into a tightly planned communication strategy that depended on carefully managed circulation, but using the advantages that online and networked media could offer.

First, they created a girl pop group called 'Mofu Mofu Dogs' (Fluffy Dogs), where each singer wore the head of an Akita dog. The group filmed a song, 'Waiting4U', which combined e-pop and barking dogs on the soundtrack, and a video incorporating shots of attractions in Akita province featuring the 'dog' singers. The track was designed to go viral, but was launched in Japan first in order to create a 'buzz' that the Taiwanese market would be attracted to. Once the track had a million views, Dentsu worked with a local public relations agency in Taiwan to write a news release that promoted the video and pop group as the latest Japanese trend. This cultural creation was then complemented by a hosted trip to Akita for Taiwanese bloggers – a key set of influencers for Taiwanese tourists – reinforcing the online promotion with the physical experience of

(Continued)

> visiting the region. The campaign also prompted the regional government to host an additional promotional trip for foreign ambassadors based in Japan.
>
> The campaign was very successful, achieving a significant increase in tourist numbers. More interesting for the purposes of this chapter, however, is the way in which circulation was so carefully analysed and constructed. The online video was created and launched in a way that would attract attention from online audiences and prompt it to go viral; releasing it online also gave it international reach because of the borderless nature of networked, digital platforms, meaning that audiences everywhere, but particularly in Taiwan, could access it without a problem. In Taiwan, an additional circulatory impetus was given through the construction of 'news' about the group's online success, tapping into the existing cultural trend of popular Japanese girl pop groups and using traditional media alongside online sources to extend the attraction of the campaign. In the end, the strategy attracted news coverage that went far beyond Taiwan and raised awareness of the Akita region in countries across the world.
>
> For more information, see http://dentsu-pr.com/our-work/0608.html

Gaonkar and Povinelli (2003: 392) argue that understanding the 'quiet work' of circulatory mechanisms requires 'an almost neurotic attentiveness to the edges of forms as they circulate so that we can see what is motivating their movement across global social space and thus what is attached to them as both cause and excess'. In other words, our analyses of the circulatory tools and strategies of public relations should go beyond their synchronic presence in specific locations, to incorporate a diachronic view of their movement, interactions and translation across space and time (Gaonkar and Povinelli, 2003). In the circuit of culture, meaning emerges in circulation, the *articulation between* moments, rather than in the moments themselves. How meanings travel through public relations campaigns, which actors or artefacts embody them, how they are translated, and how all these things influence the dynamics of power in society and culture are therefore crucial questions for understanding the circulatory work done by public relations as a promotional industry. Human beings are only one group of relevant actors: understanding the role of technologies, discourses, media systems, organisational cultures, historical events and structures of connectivity in public relations practices also helps to determine how meaning is disseminated. Following Gaonkar and Povinelli, understanding the circulatory work of public relations starts with attentiveness to the forms it takes at each moment of the circuit, and how those forms subsequently move across time and space. Below I outline some of the ways in which this happens; since the complexity of articulations in the circuit leads to endless possibilities for investigating the nature of circulation, the discussion is not exhaustive, but it offers a starting point for more in-depth analyses.

The moment of representation describes the locations in which similarity and difference between elements of culture are constructed. Representation draws on the past, but also engages in fantasy as new meanings are imagined. Hierarchies and exclusions emerge in this moment, not only in relation to people, but also as a means of distinguishing the value of different artefacts and organisations. In public relations, representation describes the process through which discourses attach value to products, services, individuals and organisations (Du Gay et al., 1997). A campaign to promote a sponsorship of a school breakfast club, for example, may represent those in poverty as victims (because they have been deprived of the resources to live adequately) or as poor parents (because their children are not fed at home) and without agency. On the other hand, the sponsoring corporation may be presented as a socially engaged, caring organisation rather than a profit-oriented enterprise, providing a solution to poverty's problems.

When representations are repeated over time and in different spaces – for example, when public relations campaigns promote messages in multiple places at the same time, or draw on widely circulating representations of social groups in their discourses – they can become part of the normative landscape that allows us to decode communication materials in a patterned and relatively predictable way. This speeds up the circulation of promoted ideas and makes them easier for audiences to relate to. At the same time, it creates a barrier for representations of society and culture that do not fit the dominant narrative: gaining visibility and attention for 'alternative' representations of events (for example, portraying war as a crime rather than a justified military intervention) is correspondingly more difficult.

As audiences respond to and align themselves (or not) with the representations of society and culture in public relations work, these representations articulate with the moment of identity, which describes the ways in which various groups of people *come to be associated with* a particular representation (Du Gay et al., 1997). As public relations campaigns impute identities to audiences and organisations (see, for example, Curtin, 2011), processes of attachment and rationales for inclusion or exclusion are constructed based on the valorisation or dismissal of individual characteristics in public relations discourses, based on lifestyle, class, ethnicity, gender, disability, religion and sexuality. Policies communicating solutions for inadequate parenting, for example, may construct the problem as a result of a lack of education (an argument based on class status), drug and alcohol addiction (class, lifestyle), cultural norms (religion, ethnicity, gender) or health issues (disability, gender). The socially responsible corporation may be identified through its commitment to local communities, a natural affinity with a particular cause, or a historically altruistic organisational culture. Public relations also produces identities for products that align with, or are easily decoded by, a certain type of person, such that the apparent fit in attributes makes the product more appealing to them (consider the stereotypical user of the most up-to-date iPhone, or the housewife who uses the latest cleaning product). Often, this is done by associating with existing widely circulating identities such as celebrity 'brands' (e.g. the Beckhams, the Kardashians), which 'lend' their (positive) identity attributes to the promoted artefacts.

By constructing or incorporating identities into its discourses, public relations abstracts them from specific locations and owners and enables them to circulate and be recognised in new and different contexts, increasing their value as promotional tools (Miège and Garnham, 1979; Edwards, 2015). In the process, desirable identities may become incorporated into organisational and individual self-narratives (for example, in mission statements or social media profiles). Here, they provide the parameters for future actions, such as decisions about what kinds of products to produce, or what brands to support. As this happens, the moment of identity articulates with the moment of production.

The moment of production is the point at which meaning is encoded into cultural artefacts through production practices and contexts. Organisational cultures, heroic individuals, available technologies, equipment, organisational networks, finance and marketing are all taken into account. The ways these factors coalesce and work together frame production in terms of norms and values that give the various activities and processes involved particular meanings (Du Gay et al., 1997). For example, when public relations practitioners develop and manage campaigns, their work is informed by the availability of circulatory technologies such as social media platforms, news distribution systems, mobile phones and phone lines, internet availability, event hardware (staging, lighting, furniture), and/or the availability of spokespeople and partners to support the campaign. The decisions they make in turn determine what kinds of meaning are encoded into the final campaign and how those meanings then circulate – at what speed, to whom and in what kinds of contexts (for example, statements on a Facebook page may be interpreted and passed on in different ways to a tweet, an Instagram post or a press release).

Once artefacts are produced, they have to be distributed and consumed, and this creates an articulation between the moments of production and consumption. Consumption is the point at which the meanings imbued in artefacts at other moments are decoded by audiences. They are interpreted, evaluated and integrated into a cycle of meaning-making that is driven by the agency of individuals based on their social and cultural milieu. The result is variable and always has the potential to subvert the meanings encoded in other moments of the circuit, particularly production (Du Gay et al., 1997). This tension has produced a range of promotional techniques to try and control meaning (e.g. audience monitoring, data surveillance, public opinion surveys) and help producers to minimise the risk of their promotional efforts foundering due to a lack of interest or relevance (Bourne, 2016). In their boundary-spanning role, practitioners are expected to understand consumers and consumption by monitoring audience perceptions, expectations and reactions to organisational activity, and appealing to contemporary social and cultural trends. By 'piggybacking' on these different forms of knowledge, they increase the currency of campaigns and make it more likely that their messages will be passed on by consumers, circulating through social media networks, word of mouth, and potentially being incorporated into new contexts. Yet despite efforts to control decoding, subversion is always a possibility, changing the direction of circulation and prompting the need for more public relations work to manage fluidity and unpredictability (Hang and Zhang, 2009).

These kinds of failures reflect articulations with the moment of regulation, because they reveal the formal and informal norms that determine what kinds of meanings are acceptable in different contexts. Regulation refers to the meanings prompted by classificatory systems that societies use to structure difference. Oppositions such as private–public, work–leisure, childhood–adulthood and civilised–uncivilised serve as the basis for ordering individuals, artefacts, identities, behaviours and values into categories. Classifications change over time and can be both normative and informal (e.g. social mores), or explicit and formal (e.g. the law). They contribute to the processes of inclusion and exclusion that form the basis of social hierarchies, and therefore constantly articulate with the moments of identity and representation (Du Gay et al., 1997). When regulatory norms are transgressed – that is, when meanings violate the accepted classification – it can produce a sense of threat, fear and 'moral panics' (Hall et al., 2013). The scale of the migration crisis in Europe during the 2010s, for example, transgressed the regulatory role played by national borders as a barrier to entry and prompted many discourses that framed migrants as a threat to the stability and values of European societies (Philo et al., 2013).

Public relations campaigns contribute to the circulation of regulatory meanings by deploying them in campaigns and thereby perpetuating their presence in a range of social and cultural contexts. For example, policymakers may use nationalistic discourses that draw on national–foreigner classifications as normative arguments to justify promises to limit immigration or curtail welfare support for migrants, while campaigns for a listed company must adhere to formal rules about information disclosure, designed to prevent insider trading. At the same time, classifications can also be challenged or newly created when public relations campaigns circulate messages that justify alternative systems. For example, female genital mutilation used to be regarded as a private and culturally determined practice, but lobbying and public relations campaigns by charities and grassroots organisations have resulted in it being criminalised in many countries, and a matter of public rather than private concern (see, for example, Equality Now, 2017). In a different context, the incorporation of corporate social responsibility strategies by organisations is in part a result of public relations campaigns that have challenged the informal regulatory opposition between markets and civil society, by demanding that organisations take seriously their impact on communities and the environment (Carroll, 2008; Kotler et al., 2012).

PRACTITIONERS IN THE CIRCUIT OF CULTURE: PROMOTIONAL INTERMEDIARIES

The circuit of culture provides an invaluable tool for understanding the detail of public relations' promotional work, but it also runs the risk of obscuring the individuals who actually construct and enact campaigns. Without practitioners the industry would not exist, so their promotional role is crucial. One important approach to understanding practitioners as promotional workers has been the idea of cultural intermediation. Cultural intermediaries are market actors – including but not limited to people in the promotional industries – working on the 'presentation and representation' of culture (Bourdieu, 1984: 359), shaping 'both use values and exchange values, and seek[ing] to manage how those values are connected with people's lives' (Negus, 2002: 505; Hodges and Edwards, 2014; Smith Maguire and Matthews, 2014). As such, their work is specifically focused on associating meanings with artefacts, and can be mapped onto the activities explained through the circuit of culture.

Promotional intermediaries are cultural intermediaries working in the promotional industries, identifying marketable 'products' and potential audiences, framing messages using a variety of forms of communication, and identifying the correct channels for circulating those messages in the right places at the right times. As the circuit of culture illustrates, their work is ideological in that it invokes or contests existing hierarchies of power – for example, when a product is advertised in gendered or racialised terms. As they analyse and deconstruct the world we inhabit for marketing purposes, they contribute to the construction of that world, creating ways for us to apprehend our environment in terms of different (commercially and politically lucrative) possibilities and desires (Cronin, 2008). In other words, the 'process of "mediation" they engage in is also a process of reproduction, of inequalities in cultural capital and relations of power' (Wright, 2005: 111). Edwards (2012b) argues that public relations practitioners should be more specifically defined as symbolically violent cultural intermediaries, since by manipulating discourses that frame markets, organisations and subjectivities in ways that appear to be common sense, they 'generate power for vested interests' (Edwards, 2012b: 439) without the target audiences being fully aware of the extent of their manipulation.[4]

Promotional intermediaries draw on popular and 'high' culture for their creative inspiration. Public relations practitioners, for example, are exhorted to be in touch with popular culture and current events for their work (Edwards, 2014b), and frequently use popular music, deploy celebrities or draw on popular cultural trends to make their campaigns stand out. They also feed back into culture, both by producing promotional artefacts that become a focus for sharing, discussion and (particularly in the case of advertising) display in their own right (Soar, 2000; Edwards, 2015), and by their own status as cultural authorities and 'trendsetters' (Smith Maguire and Matthews, 2014). By reifying their own creativity and their work as cultural artefacts, and by characterising their work as a value-free process, promotional intermediaries are able to distance themselves from instrumental objectives (McFall, 2007; Aronczyk, 2013b) and claim that they provide some kind of social and cultural value alongside their commercial role (the latter being a common strategy among public relations industry associations). Such claims become institutionalised through the presence of archives and museums dedicated to promotional work (in the UK, for example, these include company archives such as the Marks and Spencers archive, the History of Advertising Trust archive, and the Museum of Brands), as well as the transformation of manufacturing processes themselves into popular museum-like tourist attractions (for example, Cadbury World or the Guinness Storehouse in Dublin).

Integrating culture into promotional work can soften its economic or political purpose and instrumentality, because it speaks to activity valorised for its non-economic contribution to social and cultural life. The strategy also embeds objects of promotion in a wide set of contexts (for example, commercial brands may become readily associated with a certain film, or with a soundtrack), facilitating circulation, and constructs promotional tools such as a striking ad or a viral campaign as cultural forms in themselves (Edwards, 2015). These – as well as promotion-gone-wrong (see, for example, Schultz, 2017; Victor and Stevens, 2017) – may become a form of cultural currency, the subject of popular debates and sharing among audience members (Elliott and Wattanasuwan, 1998; Ilmonen, 2004).

Using the circuit of culture and the idea of promotional intermediaries to understand the detail of public relations' promotional work reveals how it is implicated in the complex processes of meaning production that underpin society and culture. It permits a focus on how public relations works with cultural norms and values to reproduce social hierarchies, simultaneously commodifying and constructing culture and revealing the 'interactional dynamics – structural and interpersonal – that produce and animate the market for cultural goods' (Smith Maguire and Matthews, 2014: 6). Formal objectives in public relations campaigns are often focused on securing resources – profit, voter support, charity donations; but framing practitioners as cultural intermediaries also reveals the importance of status and symbolic power, or the ability to claim the most valued forms of financial, cultural and social capital in a society, as important reasons for engagement with audiences. Moreover, because circulation is constant, there is always the possibility that as conditions change, voices that were previously marginalised re-emerge as dominant, and vice versa. Thus, the model helps to explain the need for the continual reinvention of promotional work and the constant reassertion and recirculation of messages: promoting something once is never enough.

CONCLUSION: UNDERSTANDING PUBLIC RELATIONS AS A PROMOTIONAL INDUSTRY

The analysis in this chapter shows that, in its capacity as a promotional industry, public relations is both a producer of meaning and a circulatory mechanism. Left static, meaning has very limited power; it has to circulate in order to generate the advantages that organisations are trying to secure by engaging in promotional activity. The business of public relations is therefore to ensure that meaning is created and campaigns devised in ways that maximise circulation. It ensures the meanings imbued in promotional discourses are pushed out into society, actively engaging individuals with existing and new understandings of the world around them. This circulatory work makes use of networks, technologies, social and cultural norms and trends, and other discursive regimes to drive the uptake of meaning, but also to control meaning so that the interests underpinning campaigns can be realised.

Like other promotional industries, public relations cannot be definitively framed as positive or negative in society and culture, since the power that it generates for different actors depends on the contexts in which it is deployed (Moloney and McKie, 2016). However, we can say with certainty that it is a vital mechanism for ensuring the continued circulation and contestation of meaning, and therefore contributes to the evolution of society and culture over time. The pertinent question for socio-cultural researchers of public relations is how this role plays into the positive and negative effects of promotion on society and culture outlined at the beginning of the chapter. As well as critically evaluating the meanings that are present in public relations discourse, it is important to ask what mechanisms enable such meanings to be transported into different locations, how they are taken up and changed by audiences, and how they prompt change or continuity in social and cultural norms. Answers to these questions will create new links between public relations and the environmental conditions outlined in Chapter 1 by helping to explain how it influences the social and cultural structures that define our environment and the choices we make about how we want to live as individuals and together. They will also speak to the ways in which society is changing, including the role played by neoliberal values as drivers and subjects of promotional activity, as well as a focus for activism; and the contemporary importance of networks and digital technologies as value-laden channels of circulation.

The perspectives outlined in this chapter also have implications for practitioners. Many aspects of public relations practice are taken for granted as good promotional tools, not least because they facilitate circulation, yet raise important ethical issues about privacy and civic engagement, 'promotional excess' and whether we have the right to promotion-free space in our lives (Moloney, 2006). The use of audience data to track and target audiences across a wider range of public and private spaces than ever before, and the co-optation of audiences' agency and sociability in viral campaigns, are cases in point. They are largely unquestioned in both practice and functional scholarship, but have significant implications for the power of public relations to influence us in ways that we do not always recognise (see Chapter 11). Practitioners could, and perhaps should, find ways of weighing up the ethical implications of using digital and mobile technologies against the advantages of access and co-optation. More broadly, they could reflect on the potentially negative impact they have on communicative capitalism (Dean, 2005), as contributors to the volume of communication that ultimately fragments collective voice. Because promotion is so embedded in the ways we engage with the world, questions like this can be brushed aside too easily. Adopting an explicitly promotional perspective of public relations helps to mitigate this danger. Ultimately, the insights that come from such analyses will permit a more holistic picture of public relations as a source of both power and resistance.

NOTES

1. Some excellent histories of promotional industries are Lears and Jackson (1994), Ewen (1976, 1996), Jackall and Hirota (2000), Schudson (1993), McClintock (1995), Fletcher (2008) and Marchand (1998). Unfortunately, histories of the industry outside the US and UK contexts are quite rare, although the new Routledge book series *National Perspectives on the Development of Public Relations: Other Voices*, edited by Professor Tom Watson, is an important new addition to the field.
2. From a governmental perspective, for example, communicating to the public about political parties, policies and decisions has become more important as democracies have matured and citizens have become more cynical. Political marketers treat the world of politics as a marketplace, where attracting voters' attention and support is achieved through various promotional techniques (Franklin, 1994; Lilleker and Scullion, 2008). Content ranges from personality-focused appeals to negative advertising, factual arguments, celebrity associations and word-of-mouth marketing, often via social media (Corner and Pels, 2003; Scammell, 2006). Rather than simply being about policy dissemination, promotional work in the political sphere involves monitoring and accommodating voters' behaviours, responses and apparent priorities in order to facilitate rapid responses from policymakers as well as to influence policy formation (Lees-Marshment, 2001; Strömbäck, 2008; Strömbäck and Kiousis, 2011), reversing the traditional view of politicians making policy and then disseminating their decisions to the public after the fact.
3. The credibility of promotion as protest is also challenged by 'communicative capitalism' (Dean, 2005), where the promise and availability of communicative technologies appear to facilitate engagement and voice on a global scale, but the sheer volume of messages circulating across communicative networks means that political action becomes transformed into contributions to the circulating mass, speaking to the 'converted' rather than challenging those who are materially powerful. Activists may use these networks to disseminate their protest, but as their promotional work multiplies, resistance correspondingly fragments and the power of a cohesive opposition to elites is significantly weakened.
4. This view of public relations' cultural intermediation may hold in some cases, but given that audiences are increasingly knowledgeable about promotional techniques, the existence of misrecognition may be over-emphasised and should be an empirical question.

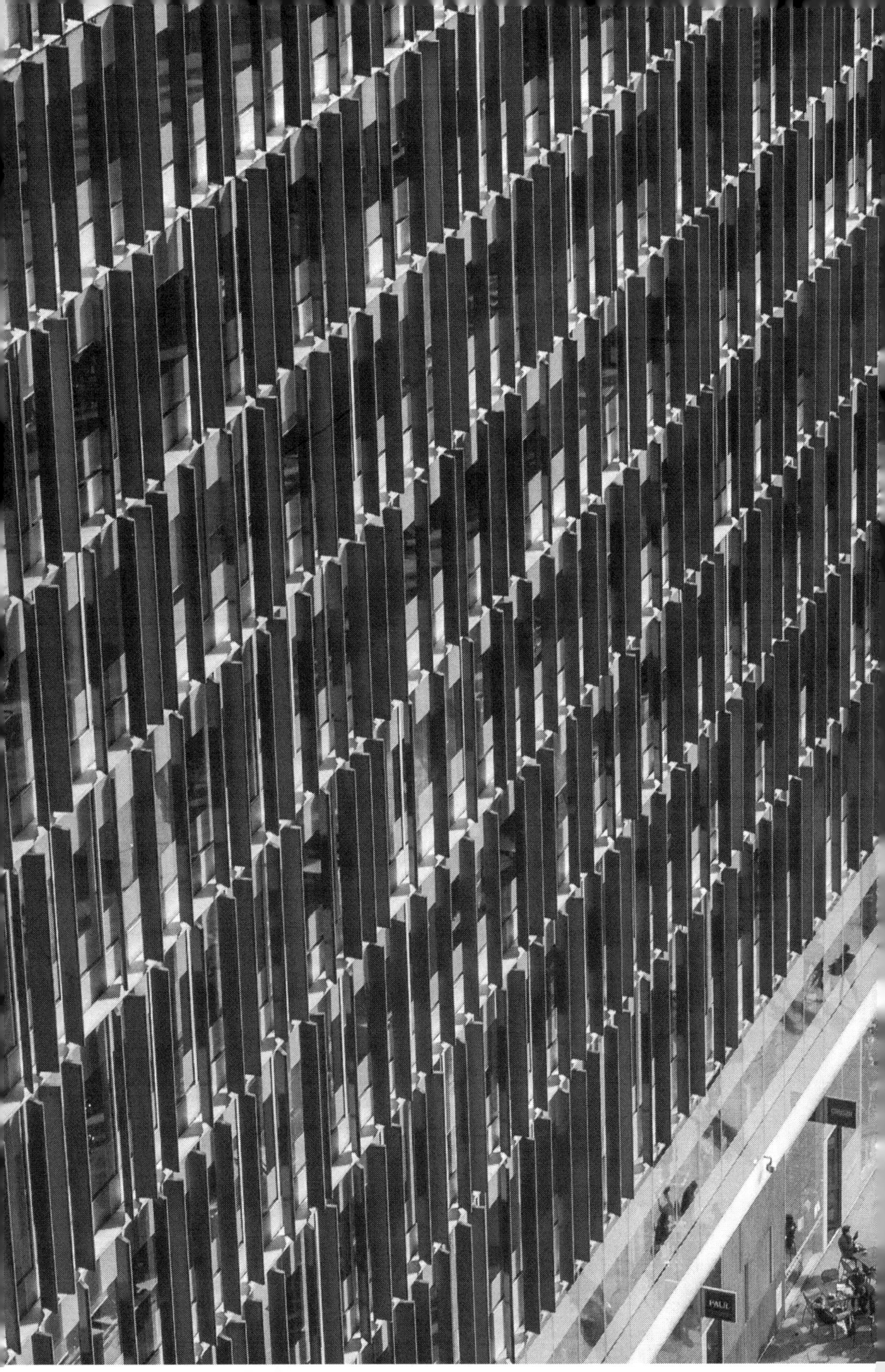
PAUL

CHAPTER 3

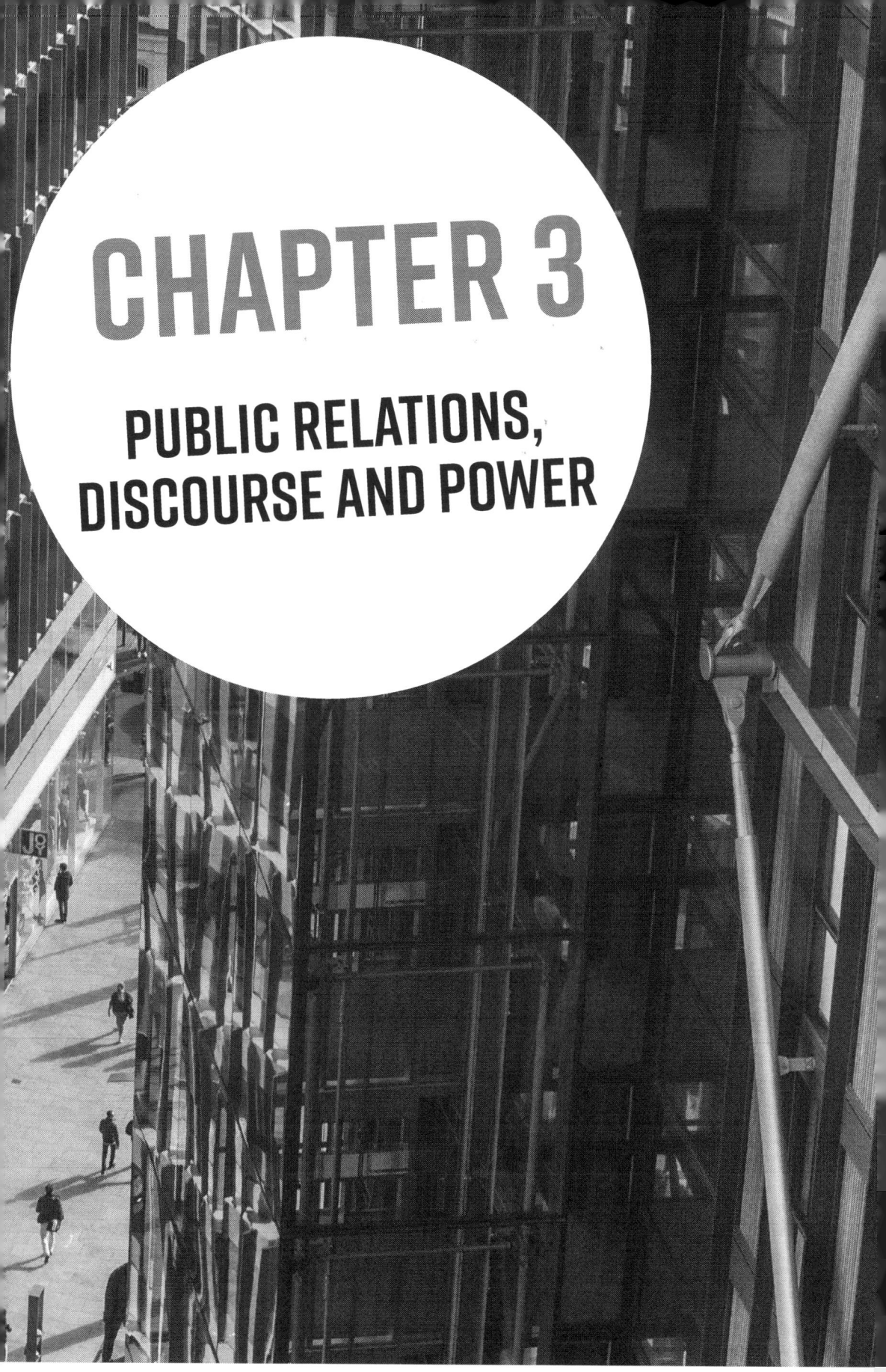

PUBLIC RELATIONS, DISCOURSE AND POWER

INTRODUCTION

The previous chapter dealt with public relations' identity as a promotional industry, and its importance as a source of meaning and a circulatory mechanism for promotional work. In this chapter, attention turns to another aspect of public relations, also central to its promotional role: the discourses it uses to achieve the promotional outcomes it promises. Discourse underpins all of public relations' effects on society and culture, because it lies at the heart of practice. Public relations is about using language effectively to frame ideas, direct perceptions, shift attention and create connections between people and organisations. The importance of this fundamental truth to socio-cultural research on public relations cannot be underestimated and is reflected in the fact that discourse is relevant to every chapter in this book. It shapes public relations' contribution to democratic life, it provides the ideas and inspiration that underpin the industry's influence on globalisation, it is a means of securing the material and symbolic resources over which elite and non-elite actors struggle, and it reveals the identity of the occupation and its practitioners.

The discourses we identify in public relations texts are a manifestation of the power of the industry, as well as the connections it has to power *struggles*. They matter a great deal to clients and practitioners alike. Practitioners spend long hours framing ideas, composing messages, writing content, checking phrases and words, all to ensure the discourses that end up circulating across audiences are the 'right' kinds of discourse, communicating messages that align with their objectives. Yet the importance of language formulation as a form of public relations practice is underplayed in empirical research, which has tended to focus on practitioner experiences and power rather than technical practices such as writing. As a result, there are still many unanswered questions about how practitioners understand and use discourse as a tool of their trade. We know little about how they work with language, how they make choices about the ways they craft texts, the roles of text and visual language, particularly in multimedia environments, and the degree to which their use of language is instinctive rather than conscious, a form of practice that has been absorbed through the rules of the occupational 'game' they have bought into (see Chapter 8).

Answering these questions requires extensive empirical research that deconstructs public relations work, challenging what appears to be self-evident in order to understand what less obvious purpose it serves. In addition, empirical work must be underpinned by a robust theoretical framework, and in this chapter my focus is on extending the theoretical tools we have to address the empirical realities of language and discourse in public relations. An important body of critical work has been carried out using Foucauldian approaches to discourse, contributing to the understanding of public relations as a powerful ideological intervention. I review the Foucauldian perspective here, and add to it by introducing two additional theorisations of discourse from the work of Pierre Bourdieu and Luc Boltanski. I aim to introduce both variety and depth into the potential for discursive analyses of public relations work, creating strong links with material and structural forms of power through a Bourdieusian lens, and addressing the importance of discourse as a route to societal agreement by using Boltanski's approach.

I begin by defining what is meant by discourse, in order to clarify the differences between discourses and other forms of language. I then review the Foucauldian perspective of discourse (Foucault, 1980, 1982) and public relations scholarship that draws on this theoretical approach. I introduce Boltanski's notion of justificatory discourse and Bourdieu's conceptualisation of language and symbolic power, along with examples of how their insights add a different perspective to the understanding of discourse in public relations. I conclude by considering what each approach offers for critical socio-cultural analyses of public relations work.

DEFINING DISCOURSE

The term 'discourse' is used widely in critical public relations scholarship, and it is worth taking the time to consider exactly what is meant by it. Discourse is certainly a linguistic 'object', but it is not purely to do with language. Similarly, discourse analysis is a form of textual analysis, but it does not deal only with texts; rather, it illustrates the complex relationship between the use of language and its socio-cultural context. Discourse has been defined in multiple ways, and there is a correspondingly wide variety of approaches to discourse analysis. However, certain core principles do allow us to identify certain important parameters of discourse that underpin the approaches outlined in this chapter.

First, discourse refers not simply to individual words or sentences, but to sequences of language, or series of statements that combine to create a particular picture of the world. Second, discourse refers to the use of language in context. Rather than understanding language as a form of communication that is abstracted and separate from the social world, the assumption is that context and language are inseparable (Titscher et al., 2000). Correspondingly, different forms of language, or genres, are used in different contexts, so that, for example, writing an advertorial piece for a women's magazine would use different vocabulary, phrasing and ideas than an advertorial for a financial publication or a political campaign speech (Fairclough, 2003). Third, discourse is a form of action through which things can be accomplished (van Dijk, 1977). It is also both a social practice and a *recontextualisation* of practice, in so far as it constructs representations, or 'socially specific ways of knowing social practices' (Van Leeuwen, 2008: 6). How these representations are constructed depends on the choices made by the speaker, the options available for 'appropriate' language, and the context (Woofitt, 2005).

Discourses consist of a series of statements that together build a coherent way of understanding social practices, and can be analysed within texts on their own terms, or in terms of their relations with other co-existing discourses in the same texts. Beyond individual texts, discourses can be analysed as they are used in social contexts. In these kinds of analyses, the focus is on the multiple discourses that inevitably co-exist because of the multiplicity of actors and situations that comprise the research site. Different actors will make different choices about how they wish to represent practices, and the contexts for practice will vary depending on the situations being observed. Thus, the discourses circulating in a public relations agency may draw on practices associated with running a business (e.g. accounting for time, securing new business), practices of collegiality (e.g. teamwork, brainstorming) and practices associated with professional identity (e.g. reporting, client presentations, training). Junior practitioners, administrators and senior managers are also likely to make different choices about how they describe the various practices, given the positions they occupy within the agency and, consequently, the different normative rules that they follow. Foucault (1981: 58) calls this combination of different discourses and practices 'a principle of grouping of discourses, conceived as the limits and origins of their meanings, as the focus of their coherence', and Fairclough (2006) notes that the relations and articulations between different discourses and practices are a crucial focus for analysis.

These parameters mean that analyses of public relations discourses have to go beyond a straightforward understanding of the language used, to more complex, contextualised investigations of their role as a purposive, ideological intervention in specific situations (Motion and Leitch, 1996). Practitioners and organisations using public relations are understood as actively making choices about how the statements they produce over time should be constructed, in light of the objectives they are trying to achieve. In the discourses they create, they draw on existing systems, norms and values to claim authority for particular perspectives of the world – or, more specifically, for the perspectives of their clients. In other words, if discourse is a way of representing social practices, then public relations discourses must be understood as structuring and prioritising different ways of knowing the world around us. This means we must pay attention not only to texts, but also to the practices that are involved in the production, distribution and interpretation of texts, and the social practices that form the context for these activities (Fairclough, 2003; Erjavec, 2005; Motion and Leitch, 2016: 144).

The three approaches to discourse described in this chapter reflect these principles. All consider how discourse relates to power, but the analytical framework that each provides is quite different. The Foucauldian approach focuses on the intersections between the knowledge produced in discourse, the presentations of 'truth' that it constructs, and the interactions between the two that produce possibilities of both power and resistance for the producers and consumers of discourse. In contrast, Bourdieu's approach to language emphasises the ways in which language is structured by, and simultaneously reproduces, the social hierarchies that mark the context in which it is produced and can thus be treated as form of symbolic power (Bourdieu, 1991). While not strictly a discursive approach, he draws on some of the same fundamental principles as the other two theories, including an emphasis on styles, language as a social practice, and the importance of language in context. In contrast, Boltanski and Thévenot's (2006 [1991]) theorisation of processes of justification and discursive orders of worth returns to an emphasis on discourse and focuses on the ways in which discourse is constructed within a certain set of logics that provide a coherent worldview. They explain how the legitimacy of these logics is repeatedly faced with discursive challenges that must be overcome. For each approach I consider the advantages they offer as a means of illuminating the power of public relations discourses.

FOUCAULDIAN DISCOURSE THEORY AND PUBLIC RELATIONS

Foucault draws attention to discourse as a socio-cultural practice, intimately connected to the circulation of power as well as being an object of power in itself. He argues that 'discourse is not simply that which translates struggles or systems of domination, but is the thing for which and by which there is struggle, discourse is the power which is to be seized' (Foucault, 1981: 52–3). Individual discourses form overarching discursive regimes (or Discourses, capitalised) that combine to produce 'regime[s] of truth' that regulate particular areas of life. Regimes of truth are structured through existing institutional norms; concepts of 'rationality' or reason that circulate in a particular arena; and the 'will to truth', or 'the way in which knowledge is put to work, valorized, distributed' (Hook, 2001: 524).

Foucault (1981) calls these regimes of truth 'orders of discourse', and they can be identified through three different elements: individual discourses, which represent the world in particular ways; genres, which communicate different ways of acting for author and audience; and styles, which communicate different ways of being for author and audience (Fairclough, 2003). The power generated through discourse is relational, in so far as it is manifest in the connections between different actors, rather than as a form of property or a tool to be wielded against others (Foucault, 1982). For example, the power that a client has over a public relations consultant would be seen as a product of the discursive construction of client need and superiority alongside service and deference on the part of the consultant, as opposed to understanding power as a product of the penalties imposed on a consultancy for non-delivery.

For Foucault, orders of discourse not only represent the world, but *constitute* it: subjectivities, institutions and relations of power among different social actors are brought into being through discourse. Within an order of discourse, truth is presented as what is considered 'reasonable' and 'normal', while forms of knowledge that stand outside the constructed order are defined as a form of madness, a 'noise to discourse' (Hook, 2001). The oppositions between 'true' and false, sanity and madness are contingent on the political, economic, social and cultural interests playing into the discourses that make up a particular order of discourse and form the conditions of possibility for 'what counts as knowledge, and the various systems through which knowledge is qualified/disqualified'

(Hook, 2001: 525). For example, public relations discourses are deployed strategically in specific contexts 'to circulate ideas, establish advantageous relationships and privilege certain truths and interests' (Motion and Weaver, 2005: 53). What is *said to be true* in different public relations texts contributes to the establishment, maintenance or contestation of hegemonic and material power through social interactions (Motion and Leitch, 1996; Weaver et al., 2006). At the same time, other voices and forms of knowledge are excluded from the regime of truth. In the professional workplace, for example, discourses tend to privilege a white, male worldview because white males dominate and have vested interests in such environments. The perspectives of other actors (e.g. women, people of colour and people with a disability), to whom the professional workplace offers different possibilities and limitations, tend to be marginalised (Acker, 2006).

Because what is presented as 'true' in discourse is intimately connected with the context in which it is produced, it cannot be separated from power, and so discourses reveal the nexus of truth, knowledge and power in that context. The 'will to truth' is a mechanism through which the 'will to power', or the realisation of dominance, is expressed. Place and Vardeman-Winter (2016), for example, show how public health campaigns reify scientific knowledge and thereby justify using the body as a site for both scientific deconstruction and technological intervention. However, in Foucault's view power is never absolute; the fluidity of discourse and the relational nature of power mean that spaces for resistance continuously emerge through challenges to normative understandings of 'truth' (Foucault, 1981). Alternative explanations and representations of events are (re)presented and other voices are given credence. Activist groups, for example, frequently counter corporate or government discourses by framing particular events in an alternative way, presenting different 'truths' about them. An oil conglomerate's positive financial results might be reframed as evidence of the continued damage to the environment that it promotes, whereas a new government policy to limit migration in the interests of national security might be reframed as contravening human rights.

Finally, Foucault argues that discourse is a form of governance, through which we are disciplined into adopting hegemonic values, attitudes and behaviours that serve the interests of already powerful groups (Foucault, 1991). In professional contexts, for example, researchers have demonstrated how discourses about professional identity and the importance of the client actively produce professionals who are willing to work long hours, adopt certain styles of dress, network and socialise in a particular way, and generally conform to the ideal professional archetype that both legitimises and secures the future of the profession (Anderson-Gough et al., 2000, 2006; Hodgson, 2002; Edwards, 2014b). In public relations, this hegemonic power generates complicity among audiences too: they participate in discourse, even if it results in their subjugation, to the extent that 'a discourse resonates with their individual or collective subjectivities and perceptions of reality' (Weaver et al., 2006: 20). Bourne (2013), for example, shows how public relations discourses and practices promoted by the financial industry generate power by promoting trust in the financial sector and its products. She explores how trust production in financial markets is an output of the discursive system of public relations across the industry. Discourses and associated practices reinforce the trust we put in finance and financial experts by privileging their expertise and excluding others (non-experts) from systems of money and capital. At the same time, public relations discourses promote finance itself as a market and a product, underpinned by trust, which in turn helps more power to accrue to the sector, while simultaneously disempowering those who invest in it. However, hegemony always leaves space for resistance to power and if audiences find discourses to be irrelevant or inaccurate in terms of their experiences of the world, they will reject them or take action against the 'truth' being promoted – sometimes turning the tools of capitalism itself against those who profit from it (MacLeod and Park, 2011).

Roper (2012) argues that public relations discourses act in a number of different ways. They may overdetermine a debate by becoming the dominant discourse; alternatively, they may colonise a debate by crowding out other arguments or perspectives (Roper uses the example of market discourses colonising debates about sustainability through the work of corporations trying to influence policy and public opinion in New Zealand). On the other hand, public relations texts may bring together (articulate) different discourses in order to generate new forms of knowledge and 'truth' about an issue. Multiple discursive strands are often identifiable in public relations texts because of their persuasive power, even though they may lead to inconsistency in the internal structure of the text itself (de Brooks and Waymer, 2009). For example, discourses of markets, consumption and pedagogy are often combined in the context of market-driven higher education sectors (Hearn, 2015; Cronin, 2016), and discourses of national security and human rights often co-exist in discussions about migration (Philo et al., 2013). Through all these different forms of discursive work, 'both sociocultural practice and the attitudes and values which support it [are] transformed' (Motion and Leitch, 1996: 299).

Importantly, public relations practitioners' work as 'discourse technologists' consists not only of textual production, but also of engagement in the discourse practices noted above. Through a wide range of background activities, such as media training, environmental scanning, analyst briefings, stakeholder engagement and the production of background documentation, they are 'actively involved in the research, redesign and training dimensions of discursive struggles to maintain or transform sociocultural practices' (Motion and Leitch, 1996: 301; see also Erjavec, 2005). In these contexts, discourse is being used as a disciplinary tool – a means of governing others – to ensure that spokespeople, journalists, analysts and stakeholders adopt and enact the individual and institutional identities that will preserve organisational power.

In summary, the Foucauldian perspective of discourse leads us to understand public relations discourses as a manifestation of power relations, analysed as social practices, rather than purely linguistic creations. The texts – the language used in the discursive events – are of course important, but not for their linguistic characteristics (grammar, syntax, punctuation). Analyses of public relations texts using a Foucauldian perspective will explore the ways in which discourses travel, investigating their intertextuality (the degree to which one text draws on others) and interdiscursivity (the degree to which a text draws on and connects different discourses), in order to understand how ideologies circulate and are contested through public relations work (Erjavec, 2005; Leitch and Davenport, 2009). These kinds of investigations would also show us the contradictions and discontinuities of discourses as they travel, and prompt questions about why these interruptions happen, as well as the potential they have for resistance. Questions about subjectivity (whose identities are privileged and whose are ignored), voice (whose voices are authoritative and visible, and whose are not), institutional power (which institutions are privileged as a source of knowledge and expertise, and which are not), and materiality (how discourse is being used as a tactic for the acquisition or preservation of material power) all become central to understanding how power emerges through public relations, and where the spaces for resistance to power can emerge.

CASE STUDY 3.1

COMMUNICATING GENDER EQUALITY? WOMEN IN INDIA

Gender plays an important role in structuring social relations in India. However, violence against women is a particular problem, recognised in the Indian government's National Policy for Women as a priority area. Article V.i of the draft 2016 document says:

> Efforts to address all forms of violence against women will be continued with a holistic perspective through a life cycle approach in a continuum from the foetus to the elderly starting from sex selective termination of pregnancy, denial of education, child marriage to violence faced by women in private sphere of home, public spaces and at workplace. It will identify and combat violence and abuse through a combination of laws, programs, and services with the support of diverse stakeholders. (Ministry of Women and Child Development, 2016: 12)

In this statement, gender is recognised as a potential focus of violence throughout a woman's life. Violence is recognised as fluid, continuous (experienced throughout the 'life cycle') and pervasive – it is found in homes, workplaces and in public. Correspondingly, solutions are systemic: better education for women and men, stronger law enforcement, improved monitoring of violence and its consequences, increased representation of women in the judiciary, integration of different agencies charged with supporting women, and increased access for all women to that support.

> The recognition of the problem is commendable, and the ambition of the proposed solutions is impressive. However, the policy is also problematic. The discourse represents Indian society as manageable, coherent, structured, and capable of surveillance and co-ordination. A discourse of modernity underpins this framing – India has systems and structures that suggest stable, rational governance (a judiciary, education, a police force, a developed economy and a government capable of dealing with major societal issues). While these institutions certainly exist, the material reality of life in India is not so streamlined. In fact, India's federalist structure, the divide between rich and poor, the gap in living standards between urban and rural communities, and the scale of poverty mean that the implementation of systemic solutions for violence against women is very difficult.
>
> Moreover, the National Policy for Women fails to mention the responsibility that men take for perpetuating many (though not all) forms of violence against women. The only mention of men's role is in Article V.ix, which states: 'Engaging men and boys through advocacy, awareness generation programmes and community programmes will be undertaken' (Ministry of Women and Child Development, 2016: 13). Thus the problem with men is that they are 'disengaged' from the lives of women (rather than being excessively involved and controlling those lives), and improved awareness and collective understanding will help to address the problem. Thus, while the policy does an admirable job of highlighting the complexity of gender equality and violence against women, it might also be interpreted as reinforcing male dominance through their erasure from most of the document.

JUSTIFICATORY DISCOURSES: LANGUAGE AND LEGITIMACY

While Foucault emphasises the ways in which power circulates through discourse, Boltanski and Thévenot (2006 [1991]) examine the ways in which discourses are used as a means of justifying social, political, economic and cultural relations and practices. Their starting point is that justification is essential to the process of living in a community: because society is made up of a diverse range of interests, our actions do not always make sense to others, and yet to live in harmony we must find ways of reaching agreement (see Chapter 1). In order to avoid conflict, we find ways of justifying our actions in ways that make them acceptable to others and grant us legitimacy. This, they argue, is a fundamental aspect of the 'social': 'persons face an obligation to answer for their behaviour, evidence in hand, to other persons with whom they interact' (Boltanski and Thévenot, 2006 [1991]: 37).

Boltanski and Thévenot (2006 [1991]) outline a number of different 'orders of worth' that act as discursive justificatory regimes. Each order of worth is defined by a particular conception of the common good, and individuals, groups, practices and relationships are ordered hierarchically in terms of the degree to which they serve that common good. Importantly, the notion of 'worth' in each order is a unifying and generally beneficial principle – all who ascribe to the order agree to it and work towards its realisation. Therefore, agreement on the 'common good' in a particular order of worth generates social stability. Seven general orders of worth have been identified, giving rise to seven 'common worlds'. In the civic world, worth is assessed in terms of contribution to collective welfare; in the world of fame, the measure of worth is public recognition; in the market world it is the ability to command a price; in the industrial world it is functionality, efficiency and reliability; in the domestic world, worth depends on reputation based on position in the social hierarchy; in the inspired world it is interpreted in terms of the degree to which an individual is unusual, creative, passionate; and in the 'green' world worth is measured in terms of contribution to environmental sustainability. The application of these orders of worth to different situations results in actors and objects (people, organisations, institutions) being ordered hierarchically based on the general principle being applied, but this inevitably leads to disagreement because people often use different orders of worth to assess the same situation. When conflicts arise, we challenge and debate the application and validity of different forms of worth in order to find resolutions to the dispute (Thévenot et al., 2000; Boltanski and Thévenot, 2006 [1991]).

Applying the framework of orders of worth to public relations discourses raises important questions about which forms of worth are privileged in campaigns, and why. The latter point is crucial, since different orders of worth legitimise different identities, actions and groups of people, and their use betrays implicit attempts to construct the world in a way that supports those who are designated more 'worthy' than others (Patriotta et al., 2011). How 'worth' is defined is therefore central to understanding the role that public relations plays in the distribution of power.

Because exercises in justification are based on particular interpretations of the common good, they must be, and are, tested in order to be accepted. In complex, plural societies more than one justificatory regime is likely to exist in the same social space (Chiapello and Fairclough, 2002; Boltanski and Thévenot, 2006 [1991]). For example, in debates about corporate social responsibility the green order of worth may be invoked (prioritising environmental sustainability) alongside the market order of worth (prioritising competitiveness and price), or the industrial order of worth (prioritising process and structure). Their co-existence provides the basis for different kinds of tests, expressed as critique, to which individuals must respond in the public arena (thus a company claiming it is socially responsible may be challenged on the basis of its environmental credentials, its ability to turn a profit, or the efficiency and clarity of its efforts).

The dialectical relationship between justification and critique means that justificatory discourses are produced in response to critique, but also generate critique as they are articulated. Critique may focus on the hierarchical order *within* a particular order of worth – so that, for example, the relative worth attached to people, groups and relationships in light of a particular common good may be contested. For example, an energy company's claims to a commitment to sustainability may be critiqued based on its ongoing extractive activities. This would be a critique from *within* the green order of worth, contesting the claim that its activities contribute to the agreed general principle of the common good (environmental sustainability). Alternatively, critique may challenge the definition of the common good on which a justification is based, dismissing the fundamental basis for claims of 'worth'. Thus, the same oil company's implicit claim that environmental sustainability is a form of common good, and therefore worth investing in, may be critiqued by those who argue instead that market flourishing is the common good to which the company should be contributing, and suggest it should spend its profits on developing new products in order to improve its competitiveness. This would represent a more fundamental critique of the legitimacy of the company's actions. Companies must respond to critiques regardless of their origin, and this dialectical engagement produces a gradually increasing abstraction of justificatory discourse so that eventually a compromise emerges that all can agree on.

Inherent in justificatory discourse is a tension between 'legitimation' and 'legitimacy' (Boltanski and Chiapello, 2005: 26). Processes of legitimation occur when actors use discourse strategically in order to justify their particular interests and position themselves in relation to others. In these situations discourse plays an ideological role, either furthering the objectives of dominant groups and reproducing existing power relations, or challenging those relations in order to alter the normative order of worth (Fairclough, 2003). Public relations is a widespread tool of legitimation. At the same time, when actors justify their positions in specific contexts, they often need to appeal to more general principles such as human rights, fair trade or democracy in order to establish their legitimacy. For example, the global human rights charity Amnesty International justifies its campaigns in terms of the need to address human rights violations and challenge other priorities, such as profit-seeking or political power (Mynster and Edwards, 2014). These principles create opportunities for more wide-ranging evaluation and critique by other groups because they introduce different notions of the common good into discussions, and thereby open up broader questions of legitimacy that may be resolved only through deliberation and reasoned agreement about the nature of justice. The co-existence of legitimation and legitimacy in justificatory discourse means that any attempt to use discourse as a means of gaining power in specific situations will likely prompt broader questions about the general principles underpinning the justifications being used.

CASE STUDY 3.2

COLLECTIVE WELFARE, SUSTAINABILITY OR PROFIT? SHELL'S SOCIAL INVESTMENT IN NEW ZEALAND

Shell, one of the world's largest energy companies, has a number of different operations in New Zealand and has faced regular challenges from local communities, particularly the indigenous Maori population, challenging its right to extract gas and oil from land and offshore sites. The activist group Climate Justice Taranaki, for example, describes the company as '[polluting] our ocean, our waterways and our air, and [threatening] marine species. They ignore cultural values, erode the social fabric that hold[s] communities together, and delay urgent actions needed to transition onto sustainable energy systems.' Their critique frames Shell's actions in terms of the market order of worth, as a purely profit-seeking enterprise, but also draws on the civic order of worth (collective welfare) to illustrate how Shell's actions ignore collective well-being and thereby reduce its 'worth'. The green order (environmental sustainability) is also integrated into the framing, again in order to illustrate Shell's poor credentials. In the discourse, the market order is opposed to the civic and green orders of worth, suggesting that while Shell focuses on profit above all else, it cannot make claims to provide collective welfare or sustainability.

In response, Shell has sponsored a range of programmes that protect New Zealand wildlife, and trains local Maori to monitor the presence and health of marine mammals. It uses the same orders of worth as its opponents to describe its credentials, but places the emphasis differently and weaves them together in order to legitimise, rather than delegitimise, its presence. The training programme, for example, is framed primarily by the civic order, reflected in the claim that it will allow local Maori iwi to 'grow their knowledge of customary practice' and fulfil their role as 'Kaitiaki or guardians of the sky, sea and land', as well as 'further enhancing the cultural understanding of their hapū or rūnanga'. The 'green' order is evident in the training objectives (long-term observation of marine mammals for protection), and the industrial order is incorporated via the implicit value attached to increasing knowledge and training Maori in scientific data collection and presentation – a presentation that allows it to be aligned with the civic priority of collective welfare. However, the market order of worth is absent; there is no mention made of the company's profit, financial success or extractive activities (even though these underpin Shell's need and ability to invest in local communities) and instead the emphasis is on its collaborative approach to working with local Maori.

Understanding the contest for legitimacy in terms of these orders of worth, and seeing how their deployment changes depending on the objectives of the organisation

> using them, provides an insight into why and how conflict arises (here, in the clash between profit, community and sustainability objectives), and where some efforts to bridge the gap between the two sides might be made (through greater involvement in community life). It also shows how some claims are never likely to be successful: the exclusion of any mention of financial success, efficiency, employment and shareholder value in Shell's discourse shows how difficult it is to marry these ideas, associated with the market and industrial orders of worth, with the more altruistic civic and green worlds.
>
> To read more, see http://www.shell.co.nz/sustainability/social-investment/kaitiaki-for-marine-life.html and https://climatejusticetaranaki.wordpress.com/about/

clarification

Justification and critique are fundamental to the ways in which capitalist society continually reproduces itself; therefore, as a tool that is directly implicated in both of the dialectical elements, public relations' relationship to capitalism comes under the spotlight when this view of discourse is adopted. According to Boltanski and Chiapello (2005), the 'spirit' of capitalism operates through three main justificatory dimensions that offer an account of what is stimulating about it (how it enthuses people, allowing them to 'blossom' and offering them personal liberation), the forms of security it offers (financial, personal and societal), and how it is consistent with justice and fairness and contributes to the common good (Chiapello and Fairclough, 2002; Chiapello, 2003; Boltanski and Chiapello, 2005). All these forms of justification can be identified in public relations campaigns, either in isolation or in combination. Corporate claims to the right to exist are framed in these terms (for example, a tobacco company might frame the value of its activity in terms of catering to freedom of choice and providing employment opportunities in local communities), while organisations working to change the economic, political and social order will challenge corporate and government activity on the basis of the same general principles, but applied in a different way (Patriotta et al., 2011). In response, corporates and governments adapt their activity and discourse, establishing new claims to legitimation in the process, which are in turn subjected to renewed critique. In this cycle, we find one important reason why public relations has thrived and why its importance has increased as the information and communication ecology of modern societies has become more complex, offering more numerous opportunities for critique that organisations must respond to.

The dialectics of justification and critique, legitimation and legitimacy can be easily applied to public relations work, since they deal with the processes by which 'stakeholder groups engage in public debates so as to handle disagreement and maintain the legitimacy of institutions relevant to their activity' (Patriotta et al., 2011: 1805). They are therefore directly relevant to the fact that public relations tends to emerge at points of disagreement or where an issue needs to be resolved through communication (L'Etang, 2008).

They also focus attention on the ways in which practitioners produce continuity and change in the social order through their work. Public relations campaigns may be produced as a response to critique (e.g. in the case of a crisis), to pre-empt critique (e.g. in order to deflect shareholder disappointment with poor financial results), or to exercise critique (e.g. to challenge an organisation's claim to a 'green', environmentally friendly identity). Campaigns valorise certain attitudes, values and behaviours, but their claims are often challenged with reference to the same or alternative orders of worth. In addition, understanding how different orders of worth compete across public relations campaigns can deepen our grasp of the consequences of adopting different understandings of the common good in democratic discussions (see Chapter 5). The relative strength of different forms of worth in a particular context, and the ways in which different forms of worth are combined in public relations discourses, show how public relations works with existing normative hierarchies to create apparently unassailable positions for the organisations it serves. At the same time, identifying the interpretations of the common good that form the basis of claims to organisational legitimacy simultaneously reveals possibilities for challenge and critique that can drive changes in the social order.

LANGUAGE AND SYMBOLIC POWER: THE BOURDIEUSIAN APPROACH TO DISCOURSE

In contrast both to Foucault and to Boltanski and Thévenot, Pierre Bourdieu's approach to language is more focused on its relationship to structural and symbolic power (Bourdieu, 1991). He identifies the existence of linguistic 'markets', or the range of languages available and used in a particular context, and argues that once a linguistic market is unified – when one language dominates all others – then a linguistic 'field' emerges. The linguistic field is structured according to existing social hierarchies, so that the types of language used by those higher in the social hierarchy tend to attract greater symbolic value than those forms used by groups that have a lower status. Linguistic fields also structure social hierarchies, in so far as the symbolic capital associated with different language types reinforces and confirms the existing power hierarchy. Class is a particularly important structuring/structured factor (Anthias, 2001), but gender and ethnicity are also important to the ways in which 'legitimate' language is acquired, assessed and deployed (van Dijk, 1996).

Bourdieu does acknowledge that language is not static and that struggles over the normative hierarchy do take place between different groups, while different types of language may dominate within subcultures. Nevertheless, the outcome of these struggles is a linguistic field that classifies groups and individuals in the social hierarchy based on their linguistic 'capital', or the ability to deploy the appropriate syntax, lexicon and semantics for the group and field to which one belongs. The linguistic hierarchy within a field in turn influences individuals' perceptions of the forms of language that are available to them, are appropriate in that context, and 'fit' with their own habitus – a set of dispositions, developed and inculcated over time that determine the way we comprehend our social environment and our role within it (Bourdieu, 1990; Swartz, 1997; see also Chapter 8 later). In this sense, language reflects social structure:

> Through the medium of the structure of the linguistic field, conceived as a system of specifically linguistic relations of power based on the unequal distribution of linguistic capital…, the structure of the space of expressive styles reproduces in its own terms the structure of the differences which objectively separate conditions of existence. (Bourdieu, 1991: 53)

Bourdieu's argument is based on the assumption that there is a clearly identifiable form of language associated with the middle and upper classes – a 'socially charged' legitimate language (Bourdieu, 1984: 226) – and that the acquisition of this language is not equally available to everyone. In part this is because of the link between language and habitus: language skills are acquired not only in the classroom (where the normative hierarchies of language are reinforced), but also in the home and through social networks, which means that who one mixes with is crucial to the language one can confidently deploy in different settings. Here, Bourdieu makes an important distinction between the *recognition* of dominant forms of language – which may be very broad among social groups because of the normative associations in the linguistic field – and *knowledge* of them (Bourdieu, 1991: 62), which is much less widely available and relates to the instinctive understanding of appropriate language in specific social milieux. Knowledge of appropriate language use comes through education and upbringing, and is difficult to acquire with ease later in life.

Bourdieu's analysis of the role of language prompts questions about the ways in which choices of language in public relations might be understood as a form of symbolic violence. In normative public relations theory, the requirement to use language appropriate to the audience is framed as a marker of effective communication, but from a Bourdieusian perspective, efforts to adapt language to a different context are underpinned by – and reinforce – particular classed, racialised and gendered assumptions about how certain groups of people communicate, what forms of speech are appropriate to them and ultimately where they are placed in the social hierarchy. When public relations practitioners try to find ways of communicating a message 'clearly' or 'effectively', they are searching for language that fits with the habitus associated with their targeted audience. From Bourdieu's perspective, such choices are not neutral or simply pragmatic; they also reinforce social hierarchies by 'fixing' the place of certain groups in society. Through language, he argues, 'a whole relation to the world is imposed' (Bourdieu, 1984: 462). Language choices both exclude and include, reifying certain forms of linguistic competence and, implicitly, the habitus associated with those competences. In public relations, indicators of exclusion and inclusion will comprise the types of vocabulary, grammar and expression used in campaign texts, the ways in which those choices are associated with particular audience identities, as well as the channels and formats (e.g. visual, text-based, multimedia, online, face-to-face) used to communicate the messages.

Bourdieu's work also provides a basis for analysing the ways in which language shapes public relations as a professional field. The language used by industry associations and public relations consultancies betrays the middle-class identities that inform its aspirations (Edwards, 2014b), while specialist firms (e.g. financial, technology or consumer consultancies) describe their competence using language that signifies their knowledge of the habitus associated with different audiences. Practitioners are expected to display a certain competence in terms of their ability to use language appropriately in business contexts, as well as the confidence to mix with a wide range of people from different professional backgrounds – from journalists, to chief executive officers (CEOs) and analysts (Public Relations Consultants Association (PRCA), 2009). Such expectations are generally presented as common-sense requirements, but they communicate assumptions about the identities of a typical 'PR practitioner'. Their normalisation masks the fact that 'writing well' or 'mixing comfortably' means using normative grammatical, spelling and 'legitimate' language norms that fit within the white, middle-class business context, rather than any kind of dialect. It also assumes knowledge of what 'writing well' means in the professional environment, often before individuals have much experience of those worlds. Moreover, the close links between public relations practice and the development of public relations degrees (Edwards, 2016a) mean that misrecognition of these requirements as objective and neutral realities of professional life begins even before aspiring practitioners enter the workplace. Degrees often require students to demonstrate their ability to write public relations materials (press releases, reports, blogs, social media posts) competently. This training in style and structure is a response to industry demands for recruits who are competent in the 'practical skills' required by the profession, ready to play the professional 'game' of public relations, and it reinforces the social hierarchies on which the profession is based (Bourdieu, 1990).

Finally, Bourdieu's analysis of language can be linked to the production of symbolic power on which social hierarchies are based. Symbolic power is attributed to the different forms of capital (financial, economic or cultural) possessed by actors in a particular field of action, through the cognitive transformation of that capital into symbolically valuable assets (Bourdieu, 1984). Because not all forms of capital attract symbolic value, only some forms can act as 'symbolic capital' and support their owners' claim to a superior place in the social hierarchy. The transformation into symbolic capital happens through language and, specifically, through the work of cultural intermediaries, the 'shapers of taste and the inculcators of new consumerist dispositions' (Nixon and du Gay, 2002: 497). Cultural intermediaries' use of language is designed to attribute symbolic value to certain ideas, identities, attitudes, values and beliefs, making them seem more valuable – and generating more status for those who possess them – than their material characteristics suggest. Public relations is an important cultural intermediary (see Chapter 2), and it is reasonable to argue that all public relations campaigns are designed to attribute symbolic value to various forms of capital, in order to make them attractive to the target audience (Edwards, 2012b; Hodges and Edwards, 2014). The associations among goods, services, behaviours and identities constructed in campaign materials make some forms of capital seem more appropriate or useful than others, having more potential to improve one's status in society. At the same time, the normalisation of such judgements means that audiences misrecognise the messages they receive as expressions of common sense, rather than seeing the ways in which they reinforce the power of dominant groups.

Bourdieu's approach to language has not been used extensively in public relations, but it can provide valuable insights that complement those of Foucault and Boltanski and Thévenot. For example, in an ethnographic study of a communications department in a national passenger rail company in the UK (Edwards, 2012b), a Bourdieusian analysis of their external communications materials revealed purposes other than simply the promotion of a product. The discourses used in campaigns, and the associated representations of 'passenger', 'journey' and even 'time', meant promotional messages simultaneously attempted to reshape norms and attitudes towards passenger rail travel in ways that both reflected a particular, middle-class, professional passenger identity and supported company objectives. In other words, the messages tried to alter the nature of symbolic power in the field of rail transport, by communicating a cultural shift in expectations of rail travel and changes in the roles and identities of rail operators, passengers and staff. Similarly, internal communication was designed ostensibly to encourage staff to offer the best possible experience to customers as a foundation for the company's success. In fact, the team couched this message in language that prompted a family-based identity and loyalty to the Chief Executive. The cultural construction of 'family', with a benevolent father-figure at its head, made the staff 'voice' subordinate and limited the space for any critique of company leadership. These deeper purposes were never stated explicitly, so the interests they reflected were misrecognised and consequently all the more likely to be accepted unreflectively by the audiences being targeted (Edwards, 2009).

CONCLUSION

In this chapter, three different ways of understanding public relations discourses have been presented. Each approach differs in its understanding of how power and discourse are intertwined and recognises that discourse is more than just text, image or the production of meaning, but should be understood as a social practice with clear material consequences. Foucauldian analyses are focused on the interrelations between truth, knowledge and power that are constructed in public relations discourse. Public relations is understood as a tool through which some are silenced and others govern, creating regimes of truth that exclude certain forms of knowledge and subjectivity while normalising and privileging others. In the process, it limits the information we have access to and the choices we are able to make about how we live our lives. In contrast, understanding public relations as justificatory discourse brings the focus back to how we reach agreement. It illuminates the part played by public relations in the processes of justification and critique that organisations and individuals must engage in, and helps to explain why organisations must continually re-establish their legitimacy in debates about the organisation of collective living. Finally, Bourdieu ties discourse back to its material origins by pointing out the links between language use and social hierarchies. Bourdieusian interpretations of public relations explore the ways in which language used in different contexts reinforces the relative power of different groups, based on structural hierarchies of class, race, gender or other aspects of identity. Structure takes precedence over agency in Bourdieu's model, such that our choices about the language we use are, to some extent, prescribed. His approach may be somewhat overdeterministic, but is a valuable reminder that the taken-for-granted approach to language in public relations is as ideological as any other of its practices.

Each of the approaches offers a different way of understanding the importance of discourse as the production of meaning at the heart of public relations work, and prompts us to consider how the practices that public relations promotes, as well as the practices it engages in, are (re)presented in discourse. Certain commonalities link all three perspectives. They all understand public relations discourse as a relational phenomenon, a manifestation and negotiation of the social relationships that we engage in on an ongoing basis. Discourses operate not in isolation, but as part of a number of co-existing 'regimes of truth', in Foucault's terms, and circulate through communicative networks (see Chapter 1) in which public relations is deeply implicated not only as a source of discourse, but also as a mechanism of circulation (see Chapter 2).

All three theories also understand language and discourse as a source of power, which reinforces the fact that inclusive communicative networks, where everyone can enjoy the capacity and opportunity to express their identity and interests by engaging discursively with others, are crucial to effective democracy. As a tool through which organisations can represent different voices and subjectivities, public relations has an important role to play here (see Chapter 5). The advantage that organisations and institutions enjoy as producers of discourse and arbiters of ideology also opens the way for critiquing the way these privileged actors dominate the public relations industry and exploring the effects of their hegemony on other voices.

In a world where communication technologies change rapidly and discourses travel far beyond the place of their inception, the circulation of discourse is the final crucial piece of the analytical jigsaw that needs to be accounted for. As Motion and Leitch (1996) have noted, public relations practitioners are discourse *technologists*; their work on the construction and enactment of discourse is done with specific objectives in mind. As noted in Chapter 2, they support the circulatory function of public relations that is indispensable to its status as a promotional industry. How they, and other actors in their communicative networks, actually put language and discourse to work through different practices is also crucial to research in this area (Motion and Leitch, 2002), and completes the picture of how broader dialectics of power and resistance emerge through the discursive dimensions of public relations work.

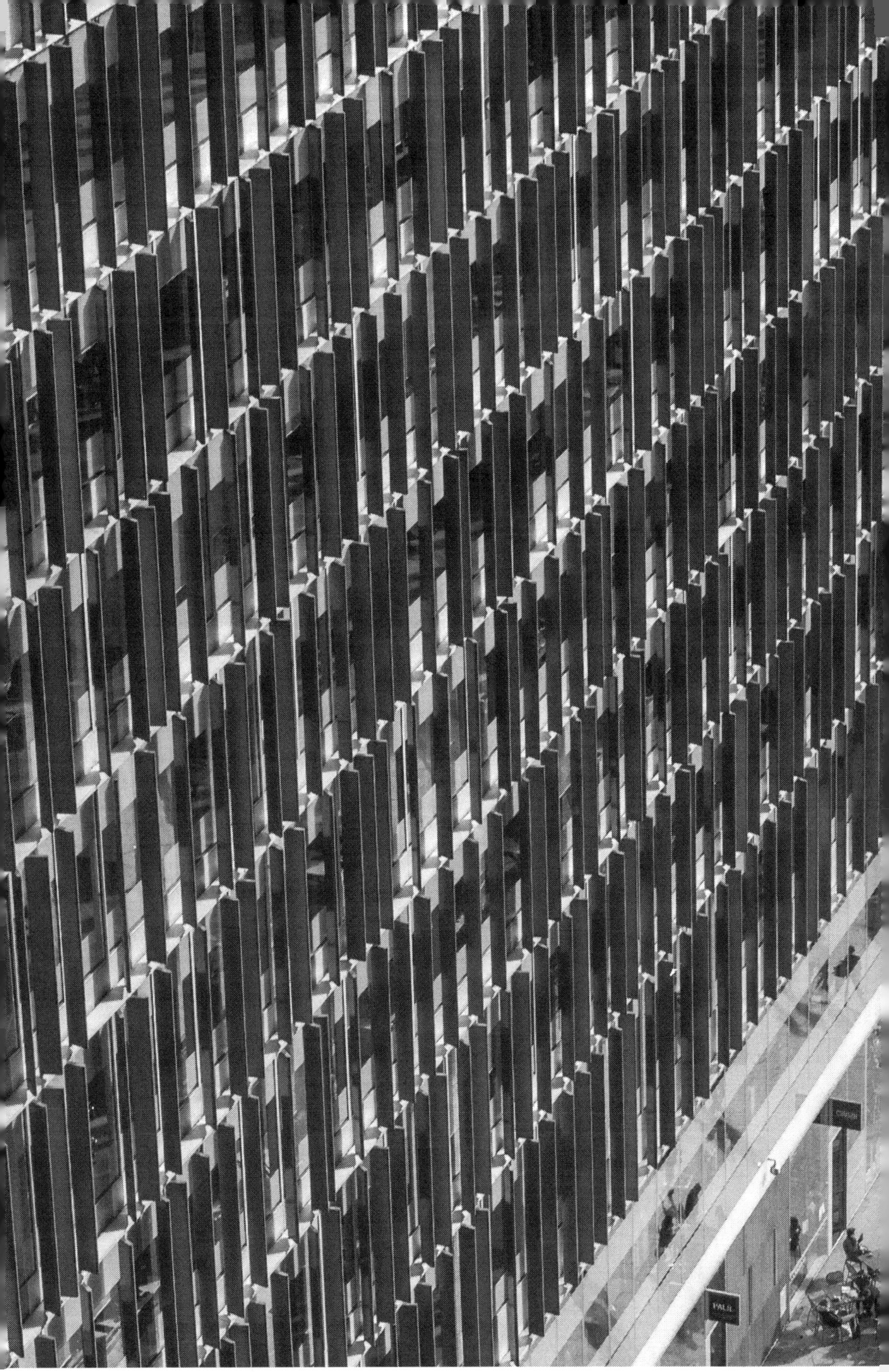

CHAPTER 4

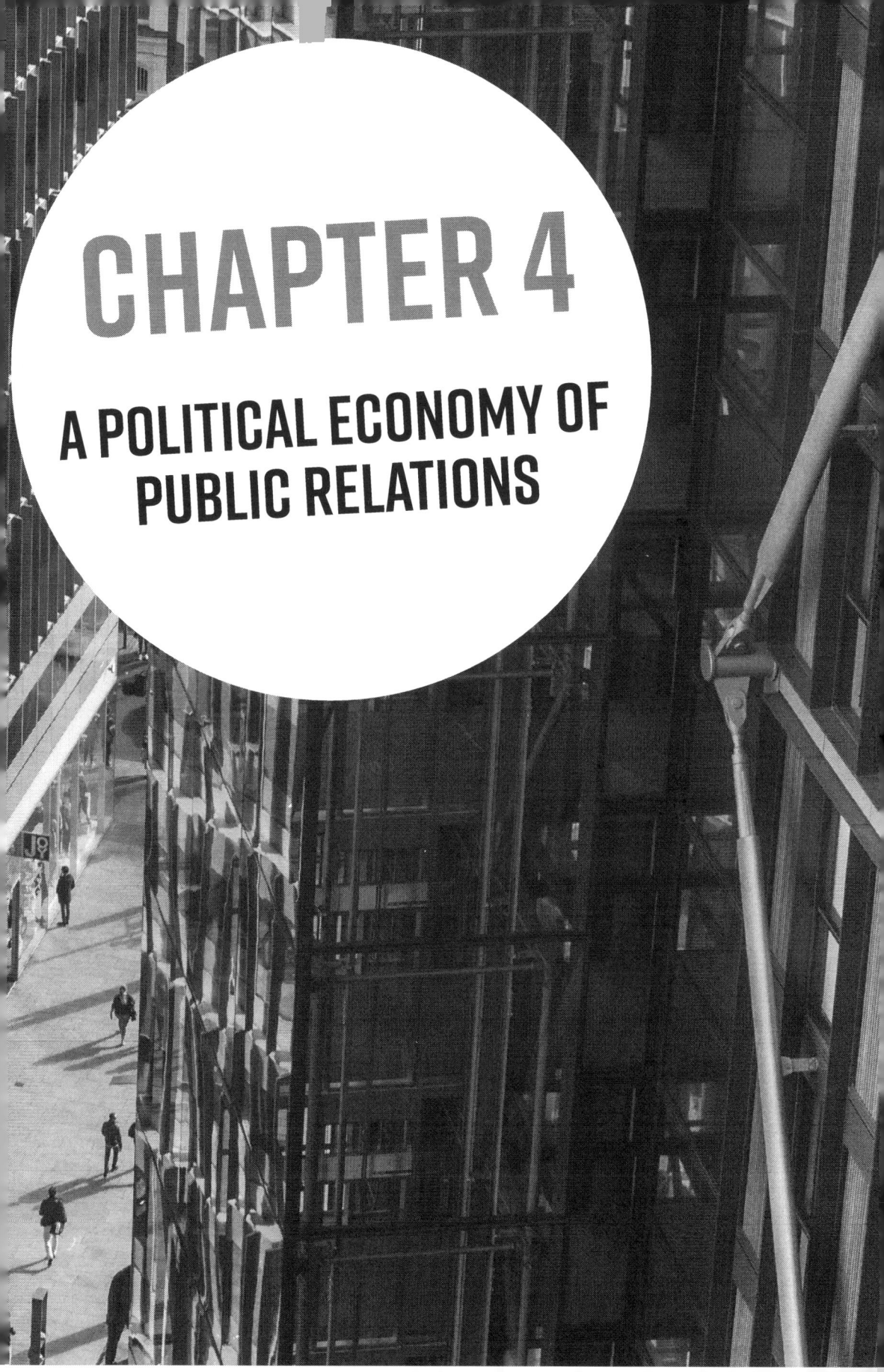

A POLITICAL ECONOMY OF PUBLIC RELATIONS

The previous chapters examined in detail the nature of public relations as a promotional industry, and the centrality of discourse in public relations practice. In this chapter, I approach public relations from a political economic perspective, to explore how it affects the distribution of material and symbolic resources. The engagement with resource distribution invokes structure and agency by focusing on how our position in society might affect our access to resources, and asking what choices we have about how we use those resources. It also addresses the changing nature of society and the reality that struggles over resources are continuous; the power to access the resources we desire is never complete because, as political and economic circumstances change, so too does our relative power as compared to others.

The starting point for political economic analyses is the assumption that the political and economic environment is an important influence on the public relations industry, and that public relations practices in turn influence political and economic arrangements. A number of scholars have adopted a political economic approach to analysing public relations work by analysing how political power and the distribution of resources generate the conditions for public relations practice in specific contexts. Many of these studies take a traditional critical approach (L'Etang, 2005) and offer a broad-brush treatment of public relations as a locus of dominance, rather than engaging with the details of practice or the structures of the industry in any depth. I take a slightly different approach in that I review the fundamental principles of a political economic analysis of communication from the perspective of critical theory, but complement this with a review of the cultural industries approach to political economy (Miège, 1987; Mosco, 2009). I integrate the two approaches in an analysis of the ways in which commodification, spatialisation and structuration are manifest in various aspects of public relations, and conclude by proposing a range of new areas for research that flow from the analysis.

PRINCIPLES OF A POLITICAL ECONOMY OF COMMUNICATION

At the heart of political economic analyses of communication lie questions about power, and particularly about struggles over the ability to control the material and semiotic resources that are needed for survival. Mosco (2009: 25) suggests that a useful way of thinking about political economy is 'the study of control and survival in social life'. Questions of control deal with the way in which individuals and groups are organised in society, while questions of survival focus on the means by which those individuals and groups generate the resources needed to survive and/or reproduce themselves. This broad definition is able to encompass a wide range of activities related to the production, distribution and consumption of resources; but perhaps the most basic question for a political economic analysis of any aspect of society is how power and wealth are related and how these relations are in turn connected to cultural and social life (Mosco, 2009: 4).

Mosco (2009) identifies some key characteristics of political economic analyses. First, political economic research focuses on social change: how social structures emerge and are constituted over time. Second, political economic research focuses on the social totality. The object of analysis is always situated in the broader context of society, and the focus is on the relations between the political sphere (the different power blocs that govern society) and the economic sphere (the material and symbolic sources of production and wealth). At the same time, political economic analyses avoid essentialising society in an ideological or material sense. Simply recognising an overarching ideology in a particular social context (for example, on the basis of the political leaning of a current government) is not taken to mean that all members of a society adhere to it. Rather, society is recognised as both a form of unity and a continually evolving, fragmented and fluid space. Third, political economic research focuses on moral philosophy in so far as social values and norms are connected to political and economic patterns of resource distribution. Finally, political economic research considers human activity, exploring the actual practices that generate – or prevent – social change. Importantly, however, a 'sophisticated political economy [insists on] the point that the interplay between economic, political and cultural practices and structures provides the context – the opportunities and constraints – with which actors struggle to mobilise material and symbolic resources' (Manning, 2001: 42).

Applying a political economic approach to analyses of the communications industries begins with an understanding of communication as a source of material and semiotic resources that contribute to the processes that structure and differentiate different groups in society and influence the 'interplay' that Manning describes – the complex context in which the social struggle for resources takes place. Political economic analyses of communications industries such as public relations will include their structures of ownership and operational processes, day-to-day practices, as well as the societal distribution of communication resources, technologies and skills, the ways in which different types of communication are produced and consumed, and who is able to produce and consume them. At the same time, the fluidity and change that characterise communications industries should be taken into account, as well as broader socio-economic and political factors including the effects of globalisation, digitisation and the rise of neoliberalism on the communications industries, their workers and their audiences; the ways in which historical events have shaped the industry; and the ways in which dominant sources of power are resisted by alternative voices, using alternative communicative tools, technologies and practices.

Mosco (2009: 2) argues that there are three starting points for political economic analyses of communication: commodification, spatialisation and structuration. Commodification is the process of transforming things that have a particular use value into things that have an exchange value – marketable products. How does the human act of communication itself become 'marketised' – a product produced for a profit, or used to generate profit from other products? We might consider the way in which content is structured, or how audiences are identified and used, or how labour is found, recruited, trained, skilled and deskilled, paid or used for free. Spatialisation refers to the processes that enable the constraints of geographical space to be overcome using media and communications technologies. What happens to the relative power of different groups in the struggle for resources when communication goes global and businesses market their products worldwide, or as the connections between space, structures of production and consumption of communication change, or as the public relations industry becomes internationalised? Questions of spatialisation would also consider how public relations work flows between different local, national and global communities and how different modes of production, transmission and consumption facilitate such flows. Structuration (Giddens, 1984) is concerned with the links between communication industry structures and the wider society. The focus here is on the power inherent in the relationship between individuals as active agents, and the social structures that shape, and are shaped by, their communicative activities. In the context of public relations, questions of structuration consider how social class, gender, ethnicity and other aspects of identity are reflected in the ways in which the different forms of public relations work are produced, distributed and consumed. We might also question how the modes of production of public relations – for example, the extensive use of digital communication and social media – themselves reproduce hierarchies of structural power.

Political economic analyses that have their roots in critical theory (see L'Etang, 2005) offer valuable ways of illustrating the macro-level dynamics of power across the communication industries, but are arguably less suited to understanding the specifics of different industries. An alternative approach, developed as a way of understanding the specific political and material struggles for resources in the cultural industries (to which public relations arguably contributes; see Edwards, 2015), was proposed by Miège (1987; see also Miège and Garnham, 1979). Miège argued that attention should be paid to the 'social logics' of the cultural industries, defined as the various, sometimes conflicting, 'processes of production and labour that contribute to the supply of cultural commodities [and] provide some stability over time while responding to the intervention of new entrants' (Miège, 1987: 274). The term 'social logics' refers to the different types of activity that make up the cultural industries. At the time Miège was writing, these included editorial production (books and publishing), broadcast production (television, radio, film, video), live entertainment, written information (newspapers and magazines) and electronic information. Today, networked technologies, multimedia and digital communication forms, and social media all clearly have an important place in the social logics of all cultural industries, including public relations.

Paying attention to these different logics permits a more detailed understanding of how traditional objects of political economic research – labour relations, employment patterns, technologies of production and consumption, interconnections across different industries and power blocs, and core–periphery relations – vary depending on the particular context and form of production and distribution under investigation. For the communication industries, the advantage of Miège's approach is that it opens the way to recognising the differences between the types of communicative work undertaken across different industries, how they are organised and distributed, and how they complement or conflict with one another. In public relations, it shifts the analytical focus from industry structures such as practice and disciplinary specialisms (e.g. financial or consumer public relations; crisis management or analyst relations) towards the specific forms of work that could be part of a public relations campaign in any area.

CASE STUDY 4.1

THE SOCIAL LOGICS OF PUBLIC RELATIONS

Table 4.1 shows some of the social logics around which public relations is organised, based on the specialisms that practitioners have identified in a UK industry survey (Chartered Institute of Public Relations, 2017).

Table 4.1 The social logics of public relations

Media relations; content creation; content curation; event management; internal communication; photography; campaign planning; social media strategy and planning; search engine marketing; media training; evaluation

Breaking public relations work down in this way, it becomes easier to see how public relations production will be organised differently depending on the social logics involved. Social media strategy and planning, for example, is likely to have a younger workforce, a fast pace of work, a rapid pace of change in styles and technologies of communication, require 24-hour availability, and combine a mixture of pre-planned and ad hoc reactive content. In contrast, media training is likely to involve ad hoc contracts, be delivered by older, more experienced practitioners and journalists, have a stable format with only slight alterations each time, and be delivered to a fixed schedule and during traditional working hours. Changes in social logics also result in hybridised forms of practice as new ways of organising production develop, characterised by change and continuity. For example, social media have fundamentally altered how, when and in what format media relations are conducted – a wider range of news

(Continued)

> sources is now likely to be included in public relations targets, including high-profile bloggers, YouTubers, and online news sites; public relations texts are made available digitally and might include video, text and spoken recordings all in the same 'package' for journalists. However, continuity persists in so far as social media channels have not displaced media relations from their foundational role in public relations work, nor altered the fact that established media outlets remain influential and key targets for public relations campaigns.

The cultural industries model also adds to traditional political economic analyses by helping to explain continuity and change as a product of industry-specific dynamics articulating with changes in political, economic, technological and social environments (Hesmondhalgh, 2013). As I show later in the chapter, these kinds of insights can support and add depth to our understanding of the broader power dynamics with which the public relations industry is engaged.

POLITICAL ECONOMIC ANALYSES OF PUBLIC RELATIONS

Although many scholars refer to political and economic contexts in their analyses of public relations work (Duhe and Sriramesh, 2009; Sriramesh and Verčič, 2009), critical political economic research grounded in the Frankfurt School is less common within the scholarly field and much of the existing work on public relations originates from outside the field. A strong tradition of critical media sociology and political communication research has led to a number of important studies, many of which focus on the intersection of morality and power as manifest in actual public relations practice. They ask critical questions about the power structures that allow the continued dominance of certain types of public relations practices – such as morally suspect campaigns conducted on behalf of despotic governments, anti-social products and environmentally damaging activities – despite the inequality they sustain (Brogan, 1992; Miller and Harkin, 2010; Cronin, 2013; Roper et al., 2016).

Within public relations scholarship, accounts of industry history and current practice show the long-standing connections between public relations and the political and economic spheres, through its development as a means of promoting business and political interests in domestic and overseas markets and maintaining a compliant electorate (Cutlip, 1994; Stauber and Rampton, 1995; Bentele and Wehmeier, 2003; Bernays, 2005 [1928]; Cronin, 2013). In the UK, for example, L'Etang points out how these dynamics have served the occupation's ability to profit from global trade as well as global conflict, allowing it to establish itself 'as the source of cultural and ideological power' (L'Etang, 2004: 221) that served the British government's efforts to extend and maintain its Empire in the nineteenth and early twentieth centuries, producing campaigns that reinforced the superiority and credibility of the Empire, its leaders, and British forms of government, administration and culture, while undermining resistance movements (Carruthers, 1995; Smyth, 2001; Anthony, 2012).

Miller (2005) and Miller and Dinan (2000, 2007) analyse how the UK public relations industry's historical connections with other loci of economic, political and social power have affected its evolution and determine its present-day structure, paying attention to the clients that helped the industry to grow and the distribution of public relations across different economic sectors over time. At an ideological level, they argue that public relations played a crucial role in the spread of neoliberal economic doctrine and, more specifically, in the successful transformation of 1980s Britain into a neoliberal, market-driven economy (Miller and Dinan, 2007). They argue that the dominance of neoliberalism today has been a hegemonic victory, 'won by argument and action' (2007: 15) and, as such, required significant investment by different power blocs in 'the machinery of information management' – including public relations – in order to win the 'battle' against other ideas of how economies might be run (see also Gandy, 1982). They show how close historical links with the interests of big business continue to shape the public relations industry and, in their view, compromise its ability to contribute to society. Because the industry's survival depended on practitioners serving their corporate clients well, its primary purpose was to persuade the public to support policies and practices that favoured commercial interests, usually by misrepresenting them as the public interest. In the process, the authors argue, public relations has subverted genuine debate and weakened democracy. In similar fashion, Marchand's (1998) account of public relations in corporate America charts the emergence of the industry as part of the need for corporations to project a 'corporate soul' that would re-establish trust in business and encourage the public to believe that corporations in fact had the public interest at heart. Already three decades ago, Gandy (1982) showed how public relations, used as a tool for securing influence through the ownership and dissemination of information, had become central to policy making in the USA (and arguably in other countries), framing problems, choices and outcomes in ways that favour those who have the strongest influence on political actors. As he noted at the time, 'corporate and foundation boardrooms are important policy centres' (1982: 135).

Connections to corporate and political elite networks remain some of public relations' most important sources of power, helping the industry expand its global presence and its involvement in all areas of business and political life (Roper, 2012; Kantola, 2014; Aronczyk, 2015). They also help to perpetuate inequality because of their exclusionary dynamics. Within elite networks, the public relations industry is now indispensable to the facilitation of other, equally exclusive interactions: practitioners enable editors to talk to senior politicians about stories, connect financial journalists with analysts and CEOs, and pit CEOs against their peers in debates. The result is that 'much elite promotional activity is aimed, not at the mass of consumer-citizens but, rather, at other rival elites' (Davis, 2003: 673; see also Leveson, 2012). What the public think is less important to political and economic elites than the opinions of their peers, because peers have the power to determine their success or failure, while the public's compliance – or lack of opposition – is all that is required (Miller and Dinan, 2007).

The relationship between public relations and the news media has been an important focus of political economic critique. Manning (2001), for example, argues that the 'gravitational pull' of capital (2001: 38) on economic and social life is influenced by public relations in its role as a representative of capital (or a source of resistance to it, when used by activists) in the media industries. Public relations affects organisational access to media institutions and journalists, and shapes the way journalists understand issues on the media agenda. Political economic analyses of this kind tend to identify the rise of neoliberalism and the consequent market-driven, structural changes to the media environment as being at the heart of some of the shifts in the relationship between public relations practitioners and journalists, including the economic and practical implications of a 24-hour news agenda across a range of platforms, intensive competition for audiences, continually evolving technologies, pressure on costs and changing audience demands. These changes make journalists much more dependent on public relations practitioners for news stories, relationships with spokespeople, access to information, and more basic types of journalistic work, including fact-checking and ensuring 'balance' (Cottle, 2003; Davies, 2008; Lewis et al., 2008). However, structural and agentic constraints in the media environment – for example, editorial policy, staffing levels, the levels of investment in investigative journalism, the pressure of time for both public relations practitioners and journalists, and the quality of their relationships – all have a mutual influence on each other and introduce an element of unpredictability in the impact of public relations in different media environments.

One assumption that underpins critiques of public relations' influence on the media is that it acts as a vehicle for the perpetuation of hegemonic ideologies (see Chapter 6). Political economic analyses of public relations tend to emphasise the power of dominant groups (Roper, 2005), arguing that discourses communicated through the industry attribute moral and intellectual leadership to elite institutions and individuals (see Chapter 3). However, hegemonic power is never completely secure (Hall, 1981, 1988a), and public relations can facilitate resistance when used by marginalised groups. Even when critique is the main objective of analysis, it is important to remember that public relations is used across all areas of the economy and includes practices that are aimed at redistributing, rather than consolidating, power.

Moloney (2006), for example, views public relations as a fundamental component of liberal democracies. While corporate and political public relations work may keep conflict latent when the public interest clashes with the interests of dominant groups, Moloney also points out the variety of ways in which public relations is used by organisations large and small, some of which encourage debate. Rather than assuming public relations audiences are easily duped (a trap that some critical political economic theorists can fall into), he notes that public relations tactics are frequently identifiable, the information communicated is often accurate and the purpose is recognisable. Audiences can actively interpret and make new meanings from public relations texts as they consume them, and the power of public relations is limited by the fact that the audience is aware of the attempt to persuade them. Nevertheless, Moloney accepts that public relations resources are less available to marginalised groups. Activist organisations rarely have the resources to invest in public relations that large corporations enjoy, while consumers are not always told whether the information they receive comes from a public relations source or not. To counter these political and economic inequalities, Moloney (2006) suggests the restoration of 'communicative equality' by educating consumers to recognise and be vigilant about public relations work, and providing training and funding to institutions that act in the public interest and challenge dominant groups.

As Miège's model reminds us, there are variations in practice within the industry, across companies, specialist disciplines, in-house and consultancy contexts, and geographical regions, and these variations are reflected in critical studies of public relations specialisms. Demetrious (2013), for example, highlights how activist groups engage in communication based on a detailed and nuanced understanding of the communicative environment, their own power and the power of their adversaries. Anti-slavery, anti-racism and anti-colonial movements have used a range of public relations techniques, including rallies, speeches and media relations, as part of their promotional toolboxes (Straughan, 2004; Heath and Waymer, 2009; Page and Adams, 2014), while in conflict societies public relations is used by groups from across the ideological spectrum to secure publicity and support and can be an important means of rebuilding civil society and improving social cohesion (Thörn, 2007; Taylor, 2010; Somerville and Kirby, 2012). Such studies are valuable in their ability to situate practice in a particular political and economic context, and illustrate the important truth that public relations work does not simply come from nowhere, but exists in a dialectical engagement with the environment in which it is used; there is significant scope for more of these kinds of political economic analyses of public relations, addressing the specifics of context and practice in a systematic way.

In the next section, I extend the theoretical foundation for political economic approaches to public relations scholarship by integrating the critical perspective with Miège's cultural industries analysis in order to address the three starting points that Mosco (2009) identifies. In each case, I consider what kinds of questions we might ask, and what we could discover, if this more complex theorisation of public relations were adopted.

APPLYING POLITICAL ECONOMY: COMMODIFICATION, SPATIALISATION AND STRUCTURATION IN PUBLIC RELATIONS

The three starting points of commodification, spatialisation and structuration ensure that attention is focused on the higher-level contextual factors that affect the evolution and use of public relations, including the increasing importance of neoliberalism as a set of organising principles for markets and organisations, the effects of globalisation and the digital age, and the importance of networks. I consider here the important questions they raise, which could extend the quality and quantity of political economic work in the field.

COMMODIFICATION

The nature of commodification done by public relations depends on the campaign being conducted as well as the social logic being considered. Media training and strategic planning, for example, do not produce public texts in the way that video or broadcast production does, while products and services must be differently commodified in order to appeal to a particular audience (consider the different ways in which washing powder, mobile phones, films and banking services are promoted). Alternatively, it may be the CEO's identity that is commodified and packaged through public relations, as a representation of strong leadership or inspirational change, 'selling' a positive future. Public relations for a charity may commodify the people in need of help, constructing them in a way that elicits sympathy and support from the donating public (Chouliaraki, 2006; Thompson and Weaver, 2014). And as a promotional industry (see Chapter 2), public relations always commodifies audiences, constructing them as a tool through which organisational success is secured rather than being understood as people in their own right (Davis, 2013). Through these different forms of commodification, the texts produced and circulated by public relations facilitate the transformation of use value into exchange value for other goods, services and ideas. They also add to the capacity of communication to enhance the marketisation processes that characterise neoliberal economies, and support the survival of capitalism (see Chapter 3).

Public relations is a relatively cheap route to commodification; individual campaigns need not be expensive, unlike advertising and branding, and there is a wide range of self-help books and websites for small and medium-sized organisations keen to do their own public relations without the help of a practitioner or agency. The question of how much value is created by such campaigns is difficult to answer, since the actual return on investment from public relations is impossible to measure. Arguments about the contribution to improved reputation, better customer loyalty or a better public understanding

of an organisation's work may be pertinent, but they do not explain the ⟨
such improvements add value to a company's bottom line. In part, this is
relations outputs are not commercial or cultural 'goods' with a specific u
value for their audience. While they are designed to be consumed (read,
they are not marketed in and of themselves (one does not buy a press
conference, or a speech by a CEO). Moreover, the audiences for public relations texts –
consumers, journalists, investors or policymakers, for example – do not purchase the
work that is directed towards them; rather, it is the organisations aiming to persuade them
of a particular point of view that make the financial investment. Nonetheless, public
relations *is* designed to influence our understanding of the world and our place within
it (Edwards and Hodges, 2011), so that we are more likely to support the objects to
which they direct our attention – whether those be a response to a refugee crisis, a new
anti-welfare policy, or a local animal charity. In this sense, public relations outputs exert
persuasive effects that commodify objects in ways that make them desirable for a particular audience, and thereby serve the institutions that deploy campaigns.

CASE STUDY 4.2

PRODUCTION, CONSUMPTION AND CIRCULATION IN PUBLIC RELATIONS

Public relations has traditionally been conceptualised as a profession that helps organisations engage with audiences, but with the advent of social media, the definition of organisation and audience, or producer and consumer, becomes increasingly unclear. In particular, the question of who is promoting what, to whom, becomes much more fraught. Audience-driven, viral public relations has become popular since the advent of social media and networked technologies, and blurs the boundaries between production and consumption in the industry. In contrast to other industries, where copying and circulating goods can be a form of copyright infringement, practitioners focus on crafting texts such as viral videos or Twitter trends, which actively prompt audiences to share content as widely as possible. Campaign artefacts are *designed* to be public, since the more public relations outputs are talked about and shared, the greater the publicity generated for the object they promote, and the more widely a desired meaning can circulate. The consumption and circulation of public relations outputs by a target audience is a mark of success, evidence that

(Continued)

> messages have been taken up and the persuasion process is underway. There is no risk of losing income as a result of audiences sharing public relations 'products'; rather, the risk exists in them *not* being shared, and the desired meaning of the texts never being taken up. At the same time, the tactic raises difficult questions about the free labour that audiences do for organisations. Given that their sharing generates awareness, and potentially income, for the organisation, should they be rewarded for their efforts, or are organisations and public relations practitioners justified in framing this type of work as audience 'engagement'?

SPATIALISATION

Questions of spatialisation relate to the ways in which space and time both shape the public relations industry, but are also shaped by the industry's activities. At issue are the ways in which public relations strategies and tactics can bring together audiences in different locations across the globe, what kinds of connections are made and between whom, which communities are marginalised by public relations and which are placed at the centre, and how such dynamics change depending on the social logic being considered. Online communication, for example, privileges those who are connected and largely ignores geographical and temporal boundaries, while media relations may be much more driven by concrete deadlines and localised engagements. Sponsorship management focuses on communication around a particular event that takes place at a very specific space and time. Executive strategy reifies the status and centrality of senior management over employees as authorities on an organisation's future, while choices about what, who and how to film for video and broadcast production will literally place some groups and individuals in the foreground, while erasing others from the space being constructed in a film's narrative.

A focus on spatialisation also prompts attention to how the structures of global public relations affect the circulation of power and finance and the ways in which core–periphery relations are structured in and through the industry (Hesmondhalgh, 2013). For example, one important dimension of core–periphery relations is the global distribution of the consultancy industry. Industry league tables illustrate how public relations resources and revenues flow towards the global West and North (Table 4.2). For example, eight of the top ten global public relations corporations in 2015 were headquartered in the USA and one was in France (Holmes Group, 2016). Only one, BlueFocus, was headquartered outside Europe and North America, in China. Even though this agency's growth rate far outstripped the others in the top ten, its revenues remain over US$100 million behind those of its closest rival.

Table 4.2 Top 10 PR consultancies 2016 by revenue

2016 Rank	Agency	HQ	Revenues (US$)
1	Edelman	USA	854,576,000
2	Weber Shandwick	USA	775,000,000
3	FleishmanHillard	USA	570,000,000
4	Ketchum	USA	530,000,000
5	Burson-Marstellar	USA	480,000,000
6	MSLGroup	France	480,000,000
7	Hill+Knowlton Strategies	USA	385,000,000
8	Ogilvy PR	USA	347,000,000
9	BlueFocus	China	245,055,843
10	Golin	UK	227,000,000

Source: Holmes Group (2016). Figures are based on 2015 revenues. With the exception of Edelman and BlueFocus, revenues are estimated because the parent companies elected not to provide revenue numbers for individual firms.

Slightly more geographical diversity is evident in the top 250 agencies for 2016 where, in total, 30 countries are present. However, North America and Europe still dominate, and only the most economically developed countries within other regions tend to be represented (for example, South Africa is the only African nation included; Asia comprises China, Japan, Korea and India). In other words, the general flow of trade and finance between developed and developing nations, from South to North and East to West, remains undisturbed (Table 4.3).

Table 4.3 Regional breakdown of top 250 public relations consultancies, 2016

Region	Number of agencies in top 250
North America	114
South America	5
Europe	104
Middle East	2
Asia	15
Africa	2
Oceania	3

Source: Holmes Group (2016).

> ## CASE STUDY 4.3
> ## CORE–PERIPHERY FLOWS OF FINANCE
>
> Revenue distribution provides another example of core–periphery relations, being highly concentrated among a small number of Western-based companies. The top ten agencies in 2016 received a total estimated fee income of US$4,894 billion, more than the total revenues of all the companies ranked 11–156 in the list ($4,888 billion; Holmes Group, 2016). Moreover, many of the elite public relations agencies are owned by global communications conglomerates such as WPP, Omnicom and Publicis, reflecting the degree to which promotional industries as a whole form a tightly connected network of institutions controlled by relatively few corporations. At the time of writing (2017) WPP, for example, is the world's largest marketing group, owns four of the world's largest advertising agencies in JWT, Ogilvy & Mather, Young & Rubicam and Grey, and owns Hill+Knowlton Strategies and Ogilvy PR, listed at 7 and 8 in the global top ten public relations agencies (see http://www.wpp.com/). It also owns the global media networks Mindshare, MEC, Mediacom and Maxus (Adbrands, 2016). The pattern of combining advertising, public relations and media agencies under one corporate umbrella is repeated with WPP's competitors. Omnicom owns advertisers BBDO, DDB, TBWA and media-buying network OMD, and runs over 200 marketing services agencies through its DAS group of companies, including sector specialists and general public relations companies such as Ketchum (number 4 in the top ten; see http://www.omnicomgroup.com/our-agencies/). Publicis Groupe owns advertising agencies Saatchi & Saatchi and Leo Burnett, media planners and buyers Starcom MediaVest and Zenith Optimedia, and public relations agencies including MSL Group (number 5 in the top ten agencies; see http://www.publicisgroupe.com/).

A second core–periphery dynamic emerges from the ways that communication conglomerates make investments and structure their operations. Contemporary changes include heavy investment in digital agencies, as well as prioritising online and networked channels of communication in campaigns (Adbrands, 2016). These investments provide channels through which work from across all sectors of the industry circulates within a 'stable' of agencies controlled by the same group (Sanders, 2002), and protect the westerly and northerly direction of the flows of capital, ideology and political influence facilitated by their work. The reification of digital communication also increases the power of audiences that enjoy access to robust technological infrastructures, sophisticated mobile technologies and the wherewithal to pay for online access, at the expense of those who have less, and less reliable technology at their disposal. Privileged audiences – most of whom are in the global North and West or belong to elites in developing countries – end up having more time, effort and attention paid to them, and arguably have better access to information as a result.

The final core–periphery trend relates to the *stratification of clients and agencies*. While large agencies may be able to take on small clients, small agencies cannot compete for the lucrative business of larger national and international clients. The scale of communications work required by multinational corporations, listed companies and larger, national organisations, and the track record that larger agencies enjoy in managing large campaigns, make it much more likely that this kind of work and its associated revenues will flow towards the already dominant agencies. At the same time, the rich communicative resources (staff, skills and technologies) that the largest agencies benefit from – and can continue to invest in because of the lucrative campaigns they win – remain out of reach of both smaller agencies and smaller clients. The volume of public relations produced by the latter is less, and this potentially limits their promotional 'voice', ability to be heard by key audiences, and ability to contest or influence political, economic and social developments that are damaging to their existence. Grassroots organisations, activists and small and medium-sized businesses are at significant risk of this peripheral status, while on a global level the interests of local organisations, industries and communities in developing countries are easily steamrollered by global corporations using public relations to push through their agenda (see Chapter 7). The risk is that public relations campaigns neglect and/or stereotype the global South and discriminate against the interests of globally marginalised populations in the service of capital. Thus, the inequitable structure of the global consultancy industry produces a wider inequality of 'voice' that reinforces global political and economic hierarchies.

STRUCTURATION

Questions of structuration applied to public relations might begin with the well-known lack of diversity in the profession and the gender discrimination that continues to exist despite the fact that it is a feminised occupation. The benefits of employment in public relations are not equitably distributed (see Chapters 8, 9 and 10): women are paid less than men at all levels of the occupation, and the field is marked by gender, race and class hierarchies that shape the opportunities available to practitioners and the texts they create (Edwards, 2014b; Chartered Institute of Public Relations, 2017). Inequity is also reflected in the industry's tendency to gravitate towards audiences that constitute 'markets' and voters, largely because most public relations work is carried out by corporates and government (see Chapter 8). Audiences that have less to offer organisations tend to be neglected until they gain enough economic or social status to justify attention. Thus, for example, the 'brown', 'pink' and 'grey' pound are phrases used to describe the fact that black, gay and ageing populations have significant disposable income and therefore need to be targeted as audiences for promotional communication.

Changes in technology, and particularly the advent of social media, drive rapid changes in public relations practice on a number of levels, and these changes also shape the way its work is consumed in different ways. Most significantly for structuration, technology has altered public relations' mode of engagement with audiences. The ability to use online, mobile and social media allows practitioners to sidestep traditional media in their efforts to communicate, exerting more control over the production of messages and communicating more directly with audiences. Connectivity across devices and platforms means that the trend towards digital communication with audiences will both continue and become more complex, as campaigns are designed to make the most of the opportunities to reach audiences in increasingly diverse ways across space and time (Zerfass et al., 2012). Consequently, practitioners are under pressure to become more familiar with and capable of using a range of digital communication platforms (Zerfass et al., 2012; Holmes Report and International Communications Consultancy Organisation, 2013), whether they manage these themselves or in conjunction with related promotional occupations (e.g. digital or advertising agencies). The dominance of online communication in public relations may also perpetuate the youth bias in the occupation: the average age of the public relations workforce is relatively young, just 28 years in the UK industry (Public Relations and Communications Association, 2016).

While the industry celebrates the ability to reach more people more effectively through online communication, such trends are also important sources of marginalisation. Technology is far from neutral: access to and deployment and use of technology are all shaped by class, gender and other primary social definers that mean the power structures of the offline world are closely replicated online (Mattelart, 2003). As online communication and social media become the norm in public relations campaigns, audiences who do not use social media, or who find it more difficult to get online, will have both less access to communication that might be relevant to them, and less opportunity to intervene in debates that affect them and their ability to act in the world. Such groups might include the elderly, people with disabilities, rural communities, or communities across the globe where traditional media and face-to-face communication still dominate. This also raises questions about how and why such communities might use communications to reassert their voice, and with what effect.

The increased use of mobile devices and social media to communicate promotional messages also means that public relations is part of the excessive marketisation of public space, and is increasingly visible in the private sphere (Klein, 2000; Moloney, 2006). The ability to engage with people via their personal devices – for example, as a form of 'pull' marketing where consumers proactively sign up to receive promotional messages (Barnes and Scornavacca, 2004) – extends the influence of public relations discourses as readily available sources of meaning about how people might live their lives, take action and construct their identity in connection with others. Decisions about the self become framed, consciously or unconsciously, in terms of the meanings commercial, government or non-profit communication attribute to different actions. Their communication addresses us not as individuals seeking to make informed decisions, but as potential organisational assets, thereby reinforcing the dominance of those institutions in our lives. Moreover, public relations' intrusion into the private sphere also allows practitioners to co-opt audiences into doing unpaid promotional work (see Chapter 2). Given the convergence of communicative technologies and platforms, the instrumental use of this 'productive sociality' (Arvidsson, 2005: 248) by public relations is likely to continue. Even if the engagement of audiences is voluntary (Hesmondhalgh, 2010), it nonetheless raises questions about how the division of labour between production and consumption is influenced by public relations' approach to promotion, how audience labour is rewarded (or not) and how aware audiences are of their role in the perpetuation of organisational power.

On the other hand, technology can impact structuration dynamics in the opposite direction. The focus on generating public discussion via 'word of mouth' viral techniques also allows public relations to contribute to processes that bring issues from the private realm into the public sphere and encourage debate, changing their social and cultural significance through its symbolic intervention and raising the profile of issues that might otherwise be ignored. Campaigns dealing with domestic violence, marital rape and female genital mutilation are examples of how injustices that happen in private spaces have been made a matter of public concern through a combination of public relations campaigning, lobbying and grassroots action. The result is that women enduring such treatment may feel more able to escape it than was previously the case. The limitations of technology notwithstanding, the fact that social media are relatively easy to access and use also gives activists an opportunity to put low-profile issues on the public agenda and make them visible to journalists, bloggers and prominent tweeters. This is a significant benefit for groups who want to use public relations to propagate their cause, but cannot profit from the global industry infrastructure described above because of their peripheral status.

CONCLUSION

Political economic analyses of public relations represent a fundamental shift away from the managerial/organisational view of public relations towards a focus on history, industry structures, cultures and practices, and their effects on the struggles for material resources that we all undertake as members of society. Their importance cannot be underestimated. In other fields of communication, political economists have revealed important information about how and why the communication industries perpetuate or challenge power by contributing to global movements of capital, labour, technology and ideology. Public relations is central to such processes, but much more work needs to be done to examine its specific effects, both in isolation as well as in conjunction with other industries.

Some work has been conducted in relation to the links between public relations and journalism, but more could be asked about the continually changing nature of these connections in a world of marketised and digitising media industries. The relationship between public relations and other promotional industries, such as advertising, branding and digital marketing, could also be re-examined from a political economic perspective, and is particularly urgent given the close links between these industries on a global scale. Answers to these kinds of questions would also inform the important but under-researched area of the structures, connections, differences and similarities between consultancies, owned by the global conglomerates, and in-house public relations. Investigations could interrogate the relative power of large public relations consultancies compared to small ones, or multinationals compared to independent agencies, by considering the clients they service, the level of fees they command, or the networks of contacts they enjoy across other power blocs. Alternatively, research on in-house public relations could examine when and why in-house teams use consultancies and when they keep work in-house, revealing their role as a driver of the global expansion of consultancy services and an important engine for public relations' global presence.

Traditional political economic analyses focus on structures, but the more nuanced cultural industries approach addresses the specifics of located practices. While broad questions clearly need to be asked about how the overarching structures of the public relations industry affect the ability of different groups to access resources that ensure they can participate fully in the networked communicative environment, Miège's approach invites scholars to drill down into how the different social logics of public relations contribute to hegemonic power and individual agency, and particularly how they both realise and limit the choices available to us. Research needs to address these logics in a way that avoids generalisations and mechanistic descriptions, and instead develops nuanced and detailed understandings of the range of work involved in the industry, the reasons why it is structured and organised in particular ways, and the drivers behind change.

Finally, this kind of analysis could contribute to our understanding of different manifestations of the industry's internal power structures. Detailed empirical work would provide robust evidence to illuminate how and why different public relations specialisms are rewarded differently, how those forms of industry stratification reflect wider social, political and economic contexts such as the norms associated with (or contesting) neoliberalism, and how gender, race, class and other dimensions of identity affect the distribution of access, skills, expertise and rewards across different specialisms and practices. As well as helping to explain the different ways in which inclusion and exclusion are produced for different practitioners, clients and audiences (see Chapters 9 and 10), including the cultural industries approach in political economic analyses of public relations will ensure we develop a more holistic picture of how the industry is implicated in wider social and cultural dynamics of dominance and resistance.

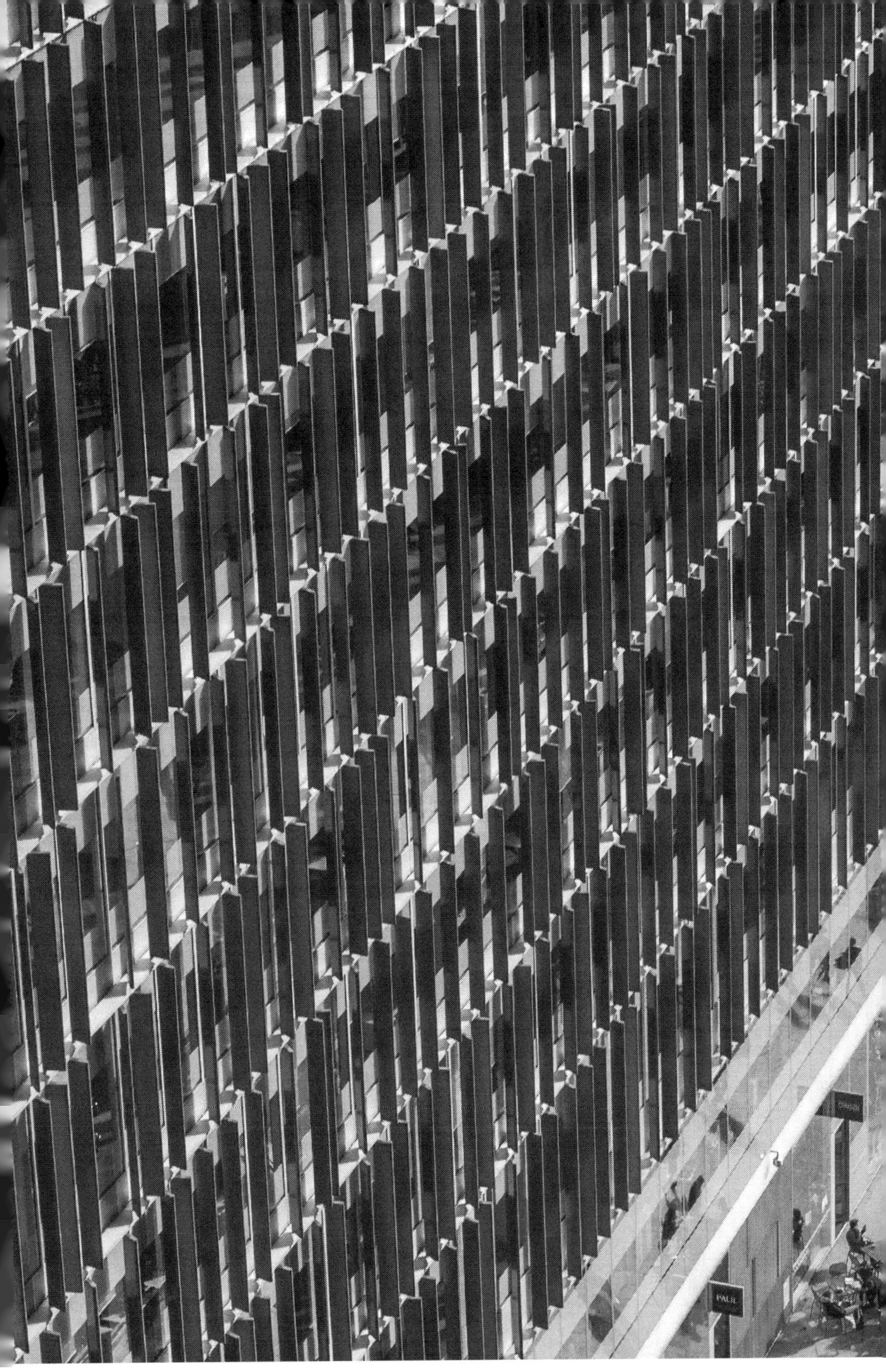
PAUL

CHAPTER 5

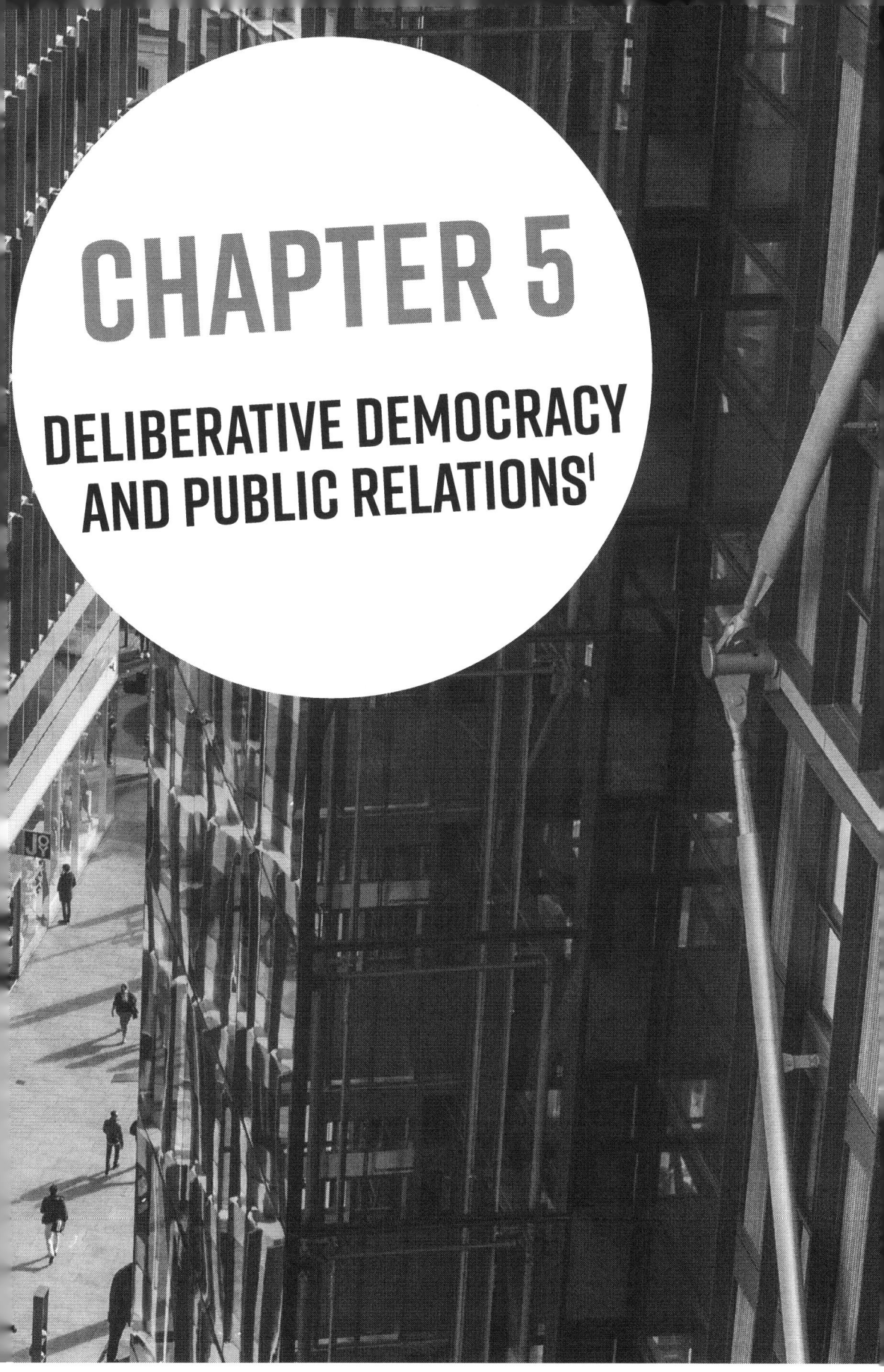

DELIBERATIVE DEMOCRACY AND PUBLIC RELATIONS[1]

In this chapter, I consider the question of public relations' effect on democracy, a powerful normative idea that guides the political arrangements of many nations. In terms of the societal debates outlined in Chapter 1, the discussion here relates to the challenges of reaching agreement about how we should live together and what kinds of structures should govern our communities. The discussion in this chapter also affects issues of agency and identity, because democratic arrangements influence the kinds of choices we are able to make about our lives, as well as the visibility and opportunities we enjoy as citizens with different identities.

Electoral-representative democracy is the model of democracy that many countries are familiar with, where representatives are periodically elected to govern civil society on our behalf. Alongside electoral representation, ongoing political debate, or 'deliberation' among citizens, is also essential for a healthy democracy (Habermas, 1984, 1989, 1996; Cohen, 1989), because it is a means for citizens to influence those who govern and call them to account. Deliberation emerges because long gaps between elections leave those in power vulnerable to the temptation to abuse their position and ignore the wishes of the electorate; as a result, while we may trust them as our representatives, we also mistrust their ability to remain faithful to their role (Rosanvallon, 2008). Through deliberation, their actions can be challenged and they must justify their decisions. Deliberation between citizens also helps us come to agreement about societal norms and values (such as attitudes to gender equality, or environmental protection), and communicate those norms to policymakers so that they can be taken into account.

While public relations is particularly important in periods of electoral campaigning, used extensively by political parties and activist groups, it is also crucial to deliberation. Not all forms of public relations are relevant here: it is difficult to argue, for example, that a campaign to sell more bubble wrap or to market concert tickets for the latest pop sensation constitutes a serious contribution to democracy. On the other hand, work done by corporates and NGOs designed to influence policymakers and input into public debates about the legitimacy or otherwise of a particular set of activities (e.g. the payment of bankers' bonuses) does affect the way we think about and discuss important political issues. So too does 'political public relations', carried out by government to communicate policy, promote parties and politicians, or win elections (Strömbäck and Kiousis, 2011; Liu et al., 2012). To provide sensible boundaries for the discussion in this chapter, the types of public relations relevant to the argument being made relate only to work that facilitates – or works against – the involvement of the populace in direct and indirect processes of government and policymaking.[2]

I begin with a discussion of the main tenets of deliberative democracy, including recent work on deliberative systems which, I argue, provides a valuable framework for understanding public relations' role in deliberation. I then discuss how we can analyse public relations as part of a deliberative system, and introduce a model of how its effects on deliberation might be analysed. The chapter concludes with a discussion of the ways in which a deliberative systems understanding of public relations can be applied to empirical research.

DELIBERATIVE DEMOCRACY

Deliberative theorists adopt a 'talk-centric' view of democracy (Dryzek, 2000; Chambers, 2012), arguing that rational, reasonable, open and inclusive debates among citizens lead to legitimate decisions on how policy and modes of governance should develop (Cohen, 1989). Deliberation takes place when there is disagreement about a particular matter on which a decision must be reached (Thompson, 2008), and is actively engaged in with a view to taking action (Chambers, 2012). Thus, deliberation is truly effective only if there is a means by which the content and results of the deliberation are communicated to policymakers and have some kind of impact (Goodin and Dryzek, 2006; Chambers, 2012).

Normative understandings of deliberation position it as taking place within the public sphere (see Chapter 6). Ideal conditions for deliberation include: equal access and status for all those entitled to participate; arguments leading to a rational consensus, based on reason rather than emotion; and participants setting aside their own interests in favour of the common good (Cohen, 1989). These requirements distinguish it from being 'mere talk', manipulation or coercion (Parkinson, 2012). Publicity – and the media in particular – is important as a means by which the content of deliberative discussions circulates among citizens, encouraging engagement from wider audiences.

The conditions associated with traditional models of deliberation present a serious problem for public relations because campaigns directly contravene them: campaigns are partisan, frequently driven by private interests, and tend to target specific rather than broad audiences. More often than not they are characterised by persuasive discourse and rhetoric, rather than rational communication. Because of this, public relations has the potential to be behind various pathologies of deliberation, including misleading the public about policy decisions; misleading policymakers about public opinion; manipulating the media agenda such that media discourses represent 'pseudo-preferences' rather than real ones (Stokes, 1998; Bohman, 2000); and more generally, engaging in 'plebiscitary rhetoric' (Chambers, 2009: 328), where the aim is to win the argument and gain power, rather than reflexively engage with other actors.

These limitations have led to public relations being largely overlooked as a deliberative force. The problem is that in practice, all sorts of organisations and groups use public relations to engage in deliberation. For the most part, actors in deliberative engagements have been understood as individuals, grassroots organisations, citizen forums and social movements, pursuing societal interests rather than individual concerns.[3] But they use public relations techniques to communicate their position to their target audiences, just as self-interested corporations and government departments do (Coombs and Holladay, 2010; Demetrious, 2013; Ashra, 2014; see also Chapter 6 following). Public relations also influences the media agenda and thus frames deliberative debates in the wider public arena (Schlesinger, 1990; Manning, 2001; Cottle, 2003; Ramsey, 2016). Ignoring a significant amount of deliberative activity because public relations is involved is clearly unsatisfactory, because it stops us asking about how it is produced, circulated and taken up by a wide range of actors, and prevents investigations of public relations' influence on deliberation in national and transnational contexts as 'a major communicative expression of competing interests' (Moloney, 2006: 78). A robust analysis of public relations' deliberative role has to make sense of these realities.

Recent work on deliberative democracy has begun to recognise that, in practice, self-interest often drives the desire to participate in deliberation and should therefore be incorporated into analyses of deliberative processes (Habermas, 1996; Dryzek, 2010b; Jacobs et al., 2010). This has opened the door for all kinds of organisations to be recognised as deliberative agents (Hendriks, 2006b; Bächtiger et al., 2010) and for public relations, as the organisational function through which deliberation is institutionally managed, to be recognised as an important influence on deliberative engagements. Practitioners draw on different discourses and use different communication styles and channels to frame deliberative discussion (Moloney, 2006). Their work has variable effects on the quality of deliberation, depending on the context in which it is being applied. These effects need to be empirically verified, and in the last section of this chapter I suggest some initial questions to guide empirical work. First, drawing on recent work on deliberative systems, I suggest a number of theoretical starting points for understanding public relations as deliberative activity.

DELIBERATIVE SYSTEMS

Deliberative systems offer a way of understanding how deliberation unfolds at a societal level (Mansbridge et al., 2012). They include both formal and informal discursive arenas, from everyday talk (Mansbridge, 1999) to deliberative forums explicitly set up to bring different parties together to debate a particular issue (Parkinson, 2004; Hendriks, 2006b; Marques and Maia, 2010). Dryzek (2009: 1385–6) suggests there are five elements in any deliberative system. *Public space* is inclusive and may take a variety of forms, including the abstract 'space' of the media, institutionally defined 'spaces' such as activist groups or social movements, and physical locations where discussion takes place, such as cafés, bars and classrooms. *Empowered space* comprises locations where institutional actors produce collective decisions, such as courts, legislative bodies, or stakeholder networks brought together to address a specific matter. *Transmission* is the means by which deliberation in public space influences deliberation in empowered space. *Accountability* is the degree to which empowered space is accountable to public space in so far as the legitimacy of decisions made may be assessed. Finally, *decisiveness* relates to the degree of influence that deliberation has on collective decisions.

Deliberative systems are dynamic decision-making arenas that address societal decisions in an 'emergent' rather than definitive way (Bohman, 2012; Mansbridge et al., 2012: 8) that reveals not only areas of conflict, but also shared values that might form the basis for agreement (Jacobs et al., 2010; Kurian et al., 2014). In practice, deliberation takes place on two levels. At the micro level, relatively small-scale and localised arenas bring different actors together to deliberate on a particular issue (Hendriks, 2006a; Parkinson, 2006; Munshi et al., 2014). At the macro level, the focus is on the ways in which public debates circulate, evolve and change across public spheres (Mansbridge, 1999; Parkinson, 2004). Publicity plays a role as a transmission mechanism that helps policymakers understand and be accountable to public opinion (Gutmann and Thompson, 1996; Goodin and Dryzek, 2006; Dryzek, 2009).

Over time, the continuous interactions between deliberative actors in a system produce changes in acceptable societal values and behaviours, based on the discourses[4] that develop within and circulate across the system (Dryzek, 2010a; Mansbridge et al., 2012). Some of these decisions may be policy-related, ultimately taken by the state, but some may simply be norms that have become a matter of general consensus, such as racial or gender equality. In other words, deliberation is focused on matters about which a decision must be made, but policy or legislative intervention is not a necessary outcome.

In the systems approach, the quality of deliberation is assessed on the basis of the system as a whole; imperfections in individual deliberative exercises should be balanced across the system, such that a 'more deliberative democracy' can be achieved (Coleman and Blumler, 2009: 38). Certain criteria for deliberative communication remain: it must be respectful of others, non-coercive, capable of connecting the particular to the general, and encourage others to reflect on their own positions (Dryzek, 2000: 167). Communication must be reciprocal, expressed in terms that others can accept (Gutmann and Thompson, 1996), and if it claims to be truly democratic, the system must be sensitive to a wide range of deliberative inputs from citizens, including those who turn to non-deliberative forms of communication in order to get their voices heard (Parkinson, 2012). However, a systems approach recognises communication as a 'mixed-motive game of strategy' (Goodin, 2005: 190) and does not require that every deliberative interaction demonstrates ideal characteristics. Rather, it recognises that some arguments may be more rational than others, some actors more altruistic, and some more partisan. The measure of deliberative quality is whether the combination of these characteristics amounts to an inclusive process of 'arguing, demonstrating, expressing and persuading' (Mansbridge et al., 2012: 5) – a system that enhances both communicative freedom, granting all citizens communicative status, and communicative power by ensuring that deliberation has an impact on decision-making (Bohman, 2012).

Dryzek (2009) argues that the degree of authenticity and inclusiveness of the elements in a particular deliberative system, and the decisiveness of that system, gives an indication of its deliberative capacity. The higher the deliberative capacity, the closer the system is to realising the ideal conditions for deliberation. The closer a system is to those conditions, the more likely it is that deliberation will ensure individuals engage effectively with each other, and that mutual recognition can develop between individuals and groups with sometimes radically different views (Dryzek, 2009). Moreover, different elements in the deliberative system have different roles to play in the process of reaching a judgement about a particular debate and those roles may shift, since systems are dynamic rather than static. Goodin, for example, proposes the idea of distributed deliberation, where 'the component deliberative virtues are on display sequentially, over the course of ... staged deliberation, rather than continuously and simultaneously present' (2005: 186; see also Bächtiger et al., 2010).

Analysing deliberation at the systemic level creates space for public relations to be acknowledged in deliberative processes. It recognises the value of self-interest to deliberation in pluralistic societies, and opens the door for partisan actors to be legitimate participants, because their contributions are contested by other actors in the system and there is less danger of their interests distorting the quality of argument (Hendriks, 2002; Mansbridge et al., 2012). In fact, Mansbridge et al. (2010) argue that self-interest is essential if a deliberative process is to properly clarify the various interests and preferences relevant to an issue: 'If members of the group can speak only as "we" and not as "I," neither they nor the other participants may be able to discover what is really at stake and forge integrated solutions' (2010: 73).

A systems approach also expands the types of discourse permitted in deliberation; alongside rationality, rhetoric, storytelling and testimony can play a crucial role as communicative styles that express the identities and positions of the different groups involved in deliberation, thereby improving representation (Mansbridge, 2003; Dryzek, 2010c; Bohman, 2012). This position aligns with rhetorical perspectives of public relations that recognise the importance of rhetorical techniques and principles as a way of interpreting public relations practice (Heath, 2001a; Ihlen, 2011; Taylor, 2011). Dryzek (2000) allocates a particular role for rhetorical communication in the process of deliberation, because it is able to help groups reach others – including policymakers – whose positions may be very far removed from their own. In addition, the emphasis on pathos and ethos in rhetorical communication encourages others to reflect on their position, thereby sowing the seeds of persuasion. He points out that rhetoric is frequently deployed in public debates, and that rhetorical arguments can and should be evaluated using rational criteria (for example, seeking concrete evidence of the speaker's claims to credibility, or considering whether an emotive message has any basis in reality). Emotion, as both a motivator for participation and a powerful vehicle for expressing an argument, is thereby incorporated into deliberation rather than excluded from it (O'Neill, 2002; Krause, 2008).

CASE STUDY 5.1

BLACK GOLD, BLACK SNAKES OR GREEN ENERGY? DELIBERATING OVER OIL PIPELINES

Oil pipelines have become one of the most fraught issues in recent times for the energy industry in the USA and Canada. A wide range of actors are involved in the debate, from the energy companies investing in pipelines and extraction infrastructure, to state policymakers, local communities and aboriginal tribes opposed to the industry. Each of the groups addresses the issue in their own way. A spokesperson from the Standing Rock Sioux tribe, for example, uses language that echoes the storytelling, spiritual traditions of her people, describing the pipelines as 'black snakes', tearing up land and clawing their way through ancient villages and burial grounds (see https://www.theguardian.com/us-news/2016/aug/18/north-dakota-pipeline-activists-bakken-oil-fields). She also uses rational arguments, pointing out the lack of consultation with tribespeople, the need to adhere to agreed processes for planning permission and the need to avoid the repetition of past mistakes. In September 2016, aboriginal tribes from Canada and the USA addressed the transnational nature of the oil industry and its infrastructure by signing a treaty to join forces in their efforts to oppose the pipelines and pledging to support each other's protest efforts across borders. This transnational co-operation extended the public space of protest and put pressure on empowered space in the USA and Canada. Their opponents in the debate, the Canadian Energy Pipeline Association, frame their arguments in terms of the need for energy and the relative safety and environmental friendliness of pipelines, but also acknowledge the need to 'listen to aboriginal concerns' – thereby recognising the validity of a very different perspective in the debate (see https://www.theguardian.com/us-news/2016/sep/22/pipelines-alberta-oil-sands-aboriginal-tribes). However, the inauguration of President Donald Trump in January 2017 also saw him sign an executive order to authorise the continued construction of the pipelines, suggesting that the decisiveness of this particular deliberative exercise was weakened significantly in the face of an intransigent political actor.

THE PLACE AND FUNCTION OF PUBLIC RELATIONS IN DELIBERATIVE SYSTEMS

In deliberative systems, public relations practitioners and other professional communicators help make expert knowledge accessible to a wide range of people by 'packag[ing] exchanges and discussions for audiences who have little opportunity to contribute' (Bohman, 2000: 48). This work is important because the wider the variety of voices and perspectives included in deliberation, the more secure any agreement reached about policy, governance or social norms will be. At the micro level, public relations practitioners make episodic interventions by managing communication about a specific issue (e.g. environmentally friendly packaging, or ethical treatment of suppliers) on behalf of organisational actors engaged in deliberation with other groups. At the macro level, public relations can contribute to deliberation in public space, when organisations provide information that helps citizens 'form their opinions and come to their policy preferences' (Chambers, 2009: 333). In both cases, pluralism in deliberative systems is improved by facilitating the inclusion of a wider range of interests, communication technologies and discourses (Dryzek, 2000; Parkinson, 2012).

Public relations acts as a transmission mechanism that ensures deliberation in public space is communicated to empowered spaces. It also furthers accountability when used to publicly challenge policy and government decisions, and when those decisions are justified by those in power. For example, activists have long used public relations campaigns to communicate their position on a particular issue, persuade audiences of the rightness of their perspective, and influence policymakers both directly and via shifts in public opinion (Straughan, 2004; Heath and Waymer, 2009; Demetrious, 2013). Profit-oriented organisations also use public relations to justify their perspectives on matters of policy and engage more effectively with citizens and stakeholders (Livesey and Kearns, 2002; Henderson, 2005; Roper, 2012). On a global scale, transnational and national NGOs use a wide range of communication materials to prompt debates and policy change on matters ranging from human rights to environmental degradation and violence against women (Peruzzo, 2009; Somerville and Aroussi, 2013; Mynster and Edwards, 2014). In these contexts, networked communication is particularly important: digital technologies provide channels that help messages travel widely and quickly, connecting different groups of citizens and potentially increasing the pressure on elites and the opportunities for change.

As a transnational industry (see Chapter 7), and through the use of networked, digital technologies that ensure communication spans the globe, public relations also plays a role in transnational deliberative systems by facilitating communication on behalf of a range of actors, or their representatives. When used as an activist intervention, it is a means by which representation can be improved for groups that would otherwise find it difficult to engage in deliberation because their identities are marginalised, even though the outcomes of deliberation may affect their livelihoods. Marginalised groups, whether they are workers in the global South or the long-term unemployed and welfare recipients in developed countries, often find that their communicative status is weak and their views are overwhelmed by other dominant voices (Moloney, 2006; Bohman, 2012). Discursive representation of different groups, of the kind facilitated by public relations campaigns, is an active process that can 'call constituencies into being … such that citizens identify and engage with different representatives on different topics in different contexts' (Parkinson, 2012: 163; see also Dryzek, 2010b). Correspondingly, public relations can play a significant role in constructing the landscape for deliberation by introducing new forms of agency and identity into the process, and potentially extending deliberation to include new geographies and constituents.

Public relations can also act as a translation mechanism in deliberative systems. Christiano (2012) argues that effective deliberation depends upon the availability of a wide enough range of interest groups with specialised knowledge about a policy domain, such that no single group can dominate discussions. Interest groups can use public relations to communicate their knowledge in a way that is accessible to those outside their field, thereby ensuring that debates include the widest possible range of relevant arguments and improving the basis for participants' decision-making. Interest groups that represent human and non-human actors affected by global issues (e.g. global warming, child poverty, gender equality) also use public relations to conduct wide-reaching campaigns that can result in their specialist expertise and research being integrated into national-level deliberations (Urbaniti and Warren, 2008). The translation role can also preserve quality and pluralism, because the range of discourses it facilitates ensures that more information about a particular issue is available from a wider range of standpoints, and thereby improves the basis for choices we make about how to live our lives, rejecting some arguments and accepting others (Dryzek, 2000).

Finally, public relations facilitates the communication that sustains network governance in deliberative systems, a role that is particularly important in networked societies. According to Papadopoulos (2012: 132), networks are 'a forum of mutual deliberation – it is expected that through reason-giving and the convincing force of justification, actors may be persuaded to change their preferences and include considerations they initially ignored'. Given that many network actors are organisations, public relations practitioners will be among those responsible for the construction and circulation of discourses that rationalise and justify the positions being adopted in specific debates, potentially initiating changes in network governance – or, in Castells's (2009) terms, network logic. As such, they can help to promote deliberative quality across networks, countering their inherent structural and communicative inequalities and levelling the discursive playing field (Moloney, 2006; Dryzek, 2010d).

On the other hand, public relations is a mechanism through which organisational bias is likely to emerge in the networked governance of the deliberative process (Papadopoulos, 2012), because it magnifies institutional voices, networks, knowledge and the value of institutional expertise in debates over the voices and preferences of individual citizens. Rather than acting as an equalising force in deliberative arenas, it can therefore enhance inequality by enabling organisations and elite individuals to occupy powerful nodes in communicative networks, as programmers and switchers that frame and direct debates, determining network logic that gives more visibility and agency to some actors, identities and issues over others (Castells, 2009), and fragmenting collective debate through tightly targeted communication (Bennett and Manheim, 2006). Urbaniti and Warren (2008: 405) point out that inequality is inherent in non-electoral domains, and as a consequence, 'the advantages of education, income, and other unequally distributed resources are more likely to translate into patterns of over- and underrepresentation'. Public relations is a competitive activity, where exploiting existing advantages in order to ensure visibility and attention for the client is a normal tactic; consequently (and their activist potential notwithstanding), campaigns may well exacerbate rather than mitigate systemic inequalities (Parkinson, 2012).

PUBLIC RELATIONS AND DELIBERATIVE QUALITY

While public relations is an important aspect of the communicative infrastructure that underpins deliberative systems, this does not necessarily mean that it enhances their democratic potential (Moloney, 2004; Coombs and Holladay, 2007). Indeed, deliberative theorists highlight dysfunctional aspects of deliberative systems where public relations reduces the quality of deliberation and democracy, and therefore makes it more difficult to reach a genuine agreement about how society should be governed. For example, if a communication campaign to gather citizen feedback on policy is driven more by the need to 'perform' engagement than to genuinely democratise policymaking by involving citizens in the nuts and bolts of policy development, then it has little deliberative value (Weaver and Motion, 2002; Freedman, 2008; Coleman and Blumler, 2009; Papadopoulos, 2012). Similarly, if organisations engage in debate without believing in the possibility of agreement, and without treating other actors sincerely as deliberative partners, then they hamper deliberation (Cohen, 1989).

In fact, the effect of public relations on deliberative quality is always context-specific. It depends on the nature of the work being undertaken, the motivations of the organisations using it and the way communication is constructed. Some public relations work obstructs deliberation, while other campaigns enhance it. The question arises: how can one assess the deliberative quality of public relations? Below I set out two conditions that can help us answer this question.

As a starting point, and to avoid the fallacy that 'anything goes' in deliberation (Bächtiger et al., 2010), we need to consider what general conditions should exist for public relations to be a deliberative intervention. Dryzek's (1990, 2000) work on discursive democracy provides some helpful parameters because it focuses on the substance of actual public relations practice – discourse production using different types of communication. He argues that deliberative discourses must deal with matters of *public* interest. Therefore, campaigns that claim to be deliberative must demonstrate a link between the particular position of the advocate and a relevant generalisable interest. Speaking only in one's own interest does not constitute a contribution to deliberation. For ease of reference, I term this condition 'the condition of generalisable interests'.

Deliberation should also be characterised by inclusivity and reflexivity. As Dryzek (2000: 77) notes, '[c]ontestation is democratic to the extent that it is engaged by a broad variety of competent actors under unconstrained conditions of the kind that deliberative democrats ... have always championed'. Participants must give their opponents the space to speak, treat them with respect, and be open to changing their own position if necessary. Thus, genuinely deliberative public relations campaigns must be open to and respectful of other perspectives – including geographically or symbolically distant groups that are not immediately relevant to an organisation, but are nonetheless affected by its work. I term this condition 'the condition of genuine engagement'.

The challenge for applying these conditions is to verify that they exist in practice; organisations make many claims about the public relevance of their work, but given the fact that they are motivated by self-interest, such claims cannot be taken at face value. In fact, the content of any public relations campaign should be regarded with a certain scepticism, since vested interests underpin all public relations work. In the first case, generalisable interests have to be expressed with reference to a particular worldview or justificatory regime (Boltanski and Thévenot, 2006 [1991]) that provides parameters for understanding what might be considered 'generalisable', as opposed to 'private'. These worldviews are reflected in the societal norms and values that form the basis for other actors in deliberative arenas (e.g. activists, community groups, scientists, other experts) to contest organisational claims to generalisability. Campaigns that genuinely engage with generalisable interests should be able to withstand such tests. Correspondingly, two requirements exist for verifying the condition of generalisable interests: public relations campaigns must be contested, and they must overcome challenges to the generalisable interests that they claim through a process of high-quality argumentation.

Verification of genuine engagement must also come from sources beyond a campaign. While the nature of engagement will be determined to some extent by the specific context, it will also be informed by the variable status of the different parties affected by an issue, some of whom the organisation may more readily pay attention to. The concept of voice as value (Couldry, 2010) is helpful here and aligns with the emphasis that deliberative theorists place on the ability not only to talk, but also to be heard in deliberative engagements (Dryzek, 2000; Parkinson, 2012: 166). Like deliberation, voice is a reflexive process for both speaker and audience, a mechanism through which we come to better understand our own life as well as others' experiences. Effective voice exists for groups and individuals if their narratives are valued in the material organisation of our social, political and economic worlds, which links it directly to the openness and respect required of public relations campaigns claiming to be deliberative. Correspondingly, the condition of genuine engagement may be expressed in terms of the degree to which campaigns value or deny voice for different groups. Couldry (2010: 10) is quite specific about what the denial of voice means:

> Voice is undermined by rationalities which take no account of voice and by practices that exclude voice or undermine forms for its expression. ... So models for organising life that place no value on voice may, when applied, undermine voice not just by failing to acknowledge it, but also by blocking alternative narratives that would authorise us to value voice.

Applied to public relations campaigns, these principles open up questions about whether audiences are consulted and their views fed back to the organisation, whether response mechanisms are built into the communicative tools used in the campaign, and whether the organisation is communicating with all audiences affected by the issue at hand, including those who are geographically distant or less immediately useful to the organisation's purpose. For example, lobbying is clearly non-deliberative if it is carried out in secret, since it violates the condition of genuine engagement. However, if carried out in a more transparent way – for example, in a forum with opposing parties – it may be more acceptable. Equally, a campaign to promote the oil industry is non-deliberative if it does not engage with local populations working at extraction sites, whose lives are directly affected by the environmental disruptions the industry causes; but if those populations are genuinely consulted and actions taken to accommodate their views, then one might argue that public relations is making a positive deliberative contribution.

The two conditions help to explain why the criteria often used to frame public relations' deliberative contribution – such as the quality of argumentation, the ethics of the speaker, the presence of symmetrical communication, or its ability to strengthen civil society by generating social capital (Heath, 2006; Taylor, 2010; Heath et al., 2013; Sommerfeldt, 2013; Schwarz and Fritsch, 2014) – are not *sufficient* for justifying it as a positive force in deliberation. Without a clear, defensible link to generalisable interests and evidence that voice is valued, public relations campaigns remain a (more or less moral) exercise in selfish advocacy.[5]

DISTINGUISHING LEVELS OF PUBLIC RELATIONS 'WORK' IN DELIBERATIVE SYSTEMS

The two conditions set out in the previous section provide normative standards against which the deliberative quality of *public relations campaigns* can be measured. However, individual campaigns are not the only route through which public relations' deliberative contribution should be understood. Just as deliberation takes place differently at micro and macro levels, in practice, public relations manifests on three levels in deliberative systems: the campaign level, the issue level and the systemic level. We must therefore also separate the aggregate balance of power that it influences through its contribution to the *overall level of deliberation* from the ways in which it facilitates deliberation *relating to a specific issue*. The three levels of analysis are linked, but as a heuristic tool their separation is a useful way of teasing apart the complex effects of public relations across deliberative systems as a whole.

First, at the *individual campaign level*, the quality of deliberative engagement can be assessed based on the content of the campaign and the approach to engagement adopted by the advocate. The empirical focus will be on *a set of campaign activities* that answer questions such as: Does the campaign clearly connect specific organisational interests to a generalisable interest? Are opponents treated as adversaries rather than antagonists (Mouffe, 1999), with respect and giving them room to speak? Is the organisation adopting a genuinely deliberative approach, reflexive and open to change?

At the *issue level*, public relations' contribution to deliberation can be assessed based on the range and balance of voices that it facilitates. Relevant questions to guide empirical work will relate to the range of voices using public relations to engage in debate *on a particular issue*, as well as the quality of engagement between them: How vibrant is the deliberation, in terms of its scope and inclusivity? How wide-ranging are the views being considered, and how are different voices recognised and acknowledged by different parties in the deliberative process? Network analytics and social media mapping are important tools at this level, since they permit us to track the different groups engaged in debate, the public relations partners they have, the significance of their roles, the resources they draw on and the communicative relationships that exist between them (see, for example, Schölzel and Nothhaft, 2016).

Finally, at the *systemic level*, questions will be concerned with the ways in which public relations enacted *for a particular organisation or institution* (corporate, government or non-profit) enhances or diminishes its power, as well as with the cumulative effect of public relations work on other institutions and processes vital to deliberation, such as the media or social movements. This level of analysis engages with structural hierarchies and the ways in which public relations enables them to either continue or change through its cumulative effect in a deliberative system. Long-term changes in social norms relating to gender, sexuality, race and disability, for example, have led to structural change in the form of equalities legislation, accessibility standards, or changes in the ways in which institutions identify us demographically (for example, by adding the category 'other' or 'prefer not to say' to questions about gender). Arguably, such changes happen after an accumulation of voice from one or several groups across society, which eventually creates a critical mass that can generate a shift in social norms, policy and practice. Such structural changes (for example, allowing same-sex marriage) simultaneously offer newly recognised groups greater agency in how they live their lives, because of the recognition that they have received as citizens (Honneth, 1996).

CASE STUDY 5.2

COMMUNICATING FEMINISM: MAKING MARGINALISED VOICES VISIBLE IN DEBATES ABOUT VIOLENCE AGAINST WOMEN

Rape Crisis England and Wales (RCEW) is a feminist organisation that exists to promote the needs and rights of women and girls who have experienced sexual violence, to improve services to them and to work towards the elimination of sexual violence (see http://rapecrisis.org.uk/historyofrapecrisis.php). It uses public relations to promote its political goal to end violence against women and girls, but faces significant challenges because it has very limited resources to invest in communication. Keeping up with the speed and volume of comment on digital platforms is difficult, and the volume of stories on sexual violence in the media means that much of RCEW's time is taken up with reactive comment, focused on single cases, rather than proactive, strategic communication that can help it achieve social and political change. Media coverage tends to demand comment on institutional failings and the merits or severity of a case, but rarely offers a chance for RCEW spokespeople to challenge broader patterns of discrimination and prejudice that underpin the scale of violence against women. As such, it was failing in its role as a transmission mechanism for communicating activist messages to empowered actors who could generate policy or organisational change.

To address this problem, in 2016 RCEW gathered a small number of recordings of survivors talking about their experiences, in order to take over the transmission role themselves and make a powerful intervention in the public debate about the impact of sexual violence on women's lives, challenging the ways in which society commonly views both victims and perpetrators. The recordings were loaded up to the RCEW website and disseminated via social media. They represented a new type of voice in discussions about sexual violence against women. In contrast to the rational, process-oriented perspectives of the judiciary, police and policymakers, survivors' voices were marked by emotion as well as rationality, and driven by direct experience rather than abstract logic. Survivors told their stories in their own words, using their own forms of rhetoric, and in doing so they challenged normative discourses about the systems, institutions and individuals involved in the perpetration of and recovery from sexual violence.

The recordings were disseminated in public space via the internet (see https://rapecrisis.org.uk/survivorsvoices_2.php) with a view to reaching other survivors,

> but RCEW's lobbying work with policymakers also meant there was the potential to disseminate them into empowered spaces. In addition, the narratives were designed to be used for training in organisations that supported survivors (social services, the police, the medical profession) in these contexts they had the potential to extend discussion about sexual violence against women and girls into more empowered spaces. While the exact impact of this campaign is hard to quantify, it does illustrate how public relations strategies and tactics can be used in deliberative systems to make marginalised voices heard, broaden the perspectives and discourses included in discussions about issues of public importance, transmit discourses across different locations, and contribute to the overall decisiveness of deliberative systems.

CONCLUSION

In this chapter, I have argued that public relations' democratic contribution is best understood in the context of 'talk-centric', deliberative models of democracy. Using the model of deliberative systems, the role of public relations as a form of deliberative engagement is readily revealed. Because it is used so widely to manage organisational discourse, public relations' effects on deliberative systems are complex and variable. They depend on what kinds of organisations are using public relations, their openness to engagement with other parties, their recognition of and connection to generalisable interests, and their ability to reflect on their own position.

Adopting this multi-level analytical approach allows us to understand public relations' effects on deliberation at one level without negating contradictory effects at another. For example, the fact that public relations at a systemic level tends to support existing power structures does not negate the good it can do when used by marginalised actors to raise their profile and access effective voice in deliberative arenas, or when enlightened corporations use it as a means of genuine engagement with audiences. The effects are different, often simultaneous, and each comprises an important component of the role that public relations plays in deliberation.

The approach can also be used to assess how well public relations' different roles in deliberative systems are being carried out. Its role as a form of transmission, for example, can be assessed in terms of how well an individual campaign reaches new and different audiences, and how widely an issue is being debated across both public and empowered space. The quality of the translation work it does can be reviewed by asking audiences how well they understand campaign messages and how those messages are prompting them to reflect differently on the arguments being expressed about a particular issue.

Finally, the network governance carried out by public relations can be reviewed by considering the range of organisations using public relations within a particular network, the relative power of the different voices it is facilitating, and the voices that are blocked or shut down through its work.

The context of deliberation provides a valuable location for understanding the ways in which structure, agency, identity and collective living are directly affected by public relations work. As societies have changed and become more complex with the advent of networks and the digital age, deliberative systems – and the role of public relations within them – also become more difficult to trace and analyse. This does not mean, however, that they should be abandoned as an object of research or practical intervention. On the contrary, such changes also provide new theoretical and practical opportunities. As a deliberative tool, public relations is not merely a vehicle for organisations to load up with neoliberal communicative 'baggage'; practitioners can exert a significant influence on how communication is constructed, what kinds of discourses are employed, how well an organisation interacts with other parties, what technologies are used, and how communicative networks themselves evolve across space and time. By understanding their work better, we can begin to imagine how the power of public relations in deliberative processes might be recognised and managed more effectively, for the benefit of society as a whole.

NOTES

1. An earlier version of this chapter was published as Edwards (2016b).
2. The idea of 'involvement' in government and policymaking is broad, rather than narrow. I do not limit it to engaging in formalised political processes such as being a member of specific policymaking bodies, or making a submission to a consultation, since this would be an unreasonable constraint on the kinds of public relations involved. Instead, 'involvement' is conceptualised simply as the ability to speak about issues relevant to one's life and be heard by others, including those people and institutions with formal decision-making power.
3. Discourse is defined here, following Dryzek (2002: 121), as 'a shared set of assumptions and capabilities embedded in language that enables its adherents to assemble bits of sensory information that come their way into coherent wholes'.
4. Note that there is no *obligation* for reflection and engagement to be an outcome of public relations if it claims to be deliberative. They are natural outcomes of a properly open and respectful debate.
5. Both the conditions are applicable to public relations in the context of transnational deliberation. The condition of generalisable interests should include the interests of communities in other countries whenever they are affected. Similarly, the condition of genuine engagement means the voices of those communities must be valued by public relations campaigns wherever possible and necessary.

PAUL

CHAPTER 6

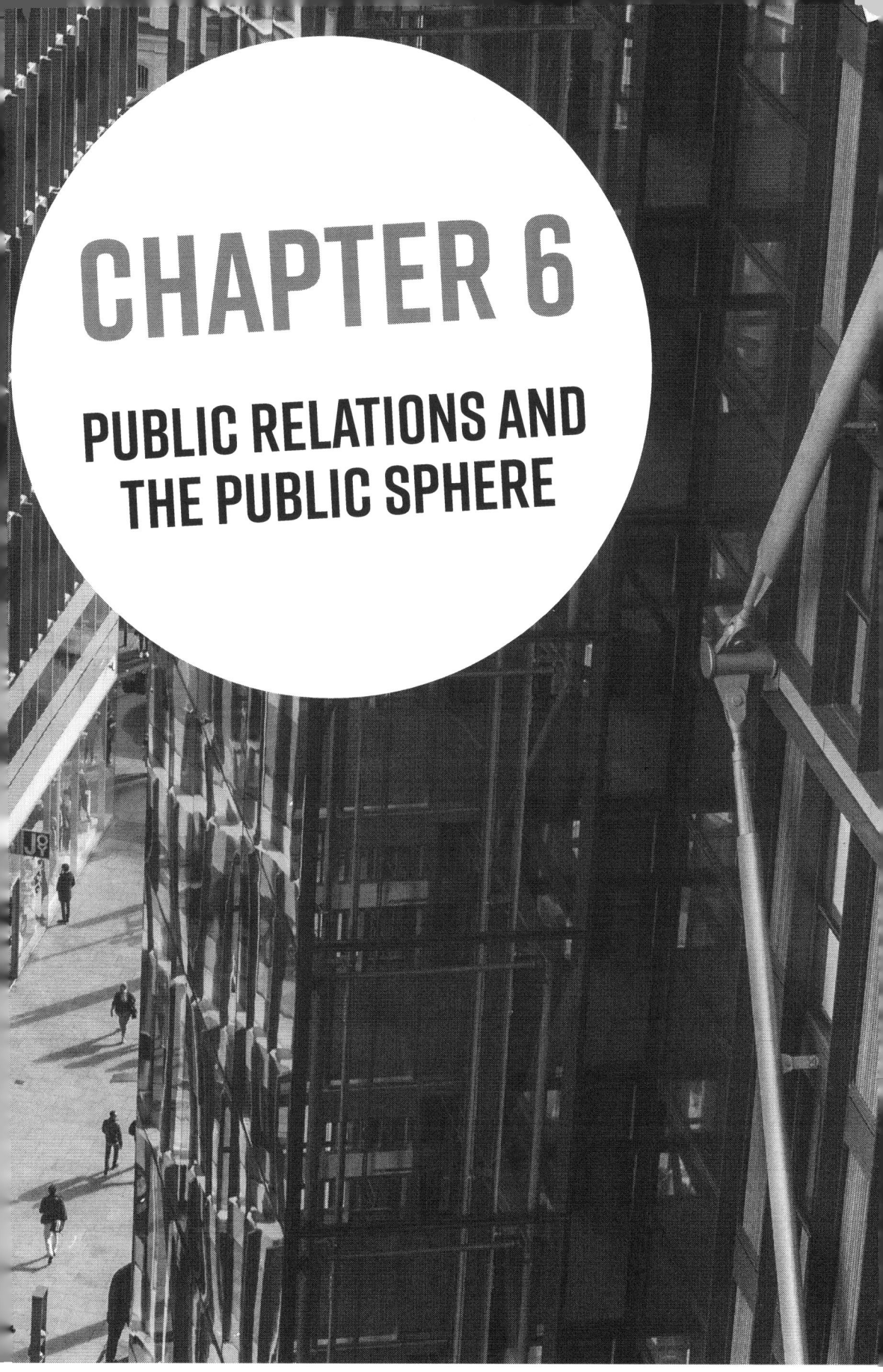

PUBLIC RELATIONS AND THE PUBLIC SPHERE

This chapter is the second in the book to deal with the question of how we reach agreement about living together in relative harmony, the priorities that we construct to govern our collective lives, and the recognition that groups and individuals receive as members of society. In Chapter 5, I discussed the role of public relations in deliberative democracy, focusing in particular on deliberative systems. In this chapter I return to the theme of deliberative democracy, but address public relations' relationship with the public sphere, particularly in terms of the historical critique of its influence on the media. The ways in which public relations interacts with the media in the context of the public sphere have been a focus of research for many decades and I do not review the whole debate here (for a review of the literature, see Macnamara, 2014b). Rather, in the next few pages I argue in favour of a broader and more multi-faceted conception of public relations in/and public spheres, by building on changing theorisations of the public sphere and considering the implications those changes have for public relations.

The idea of the public sphere is an important focus for socio-cultural research in public relations because it symbolises an important (though contested) location where the industry affects the quality of democratic life. In Chapter 5, I elaborated on how we might understand this effect in analytical terms; in public sphere discussions, the focus has been on the actual practice of public relations and its effects on the quality of public discourse and debate. Reflecting this, the current chapter moves us from an abstract conceptualisation of public relations in democracy to a more concrete engagement with campaign work. That said, the arguments remain theoretically grounded.

The connection between public relations and public spheres is also important because participation in public spheres is grounded in the recognition of citizens as having the right to speak and be visible in debates about public life; issues of identity, who is recognised in this way, and who is excluded, are therefore central to the debates presented here. They can extend current approaches to public relations' role in civic life by addressing the possibilities for agency that public relations might facilitate in democratic contexts, alongside existing arguments about the social capital to which it contributes.

I begin the chapter by providing an overview of the idea of the public sphere as first envisaged by Habermas, paying particular attention to the role of the media, which has been an important focus for the critique of public relations. I review existing scholarship that counters this critique, defending public relations as a positive influence on the quality of democratic debate. In the second half of the chapter, I reflect on the ways in which the idea of the public sphere has evolved and how the changing media and communications landscape has created opportunities to recognise arenas of debate and discussion that exist outside mainstream media. This leads to a range of new questions that can be asked about public relations and its influence on contemporary public spheres, deliberation and civil society.

THE PUBLIC SPHERE

Habermas (1989) originally argued that the public sphere emerged as a space in which citizens deliberated about political issues and public opinion during the eighteenth, nineteenth and twentieth centuries. Originating in places where the bourgeois elite gathered to discuss politics and society, the public sphere expanded as literacy levels increased and the print industry grew. A more inclusive public sphere developed as new social groups acquired the knowledge and capacity to engage in informed debates as equal citizens. However, Habermas argued that this diversity also reduced the rationality and quality of public sphere debates, and that the gradual commercialisation of the media industries compromised their role as a source of information and transmission of public opinion to those in power (Calhoun, 1992).

Habermas argued that free and independent media are indispensable to the quality of democracy achieved through the public sphere, since media outlets are the main channels through which citizens obtain information about how they are being governed, the decisions that are being made on their behalf and the different arguments they need to consider when developing their opinions. The media facilitate social relations across and within public spheres; they are a means by which society can move towards 'unity in diversity' (Fuchs, 2014: 64), bringing people together both physically, in particular spaces, and metaphorically, through the communication of different perspectives on a particular issue. As the 'fourth estate', the media also represent the voice of the public to power. Journalists monitor and critique the actions of those who govern and ensure they are held to account by publicising those actions outside the relatively elite, empowered spaces that are beyond the reach of many citizens (Hampton, 2012). As such, the media act as a transmission mechanism that helps policymakers understand and be accountable to (reasoned and well-argued) public opinion (Garnham, 1992; Goodin and Dryzek, 2006; Dryzek, 2009).

As long as the media remain independent of political and economic manipulation, they can claim to be a trusted means through which citizens can monitor those who govern, engage in debates about politics and governance, and ultimately hold power to account. However, Habermas (1989) argued that as the media expanded they became more powerful as industries in their own right, and commercial concerns started to become more important. At the same time, politicians, political parties and organisations became more adept at using the power of publicity to persuade audiences to support them. The increasing influence of business and private interests on the media agenda has been one of the most important factors in the decline of the public sphere, gradually eroding the independence of the media and transforming them into a 'vehicle for established power' (Lunt and Livingstone, 2013: 89; see also Habermas, 1989).

PUBLIC RELATIONS AND THE MEDIA IN THE PUBLIC SPHERE: COMMON CRITIQUES

While the idealised role of the media may be oversimplified – media institutions have long been commercial in their orientation and partisan in their coverage, and the way news is created is complex and variable (Schudson, 1989; Curran, 2002)[1] – it retains its power as a normative objective for professional journalism (Franklin et al., 2012; Hampton, 2012). It also inevitably positions public relations as a negative influence on the public sphere, the source of vested interests in the news agenda that corrupt the integrity of the public sphere through the core function of media relations. The term 'media relations' describes the work done for corporate, political and non-profit organisations to influence how journalists publicise stories that organisations and governments want the public to know about. Press releases, interviews, press conferences, tweets and other media-directed communication all frame stories in ways that support, rather than challenge, the power of the organisations deploying them. Media relations also involves shutting down negative stories, managing them off the news agenda by negotiating with journalists behind the scenes, preventing access to spokespeople, or simply misleading journalists through false or misdirected information (Blumler and Gurevitch, 1995; Davis, 2002; McNair, 2004; Macnamara, 2014a).

Aside from the existence of media relations as a proactive means of intervening in the news agenda, other factors have tilted the balance of power in the public sphere away from journalistic independence and in favour of public relations. Digitisation, the advent of the internet and the growth of online media have generated enormous pressures on media organisations. Journalists have less time to fill more space and must become multi-skilled, working across media channels, adapting their writing for multiple outlets and keeping track of the rapidly changing information environment (Deuze, 2004; Bull, 2010). In a time-poor, convergent media environment, public relations practitioners make journalists' lives easier by providing easily accessible stories that can plug gaps in the news agenda. They are adept at understanding and responding to journalists' requirements to make their stories more appealing (Gandy, 1982; Sallot and Johnson, 2006; Waters et al., 2010). Press releases are written as if they were news articles, videos mimic genuine news footage, and background information is provided. Practitioners make the complex communication environment more manageable, facilitating access to people within organisations, responding to media requests faster and more efficiently than would be the case if the journalist were trying to reach people independently. The colonisation of the media by public relations can even extend to behind-the-scenes activities such as fact-checking, story formatting and providing balance (Lewis et al., 2008).

From a Habermasian perspective this work makes journalists vulnerable to manipulation and weakens their capacity to monitor and challenge elite power, producing a news agenda where vested interests dominate and other issues are obscured (Davis, 2007, 2009;

Macnamara, 2014b). However, whether ideal or not, public relations practitioners are now established actors in media structures and processes. In practice the relationship between public relations practitioners and journalists is frequently co-operative, with senior practitioners seen as good contacts rather than gatekeepers and obstructions (Macnamara, 2014a). For this reason, McNair (2004: 337) suggests that public relations is 'part of the infrastructure of modern political communication' and that 'spin and anti-spin' exist in a dialectical relationship, always in tension with each other so that public relations work never secures power on behalf of its architects, but attracts counter-arguments and critique as part of the natural order of political communication.

DEFENDING PUBLIC RELATIONS IN THE PUBLIC SPHERE

Some defence of public relations as a valid actor in the public sphere is possible. First, not all organisations using public relations are self-interested or already among the powerful elite. Leitch and Neilson (2001) suggest that systems organisations (driven by strategic action) co-exist with lifeworld organisations (grassroots movements, activists, social movements), which are relatively unstructured and emerge from civil society rather than a market opportunity. Lifeworld organisations use public relations to engage in debates as a means of challenging elite power in the interest of the common good. In this context, public relations is an important channel for bringing marginalised issues and voices to the attention of the media and the public. While all organisations are driven by a degree of self-interest (Mumby, 1988), it seems sensible to regard those with an inherently altruistic purpose as legitimate participants in the public sphere (Auger, 2013).

Second, public relations allows organisations to communicate their position on societal issues (McNair, 2004) and exercise their right to express a view on matters of policy and governance that affect their operations, because they are active contributors to deliberation and community life (Grunig, 2000; Auger, 2013). For example, Starck and Kruckeberg (2001) argue for a communitarian perspective of public relations where organisations recognise society as the 'greatest stakeholder' (2001: 59), and base their communication activity with audiences on mutual respect and openness to change. Hiebert (2005: 3) claims that the 'only possible solution [for ensuring fair access to the public sphere] is public relations, not in terms of spin or propaganda but in terms of developing real public relationships in the public sphere', while Jensen (2001: 134) argues that public relations is 'concerned with issues and values that are considered publicly relevant, which means relating to the public sphere', and suggests recognising a new 'functional public sphere' dealing with issues of organisational legitimacy and identity, where public relations has a more obviously legitimate role.

This line of defence builds on arguments for recognising public relations as a means of developing a healthy civil society, which Habermas (1996) argues is essential to a robust public sphere. As a space where 'individuals and groups are free to form organizations that function independently and that can mediate between citizens and the state' (Downey and Fenton, 2003: 190), civil society mediates between private and public spheres. Taylor and Doerfel (2005: 122) argue that public relations 'with its ability to create, maintain, and change relationships is at the nexus of civil society development'. One of its main contributions is the provision of social capital, or the development of networks and trust between organisations and their audiences that facilitates social cohesion (Verhoeven, 2008; Taylor, 2011; Jin and Lee, 2013; Sommerfeldt, 2013). As rhetorical and dialogic approaches to public relations suggest, its advocacy underpins social cohesion by facilitating the co-creation of meaning about social issues (Heath, 2001b: 32), and thereby helping to create a 'fully-functioning society' characterised by robust and ethical debate (Heath, 2006). Willis (2012) suggests treating stakeholder relationships as a 'social commons' where engagement is based on 'social consensus, equity, moral legitimacy and transparency in decision-making' (2012: 118). His position echoes the German communication science tradition, where organisations are understood as social actors, rather than only functioning as market-driven entities (Saxer, 1993; Ihlen and Van Ruler, 2009). The resulting dialectical, reflexive debates, produced through 'good organisation[s] communicating' (Heath, 2001a: 39), constitute a form of institutionalised democracy according to Heath, essential if public relations is to make a positive contribution to society (Heath et al., 2013). Empirical research on cases where public relations is used by civil society organisations as a tool for engagement does suggest that public relations can play a positive role when used for connection and relationship building as part of efforts to strengthen civil society (Hon, 1997; Doerfel and Taylor, 2004; Henderson, 2005; Somerville and Aroussi, 2013).

Arguments in favour of public relations are only partially successful because, like the idea of the public sphere itself, they are normative ideals. While they point out the potential for public relations to contribute to a dynamic public sphere by building engagement and trust, they fail to address the fact that this is not always the case. Nor do such arguments address the important critique about the negative impact of public relations on the media agenda. The weight of evidence in favour of understanding organisations and their communication as fundamentally self-interested entities, engaged in strategic, rather than communicative action (Habermas, 1984; Roper, 2005), is too strong to be put aside even if some organisations are genuinely concerned about societal issues. Questions must be raised about its effect on the quality of the public sphere because it is not always designed to open up debate, and both professional and academic claims to symmetrical communication and dialogue between organisations and audiences are not always borne out in practice (Dozier and Lauzen, 2000; McAllister-Spooner, 2009; Meisenbach and Feldner, 2009; Willis, 2014).

For example, research has shown that the interactive potential of social media is rarely taken advantage of by practitioners, who adopt 'broadcast'-style approaches to communicating even when using Web 2.0 technologies (Hickerson and Thompson, 2009; Kent, 2013). Macnamara (2013) notes the lack of investment in the work of listening by organisations, and the need to take seriously the time and resources required to listen effectively. Others point out that the strategic segmentation of publics for the purposes of focused and effective communication (Grunig, 1992; Toth, 2006) works against openness and inclusivity, and obstructs one of the main objectives of public sphere debate – the development of consensus and the formation of a 'general' public with a collective voice (Leitch and Neilson, 2001; Leitch and Motion, 2010). More generally, stories abound of public relations campaigns that reframe disasters as opportunities, shut down opposition to corporate activities, falsify earnings, or offer appeasement to corporate victims with one hand while continuing their anti-social activities with the other (Ice, 1991; Stauber and Rampton, 1995; Michie, 1998; Mickey, 2002; Miller and Dinan, 2007; Roper, 2012).

In the end, constructing a positive role for public relations that ignores these realities does not move us very far on in what has become a polarised debate about whether public relations is good or bad for society and democracy. Given the ubiquity of public relations in modern promotional culture and its influence on the ways we understand and interpret the world (see Chapter 2), we need to find a different way of understanding the roles and effects that it has in the public sphere. Critiques of Habermas's original idea of the public sphere have led to important additional theoretical insights and a second, more refined version of his ideas (Habermas, 1996). These refinements, and the advent of online communication as an important channel operating alongside the media, open up new ways of thinking about public relations in the public sphere because they enable us to position its activity in the context of late modern, networked societies where debate and discussion are more fragmented and fluid than Habermas initially envisaged.[2]

DEVELOPMENTS IN PUBLIC SPHERE THEORY

PLURALITY, TRANSNATIONALISM AND DISCURSIVE VARIETY

An important critique of the original theory of the public sphere relates to the way in which the idea of the 'public' was presented. Because the origins of the public sphere were exclusionary, emerging in spaces where women and other marginalised groups were not permitted, debates in these places could not be regarded as representative of the 'public' because they would not include all those affected by the issues at hand (Fraser, 1990). To address this problem, critics adopted the principle of plurality of participants and discourses as the starting point for conceptualising the public sphere. Fraser (1990), for example, proposes the co-existence of multiple public spheres, populated (physically or virtually) by different groups. She introduces the idea of counter-public spheres, where marginalised groups develop their positions on issues through discussions among themselves, and also collectively challenge other public spheres, including the dominant public sphere (Fenton and Downey, 2003).

Recognising the variability and multiplicity of public spheres allows for more fine-grained analysis of participants and their motivations, as well as the issues being debated within and across them. Breese (2011), for example, suggests that deliberation within public spheres varies along two types of continuum: from political to civic focus and from face-to-face to mediated engagement. Deconstructing debates in this way helps reveal how understandings of 'public' and 'private' issues change over time and come to be a focus for collective agreement, according to the ways different ontologies and epistemologies become visible as challenges to the status quo (Asen and Brouwer, 2001; Fenton and Downey, 2003; Dahlberg, 2007). Environmental campaigns, for example, often focus on changing the status of environmental protection from being an issue of individual choice to one of necessary collective and institutional change, thereby justifying it as a topic for public rather than private discussion.

Other scholars have argued that the advent of globalisation and networked societies has extended public spheres beyond national boundaries, weakening the validity of public spheres defined in terms of geographically and politically bounded nation states (Fraser, 2007). By contrast, in contemporary transnational public spheres 'emerging communities of interest' engage in political participation '"below" and "above" the nation state' (Guidry et al., 2000; Bohman, 2004; Cammaerts and Van Audenhove, 2005: 148). Publics both interested in and affected by political and economic decisions – and thus entitled to participate in public sphere debates – now extend far beyond national territorial boundaries and reduce both the legitimacy and efficacy of nationally bounded public spheres (Fraser, 2007). Transnational (or more transnationalised) public spheres would ideally integrate geographically and temporally distant issues and publics into debates (Couldry, 2014), and communicate the results of deliberation to transnational bodies that have the power to change existing structures if required – demonstrating the principles of translation and capability, in Fraser's (2007) terms.

Habermas accommodates these critiques in his later work (Fenton and Downey, 2003), in part at least, by reinterpreting the public sphere as a normative, but abstract location where debates take place in the context of 'structures of undamaged intersubjectivity found in nondistorted communication' (Habermas, 1996: 148). These debates are framed by the 'ideal speech situation' as a 'regulative idea' (Mouffe, 1999: 748) that specifies the procedural conditions for effective public debate: inclusivity; equality between participants; the universal right to question the topics of discussion; and the universal right to challenge the process of deliberation. Habermas also argues that public sphere debates should be characterised by communicative reason, or critical and rational argumentation that allows us to reflect on our own and others' positions, and communicative action, or an approach to interaction with others aimed at developing mutual understanding (Habermas, 1996). Communicative reason and communicative action stand in contrast to instrumental reason and strategic action, which each assume that engagement has a specific goal, determined by individual rather than collective interests and achieved through coercion or manipulation rather than the development of common consensus (Lunt and Livingstone, 2013).

However, a number of scholars have argued against the continued emphasis on rationality in Habermas's revision of the public sphere (Dryzek, 2000; Lunt and Stenner, 2005; Krause, 2008), on the grounds that it neglects the value of emotion as both a source of motivation for engagement in deliberation and a tool for argumentation. Mouffe (1999) points out that the focus on rationality makes social stability dependent on an inevitable reduction in the number of voices involved in public debates, and fails to recognise the power dynamics that are fundamental to contestation. Rather than enabling participation, the requirement for rationality erases the inherent pluralism of the private realm and ignores the fact that many groups express their positions in emotional rather than rational terms. Building on Mouffe, Dahlberg (2007) notes the mutually constitutive nature of radical (excluded) and dominant (included) discourses in public spheres, and the continuous inter-discursive contestation between the two sets of discourses as struggles over cultural and material power. Ramsey (2016) suggests that Mouffe's agonistic pluralism, where disagreement and self-interest are accepted as part of the fabric of democratic discussion, could offer a more productive framework for public relations work.

CASE STUDY 6.1

THE PUBLIC NATURE OF PRIVATE MATTERS: CAMPAIGNING FOR GAY MARRIAGE

Debates about same-sex marriage have been heated in recent years, attracting passionate and committed actors who believe deeply in one side or the other of this controversial topic. Public relations campaigns have been developed by the Catholic Church, civil liberties association and gay rights activist groups. In strict Habermasian terms, the campaigns could only be properly regarded as legitimate public sphere interventions if they were rational, rather than emotional, and focused strictly on public issues (the effect on social norms, the infringement of human rights, principles of equality

(Continued)

and freedom of choice) rather than private matters (the preference for marriage in the context of a specific relationship, the desire to have children within marriage rather than outside it, the desire to publicly demonstrate a commitment). However, in the context of the ideas set out above, all the campaigns would be legitimate, regardless of the approach they took (emotional rhetoric or rational argumentation, or both). Struggles to make private issues a matter of public concern (for example, the desire of gay couples to choose marriage), which are a frequent focus for activist campaigns, can also be recognised as part of the deliberative process.

THE ONLINE PUBLIC SPHERE

The idea of online public spheres has emerged since the advent of the internet and networked societies have reconfigured the way we socialise, connect with each other and with institutions, and led to more fluid understandings of space and time (Castells, 2009; see also Chapter 1). Channels of access to information for citizens, and the outcomes of accessing that information, have changed. We connect with different people in variable ways that result in a wide variety of online and offline actions (Dutton, 2009). However, the effects of the internet on the quality and scope of public discussion are not straightforward, since technologies of all kinds are themselves shaped by the socio-political and socio-economic contexts in which they emerge (Mattelart, 2003; Thornham and Gómez Cruz, 2018).

Some scholars have celebrated the open, accessible and mobile nature of the internet as an 'opportunity structure … in the realm of informal political processes and social movement organisations' (Cammaerts and Van Audenhove, 2005: 183). This optimistic view of the online public sphere frames it as a 'public space' where debates of all kinds can take place between a wide range of people (Papacharissi, 2002). Anyone with the right skills and technology can access any kind of information, and networked connectivity promotes connections between individuals and groups across social strata, thereby breaking down class and other social divisions and promoting engagement, discussion and debate (Benkler, 2006). These factors promote active engagement on the part of the audience as both information publishers and deliberative participants (see Chapter 5), which in turn has the potential to enhance civic participation and the quality of deliberative democracy. People can connect across different geographies, social identities and time zones to create communities of common interest that approximate counter-public spheres (Dahlberg, 2007).

However, there are many limitations to this perspective. Case studies demonstrate that it may be possible to approximate public sphere debates online, but it involves careful management of both content and technology, as well as the existence of a public that actually wants to engage in reflexive, deliberative debates (Dahlgren, 2005; Poor, 2005; Birchall and Coleman, 2015). Moreover, Papacharissi (2002) argues that while the internet provides public space, it does not constitute a public sphere in Habermasian terms because the parameters for public sphere communication are not met online. Discourse can be partisan and emotional as often as it is rational and objective; not everyone is able to participate online; and there is no guarantee that online discussions have an effect on political arrangements. Online communication is often one-way rather than dialogic, and the English language dominates, undermining any claim to transnationality (Cammaerts and Van Audenhoven, 2005).

Online structures also tend to generate fragmentation rather than cohesion – we may more often preach to the converted in silos of mutual interest, rather than engage in the reflexive debates with people from different groups that should characterise deliberative democracy (see Chapter 5); offline power hierarchies continue to influence patterns of online access and visibility, limiting the space for genuinely deliberative engagement (Dahlberg, 2001). Fuchs (2014), for example, advocates media reform, with active subsidies for participatory media that will counter the dominance of existing hegemonic institutions online. Increasingly, search engines and algorithms are an important source of power, controlling access to information (Dutton, 2009), and Dahlgren (2005) suggests that even where deliberation takes place online, it will remain relatively impotent unless there are structural mechanisms to connect it to the material socio-political and economic infrastructures that are the focus of debate and, potentially, reform. Papacharissi (2002) suggests that instead of adopting the idea of a public sphere, the internet should be recognised as a 'virtual sphere', a set of 'culturally fragmented cyberspheres that occupy a common virtual public space' (2002: 22), structured by the power and economics of the material world, yet affording opportunities for transformative, political discourse.

NEW DIRECTIONS FOR UNDERSTANDING PUBLIC RELATIONS AND PUBLIC SPHERES

Recognising multiple public spheres, situating debates between as well as within them, relaxing the requirements for rationality, and the movement of debate into online spaces, all broaden the scope for understanding public relations' variable participation in public spheres. They highlight gaps in our existing knowledge about the detail of that participation, how it varies and its corresponding effects on structural power, our ability to make informed choices about our lives, and our ability to reach agreement with each other about how we live together. New questions arise focused on public relations' role across as well as within different public spheres, and below I suggest a number of different areas where new research directions might evolve.

VARIABILITY IN ACCESS, PRACTICE AND INFLUENCE

Access to public relations resources, variability in public relations strategies and tactics and in its relative influence on news agendas all merit further attention. While public relations has been criticised for distorting the news agenda, not all forms of public relations may have equal opportunity for this kind of influence, and some journalists may enjoy better access to public relations as an information source than others. Financial journalists, for example, may have more access to public relations sources than environmental journalists, and we need to understand what factors play into this privilege, as well as the effect it has on the information that can be accessed by the public. Consumer public relations may seem less important to mainstream news outlets than corporate or business public relations, even if some of the information they communicate is relevant to a wider news agenda (such as the introduction of new regulations to protect consumers, or an intervention by a consumer activist group to protect consumer rights). On a broader scale, the influence of public relations on deliberation will vary depending on whether it is trying to influence the 'dominant' public sphere, or is speaking from the margins. In the latter case, public relations may only be visible if public debate is particularly vibrant. Finding out more about the empirical reality of public relations in public spheres will help us understand when and why public relations resources tend to be devoted to high-profile debates, what other issues miss out, and with what effect. It will also illuminate how practitioners engage with media and audiences differently depending on the type of public sphere they are addressing (for example, in a feminist-oriented public sphere, where the primary focus is the struggle over women's rights, as compared to a transnational public sphere where issues relate to equity in global trade arrangements).

POWER DIFFERENTIALS ACROSS PUBLIC SPHERES

If there are multiple public spheres, then there is clearly more to say and understand about the ways in which power differentials affect the formulation of public relations strategies and tactical choices in these different spaces. Marginalised publics in counter-public spheres may well adopt different kinds of tactics than groups engaged in dominant public spheres (Demetrious, 2013); what kinds of tactics they use, which are most effective, why and how they attract audiences, are still areas where we have limited knowledge on a general analytical level, although individual case studies do provide useful insights. Still, knowing how and why they strategise in different ways, and how their choices change as the communicative, political and social landscape evolves, is important to our understanding of the role that public relations plays in society and culture. Power differentials across public spheres may also be reflected in the uptake by institutional actors of arguments communicated by different groups. If so, then understanding how access to elite power (or lack of it) influences the relative importance of different campaign tactics, including the use of different communication channels to reach audiences, is also an important area for research.

CASE STUDY 6.2
INEQUALITY IN TRANSNATIONAL PUBLIC SPHERES: THE WAR IN SYRIA

The Syrian civil war, which began in 2011 and at the time of writing (2017) continues to wreak havoc, has been paralleled by a transnational debate about the ways in which the conflict might be resolved. Political actors include the United States and Russia, both of which have become deeply involved in the conflict, both directly through military support for each side and indirectly through public diplomacy interventions. As well as these major powers, regional and global organisations such as the United Nations, the UN High Commissioner for Refugees, the European Union, international human rights organisations such as Amnesty International, aid organisations such as Médecins sans Frontières, Save the Children and Oxfam, all use public relations in different ways to publicise the human, political and economic impact of the war, urging action and attitudinal change that will bring the conflict to an end. International media cover the progress of the war: each new attack and bombardment is publicised through mainstream outlets as well as local bloggers and journalists. Citizens still living in Syria provide eye-witness accounts of life inside the war zone that are integrated into the media coverage and sometimes facilitated by NGOs working with them.

Arguably, the result of all this publicity is a transnational public sphere – but not all voices are necessarily given the same attention. On the one hand, those organisations that have access to communication skills and resources – for example, the US and Russian governments, global institutions such as the United Nations, large NGOs, the Syrian government – will find it easier to get their message out to the wider world. On the other hand, those who do not have such easy access will find it harder, including those most directly affected by the war: civilians trapped inside besieged cities, refugees attempting to flee the country, and various opposition groups. In chaotic circumstances, public sphere norms inevitably break down for such groups. Their ability to both create communication that will get noticed and give them voice, as well as to access communication from organisations that could alleviate their suffering, may be almost non-existent. As a consequence, and despite the active use of public relations by many of those involved, the legitimacy and efficacy of even this most transnational of public spheres is deeply compromised.

TRANSNATIONAL PUBLIC SPHERES AND PUBLIC RELATIONS

The increasing importance of transnational public spheres focuses attention on the importance of public relations campaigns conducted by multinational corporations, NGOs and governments across national boundaries and in the context of global power hierarchies. Campaigns targeting global economic and political institutions – or conducted by them – can be analysed as connected campaigns focused on common issues (see Chapter 5). Important questions then arise about their intertextuality and the degree to which they engage established and new audiences in effective debate. Understanding the role played by global public relations agencies is crucial, given that the campaigns they develop can facilitate or block transnational deliberation about global issues such as climate change, labour rights or food and water security, by bringing some issues to the fore and ignoring others. Research could investigate the kinds of media they target, the tactics for direct audience engagement they use, and the effect of these choices on the social and cultural impact of their communication. Given that online communication is fundamental to transnational public spheres, finding out more about how public relations practitioners use online channels to reach remote audiences affected by the issues being discussed, and how online dissemination affects the inclusion and exclusion of different populations, will illuminate questions about the integrity and functionality of transnational deliberation. In relation to the vexed question of the decisiveness of transnational public spheres, understanding the degree to which public relations supports processes that communicate deliberation back to institutional powers capable of initiating change is also vital.

PUBLIC RELATIONS AND THE CHANGING MEDIA LANDSCAPE

The 'relatively clustered' public sphere of the traditional mass media has become both extended and dispersed (Dahlgren, 2005: 152), so that in the contemporary media landscape, journalists are no longer the only watchdogs of power or the sole arbiters of information that reaches the public domain. Consequently, the institutional and political economic dominance of mainstream media on information ecologies is lessened. Other actors in the virtual sphere now also monitor, challenge and unmask abuses of power by those who govern, resulting in a 'fifth estate', where the mainstream media have become part of a network of institutions that people look to for information, rather than a stand-alone source (Dutton, 2009). The structures and norms of journalism have also changed, with dominant national and global news organisations now joined by a vibrant, global online journalism sector (Dahlgren, 2005; Waisbord, 2013). Audiences have the potential to contribute to the news agenda,[3] and indeed the idea of 'news' itself becomes more contested when an agentic, engaged audience begins to publish and share information actively in order to contribute to public discourse (Benkler, 2006). Perceptions of the quality and reliability of online information are based not only on the symbolic authority of the established media, but may come from verification via social networks, testimonials available online, and even the format and layout of the content (Metzger et al., 2010; Chung et al., 2012).

In this more open environment, public relations' effect on the traditional media agenda is potentially less impactful, because media organisations compete with other sources of authority and expertise, from citizen voices to NGOs, from activist groups to terrorist cells (Lüders, 2008), all of which use public relations to circulate information and interpretations of current events. Understanding public relations' effects on news formation and distribution therefore requires a more nuanced approach than simply focusing on traditional news media. It must take into account the fact that public relations works with a wide range of actors involved in news production and circulation and can be a source of resistance and change, as well as continuity. Existing research does not really address the varied role public relations plays in the development of contemporary news agendas through its engagement in dominant and counter-public spheres. More empirical work is also needed to understand whether a strong critique of public relations' influence on news is still merited and, if so, what form that influence takes in contemporary, networked and digital communication environments.

THE IMPORTANCE OF UNMEDIATED COMMUNICATION

As new tools such as social media, mobile media, websites and blogs enable organisations to reach audiences directly and independently of journalists and media outlets, questions arise about how public relations takes advantage of the normative 'mediated sociality' that characterises our lives (van Dijck, 2013). While unmediated communication will not replace work designed to intervene in the news agenda, it is important to understand how the two types of strategy are used, both separately and in combination, to influence citizens and those in power. Reaching audiences with unmediated communication will have important effects on the information environment that citizens negotiate and use to make decisions. If influencing audiences via the media merits a focus for critique, then directly influencing audiences, without the potentially moderating influence of third parties, is surely an important realm for critical scholarship. We need to find out how much influence direct tactics have on the ways that audiences think about the debates they are engaged in, and analyse the degree to which direct communication offers relative freedom to dominant institutions to further their power, without the potentially mitigating effect of a journalist's gaze. The scale of public relations' reach through direct tactics is also important: how widely such tactics circulate, and what audiences they reach that other media do not or cannot address (if any), are important aspects of public relations' effect on contemporary public spheres. Equally important for deliberation is the degree to which public relations' direct communication is inclusive: Do campaigns target only audiences that can help the organisation deploying public relations, or do they expand the realms of deliberation by reaching all those affected by an issue?

PUBLIC RELATIONS AND MEDIA INDUSTRY HIERARCHIES

Finally, given the supportive role that public relations plays for journalists short of time and resources, questions could be asked about the changing nature of media relations and its effects on the distribution of power within and across different media outlets. As media ecologies become more open, the power of public relations will be reflected in how much attention smaller online news outlets receive from practitioners, as compared to more popular sites, under what circumstances and with what effect on their news output. Public relations materials may also influence the relative power of media institutions – for example, online versus offline outlets, small versus large media organisations, and local, national or global news outlets. Other issues address the relationships between public relations practitioners and journalists, including the different kinds of engagement that take place in relation to mainstream outlets and alternative online sources. Institutional history may carry more weight and support the ongoing dominance of traditional media outlets, ensuring journalists receive better information, more promptly. Similarly, understanding how the quality of face-to-face relationships between public relations practitioners and journalists compares with that of relationships built via social media, across time and space, will also inform the ongoing influence of public relations on media hierarchies, and thereby on contemporary public spheres.

CONCLUSION

The public sphere remains an important concept through which we may understand processes of deliberation in contemporary societies. Its original framing, and particularly the emphasis on a free and independent media, has had important consequences in terms of the normative understanding of public relations as a largely negative influence on public sphere structures and dynamics. As discussed above, the challenges are difficult to counter because of the inherent nature of the occupation. It is designed to realise self-interest, and empirical evidence shows that it does so in a way that can damage democracy.

However, changing theorisations of public spheres have opened up opportunities for public relations' role to be understood differently. This does not mean that we have a way of justifying it as a positive influence. On the contrary, in many ways the discussion of new areas for investigation presented in this chapter suggests that there are many new routes through which we might understand public relations as a negative factor in public sphere deliberations. These pick up on the challenges outlined in Chapter 1, including the ways in which public relations might reinforce structural norms through its influence, or alternatively, provide new avenues for agency by improving interpersonal and online connections and forms of social capital that can prompt action. As a vehicle through which marginalised groups can access voice in the public sphere, the industry can also create changes in the ways different identities are privileged in civic life, by bringing greater public attention to some and challenging the dominance of others. Finally, we have to return to the vexed question of the relationship between public relations and the media. In a networked and digital media landscape, dominance fragments but may reappear in unexpected spaces, and may be enhanced by public relations supporting some outlets over others. Equally, the optimistic analysis of co-operation between public relations practitioners and journalists may apply in some circumstances, but friction is likely to persist, and we must resist the notion that the fragmented and fluid contemporary media ecology necessarily equalises power across the two occupations.

Overall, the variability of public spheres and media landscapes in the contemporary world inevitably means that the effect of public relations will be unpredictable. We may be able to identify some patterns, but they are unlikely to hold for long periods. In light of this, public relations should perhaps be understood first and foremost as a source of flux and change in public spheres. Through this more expansive interpretation of public relations' role, we will be able to expand our understanding of the depth, scope and range of its influence, and explore its effects in a more nuanced and detailed way.

NOTES

1. Curran (2002) provides an excellent history of the media and its relation to power, showing that the neutrality of the media has varied over time. For example, partisanship was the norm for many newspapers in the nineteenth century, while the inevitable tension between the political class and journalists has led to regulation that prevents the media from critiquing politicians and their parties. That said, the basic principle that the media are a vehicle through which misuse of power can be exposed, and citizens mobilised, remains an important pillar of professionalism in the journalistic field.
2. It is worth noting that much research on the public sphere remains limited to Western, developed nation contexts, and there is a clear need to 'de-Westernise' this area of research, including relevant work on public relations.
3. Peters and Witschge (2015) note that audience participation in news production is not necessarily the same thing as citizen engagement. They distinguish between participation *in* news, where audiences submit content or are otherwise engaged in news production, and participation *through* news, where their contributions help to set the news agenda, and consequently have a more significant influence on the way that public sphere debates unfold.

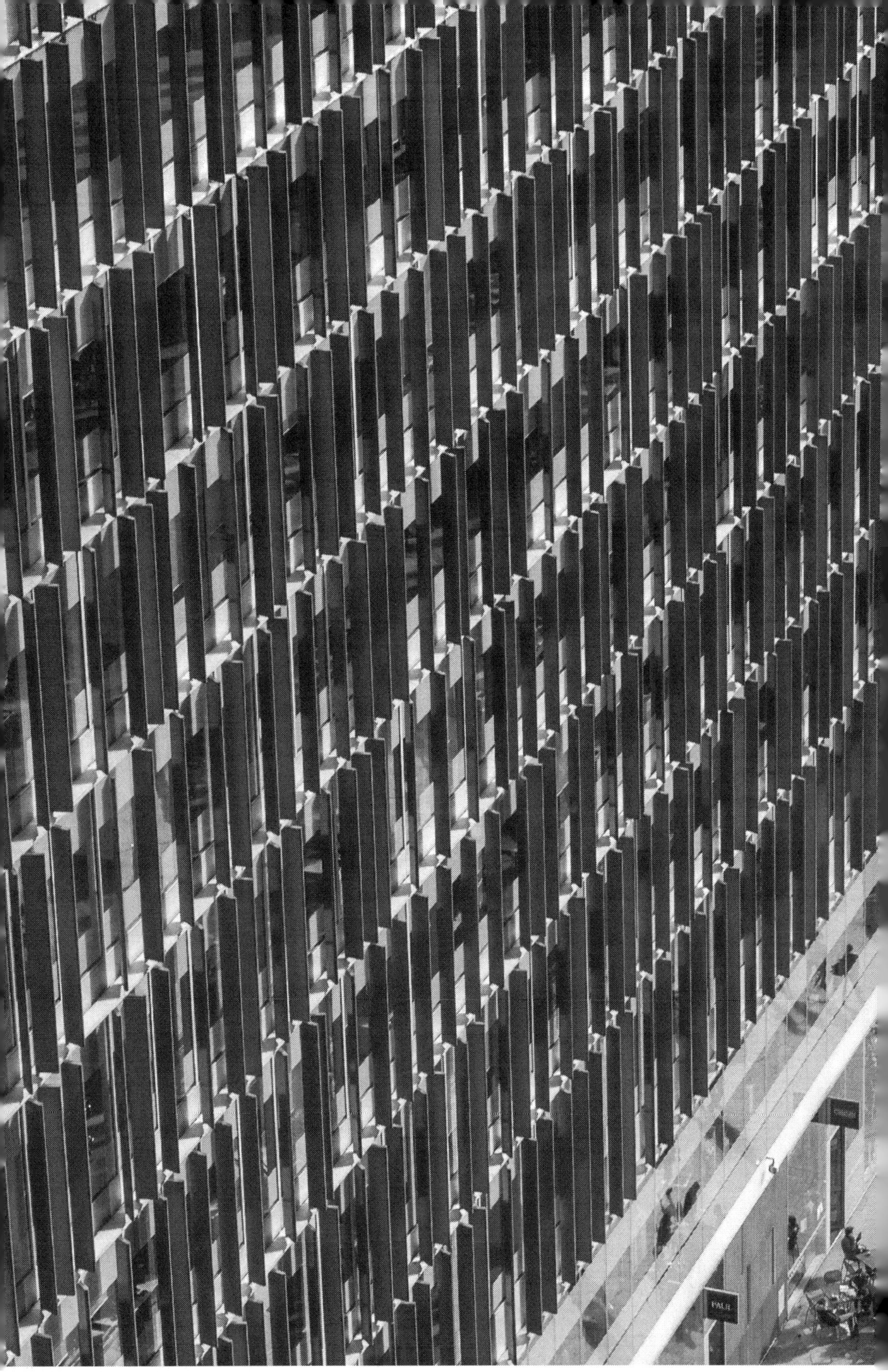
PAUL

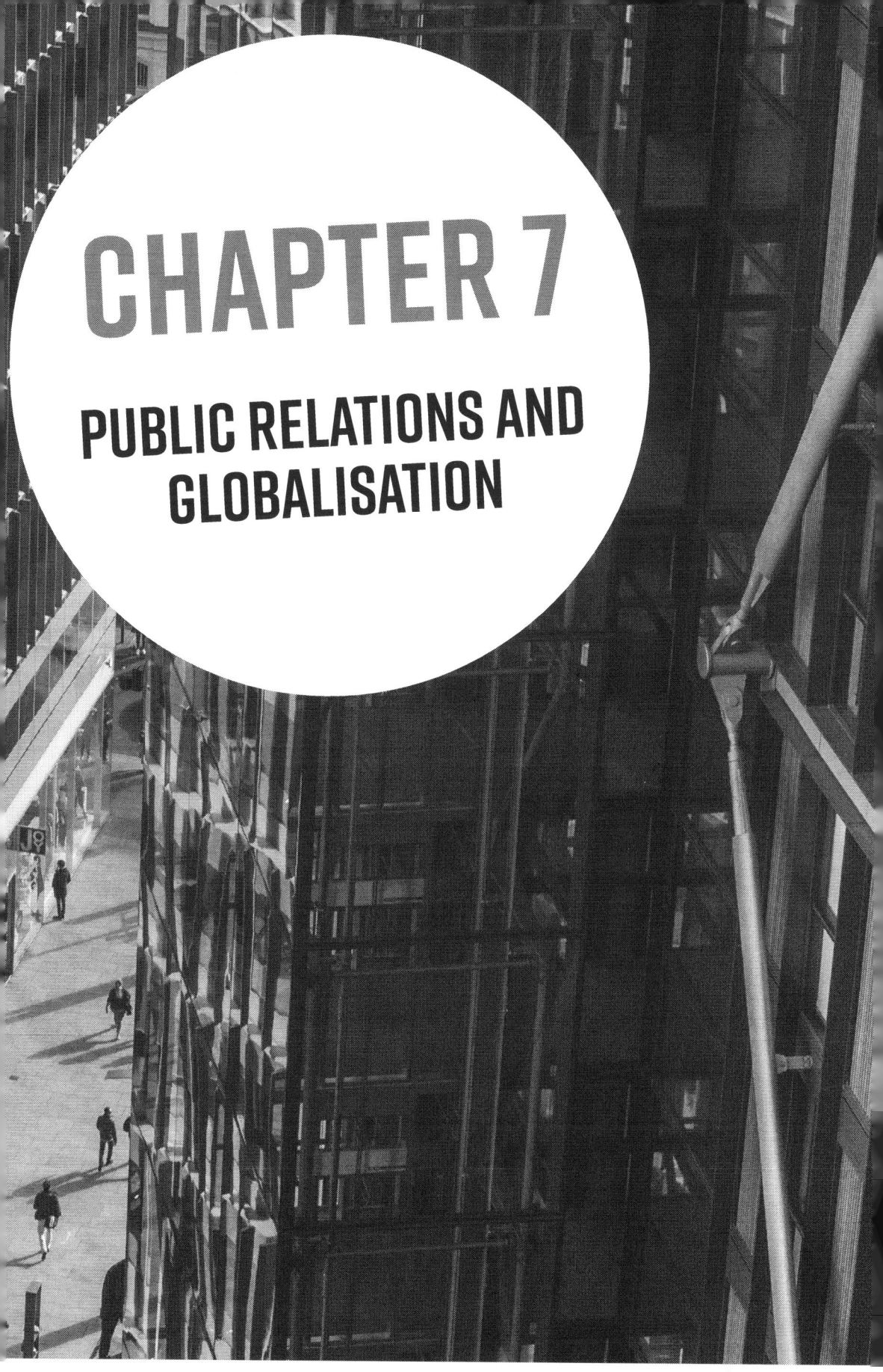

CHAPTER 7
PUBLIC RELATIONS AND GLOBALISATION

Contemporary forms of globalisation are crucial elements in socio-cultural analyses of public relations, because they constitute some of the biggest changes in the environment with which organisations must engage. Organisations frequently operate in global marketplaces, they create websites that are visible to audiences all over the world, and their communication is no longer limited to specific times or places because it travels instantaneously far and wide over transnational, digital networks. Globalisation has expanded the market for public relations among corporate and government organisations facing these challenges, supporting the growth of international agencies that can run campaigns in multiple countries simultaneously. It has also offered opportunities for non-profit, activist organisations to expand the international audience for their cause and generate greater momentum for change.

Globalisation is not a new phenomenon; movements of people, capital, information and power between geographies have influenced national and transnational economies, polities and cultures for hundreds of years, and the history of the communications industries in particular is marked by the desire to connect different countries and regions (Bauman, 1998; Harvey, 2001; Thompson, 2003). Modern forms of globalisation differ in the speed and sophistication of the technologies that enable connection, but they have their roots in complex histories of exploitation and resistance between different nations. As a result, the manifestation and effects of globalisation today are multiple, and it is impossible to label it definitively as either good or bad (Bardhan and Weaver, 2011a: 4–5). Rather, globalisation both opens up and closes down possibilities for living in different ways, depending on where people are located in global economic and political systems (Castells, 2000, 2009). What Dirlik calls global modernity both 'unifies and divides ... it does not do to emphasize one or the other' (Dirlik, 2003: 277).

The global public relations industry is exemplified by the presence of multinational agencies in more than half the countries across the globe, the extensive use of public relations by multinational companies, and the presence of transnational public relations associations that claim to connect practitioners and organisations on a global scale and proselytise about the economic and social good public relations can do (e.g. Asia-Pacific Association of Communication Directors, 2016; European Association of Communication Directors, 2016; Global Alliance for Public Relations, 2016). It is relatively unaffected by global crises and economic downturns and is continually expands into new geographies. In scholarship and practice, the 'global industry' is constructed as both an object of research and barometer of success (Sriramesh and Verčič, 2007; European Communication Monitor, 2016; Holmes Group, 2016; USC Annenberg Center for Public Relations, 2016).

However, despite this global presence and the fact that international public relations is a long-established area of practice, theory on public relations and globalisation has, until recently, reflected a hegemonic model of globalisation where knowledge flowed from 'West to rest'. North American history, practice and theory of public relations has been taken for granted as the global benchmark. Even in countries where public relations has been well-established, a lack of local textbooks has meant that public relations education is US-centric and reflects Western values, particularly ideologies of democracy, marketisation, consumption and self-promotion, all of which have been linked to the growth and spread of the occupation (Sriramesh, 2002, 2009; Bardhan and Weaver, 2011a). More recently, however, the Western, modernist emphasis in public relations theory and practice has been challenged and a wider variety of perspectives is now available in both academic and practitioner-oriented publications (see, for example, Macnamara, 2005; Sriramesh and Verčič, 2009; Vilanilam, 2011; Tench and Yeomans, 2014). New ways of thinking about and doing public relations in transnational contexts are emerging, and in this chapter I address some of those changes.

I introduce an analysis of public relations and globalisation that recognises the indeterminacy of the relationship between the two, taking into account dynamics of history, power, change and continuity in the role that public relations has played in the progress of contemporary globalisation. After outlining some of the main normative and critical approaches to globalisation, I adopt a dialectical approach to consider public relations' role in the global circulation of structures, cultural norms and discourses. Drawing in particular on Appadurai's (1996) model of cultural flows, I explore how public relations may be understood to *produce* globalisation in the ways it sustains networks and systems of governance, but is at the same time a *product of* globalisation, its own structures and practices inextricably entwined with the flows of capital, finance, technology, people and ideas that it simultaneously produces.

GLOBALISATION

Globalisation has its locus in the changing nature of interactions between people, organisations and institutions. Giddens (1999: 12–13) argues that globalisation is 'a complex set of processes [operating] in a contradictory or oppositional fashion', with effects on cultural norms and traditions, family life and democracy. As time and space have become disconnected from each other (or 'distanciated'), instantaneous connections with others are now possible across vast distances, so that relationships are no longer limited to physical encounters. This flexibility, and the accompanying 'disembedding' of social activity from specific places via communication channels such as social media, means that we are exposed to new information about the world so that 'social practices are constantly examined and reformed in the light of incoming information … thus constitutively altering their character' (Giddens, 1990: 38). The relationships that result from these changes are stretched across geographical space (extensity); networked across multiple spheres of activity (intensity); executed rapidly in a time-frame set by the possibilities of technology rather than by the constraints of distance (velocity); and marked by an increasingly visible and significant connection between local and global events (deepened) (Held and McGrew, 2007b: 2–3).

The emergence of contemporary forms of globalisation is tightly linked to the spread of capitalism, particularly since the collapse of socialism in the last decades of the twentieth century. Harvey (2001) argues that globalisation is the consequence of capitalism's need to resolve its cyclical existential crises by creating infrastructures that allow it to overcome the limitations to growth imposed by geographical space. The influence of transnational corporations on economic and political decision-making is one manifestation of this territorial growth, but it is also reflected in the ways in which globalisation discourses tend to present ideas of progress and modernity. They frequently reify technological advancement and economic progress as desirable forms of 'development' and the key to participation, largely reflecting Western experiences of modern society and relegating alternative modernities to the status of being incomplete or insufficient (Dirlik, 2003; Kaur, 2012).

Alongside the spread of capitalism, the growth, technological development and diffusion of global media and communication systems have been crucial to contemporary globalisation (Thompson, 2003: 246). Networked, digital forms of communication have changed not only the way that communication flows between physical locations, but also the ways in which relationships, identity and belonging are expressed and structured across time and space for communities across the world, and altered the connections between culture, economy and politics (Silverstone, 2006; Castells, 2009, 2012; Couldry, 2012). These connections, which facilitate extensity and intensity, are due not only to innovations in the physical and technological infrastructure of communication systems – for example, the hardware and software that make the internet and mobile telephony possible – but also to the growth of a 'transnational promotional class' (Aronczyk, 2013b), including the global public relations industry, which helps to disperse discourses that both promote and contest social, political, economic and cultural norms across time and space.

The networked, extensive and intensive characteristics of globalisation create uncertainty and fluidity in the global environment, which alters the circulation of power. Expert systems have developed as organising structures of globalisation that help us understand and navigate its complexity (Giddens, 1990: 27), and public relations encourages us to trust the organisations that constitute such systems (e.g. financial institutions, scientific authorities, research foundations) as we make sense of the world (Bourne and Edwards, 2012; Bourne, 2017). Globalisation is also entrenched and resilient because it is constituted through networked systems. Held and McGrew (2007b) identify 'deep drivers' of globalisation that have produced its contemporary manifestation: the interconnectedness of global communication infrastructures (see also Thompson, 2003; Castells, 2009); the development of global markets; the global division of labour; the diffusion of democracy and consumer values; and the growth of migration. These systemic roots mean that globalisation survives even in the face of enormous challenges such as 9/11 and the subsequent 'war on terror', as well as the global economic recession from 2008 onwards (Held and McGrew, 2007b: 4).

CRITIQUES OF GLOBALISATION

In the face of popular discourses of globalisation that unproblematically celebrate connection, participation and market-driven success, critics emphasise its divisive reality, exposing its political character and the ways it perpetuates power for some groups over others (Fairclough, 2006). Some have taken issue with its effects on democratic forms of governance and social justice on a global scale. Socio-economic, gender, racial and environmental inequalities continue to be a major feature of globalisation (Bauman, 1998; Steans, 2003; Benería et al., 2016), while the transnational hegemony of neoliberal politics and economics structurally embeds the dominance of transnational corporations and disempowers national governments (Zoller, 2004; Castells, 2009; Dutta and Pal, 2011).

Because the effects of globalisation are so dispersed, it also undermines the legitimacy and efficacy of national-level public spheres, which can neither include distant populations affected by a particular event, decision or policy, nor provide effective opposition to the complex global systems of power and governance that extend beyond the nation state and are exemplified in organisations like the World Trade Organization, the United Nations and the World Bank. At the same time, the reduced capacity of nation states to exert sovereignty over economy and politics in a networked world has led to a corresponding rise of nationalism and territorialism that increases rather than reduces division, leaving some of the world's most vulnerable people – frequently located in the global South – at risk (Dirlik, 2003; Benhabib, 2004). Instead, critics suggest, the development of justice in a globalised world requires a 'transnationalised' public sphere (or spheres) (see Chapter 6), where the dispersed effects of political decision-making beyond national borders can be acknowledged, and where previously neglected voices can be incorporated into law- and policymaking processes (de Sousa Santos and Rodríguez-Garavito, 2005; Fraser, 2007; Held and McGrew, 2007a). There is certainly scope for existing media and communication systems, including public relations, to become more transnational in nature, cognisant of the complexities in the global environment and offering more effective visibility to marginalised groups, rather than reproducing stereotypes (Pal and Dutta, 2008; Holtzhausen, 2011; Mellese and Müller, 2012; Couldry, 2014). As Kwami (2016: 151) notes, 'the margins constitute a multiplicity and continuum of spaces that is not static, with people situated in multiple intersections of the margins in different contexts, sometimes oscillating between centers and margins'.

Postcolonial theory offers an important contribution in this debate, locating globalisation in its longer history of colonial occupation and trade and thereby acting as a counterbalance to globalisation's celebratory and future-focused narratives (Schwartz-DuPre and Scott, 2015). Colonial histories continue to structure global power relations between states and communication often plays a critical role in protecting power, 'othering' the global South and East and constructing the world in ways that maintain the economic and political superiority of the West (Said, 1994; Hanchey, 2016; Edwards and Ramamurthy, 2017). Studies show how resources such as land, valuable minerals, water and labour are co-opted in the service of Western-based transnational corporations, and how indigenous culture is dismissed by claims of the need to 'modernise' in ways that reflect Western norms and expectations – almost always with little regard for the long-term economic, cultural and environmental traditions and well-being of local communities (Dirlik, 2003; Dutta and Pal, 2011). With these interventions in institutionalised knowledge and practice, postcolonial theory highlights the tensions inherent in globalisation at the local, national and international levels, including the co-existence of power and resistance, the hybridisation of cultures alongside the continued importance of difference as a structuring factor in global arrangements, the importance of mobility and the distribution of privilege and disadvantage (Shome and Hegde, 2002; Krishnaswamy, 2008; Parameswaran, 2008). While many structures and flows do privilege those who are already dominant, pockets of resistance also thrive, and adopting a subaltern approach to writing globalisation 'from below' can reveal these alternative forms of power (Dutta, 2015; Hanchey, 2016; Kwami, 2016).

Regardless of how one interprets its effects, scholars generally agree on several key features of globalisation: greater interconnectedness; increases in nationalism and regionalism; heightened uncertainty, unpredictability and risk; attempts to mitigate risk through mobility strategies that overcome space and time; the transformation of relationships to extend over space and time; a corresponding change and diversity in the lived experience of space and time (which shrink for some, but extend for others); and increasing hybridity of people, cultures and values even in the most local of spaces. Dialectics of local–global, mobility–fixity and hegemony–resistance generate tensions that ensure continuity and change in the way the world is organised. For example, the primacy of nation states as a locus of political and economic power is questioned as the most fundamental unit through which regional and international governance are managed, but national culture is a tool for participation in the global economy; clear and strong borders between nations no longer exist, but new types of borders are constructed through the regulation of movement; the superiority of Western cultures and forms of modernity is challenged and other cultures become more visible and legitimate, but the West continues to dominate in economic and political contexts, supporting the normative pre-eminence of their cultural assumptions and products.

MOBILITY, FLOWS AND FIXITY

One of the most important sources of tension in contemporary globalisation is the mobility–fixity dialectic. Mobility – of people, capital, information and ideas – lies at the heart of contemporary globalisation (Appadurai, 1996; Harvey, 2003), but is always coupled with fixity. As Harvey (2003: 99) notes, 'fluid movement *over* space can be achieved only by fixing certain physical infrastructures *in* space', such that the mobility of anything depends on permanent infrastructures that facilitate movement (airports, ports, undersea cables, newspapers, computer networks, banks). Mobility is also a locus of the inequalities produced by globalisation, since once the advantages of a new location are exhausted, people and assets move on, leaving those who cannot move to cope with the sometimes drastic consequences of the departure – a reality that is illustrated vividly by landscapes of abandoned factories, polluted waterways and emptying towns, following the decline of industrial production in cities across the globe (Harvey, 2001).

Bauman (1998) points out that mobility is a form of privilege (some people and resources are able to move between nations and places, some are not), a channel through which privilege can be obtained (some people can move themselves or their assets in order to secure the benefits of globalisation, others cannot), and a means of imposing disadvantage through exclusion (some people are actively prevented from moving so that the privilege of others is protected). For refugees, whose journeys comprise some of the most visible and concerning expressions of the mobility–fixity dialectic, moving may lead to integration, but is equally a source of dislocation and further exclusion through fixity. Refugees' mobility may be interrupted by (or indeed conclude with) long periods of immobility in camps, or be stymied by state mechanisms such as border controls and requirements for identity documents that prevent their integration into new spaces and communities and leave them without any place to belong (Benhabib, 2004). On the other hand, specific places can also be highly agentic. As Escobar (2001: 141) notes, we should recognise the 'continued vitality of place and place-making for culture, nature, and economy', alongside the importance of contemporary mobilities.

Appadurai's (1996) model of global cultural flows describes the ways in which mobility of all kinds underpins globalisation. He identifies five types of flow that characterise contemporary forms of globalisation and facilitate the movement of culture – understood as expressions of difference and identity – across time and space: ethnoscapes describe the movement of people; technoscapes reflect the movement of all forms of technology; financescapes describe the movement of capital; mediascapes relate to the distribution and circulation of information and knowledge; and ideoscapes relate to the dissemination of more expressly political ideas. The emphasis on flow notwithstanding, Appadurai does not forget the locatedness of the lives through which they are interpreted and taken up. 'Scapes' are 'perspectival constructs' (Appadurai, 1996: 33), informed by history, politics and language and experienced differently depending on the location in which they are lived (a refugee experiences migration very differently from a sponsored corporate manager, for example, while a mobile phone offers very different possibilities for inhabitants of New York as compared to a rural community in the Democratic Republic of Congo).

Relationships between the flows – the ways in which they align or clash with each other – produce the disjunctures between economy, culture and politics that are fundamental to the complex dynamics of globalisation. In this sense, the flows produce possibilities for the exertion of both power and resistance by institutions, communities and individuals. They are also productive in that they provide the raw materials for the exercise of imagination, 'a form of work (in the sense of both labor and culturally organized practice), and a form of negotiation between sites of agency (individuals) and globally defined fields of possibility' (Appadurai, 1996: 31). Imagination, in Appadurai's model, is more than just thinking differently about the world; it incorporates negotiating new and different practices, implementing them, and challenging existing arrangements in the process. It is a source of productive tension because while it provides an impetus for action and change, new practices also inevitably clash with traditional norms of what is right and possible in specific contexts. All cultural flows have a role to play in imagination, but mediascapes and ideoscapes are most specific to the diffusion of ideas and ideologies, and digital media are particularly important as a source of 'new resources and new disciplines for the construction of imagined selves and imagined worlds' (Appadurai, 1996: 3).

GLOBALISATION AND PUBLIC RELATIONS

Public relations is a product of globalisation, and particularly of time-space distanciation, since its growth over the last three decades is due in no small measure to the spread of market principles of competition and choice, which created openings for organisations to use strategic communication as a means of overcoming the material limitations of time and space in their efforts to expand into new markets (Miller and Dinan, 2007; Davis, 2013). It also produces globalisation in so far as it disembeds relationships by providing rationales and publicising technologies for connecting with temporally and geographically distant individuals. It is a source of uncertainty and reflexivity, introducing new knowledge to our repertoire that destabilises the status quo, but simultaneously supporting those expert systems that help us make sense of the world. These effects of public relations work influence the global cultural flows described above, which communicate 'differences, contrasts and comparisons' as they circulate (Appadurai, 1996: 12). They structure knowledge and relationships in new ways and play into the 'mutual contextualizing of motion and mediation' (Appadurai, 1996: 5) that is inherent to globalisation.

Analysing public relations' relationship to globalisation in this way represents a shift from normative framings in public relations scholarship, which tend to focus on the need to integrate a broader range of cultural perspectives into public relations theory, practice and education (Sriramesh, 2009; Sriramesh and Verčič, 2009, 2012). It extends both critical approaches that challenge public relations' role in sustaining the hegemonic power of transnational corporations, institutions and governments and the neglect of marginalised voices (Roper, 2005, 2012; Dutta and Pal, 2011; Holtzhausen, 2011; Bourne, 2013), and critical cultural approaches that focus on the production of meaning (Curtin and Gaither, 2007). Instead, it is a way of 'unmanaging' public relations and globalisation (Elmer, 2007) and embracing complexity, and in the remainder of the chapter I unpack the tensions and contradictions of public relations that are revealed through this approach.

CASE STUDY 7.1
CONTESTED IDEOLOGIES: COMMUNICATING FAIR TRADE?

Communicating about fair trade movements is a good example of how the complexity of globalisation is reflected within and between discourses produced by public relations. The fair trade movement is focused on intervening in global trade systems to make them more equitable and deliver fairer rewards to producers in the global South. It does this by encouraging consumers in the global North to consume ethically by buying products that feature a fair trade logo (of which there are many different kinds). The movement reflects a clash between the ideology of global trade as a fair mechanism for the distribution of wealth, and the reality that in fact, developing communities are disadvantaged because of their relative lack of power in global finance and trade arrangements.

The organisation Fairtrade UK emphasises the fact that consumers can 'change the world' through their behaviour (see http://www.fairtrade.org.uk/en/what-is-fairtrade), and quantify the impact of their work through formal and informal evidence for audiences to review (statistics and individual producer narratives about how Fairtrade has benefited their communities, as well as images of smiling producers in fertile fields – see www.fairtrade.org.uk). Their communication helps to make subaltern voices visible in the global marketplace, and fair trade products have been integrated successfully into mainstream food and clothing outlets in many countries.

However, the movement has also been criticised for buying into the very system of production and consumption that it claims to challenge. By associating activism only with consumers in the global North, fair trade organisations do not displace the basic division between the North as the locus of wealth, choice and consumption, and the South as a locus of poverty, disadvantage and production. Images of smiling producers, liberated through the generosity of wealthy (Northern) consumers, do little to change colonial discourses that positioned the global North and West as a civilising influence on colonised nations and a means of enabling their 'development'. Fair trade arrangements are also contested in practice: the premium that fair trade organisations pay to their producers over and above the market rate does not always go to those who work on the farms and in the factories, many of whom are seasonal or part-time and have no formal stake in the organisation (see, for example, Wydick, 2014). In this sense, 'fair' trade is not always as fair as it claims to be.

I address three areas: structure, culture and discourse. I interpret 'structure' in political economic terms, as the ways in which public relations is organised as a global industry (see Chapter 4), including 'moments of fixity' (offices, people, artefacts) that co-exist with its movement across different geographies, and the connections it has with other powerful institutions (corporations, governments, NGOs). By 'culture', I mean the ways in which public relations is a vehicle for the circulation of meaning (see Chapter 2). As for 'discourse', I consider the transnational scale of public relations' contribution to cultural flows through language. I prioritise a dialectical, relational approach to communication that assumes it is non-linear, contradictory and riven with tensions that arise from the different forces that shape content, processes and outcomes (Martin and Nakayama, 1999). The approach aligns with the networked complexity of globalisation, but also destabilises the idea of a definitive understanding of public relations and globalisation, instead offering the possibility of '"knowing" [public relations] as a dynamic and changing process. We can begin to see epistemological concerns as an open-ended process ... that resists fixed, discrete bits of knowledge' (Martin and Nakayama, 2010: 66). In other words, the approach does not simplify things – but it does enable a more comprehensive and realistic assessment of actually existing public relations practice on a global scale.

PUBLIC RELATIONS AND GLOBAL STRUCTURES

Historically, American and European companies dominated the control of communications infrastructure, and the colonisation of the global South and East in trade arrangements generated the greatest financial rewards for the global North and West. Consequently, the formalised practice of public relations emerged first in industrialised nations (Cutlip, 1994; Bentele and Wehmeier, 2003; L'Etang, 2004). This historical advantage has had a lasting legacy: the majority of today's global public relations corporations are headquartered in developed countries – mainly the USA or Europe (Holmes Group, 2016) – and most public relations work is carried out for profit-seeking corporations and governments (see Chapter 4). Agencies extend their presence into developing countries as they see potential markets emerging, by setting up new offices or investing in local companies, and sending managers to run their branches and train local staff in (Western) public relations techniques. By contrast, countries where markets are still to develop, or where political and economic arrangements are less stable, tend to be neglected (Sriramesh and Verčič, 2007).

As a commercial and political function, public relations benefits from and sustains global trading structures by helping countries, companies and audiences to engage with each other on a global scale. The geographical distribution of the industry reflects the fact that it locates offices in places that facilitate the movement of capital, the backbone of globalisation (Harvey, 2001), promoting markets, goods and services in new locations as growth wanes elsewhere. Its industry structures ensure it contributes to financescapes that flow towards the North and West of the globe from the South and East, since its own revenues accrue to

Western-based headquarters. However, it also contributes to financescapes through its work promoting capital and consumption on behalf of other industries, not only in countries that are already deeply engaged in the global economy, but also in those that wish to engage, newly capable of participating in the requisite relationships that globalisation designates as desirable – international trade, consumption, and political alliances (Dirlik, 2003). In the process, it facilitates the expropriation and exploitation of marginalised communities and economies by transnational companies, because it frames their presence as a necessity for participating in and securing benefits from the global economy (Munshi and Kurian, 2005; Pal and Dutta, 2008). Public relations co-opts global audiences too, encouraging material support (in the form of consumption, investment or votes, for example) for companies and governments invested in global trade.

The picture becomes a little more complicated when a dialectical lens is adopted. While there is no denying the dominance of the West, it does fragment once the dynamics of mobility and flow are taken into account. As noted in Chapter 4, the only non-Western agency in the global top ten for 2016 was BlueFocus, headquartered in China, but that company had a growth rate of 36.7% as compared to rates of under 10% for the other nine agencies on the list (Holmes Group, 2016). As the Chinese economy becomes more open and internationally competitive, Chinese influence on public relations industry structures may provide a counter to the West, both financially and ideologically. This interaction between financescapes and ideoscapes means that public relations may facilitate the movement of finance *away from* the global West and North. New offices require significant investment in the host country economy, employment of local staff, and if successful, may result in expansion. Local clients are successfully promoted overseas, bringing in foreign exchange, creating new employment opportunities and supporting the balance of trade for developing countries.

CASE STUDY 7.2

ON THE PERIPHERY OF GLOBALISATION: JAMAICA'S WATER PROBLEM

The inequitable structures of global commerce and the legacy of colonialism are frequently felt on the periphery of globalisation, but normalised through public relations. In Jamaica, the country's water system exemplifies the importance of geography on globalisation and the benefits one can receive from it. In 2015, Jamaican citizens were suffering the effects of a long-standing and chronic leakage problem in the national water supply. According to the government-run National Water Commission (NWC),

(Continued)

which is in charge of the water supply, over half the water supply in the city's capital, Kingston, and the surrounding region, was literally going down the drain, causing major problems for residents and businesses alike.

The problem continues in 2017, despite practical and communicative interventions to try and address it. From a communicative perspective, the NWC has made the most of globalised communication infrastructures to deliver professional communication through its public relations staff. They actively use Facebook, YouTube and Twitter to tell customers about the maintenance work they are doing, as well as to encourage responsible use of water, and suggest that customers 'join our online family' (see http://www.nwcjamaica.com/default). The impression is of an active, caring, customer-oriented company that aims to be the best water services utility in the Caribbean.

However, the upbeat tone of the communication belies the difficulties that underlie the problem. The legacy of British colonisation has offered the country precious little in terms of ongoing support for its survival, and it is now firmly located on the periphery of globalisation. The country is heavily indebted, poverty is high and the water shortages have knock-on effects on poor standards of health and sanitation. The funds to improve infrastructure are not available, which means the country is both subject to surveillance by global institutions such as the United Nations Environmental Programme, and dependent on overseas funding from the International Monetary Fund (which comes with attendant conditions for economic restructuring) as well as countries such as China and Israel. Jamaica's urban population, many of whom moved to the cities to find work as the agricultural sector declined in the face of global competition, struggle with the biggest problems because of the levels of demand. Droughts and hurricanes also regularly visit the island, putting the population and the water supply at further risk.

Unlike the local population, who are permanently positioned on the periphery of globalisation, overseas tourists would never guess at the scale of the issue. Their existence is mobile, rather than fixed; they therefore enjoy the privilege of choosing to visit, rather than having to stay. Because they come expecting sandy beaches, lush green forests and Jamaican culture, the tourism industry focuses on delivering just that. They are accommodated in locations beyond the realities of poverty, water outages and poor sanitation. Hotels use their income to invest in back-up water storage facilities, so that the brief sojourn that wealthy visitors have on the island is undisturbed. However, given the scale of the problem, how long their privilege can be sustained remains an open question.

For more information see Kebede (2015) and Josephs (2013).

While structure is interpreted here as political economic structure, it cannot be reduced to the movement of money and capital via financescapes. Appadurai's model prompts us to consider how different cultural flows intersect and have to be analysed in conjunction with each other. In the case of public relations, its contribution to financescapes is not possible without participation in technoscapes, particularly digital channels, which transport public relations messages, facilitate financial transactions and enable communication between local offices and global headquarters as well as between practitioners and their clients. Efforts to integrate with local communities and adapt to culturally specific norms and values by agencies and their clients also involve public relations in the circulation of mediascapes and ideoscapes, and may result in corporate social responsibility initiatives alleviating poverty and disadvantage at a local level. Just as important as these counter-movements of capital and finance is the public relations carried out by activist organisations that protest against existing inequality and call on organisations and governments to recognise and act on the needs of subaltern groups, addressing the effects of global structures 'on the ground', in fixed locations, at particular times, and on communities that may not enjoy the privilege of mobility (see, for example, Clean Clothes Campaign, 2017). When it engages in this way with the fixity rather than mobility of capital, public relations has the potential to prompt a redistribution of structural power away from dominant groups.

PUBLIC RELATIONS AND GLOBAL CULTURE

The dominance of the West in the global industry extends to the role public relations plays as a form of cultural industry (Edwards, 2015), facilitating the spread of cultural values through ideoscapes and mediascapes. The identity and success of public relations depend on ideological norms being taken up by both audiences and organisations (Sriramesh, 2009) – notably, democracy, marketisation, consumption and self-promotion, among other ideas. By communicating opportunities to choose between goods, services, schools, hospitals, political parties, policies and many other things, the very existence of public relations helps to constitute the norms on which it depends, and to transmit those norms across time and space through different campaigns. Moreover, because the majority of public relations clients are located in developed countries in the West, most public relations campaigns will be shaped by the cultural assumptions that shape Western society and modernity, and implicitly disseminate these assumptions more widely (Hanchey, 2016). In the context of development communication, for example, public relations materials often implicitly equate development with Western lifestyles, individualism, technological progress and market participation, and construct alternative ways of being as insufficiently 'modern' (Dutta-Bergman, 2005; Dutta and Pal, 2011; Kwami, 2016).

Countering this 'West-to-rest' dynamic is the development of the kind of global modernity that Dirlik (2003) describes, where different kinds of social and cultural arrangements are more readily recognised as a valid part of global landscapes. Adapting to different cultures is important to the practice of international public relations. Zaharna (2001), for example, argues that practitioners should adopt an 'in-awareness' approach to public relations in other countries, thoroughly understanding the culture before they try to communicate. This normative approach – where culture is an object that must be understood before communication can be effective – characterises many texts that argue for the incorporation of culture into public relations theory, and has a parallel in the more widely recognised concept of 'glocalisation', where global communication campaigns are made relevant to local communities. Both concepts can also be useful within countries, where practitioners may still need to communicate across different cultural groups (Grunig et al., 1995; Sriramesh, 2009; Bardhan, 2011). However, they do not fully embrace the ideas of fluidity, circulation and change that are so fundamental to globalisation, because culture is framed as fixed (located within a nation), objective (identifiable and able to be learnt) and unitary.

In contrast, a constructivist interpretation of culture as the production of meaning (see Chapter 2) reveals how public relations knowledge and practice become more fragmented and fluid in the context of global modernity. Struggles over meaning between different global communities reflect the tensions that exist between hegemonic institutions, non-profit organisations and activist communities, all of which use public relations to reframe cultural norms in ways that privilege their perspectives. The production of 'global' culture through public relations work (Edwards, 2015) and resistance to its oppressive tendencies illustrate the inherently political nature of the circulation of meaning across transnational campaigns (Bardhan, 2003; Curtin and Gaither, 2007; Holtzhausen, 2011; Sriramesh and Verčič, 2012).

The political and contested dimensions of culture (Williams, 1958; Hall, 2000) are one reason why transformation and change are so central to globalisation, and reflect Appadurai's argument that the work of imagination is most productive when cultural flows intersect, clash and generate tensions that must be resolved. Public relations has the potential to play a role in these dynamics because '[p]ublic relations action and communication occur at the junctures (spaces) of global forces and the cultural realities of a locality' (Bardhan, 2011: 80). These dynamic, 'transcultural' spaces are locations where cultures intersect, and are constituted by the interactions between people as they create new meanings through dialogic communication and interaction, questioning and reflecting on each other's assumptions, values and worldviews (Dutta, 2015). The result is the construction of third cultures and/or third realms – alternative spaces where negotiated meanings provide the basis for longer-term relationships (cultures) or shorter-term collaboration (realms) (Casmir, 1978, cited in Bardhan, 2011).

Viewing public relations as a means of resolving the tensions between local and global cultures privileges subaltern voices that can reframe globalisation in transformative terms

(Dutta et al., 2012; Dutta, 2015). From a postcolonial perspective, they reflect the potential for public relations to facilitate changes in the direction of globalisation, by offering ways to resist hegemonic meanings that do not translate into lived experiences (Shome and Hegde, 2002; Dutta, 2011). When public relations is used to give voice to silenced or ignored subaltern populations, whose lives are continually sidelined by global systems of governance, it facilitates their resistance to threats against their culture as a result of globalisation processes. These populations are as integral to globalisation as the privileged, transnational class who benefit, and whose experiences dominate globalisation narratives. Their resistance often emerges in local contexts, but when it is picked up by ideoscapes, mediascapes and technoscapes, it has the power to create change in the global order.

CASE STUDY 7.3

PUBLIC RELATIONS AS FLOW: THE 2016 EU REFERENDUM IN THE UK

Looking at public relations work focused on specific issues is one way of understanding its influence on cultural flows. In 2016, the United Kingdom held a referendum on whether to remain in the European Union. Much of the debate focused on the numbers of EU migrants coming to the UK to work and live, and reflected the tensions between ethnoscapes (movement of people between EU countries), financescapes (the fact that people were moving to find work and better pay), ideoscapes (the clash between nationalistic approaches to British identity and economy, and a more globalist philosophy tied to participation in EU trade), and technoscapes (Britain is systemically connected to Europe through technologies that facilitate all kinds of cultural, economic and social connections). The discourses about migration were carried by mediascapes across the globe. In the UK, for example, the government focus on limiting migration was reflected in online and offline national newspaper coverage. It was challenged by press releases from other organisations such as the Centre for Research and Analysis of Migration (http://www.cream-migration.org), which released a study highlighting the benefits of migration. Research reports from other European countries and think-tanks (e.g. http://openeurope.org.uk) played into the debate, often highlighting statistics showing that migrants tended not to be a drain on local economies. These reports, along with other coverage of the debate, were picked up by news outlets in more distant countries elsewhere (e.g. http://www.africa-news.eu), connecting the debate to populations beyond Europe. Since the referendum (in which

(Continued)

> the population narrowly voted to leave the EU), the debate has continued across national and international media in the context of negotiations about 'Brexit' (Britain's exit from the EU), communicating the various ideologies reflected in the debate to global audiences, with corresponding effects on the 'imagination' work associated with the idea of moving to the UK. This includes people's perceptions as to whether it is worth migrating to the UK (ethnoscapes), whether they might be able to find work if they do (financescapes), how they might be perceived if they were to move there (ideoscapes), and how they might be able to find out more about what possibilities exist (mediascapes and technoscapes).

PUBLIC RELATIONS AND GLOBAL DISCOURSE

As disciplinary tools, discourses present certain values, attitudes, behaviours, subjectivities and forms of knowledge as more important than others, and become part of wider ontological and epistemological struggles that arise from the tensions inherent in globalisation (Weaver, 2001; Fairclough, 2006). As members of the transnational promotional class that Aronczyk (2013b) has identified (see Chapter 4), public relations practitioners construct discourses about different aspects of our lives, which both constitute mediascapes and ideoscapes and circulate through them (Edwards, 2011). Because digital communication technologies transcend physical space and overcome temporal limitations, public relations discourses always have the potential to circulate globally – even if the original campaign they were associated with was not intended for a global audience. Indeed, audiences themselves circulate messages more widely through their own online and offline networks.

The mobility of public relations discourses is countered by moments of fixity, when they are integrated into local contexts through concrete public relations tools that materialise in specific places, including events, press releases, interviews, media stories, blogs, viral videos and many other artefacts. The form these artefacts take is shaped by the possibilities opened up by technoscapes and mediascapes – new communicative trends circulate via the global industry (social media, viral communication) and new media outlets emerge (citizen journalists, bloggers, online news outlets, non-Western TV channels), influencing the ways in which discourses are taken up and interpreted.

Local manifestations of ideoscapes, technoscapes and ethnoscapes influence how public relations discourses are crafted. For example, messages may need to be tailored to the expectations of local customers, supporters and citizens (a pro-refugee campaign may have to be framed in relation to nationalistic anti-immigration rhetoric; optimistic messages about a company's overseas expansion may have to accommodate fears of local job losses), while choices about channels and styles of communication must be acceptable and practical for the local target audience (a social media strategy would be useless in an environment where internet connectivity is low). Global economic, political, social and cultural trends also provide the backdrop for local interpretations of public relations messages. For example, positive stories of protection for local jobs will be interpreted in light of what employees know of the fate of other industries affected by globalisation; altruistic individuals will assess the claims made by charities against their knowledge of various forms of injustice in the wider world; and voters will decide whether a government's efforts to change international legislation are credible, based on their past history of success or failure in international negotiations.

The production, circulation and reception of public relations discourses will always be marked by the overarching local–global, mobility–fixity and hegemony–resistance dialectics that characterise globalisation, but other tensions will also play out in different contexts, precisely because discourses open up new ways for people and organisations to understand the possibilities and limitations that globalisation brings. They might include digital–analogue, profit–non-profit, sustainability–economic growth, risk–security, as well as many other combinations. They characterise public debates when different discourses are communicated by organisations with opposing views on a particular issue (for example, in debates about addressing the global refugee crisis). Public relations discourses can represent and justify global institutions and structures (for example, the position of the UN High Commissioner for Refugees on the status and entitlements of refugees, or the standing of refugees in international law), but also contest them (for example, when activists try to broaden the definition of a refugee in order to provide sanctuary for more people). Dialectical tensions may also be observed *within* public relations discourses. Hegemony is always incomplete (Hall, 1981), and inherent in the assertion of superiority is the (implicit) presence of 'other' (marginalised) groups, individuals and ideas (for example, promoting smartphones as an essential means of connection and sociality implicitly 'others' those who cannot access or use one as backward, 'outside' modern society, or 'difficult' to reach). As postcolonial theorists point out, 'othering' contains the seeds for resistance, and provides a basis for contesting hegemonic ideas and subjectivities.

CONCLUSION

By 'unmanaging' the relationship between public relations and globalisation, we arrive at a place where there is no definitive way of understanding it. Framing it in terms of flows, mobility and fixity, and dialectical tensions, offers many different starting points for analysing questions of how public relations affects and is affected by the opportunities and problems of globalisation. This analytical fluidity allows us to address the variability of public relations work in the processes and practices of globalisation. Its effects on structure, culture and discourse are powerful but not always predictable, and so understanding, investigating and potentially mitigating them is an ongoing task. Appadurai (1996) argues that globalisation is characterised by a mutually contextualising relationship between motion and mediation, where the imagination facilitated by global cultural flows interacts with the voluntary or involuntary migration prompted by globalisation, acting as both a prompt for movement and a resource for living in new places. This very human dimension of globalisation is also of particular interest for socio-cultural analyses of public relations, and begs the question of public relations' role in both motion and mediation. How does it prompt and facilitate movement, and what kinds of resources for imagination does it provide to migrant populations, helping or hindering their survival?

Rich empirical work on public relations is necessary, with a view to analyses that address how practices located in a specific place and time articulate with global flows that can transport outputs and outcomes elsewhere. Such analyses will reveal how public relations used in the service of hegemony may generate tensions in the financial, technological, communicative and cultural networks that perpetuate globalisation. They will also show how public relations may act as a means of resolving such tensions by creating platforms and providing discursive resources for marginalised populations to use as they assert their right to be heard in those same global systems. The focus is not on identifying a normative model of public relations 'best practice' for globalisation, but on seeking a better understanding of actually existing practices of public relations. Identifying the connections between the global flows that public relations engages will lead to a better comprehension of how it prompts the emergence of imagination as a response to the discontinuities, clashes and tensions generated by its actions. Analysing the production and reception of public relations at fixed points in space and time, but with reference to the cultural flows that they depend on, will also reveal the ways in which the tensions it generates manifest in struggles over everyday forms of inequality and privilege.

The call to embrace a wider perspective is not new – other scholars have urged the same kind of change (McKie and Munshi, 2007; Pal and Dutta, 2008; Dutta, 2011; Weaver, 2011). But it remains necessary because as global capitalism faces new challenges it adapts and develops in order to survive (Boltanski and Chiapello, 2005), and public relations becomes implicated in new forms of global injustice and resistance that need investigation. Currently, precious little research on inequality in public relations is truly international. Both theory and empirical work need to become more global, open and inclusive in their scale and scope, integrating voices and worldviews from the margins (Ganesh et al., 2005; Mumby, 2005; Dutta et al., 2012). This would open the way to considering the ontological diversity of public relations – what it is and does in different spaces and at different times across the globe – and to reflecting on the oppositions inherent in its globalised practice. There is also an urgent need to understand the dynamic interactions between the different forces that act upon public relations – and upon which it acts – in contemporary forms of globalisation. These kinds of insights will reveal the spaces where public relations could act to mitigate some of the most trenchant difficulties of globalisation: the achievement of transnational justice and human rights, the protection of the environment, the search for a more peaceful and stable international political system, and the creation of a sustainable future for all, to name a few. Findings ways to drive positive change in these and similar arenas may be the key to carving out space in which public relations can contribute to a more equitable future for a globalised world.

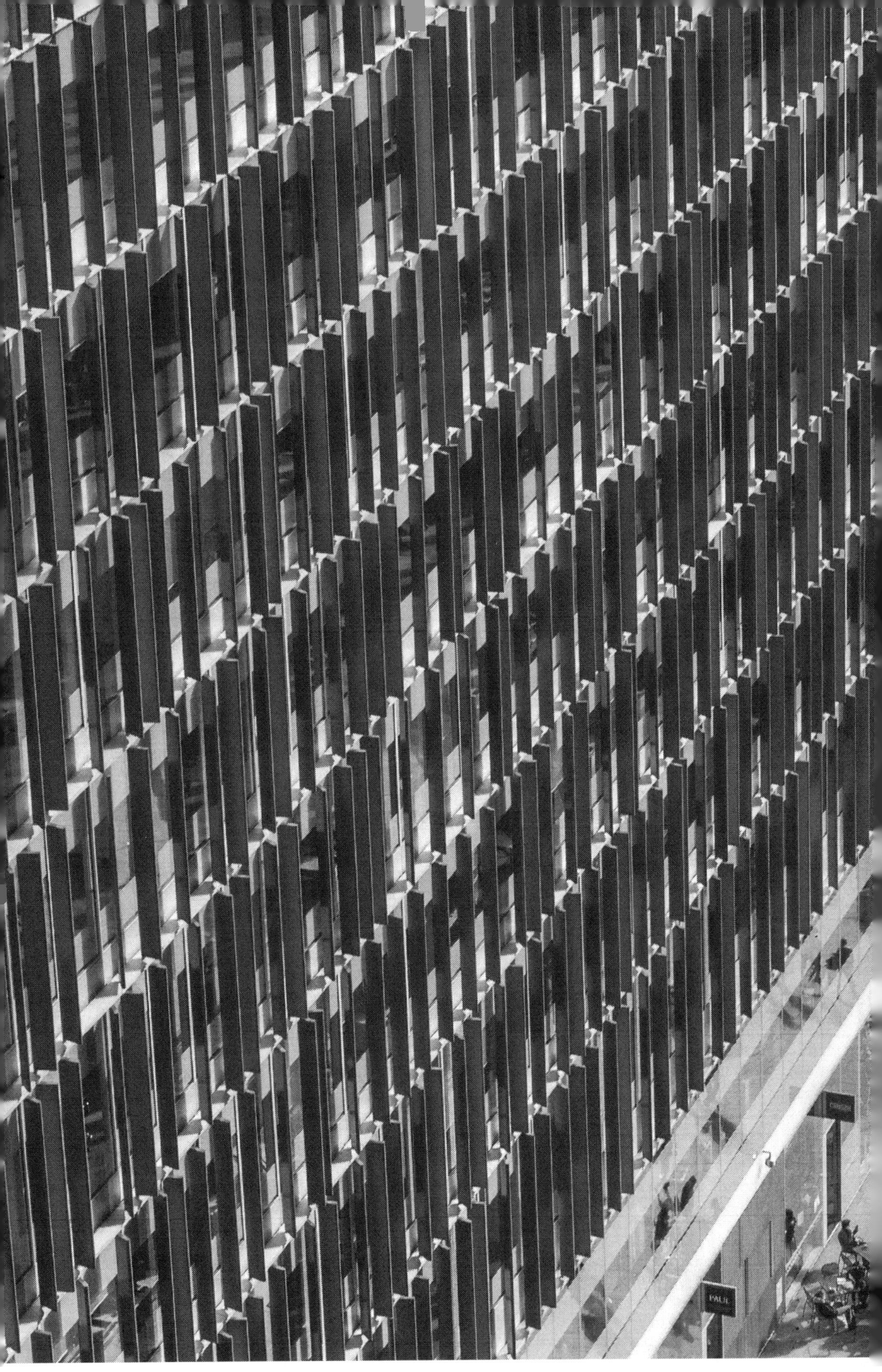
PAUL

CHAPTER 8

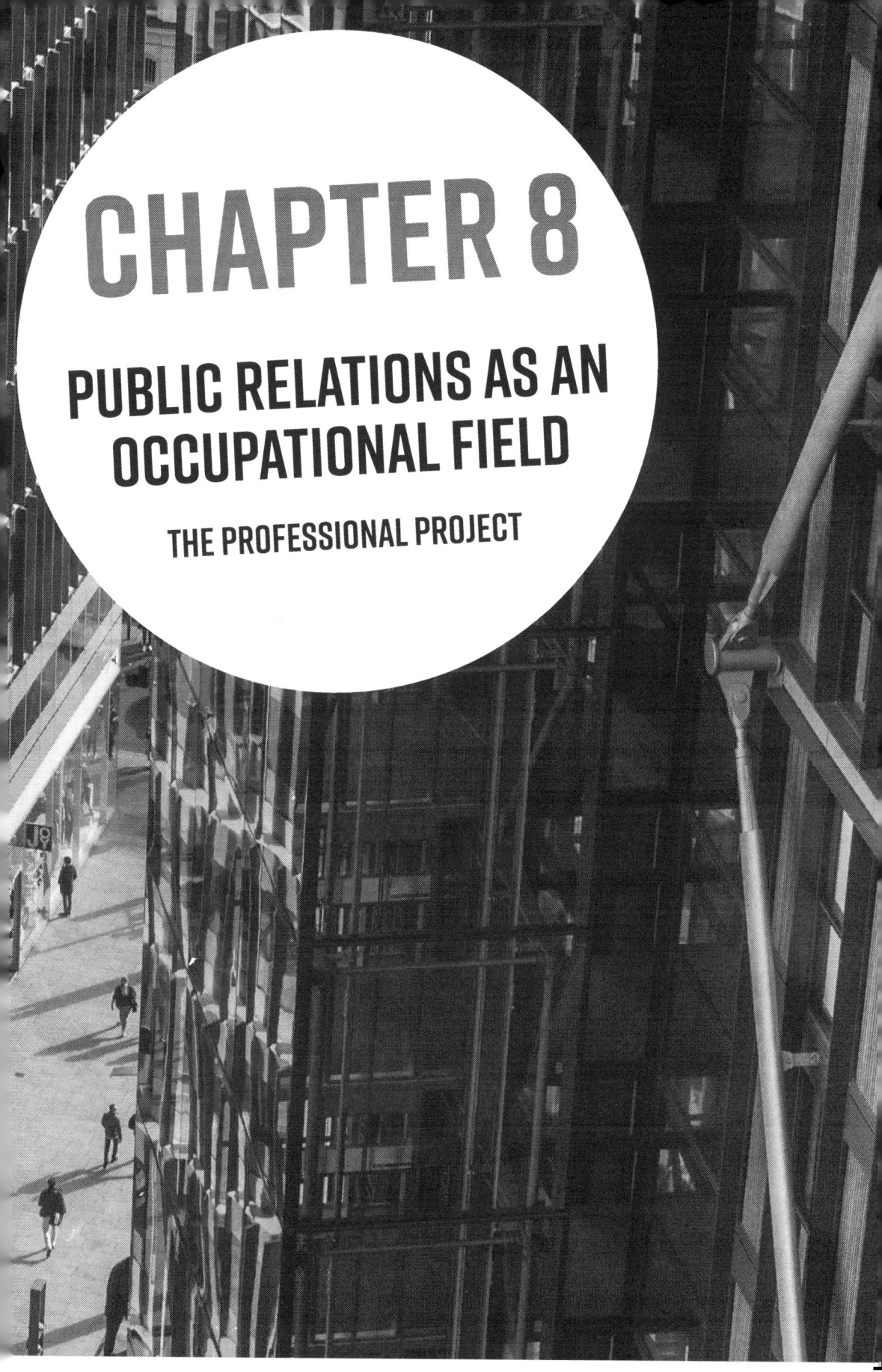

PUBLIC RELATIONS AS AN OCCUPATIONAL FIELD

THE PROFESSIONAL PROJECT

This chapter moves the focus from an outward-looking analysis of public relations in society to an examination of the internal dynamics of the field. The industry is a justifiable object of research from an economic perspective, since it generates billions of dollars each year in revenue and employs hundreds of thousands of practitioners across the globe (Muzi Falconi, 2006; USC Annenberg Center for Public Relations, 2016). However, economics is not the sole reason for an interest in the occupational field; alongside its financial clout, we should be interested in it because it provides the social and cultural context within which practitioners' working lives unfold, and its configuration affects the way they work and engage with the world beyond their occupational boundaries (Hodges, 2006).

The public relations industry started to grow rapidly in the 1980s, particularly in developed Western countries. At the time, Keynesian economics was perceived to be failing, and belief in free markets was replacing belief in the state as the best way to manage the economy and society (Harvey, 2005). The subsequent phases of deregulation and the removal of trade barriers increased competition between industries and organisations, and placed new pressure on organisations to inform customers and clients about what they offered and why it was needed. Public relations came into its own in countries and markets across the world as a function that could not only support the marketing of products and services, but also explain their complexities and build organisational reputation to generate competitive advantage in the longer term (Miller and Dinan, 2000, 2007; Moloney, 2006; Sriramesh and Verčič, 2009). The turn towards neoliberalism and unfettered competition also prompted a shift within organisations, so that their operations became framed less in terms of bureaucratic processes and public service, and more in terms of customers, their needs and their satisfaction (Du Gay and Salaman, 1992). Customer 'sovereignty' now permeates the operational logic of both private and public sector organisations, and has also supported the growth of public relations, which positions itself as a profession that can help all kinds of organisations understand and engage with their customers more effectively (Edwards, 2014b).

Research into occupational fields[1] is long-standing, but has attracted only limited attention in public relations scholarship (but see Pieczka, 2000; L'Etang, 2004; Pieczka and L'Etang, 2006; Trenwith, 2010; Edwards, 2014b; Fitch, 2014). In this chapter I consider the different ways in which the modern public relations industry operates, and reflect on the nature of its professional project, and examine how norms associated with professionalisation and professionalism affect its structures and practices. Public relations fits into the category of knowledge-based occupations, alongside other modern occupations such as management consultancy, project management and recruitment (Muzio et al., 2011; Edwards, 2014b). Knowledge-based occupations have been identified as an important and relatively new group of occupations that differ from traditional professions in that they have a fluid body of occupational knowledge, few barriers to entry, optional professional training and are inseparable from organisations in practice (Kipping et al., 2006). These conditions form the basis of their engagement with professional status and are important to understanding how public relations has evolved.

The evolution of professional fields is not a uniform process, but changes according to the context in which occupations emerge (Brock and Saks, 2016). Most of the sociological literature on professions and professionalism is based on elite occupations, often in the United States and United Kingdom; however, the findings illustrate how important the immediate regulatory, competitive and industry contexts are to the ways in which occupations develop. The models on which most sociological studies of professions are based, including the analysis in this chapter, should be regarded as open to contestation and verification in other locations, and international divergences should be expected (Adams, 2015). I begin by introducing some key developments in the sociology of the professions literature to establish the theoretical framework for the chapter. I apply the idea of a professional project to public relations, reflecting in detail on the ways in which the field makes public claims to jurisdiction and legitimacy, and how its structures and discourses discipline practitioners by establishing what makes a 'good' public relations practitioner and what kind of work counts for success in the field. I reflect on the importance of professional discourse as a technology of the professional project, before returning to the relevance of the industry to socio-cultural research in the conclusion.

STARTING POINTS: SOCIOLOGY OF THE PROFESSIONS

The analytical framework adopted in this chapter is drawn from neo-Weberian and Foucauldian analyses of professional fields, which highlight the ways in which the occupational dynamics of the field are built around the need to legitimise its work and increase its status *vis-à-vis* its competitors (Larson, 1977; Abbott, 1988; Brock and Saks, 2016). Early research in the area focused on defining and explaining how and why elite occupations (e.g. law, medicine) secured and retained their superior social status. Professional status was recognised as something that generated significant individual and group rewards; consequently, the hallmarks of professions and professionalism became an important focus and were identified as formal training, ethics and codes of practice, a public service ethos, closed membership, powerful industry associations and different specialisations.

The 'trait' perspective ran into difficulty because many traits were shared by other occupations that did not attract the same kinds of rewards, and it was almost impossible to establish comparative data that could confirm the typologies being suggested (Wilensky, 1964; Evetts, 2006). Attempts to create taxonomies of professions that accommodated variability resulted in the identification of professions, semi-professions (e.g. social work, teaching) and aspiring professions – but similar difficulties plagued these categorisations. Nonetheless, the naturalistic investigations of professional life on which they were based led to new directions for research that proved more fruitful. A focus emerged on professional fields as mechanisms for maintaining intellectual and organisational superiority in order to generate status and authority for their members,[2] and what is now known as the neo-Weberian approach produced a focus on mechanisms of social closure in the occupational marketplace, sanctioned by the state and other institutional actors (Saks, 2016).

Research on power and status in the professions began to pay greater attention to the links between fields and their wider socio-political and economic contexts, the importance of jurisdiction and legitimacy, and helped to explain how and why occupational hierarchies emerged (Johnson, 1972; Abbott, 1988; Friedson, 2001). Struggles over jurisdiction and legitimacy have come to be understood as expressions of a 'professional project', an ideologically driven, collective effort to achieve social mobility for an occupation's members by controlling internal structures, practitioner roles and external reputation (Larson, 1977: 67). Professional projects are designed to acquire and protect professional jurisdiction and legitimacy, since these two things underpin claims to the right to operate in a particular market. They emerge because occupations are inherently competitive, and the struggle for exclusive control over jurisdictions is 'a fundamental fact of professional life' (Abbott, 1988: 2). Professional projects are also focused on occupational self-interest, in so far as they pursue legitimacy and exclusive jurisdiction in order that the rewards they receive (higher salaries, social prestige) can be both increased and justified.

More recent work has begun to explore the ideological and socially constructed nature of professions as a means of governance and control (e.g. Fournier, 1999). Radical shifts towards a Foucauldian understanding of professions emphasise the importance of discourse in professional projects. They have shown how the meanings of apparently straightforward terms such as 'profession', 'professionalism', 'client' and 'professionalisation' are implicated in the circulation of power in occupational fields, because of their connections to the complex organisational and occupational demands of managerial work environments and commercial markets (Evetts, 2003; Noordegraaf, 2007; Faulconbridge and Muzio, 2008). They have also focused on the ways in which professionals themselves are disciplined by occupational discourses to behave in ways that serve the profession's objectives. Discourses of professionalism are particularly important, since they act as 'a powerful instrument of occupational change and social control at macro, meso and micro levels' (Evetts, 2013: 784).

In the remainder of this chapter, I draw on the idea of the professional project and disciplinary discourses to elaborate on the nature of public relations as an occupational field driven by professionalisation and professionalism. The discussion focuses in particular on the social and cultural processes of jurisdictional control and claims of legitimacy that the field makes in pursuit of long-term security and status.

PUBLIC RELATIONS' PROFESSIONAL PROJECT[3]

An important part of the context for public relations' professional project, and the territory for its claims of jurisdiction and legitimacy, is the institutionalised importance of a robust, positive organisational reputation as a source of competitive advantage. This is accompanied by an assumed need to proactively manage events that threaten reputation (customer complaints, crises) so that an organisation's relationship with its customers remains intact (Cornelissen et al., 2006; Christensen et al., 2008). The public relations industry has promoted these ideas in its definitions of what public relations is for, and the widespread adoption of public relations across all industries suggests that the idea of protecting organisational reputation is now well established. The result has been rapid growth in the use of public relations, as well as a widening of the scope of its operations. As a result, public relations is itself a highly competitive arena: consultancies and practitioners vie for status, and the industry is engaged in an ongoing struggle to protect territory from encroachment by other promotional disciplines (Hutton, 1999; Toledano, 2010).

The institutionalisation of reputation represents lucrative territory for promotional industries, and is not the exclusive domain of public relations. On the contrary, the dynamics of public relations' professional project are characterised by constant struggles over its public claims to jurisdiction in the management of reputation, as well as over internal hierarchies of power that shore up the occupation's legitimacy (Bourne, 2016). These are visible, for example, in the public relations trade press, where stories often focus on new trends, the changing landscape for practice, threats from other occupations, and justifications of public relations' effectiveness. Jurisdictional control is necessarily abstract and discursive. It does not translate neatly into the complicated realities of practice, since jurisdiction is a conceptual space that must be contested every time it is applied (Pieczka, 2000). The result is that jurisdiction and legitimacy are based on a set of *generalisations* about an occupation, since '[d]ifferences of public jurisdiction are differences between archetypes' (Abbott, 1988: 61). Nor are jurisdictions ever permanently settled, because occupational environments change continuously, presenting new challenges in the process; professional projects are therefore always 'under construction' (Abbott, 1988: 39; Fournier, 1999; Hodgson, 2007).

Jurisdictional control has social dimensions, in so far as occupations make public claims to other groups about what their profession is and does (Abbott, 1988). Advances in knowledge and technology, for example, may result in competition over new territory and redefinition of tasks in ways that challenge the social dimension of jurisdiction (consider the advent of the 'citizen journalist', facilitated by Web 2.0 technologies, as a challenge to the journalistic profession, or the rise of digital communication channels to become a central, strategic pillar of public relations work rather than a technical task – see, for example, Zerfass et al., 2017). Clients may change, and new types of problems evolve. Public relations, for example, faces regular jurisdictional challenges from digital marketing, internal communications, social media and event management specialists (Hutton, 2010).

Jurisdictional control also involves cultural adjustment to structures and hierarchies within the field and to practitioner identity and conduct, so that public claims are reflected in practice. For example, changing social norms may produce shifts in occupational roles and responsibilities that challenge the cultural dimension of jurisdiction (the entry of more women into professional fields such as law and medicine, for example, has challenged the status of these occupations as male-only domains). Public relations practitioners may find themselves under unexpected pressure for inappropriate practice as the context for their work evolves; for example, norms around the representation of 'race' and gender have changed as a result of equality and civil rights movements, while the 'behind the scenes' work of lobbying, which used to be acceptable, is now faced with public demands for transparency, leading to registers of lobbyists and industry codes of conduct being established in the UK and elsewhere.

CASE STUDY 8.1

DEFINING PUBLIC RELATIONS' JURISDICTION

One of public relations' most difficult challenges is defining its jurisdiction. It is easily linked to other forms of promotional work, yet being clear about its authority over specific tasks is essential because it enables practitioners to explain and legitimise their role, and consultancies to compete for clients and grow the industry. In recent years, a strong focus has emerged on defining public relations as long-term relationship management. In the digital age, this has been extended to incorporate the idea of engaging in 'conversations' with stakeholders so that companies can keep track of what they are feeling and thinking, and monitor new trends in the marketplace. These discourses are evident in consultancy websites, where they act as a means of persuading clients of the value of public relations. Global agency Edelman, for example, argues that we are in a new era of public engagement, 'pulling information from a variety of sources, experts and networks. Consumers demand a dialogue, and expect an empowered role with the brands they interact with, and the communities they touch' (Edelman, 2017). Hill+Knowlton, on the other hand, argues that businesses live in a 'purposeful age', where 'companies and institutions have the opportunity to join a meaningful conversation around things that matter, take their place in culture and demonstrate their responsibility to society' (Hill+Knowlton, 2016). In both cases, public relations is positioned not as an exchange or transmission of information, but as a way of using communication strategically in a

> complex environment in order to achieve legitimacy and advantage. Raising the bar for public relations in this way also helps set it apart from other promotional functions, and makes it appear more professional because of the allusion to a complex and sophisticated understanding of the communications environment (conducting long-term engagement successfully is arguably more complicated than selling or creating an ad). It serves the professional project by discursively constructing an arena for public relations work, despite the fact that public relations practice is not always so easily identified or segregated from other promotional activities.

THE SOCIAL DIMENSION OF JURISDICTIONAL CONTROL IN PUBLIC RELATIONS: CLAIMING PROFESSIONAL STATUS

The social dimension of jurisdictional control pursued in professional projects involves public claims that must be confirmed by a range of institutions including government, the legislature, academia, the media, clients and competing organisations (Fournier, 1999). Correspondingly, jurisdictional claims are made in 'arenas' where these institutions operate: the arena of the legal system; the arena of the workplace; and the arena of public opinion, including the media (Abbott, 1988: 59–62). Industry associations may proactively promote their work online and offline, but also respond to media stories about their profession, lobby governments about relevant policy initiatives, and reassert their value to clients and their difference from competitors on an ongoing basis.

In the case of knowledge-based occupations like public relations, their efforts to make claims in these arenas are complicated by the fact that their territories are 'ambiguous domains, in which expertise can no longer be isolated from other experts, decision makers or clients' (Noordegraaf, 2007: 780), and so their jurisdiction is difficult to define. The fact that their work is deeply embedded within organisations produces a 'corporate professionalisation project', where occupational claims to professionalism are combined with efforts to establish legitimacy in organisational (mainly corporate) contexts in order to respond effectively to changing markets for their services (Muzio and Kirkpatrick, 2011). Asserting professional authority by mixing occupational and organisational imperatives in different ways depending on the demands of the situation produces new, dynamic and hybrid arrangements of professional practice and identity that combine civic interests with market-driven logic (Hodgson, 2002; Aldridge and Evetts, 2003; Noordegraaf, 2007). Indeed, Noordegraaf (2015) goes so far as to argue in favour of the term 'organizing professions', based on the fact that hybridisation has evolved to full incorporation of organisational and managerial tasks into normal professional practice.

In these contexts, claims to status and jurisdiction may privilege attributes associated with traditional professions (delivering a public service, independence and objectivity, specialist knowledge and elite education), but simultaneously emphasise the alignment of occupational identity and practice with the needs of organisational environments (e.g. increased managerialism, accountability and commercialisation). The discourses and practices of public relations consultancies and associations reflect hybrid strategies, for example by combining the argument that they provide knowledge for consumers and citizens to make necessary choices with the justification that their work helps organisations to achieve their goals. The result is a discourse that suggests a 'win–win' situation, where public and private interests benefit from public relations work (Edwards, 2014b).

An abstract and exclusive body of knowledge is an important cornerstone of jurisdiction, since it provides the foundation for claiming exclusive territory against competing occupations. Even in knowledge-based occupations, where activities are intertwined with other disciplines, efforts are made to establish models, systems and processes that suggest exclusive expertise (Alvesson and Johansson, 2002; Hodgson, 2002; Kipping et al., 2006). In the case of public relations, for example, degrees can be certified by industry associations as long as they contain specified elements of training, while industry associations often run certified training courses as a standard service for members. Pieczka (2006) has shown how practitioners engaged in such training define and control practice in ways that reinforce their occupational identity and differentiate them from competitors. Public relations scholars have also contributed to this process in so far as the normative research tradition has attempted to clearly define public relations, its tasks and practitioner roles, models of practice and unique attributes that differentiate it from other promotional occupations, particularly marketing (Grunig, 1992; Sriramesh and Verčič, 2009; Hutton, 2010; Tench et al., 2013).

Another crucial element of jurisdiction is the control of tasks, which Abbott (1988: 84) terms the 'central organizing reality of professional life'. The body of knowledge claimed as the profession's own logically produces constructions of expertise, or 'modes of rhetoric' (Grey, 1998: 571), that suggest a certain domain of activities. These delineate the profession's territory and help to manage practitioners' and clients' expectations of practice. In public relations, practitioners actively construct expertise through narratives that explain their tasks to fellow practitioners and to potential clients (Pieczka, 2006), while the claim to exclusive knowledge about how to 'manage reputation' and 'relationship management' – articulated by industry associations and consultancy websites – opens the door to practitioners being involved in, and competing for, a very wide range of tasks, since most activities in an organisation have the potential to affect reputation (Edwards, 2012b; Bourne, 2016).

THE CULTURAL DIMENSION: STRUCTURING THE FIELD

Professional projects also involve work within the occupational field so that it reflects the public claims to legitimacy being made in other arenas. Efforts to structure occupational fields involve constructing a division of labour for tasks, as well as associating prestige with professional activities via status symbols and formal mechanisms such as elite education, certification, accredited training and licensing.

In public relations, task structure is relatively clear: there is a hierarchy between managerial and technical roles. Strategic thinking, senior management consultancy and client engagement are all associated with managerial work, while practical work such as populating and responding to social media feeds, selling stories to media outlets or other news sources, booking and briefing suppliers, managing events and monitoring media are linked to less prestigious, junior roles (Gregory, 2008). Professional associations such as the UK's Chartered Institute of Public Relations (CIPR) specify competencies and standards of practice in formal documents, training courses, processes of certification and validation. Hierarchy is translated into status on consultancy websites, where senior practitioner profiles frequently mention their educational background as well as membership of professional associations, while images of junior practitioners are rarely narrated.

The taken-for-granted hierarchy creates a career path for practitioners, but it also attributes value to individuals, setting expectations of the kinds of skills that are worth more (and therefore attract greater rewards), what clients can expect from practitioners at different levels, and how valuable individual practitioners are to the occupation. The more specialist and strategic the knowledge, the more unique and irreplaceable the practitioner, while the formulaic nature of technical tasks means that if a junior practitioner moves on, another can easily take their place. This stratification is an important form of inequality, given that racialised, classed and gendered hierarchies within public relations (see Chapters 9 and 10) mean that white men tend to dominate at managerial levels. Saks (2015) argues that the links between structural inequalities within professional fields and broader socio-economic hierarchies act as a form of social control by influencing access and visibility to professional skills for different social groups, and ensuring that opportunities to pursue a professional career are restricted.

The 'professionally engendered' inequalities identified by Saks (2015) are central to the social and ideological power of professions. In the case of public relations, this power is reinforced by the occupation's alignment with neoliberal norms and the need to orient towards organisational interests, including market imperatives that guide many, if not most, organisations using public relations. Correspondingly, occupational specialisms and rewards are stratified in ways that reflect the hierarchies characterising neoliberal economies. Most practitioners work in the for-profit sector, where the highest salaries are paid (Chartered Institute of Public Relations, 2015; Griggs, 2015; Public Relations and Communications Association, 2016). The public sector is a significant employer, but arts and culture and not-for-profit organisations employ the fewest practitioners and also pay lower salaries (Public Relations and Communications Association, 2016). Public relations consultancies and associations also tend to foreground market-related discourses when they justify the occupation's contribution to organisations: the need to manage risk, engage with customers, and keep up with a competitive and rapidly changing information landscape in order to understand customer opinions, needs and desires (Edwards, 2014b).

INTERNAL WORK: DISCIPLINING PROFESSIONALS

Successful professional projects justify their work and status not only through structural and systemic mechanisms, but also by effectively disciplining practitioners into acting in the interests of the profession and buying into the professional project of their own volition. As Waring (2014: 695) notes, 'socialisation and identity formation are significant because they bind individual professionals to shared norms and values around autonomy and collegiality, especially the idea of not being critical of colleagues or damaging professional reputations'. Both discourse and practice are important to disciplinary processes. The wider social context has an important influence on the types of 'ideal' practitioner identities that circulate: the normative status attached to certain types of resources (e.g. elite education, cultural knowledge, financial wealth, linguistic ability, digital skills) leads them to be valued more highly within the professional context as well (Bourdieu, 1992; Edwards and Pieczka, 2013). In recruitment and promotion, it becomes 'common sense' to perceive graduates from the 'best' educational institutions, professionals who have excellent networks of contacts, new recruits who demonstrate instinctive confidence in the business environment, and those who are adept at social media as 'better' or more suited to public relations than others.

Through these normative associations, practitioner background, personality and embodiment all become associated with a performance of professional identity suited to the objectives of the professional project (Bolton and Muzio, 2007; Sommerlad, 2008). Occupational elites (the largest consultancies, industry associations, practitioners in transnational companies) play an important role as actors who enable these associations to circulate in the discourses they produce (Waring, 2014); the result is an occupational habitus that disciplines practitioners into conformity with the rules of the professional 'game' they have engaged in (Aldridge and Evetts, 2003; Evetts, 2011), but that also tends to reflect attributes that are linked to success in wider social hierarchies – as illustrated in public relations by descriptions of successful practitioners in the trade press and on industry websites (Edwards and Pieczka, 2013). The public relations habitus is communicated through normative understandings of what constitutes 'professional' behaviour and embodiment, including modes of dress, speech and interaction, which tend to reflect a white, middle-class, youthful identity (Edwards, 2014a). At the same time, the advent of privatisation and an age of austerity have meant that in public relations, as elsewhere, practitioners who work on financially lucrative contracts, or who can generate significant new business through their contacts, may be perceived as more valuable than colleagues whose 'return' is less impressive (Hanlon, 2004; Edwards, 2014b).

The focus on individuals as marketers in their professional roles is a hallmark of the neoliberal economic and political context for professional work: 'Firms now constantly encourage individuals to build relationships with other professionals and clients in an attempt to place themselves in a social space where people think of them when potential business arrives' (Hanlon, 2004: 203). The need to demonstrate networking capability and sociability, which is widely promoted as an attribute of the ideal public relations practitioner (Chartered Institute of Public Relations/Public Relations Consultants Association, 2013), has become increasingly important as a criterion for success, but is also a potential mechanism for excluding practitioners whose networks may not be as extensive or targeted as those of the occupational (usually white, male) elite (Anderson-Gough et al., 2006). Being sociable, having networks and demonstrating an interest in media and current affairs (another ideal characteristic of public relations practitioners) must also be visible, so practitioners are likely to use social media, blogs and other forms of public commentary as an investment in their professional identity management (Lair et al., 2005).

While they have nothing to do with task-related skills, practitioner background, personality, embodiment and networks are nonetheless implicit criteria for entry and progression to professional fields, since they demonstrate the ability of an individual to fit in with the occupational archetype, serve occupational interests and communicate professionalism to clients (Alvesson, 1994; Grey, 1998; Anderson-Gough et al., 2006). They become understood as objective forms of merit, sorting 'good' professionals and those who 'fit' from those who do not meet the required standard (Sommerlad, 2007; Logan, 2011; Edwards, 2013). Because such characteristics are more available to the 'unencumbered (white) man' (Acker, 2006: 450), and affect decisions about recruitment and progression, they contribute to the middle-class, gendered whiteness that characterises public relations industries in developed countries. In this way, professional projects perpetuate organisational and occupational 'inequality regimes', differentiating between employees along 'race', class and gender lines (Acker, 2006). This is as true for public relations as it is in other occupational contexts, and is reflected in the lack of diversity across the field and in different geographies. It is particularly noticeable at more senior levels, where white males dominate while women and people of colour are disproportionately absent – reinforcing the fact that the ability to 'fit' can be more important than objective forms of merit in recruitment at this level (Becker et al., 1999; Davidson and Burke, 2004; Castilla, 2008; Edwards and Pieczka, 2013).

DISCOURSE AS A TECHNOLOGY OF PUBLIC RELATIONS' PROFESSIONAL PROJECT

The occupational archetypes, habitus, claims to jurisdiction and legitimacy, structures and disciplinary mechanisms described above all circulate through discourse, and recent sociological research has paid significant attention to occupational discourses as crucial mechanisms through which practitioners can be managed, occupational jurisdiction secured and organisational compliance encouraged (Anderson-Gough et al., 1998; Aldridge and Evetts, 2003; Cohen et al., 2005; Ashcraft, 2007). As ideological social practices, discourses produce meanings that sustain particular versions of reality through which some identities are privileged and others disadvantaged (Mumby and Stohl, 1991; Fairclough, 2003). Categorisation by 'race', class or gender, for example, is in essence a discursive, disciplinary exercise with which individuals may or may not conform (Anthias, 2013). What is absent from particular discourses is as significant as what is present; presence and absence work together to define how power is distributed (Mumby and Stohl, 1991; Fairclough, 2003; see also Chapter 3 earlier).

Discourses in professional projects circulate through formal and informal channels. They are visible in texts written by industry associations that educate prospective entrants and clients about what to expect from the occupation. Similarly, texts produced by professional consultancies describe their work, staff and clients in archetypal terms. Informal interactions, on the other hand (for example casual or work-focused conversations between colleagues, discussions in meetings), can also act as sites where discourses are combined to construct complex normative identities and practices in relation to material circumstances (Kuhn, 2009). These texts and interactions communicate habitus by explaining the rationale and purpose of the occupation, defining 'professionalism' and setting out expectations of its practitioners as (successful) 'professionals' (Alvesson and Johansson, 2002; Hodgson, 2002; Leonard, 2003; Gunnarsson, 2009).

PROFESSIONALISM AND PROFESSIONALISATION

One powerful overarching discourse that marks occupational fields, including public relations, is that of professionalism and professionalisation. As a competitive strategy to establish legitimacy and jurisdiction, professionalisation is 'better understood as a claim, more or less successful in social confirmation' (Alvesson and Johansson, 2002: 243), that can lead to formally recognised professional status and deliver corresponding rewards. In knowledge-based occupations like public relations, claiming professionalism as part of the process of professionalisation helps to reinforce the value of the occupation beyond organisational contexts, but is also part of the ongoing struggle for legitimacy in their imprecisely defined operational arena. Concerns about the professionalism of public relations are long-standing among both practitioners and scholars, but have generally focused on measuring some kind of professional standard in practice, rather than focusing on how professionalism is constructed and discussed. The implication is that public relations is progressing towards being more professional, and once this professional standard is achieved, it will be more widely respected (Lages and Simkin, 2003; Merkelsen, 2011; Yang and Taylor, 2013). Questions about the perceived professionalism of the occupation are regularly included in industry surveys (although what professionalism actually means remains unclear), reinforcing the fact that being professional has a positive effect on status and is something that practitioners should be concerned with (e.g. Public Relations Institute of New Zealand, 2014; Chartered Institute of Public Relations, 2015).

CASE STUDY 8.2
PROFESSIONALISING PUBLIC RELATIONS IN CHINA

Public relations is a relatively new industry in China, but is growing rapidly. As it grows, it needs to secure status both within the country and in international markets, since international brands that want to gain a foothold in China are important potential clients for the local industry. The China International Public Relations Association (www.cipra.org.cn) presents a narrative that introduces international audiences to the industry in China. It describes its role as:

> engaged in the PR theories study & practices, promoting the professionalization, specialization, and standardization of China PR industry; developing public diplomacy and opening up broad channels for foreign exchange and cooperation, and providing consulting services for organizations both at home and abroad, so as to serve for the policy of reform and opening up to the outside & Chinese economic development. (China International Public Relations Association, 2016).

The narrative is heavily inflected with claims to professionalism, including allusions to a body of knowledge, formal structures and standards for practice, serving the public good, and a client orientation. The association also provides a 'National Test of Occupational Qualification of PR Practitioners', hosts annual seminars and promotes a focus on high-quality practice. The association's and industry's status is also implied through a list of clients with elite status themselves ('top enterprises both local and national', 'PR professional corporations', 'senior PR practitioners, experts and scholars'). These statements all support the claim to professionalisation, but also reify the idea of professionalisation itself as a desirable status, which the industry and its members must work towards.

Like archetypes more generally, the concept of professionalism itself is not an absolute truth, but varies depending on the context. It has been described as an 'occupational value' (Evetts, 2011) and is an important resource for occupations and organisations alike. Definitions of professionalism become part of the 'rules of the game' that practitioners buy into, nurturing a collective identity and normalising certain practices that help define expectations for clients (Fournier, 1999; Evetts, 2003, 2006). Industry narratives tend to paint professionalism as a necessary and positive attribute, but as Evetts (2013: 787) points out, it is a particularly invasive ideological tool because '[t]he expectations by self and others of the professional have no limits. For the professional, of all kinds, the needs and demands of audiences, patients, clients, students and children become paramount. Professionals are expected and expect themselves to be committed, even to be morally involved in the work'.

Ideas about what professionalism consists of are driven both by social norms associated with established professions, and by the needs of organisational clients. Normative ideas have their origins in the early trait-based definitions of professions and appeal to concepts such as ethics, public service and objective expertise. In public relations, for example, the development of professionalism in the UK included making claims to traits associated with traditional professions (e.g. delivering a public service) in order to improve the occupation's status (L'Etang, 2004). As the occupation has grown, the balancing act of accommodating both occupational and organisational interests in the idea of 'professional' public relations has become more obvious, and today occupational credentials (e.g. the chartered status conferred on the CIPR and, through the association, to qualifying members) sit alongside arguments about the value public relations provides to organisations as evidence of legitimacy and jurisdiction (Hanlon, 2004; Pieczka, 2008; Edwards, 2009, 2014b; Merkelsen, 2011).

The discourses produced by major consultancies are particularly important as 'sites for professional development', shaping identity and practice by specifying forms of merit that define how professionals, identities, behaviours and tasks are to be assessed and rewarded (Sommerlad, 1995; Faulconbridge and Muzio, 2008; Muzio and Kirkpatrick, 2011: 391). Professionalism is often articulated through organisational identity (e.g. the identity of Edelman, Weber Shandwick or Hill+Knowlton) as a locus for elite expertise in a commercial market and a guarantee of value for clients (Alvesson and Johansson, 2002; Evetts, 2003; Noordegraaf, 2007; Kipping, 2011). Especially in consultancy discourses, the client looms large as a measure of professional 'fit': practitioners who can deliver high-quality client service, demonstrate capabilities related to client needs, and evidence industry experience are likely to be more successful (Anderson-Gough et al., 2000; Muzio et al., 2011: 446). Perceptions of compatibility, trust and reliability emerge from shared identities between practitioners and their clients, grounded in similar values, practices and forms of embodiment (Grey, 1998; Hanlon, 1999b). Over time, these two sets of norms combine to produce an occupational habitus that reflects the behaviours, values, attitudes and forms of capital that characterise the social location of both elite practitioners and typical clients.

EXCLUSION IN PUBLIC RELATIONS' PROFESSIONAL PROJECT

It is inevitable that 'larger social forces have their impact on individual professions through the structure within which the professions exist, rather than directly' (Abbott, 1988: 33), and professional projects tend to reinforce existing hierarchies of power. The dynamic flows both ways: individuals tend to seek out occupations in which the 'rules' resonate with their personal habitus, because it reinforces their view of the world (Bourdieu, 2000). As a result, professional projects tend to orient towards preserving, rather than changing, the status quo (Atkinson, 1983). Public relations' professional project may be fluid, but it is 'the product of a dialectical relationship with its environment' (Hanlon, 1999a: 3) and it has marked exclusionary effects because of this.

The norms established through the combination of traditional credentialism (where certain traits such as education and cultural knowledge are presented as evidence of status), task control and client sovereignty are integral to the effort to win externally sanctioned legitimacy, but also perform a form of 'dual closure' (Ackroyd, 1996) in professional fields, which both limits access to the occupational market and stratifies work within the field. For those who have the capacity to 'fit' the desired archetype, professionalism is a double-edged sword, where access to rewards and status is dependent on subjection to occupational discipline (Hodgson, 2002: 806). The identities of those who 'fit' less well correspond to social groupings that have less opportunity to obtain appropriate credentials (e.g. women, ethnic minority groups, working-class people and people with a disability), leading to their exclusion (Bolton and Muzio, 2007; Sommerlad, 2008, 2009 see also Chapters 9 and 10).

These dynamics have always been part of the occupational field. During its early development, entry to public relations in the UK was limited to those who had an appropriate class background and (frequently) public service career history, which meant membership privileged white males for many decades (L'Etang, 2004, 2015). Classed, gendered and racialised identities of public relations practitioners are still reflected in the form of whiteness, which dominates the field as a form of property, allowing those who possess it access to occupational privilege in ways denied to those who cannot claim it (Harris, 1993; Logan, 2011; Carbado and Gulati, 2013; Edwards, 2013).

From this perspective, the question of who practises public relations can only partly be answered by details of job descriptions, roles and specialisms. In addition, the question must be reframed in terms of who is *allowed or expected to* practise public relations, and why. This reveals how for some practitioners (women and ethnic minorities in particular) that even their own subjection to the demands of the professional project cannot guarantee success (Bolton and Muzio, 2007; Froehlich and Peters, 2007; Sommerlad, 2009; Daymon and Demetrious, 2010; Fitch and Third, 2010). Assumptions about their gender, race and class may result in perceptions that they are not suited to being a public relations practitioner, while their inclusion may appear to devalue the occupation in relation to fields where membership is more exclusive and stratified, because they are positioned lower in social hierarchies than is desirable for the professional project, contributing to their marginalisation within the field (Aldoory and Toth, 2002; Aldoory, 2003; Edwards and Pieczka, 2013; Fitch and Third, 2013; Edwards, 2014a). Even those who succeed in entering public relations and progressing in their careers despite these barriers may remain subject to discriminatory practices and micro-aggressions, or 'brief and commonplace daily verbal, behavioral and environmental indignities' (Sue et al., 2007: 273) that reinforce their 'otherness' and cast doubt on their right to belong (Tindall, 2007; Edwards, 2013).

Thus, the identities of professional 'others' are immediately relevant to the ways in which the occupation preserves its exclusivity and jurisdiction. Indeed, Witz (1992) argues that the term 'profession' is itself gendered, because it has historically referred to male-dominated, class-privileged occupations. Professional projects, she argues, are political projects of closure. Ashcraft et al. (2012) have suggested that professional projects may be understood as a form of occupational branding, grounded in dialectics of inclusion and exclusion of different bodies of knowledge, as well as different bodies. From this postcolonial-inspired perspective, occupations are recognised as constituted by their 'other', the elements of work and identity that are denied (even when they are present, such as women's strategic creativity in the context of public relations roles normatively defined as task-based and functional: see Creedon, 1991). As Ashcraft (2007: 28) notes, 'discourses of difference function to organize occupational identity and thus to reproduce occupational segregation'. The challenge for public relations research is to identify how difference is articulated and marked by the professional field, what purpose it serves and what effect it has on the claims to jurisdiction and legitimacy that characterise its professional project.

As social and cultural norms shift over time, some level of change in public relations' habitus and practices will also be inevitable, and the basis for claims to legitimacy and jurisdiction will have to change. For example, the increasing normativity of digital and mobile communication will require improvements in the level of digital skills among practitioners, so that public relations' claim to expertise in contemporary communication flows and audience understanding can be sustained. On the other hand, changes in social norms that do not serve the project will be slower to filter through. Despite increases in the normative importance of change in equality and social mobility, for example, the profession has seen very little change in practitioner diversity: dominant groups are still favoured in recruitment and promotion. To some extent, this may be because disturbing the 'fit' between client and practitioner by introducing practitioners who do not conform to a normative occupational identity may be perceived as a risk to claims of legitimacy and jurisdiction (Edwards, 2014b). The danger of institutionalised discrimination is very real here, but while the occupation spends a good deal of time attempting to implement functional remedies that will increase the numbers of practitioners from marginalised groups, there seems to be little reflection on the deeper reasons why their under-representation is stubbornly persistent. The degree to which the occupation might be a locus of social change, rather than a place for the continuity of hegemonic power, arguably depends on a much more reflexive engagement with this problem (see Chapter 9).

CONCLUSION

Analysing public relations as an occupational field adds another dimension to the ways in which we might understand its influence on social structures and individual agency. The changing environment for public relations means that its professional project is constantly underway, but within the field structures tend to be reproduced and opportunities for agency among practitioners are limited because they must buy into the professional 'game' in order to succeed, obeying the implicit and explicit rules about being a 'public relations professional' in their daily practice. Innovation may emerge in some situations, based on their previous experience and future ambitions (Bévort and Suddaby, 2016), but success tends to lead to norms being replicated so that even necessary changes in practice are slow to emerge, despite fast-moving business environments (Bruce, 2017).

As noted in the introduction, there has been little research on public relations as an occupational field, or on the enactment of its professional project. Yet the occupational field provides a filter through which society and culture affect the lives of practitioners, their agency and the choices they are able to make about their working lives. The field's hierarchies are built on social norms, their claims reinforce difference, and they perpetuate their success based on exclusionary mechanisms, often framed as merit. Understanding how this happens will strengthen the pursuit of equity for practitioners and audiences. At the same time, public relations, like other occupational fields, acts as an institutionalising influence on society and culture, and individual practitioners play a significant role as vehicles through which this influence circulates. The institutionalised 'logics' of the field only have agency if they are enacted, and the ways in which practitioners tailor and/or reproduce them as identity scripts are fundamental to micro-level processes of stability and change (Bévort and Suddaby, 2016). Moreover, in globalised professional fields like public relations, elite transnational practitioners who move between countries and clients are likely to play a vital role in the transmission of professional habitus and discourses across the globe, through their formal and informal interactions with colleagues, clients, governments and regulators (Harrington, 2015).

The professional project of public relations acts as an ideological framework that furthers the status and power of the field. Using the professional project as an analytical lens complicates ideas about power in public relations, taking them beyond campaign effects, practitioner status and meaning production. Public relations engages with power on its own behalf and practitioners are called on implicitly or explicitly to play their part in the collective endeavour to gain status and rewards. By asking the question 'What's in it for public relations?' this self-interest is revealed: a successful public relations campaign may shore up the power of a client organisation over its stakeholders, but it also demonstrates the value of public relations as a means of securing organisational interests. Similarly, the socio-cultural meanings communicated through public relations campaigns (for example constructing consumers as partners in an organisational relationship) reinforce customer sovereignty by suggesting that communication between organisations and their audiences is indispensable, and thereby justifies public relations' role over the long term. By peeling back the layers of discourse and practice that mask this self-interest, we can significantly improve our understanding of why the field is defined and enacted in certain ways, why diversity is so intransigent despite talk of openness, and why practitioners comply with professional norms that may grant them status, but also disempower them in day-to-day professional life.

NOTES

1. I use the term 'occupational field' rather than profession or professional field, because the term 'profession' is so contested and potentially raises more definitional problems than it answers (Evetts, 2013). 'Occupation' is broader and can accommodate the specifics of public relations. The terms 'professional project', 'professionalism' and 'professionalisation' are retained, however, since they accurately describe the processes that occur within the field as it tries to be perceived as 'professional'.
2. Fields can be defined in general terms as sets of continually evolving relationships between organisations and individuals whose activity is connected by the same field-specific logic (Bourdieu, 1992). In the case of professions, fields are focused on a defined set of practices, behaviours and values, often codified by industry associations.
3. This chapter focuses on public relations' professional project since the 1990s. See L'Etang (2004) and Pieczka and L'Etang (2006) for a comprehensive overview of the historical development of public relations as a profession, and also Ewen (1996) for a social history of public relations in the US context.

PAUL

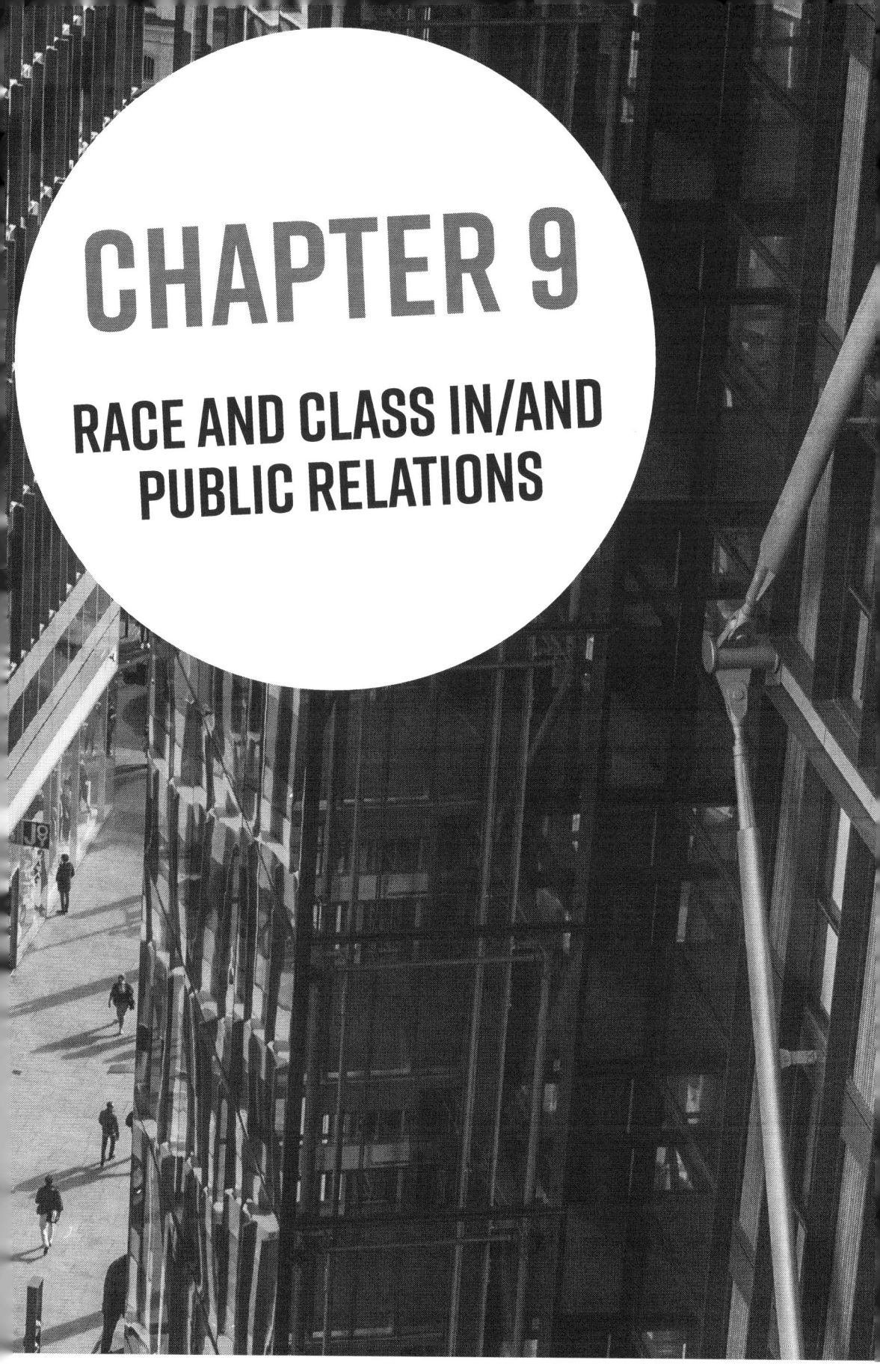

CHAPTER 9
RACE AND CLASS IN/AND PUBLIC RELATIONS

A major focus for socio-cultural research in public relations is how the occupation perpetuates power in different contexts. Power in any society is intimately connected to identity, in that those who have power are also able to claim privileged identities, which in turn give them greater access to power. 'Race'[1] and class are two of the most important dimensions of identity, or 'primary social definers' (Anthias, 2001) on which discrimination is based, socially constructed categories that have for centuries provided the basis for the inclusion and exclusion of communities in countries across the world and continue to be invidious mechanisms of deprivation.

Both categories are implicated in the fundamental questions about society that were raised in Chapter 1. They act as normative structures imposed on people's lives and constrain (or facilitate) opportunities in all walks of life. Both race and class manifest in context-specific structures of hierarchy and exclusion, but generally those people from lower classes and of a darker skin colour will be more regularly excluded from a range of social contexts and find access to financial, cultural and technological resources more limited. In the face of this systemic discrimination, struggles for recognition have resulted in formal measures to address inequality. In many countries, equality laws and equal opportunity policies in organisations and industries suggest that there is now a level playing field for accessing social, cultural and economic resources. In a 'post-racial' world where discrimination is officially illegal and overt forms of racism often meet with societal disapproval, it can be tempting to believe that race is an irrelevant identity category and racism is no longer an issue (Bonilla-Silva, 2010; Carbado and Gulati, 2013). At the same time, theories highlighting the fragmented, fluid and networked nature of society, and the celebration of individual agency (see Chapter 1), suggest that static categorisations such as class now play a smaller role in determining our life paths, with greater emphasis placed on personal choice, access to knowledge, and symbolic, rather than material, conditions of existence (Beck et al., 1994, 2003; Castells, 2000).

However, discrimination is a tool to realise power; and struggles for power only change, they do not disappear. Identity categories such as race and class are socially constructed and the meanings associated with them renew the bases of discrimination over time, justifying the inclusion of some and the exclusion of others (Goldberg, 2015). Nonetheless, when excluded communities and individuals find strength in the common injustices they suffer, they use campaigns, communication and promotional tactics to resist the denigration of their identities, challenge exclusion and insist on recognition (see, for example, Gabriel, 2015; Giroux, 2015; Melanin Millennials, 2017). These interventions help to validate their identities as important social and political actors, reassert control over how their identities are represented, and pose questions about how to fight against racism and class discrimination.

Race and class in public relations do not suddenly come into existence when we recognise moments of discrimination, or a need for a campaign targeted at a specific ethnic group. As systems, they are permanently embedded in the construction of public relations identities, discourses and actions. Just as models of campaign planning and development, approaches to evaluation and practices of segmentation are the backbone of day-to-day public relations work, so are race and class fundamental to the structures of public relations that give rise to that work. Much work on race and class in public relations, and particularly work on the marginalisation of people of colour, has tended to maintain the position of marginalised groups as the 'other', an excluded audience/practitioner/practice that is deserving of inclusion on the basis of moral, ethical or business arguments. This approach is misplaced. The reality is that race and class processes have always been *integral to* public relations, but left uninterrogated by mainstream research and practice, or treated as an important exception to the norm by critical scholars. If we understand race and class as constitutive of public relations, then the focus on these processes in recent scholarship has simply made explicit that which was always there.

The focus of this chapter is on the roles played by public relations in the construction and perpetuation of race and class as structured, systemic forms of discrimination, and in the ways they are resisted. I begin the chapter by discussing some of the definitional debates that circulate around the ideas of race and class as systems of discrimination rather than disconnected, individual acts of prejudice, before considering the range of scholarship that has addressed how they are reflected in the public relations field, its practitioners' identities and the work it carries out. The chapter concludes with a consideration of how we might expand studies of race and class in public relations, including a focus on the occupation's potential as a space where resistance to existing power relations can be exercised.

RACE AND CLASS AS SYSTEMIC DISCRIMINATION

Both race and class are socially constructed categories that act as 'different ways of organizing, clustering, arranging and classifying concepts, and of establishing complex relations between them' (Hall, 1997a: 17). These relations help to establish a particular position for individuals in society, and thereby affect their access to a range of resources including education, wealth, social networks and employment (Bourdieu, 1984). Class is grounded in economic status, including inherited family wealth, but also wealth earned in the course of employment. It is often measured on the basis of employment status (e.g. white-collar professional, skilled manual worker, unskilled manual worker, employed or self-employed), although class is also expressed culturally and symbolically (Oesch, 2006; Savage et al., 2013). Race, on the other hand, is based on 'physical variations singled out by the members of a community or society as socially significant' (Giddens, 2006: 486). There is no biological basis for racial categories; rather, they are based on attributes such as skin colour, embodiment, accent and lifestyle, and categorisations can change depending on the social context (Brown, 2015).

One useful way of understanding race and class is as *processes* of social control that evolve over time, and through specific events, to serve the interests of the powerful. For example, Skeggs (1997: 5) argues that 'class is a discursive, historically specific construction, a product of middle-class political consolidation, which includes elements of fantasy and projection'. The idea of fantasy and projection emphasises the fact that the dominant middle and elite classes repeatedly spectacularise 'inferior' classes (e.g. in reality TV shows or soap operas) in ways that betray their fascination with the 'other' in relation to whom they must define themselves. As Hall (1997b: 237) has noted, 'Marking difference leads us, symbolically, to close ranks, shore up culture and to stigmatize and expel anything which is defined as impure, abnormal. However, paradoxically, it also makes "difference" powerful, strangely attractive because it is forbidden, taboo, threatening to cultural order'. The importance of understanding racism as a process is crucial, because it helps to explain the reasons why racialisation is so entrenched in a 'post-racial' world, where racism is often treated as incidental bias against individuals (with correspondingly individualised solutions), rather than against a whole group (Bonilla-Silva, 2010).

Coates (2008: 209) defines racism as 'neither an event nor a specific series of events ... [it] is a process of structured events which over time demonstrate a system whereby groups and individuals are racialized'. In other words, to be racialised or classed is to be subject to a long-term process of marginalisation across multiple social locations. Race and class are systemic in so far as they produce discrimination in patterned ways *across* contexts: privilege tends to accrue to the same groups of people across different environments, while others are more consistently at a disadvantage (Hall, 1988b; Brah, 1994; Ahmed, 2000; Delgado and Stefancic, 2001). The process will differ depending on national, professional, community or cultural contexts. For example, being working class or a person of colour may not be an issue within one's own community, but may make one feel like an outsider in a university or professional context (Reay, 2008; Sommerlad, 2008; Gabriel, 2016); constructions of class and race will also vary depending on the national context. In Brazil, for example, the national census has five categories for race – white, brown, black, yellow and indigenous – and categorisation is usually based on phenotypical attributes including skin colour, as well as socio-economic status (Htun, 2004). Race is more fluid here than in other categorisations, which may be based on ethnic heritage or biology – for example, the historical 'one-drop rule' in the United States (see Hickman, 1997).

Race and class categories are most often called out and made visible when associated with disadvantaged groups, but the reality is that all of us are racialised and classed. However, privileged identities are used as a normative benchmark, universalised and unmarked, attracting no stigma, and repeatedly reproduced through discourses and representations that normalise their existence and implicitly or explicitly stigmatise 'others'. The result is that these categories – whiteness,[2] the middle class – become invisible to dominant groups because they simply reflect the world 'as it is'; there is nothing to remind them of their social location in relation to 'others' (Owen, 2007). In contrast, being identified as the 'other' (working class, or a person of colour) is to have one's identity linked to stereotypes of degeneracy, immorality, uncontrolled passion, anger and lower intelligence (Skeggs, 2005; Tyler, 2008). The characteristics align with long-standing constructions of the 'other' as a threat to civilised life, an uncontrolled and irrational presence that has the potential to undermine the integrity of existing social arrangements. Framing 'deficiency' in terms of individual attributes such as these masks the systemic processes and experiences of racism and class discrimination, presenting the 'deficiencies' of 'other' groups as a matter of individual choice rather than structural disadvantage, and justifying different forms of social control (e.g. managed access to education and financial resources, stricter formal and informal monitoring of behaviour). Such attributes also act as a foil for higher-status groups, whose identity is associated with civilised, controlled and rational behaviour (Hall, 1997b; Cole, 2004; Coates, 2008; Fanon, 2008 [1952]; Gillborn, 2012).

While privileged individuals may not recognise the construction of their advantage (McIntosh, 1997; McKinney, 2005), to those who are 'othered' the arbitrary nature of disadvantage is highly visible, because they occupy a liminal space between marginalised and dominant groups (Ladson-Billings, 2000; Reay, 2008). Their double-consciousness (Du Bois, 1989 [1903]) – the ability to 'recognize the recognitions of others' (Skeggs, 1997: 4) – produces options for adopting strategies to counter or circumvent their position (Ladson-Billings, 2009; Carbado and Gulati, 2013). This, and the agency associated with 'performing' identity (see Chapter 1), offers space for resistance to emerge in response to discrimination, and for actors to negotiate ways in which they can maximise privilege and minimise disadvantage (Rampersad, 2014). Moreover, the interactions between categorisations (e.g. being black and middle class or white and working class) can also provide options for resistance, since the resources associated with one categorisation of identity (e.g. education, financial resources, ability to 'fit' the racial norm) may be used to counter discrimination based on a different categorisation (e.g. Fraga et al., 2006; Carastathis, 2008; Hulko, 2009; Tackey et al., 2011). In the context of public relations, for example, practitioners may be marginalised on some identity categories, but are generally highly educated, earn well and are working in a middle-class profession, all of which are forms of capital that place them among other, more privileged groups in society and give them access to resources that can offset the negative effects of race and/or class.

Race and class are relational structures of inequality: they determine the relative power of different groups in the social world, based on the differences between them that are discursively constructed to 'matter'. These discursive constructions include what we say about the identities associated with different groups, who is included and who is left out, whose identity matters and whose does not, whose forms of knowledge are privileged and whose are not (Skeggs, 1994, 2005; see also the discussion of black feminism in Chapter 10). They are entrenched in part because of their long history: Owen (2007), for example, argues that the racialisation of non-white identities is underpinned by the historical dominance of whiteness as an economically, politically and culturally privileged identity, which has its legacy in contemporary presumptions about its superiority that underpin communicative action. The globalised privilege that whiteness accrued through colonisation has also resulted in 'pigmentocracy' – privileged status for those with lighter coloured skin – in countries where the indigenous skin colour is not white (Rampersad, 2014). The history of economic, social and cultural deprivation for racialised groups also means that race and class are often conflated. Racialised groups are assumed to belong to lower classes, and discrimination emerges as a result of the intersection between the two categorisations,[3] rather than on the basis of one or the other (Weber, 2001; Skeggs, 2005).

Relational inequalities result in differentiated access to forms of capital – economic, cultural and social – some of which become legitimised as symbolic capital and thereby confer symbolic power on their owners (Bourdieu, 1984; Savage et al., 2013; Rampersad, 2014). Not all owners of capital are equal: marginalised individuals who possess exactly the same type of capital as someone with a privileged identity – a university degree, for example – may find they are questioned or doubted because racialisation and class discrimination position them in ways that suggest they do not have the right to claim such capital (Puwar, 2004; Sommerlad, 2008; Edwards, 2013). The forms of capital that define status will also differ depending on the context. Yosso (2005), for example, notes that some forms of cultural capital specific to ethnic communities are ignored in mainstream models, and in professional fields some types of capital are valued over others (see Chapter 8). In public relations, for example, universally recognised forms of capital such as a degree and a middle-class background sit alongside strong networks of media contacts and diverse cultural knowledge as important assets (Edwards, 2014b).

The complexity of race and class as systems of discrimination is reflected in the many different ways they are evident in public relations. In the next section I examine research that illustrates some of the ways they are present in the field.

ADDRESSING RACE AND CLASS IN PUBLIC RELATIONS

In general terms, the notion of professionalism is itself a classed term, given the historical association of professions with elite occupational groups and social status (see Chapter 8). Indeed, in so far as it pursues a racialised and classed professional project, the occupational field of public relations may be understood to exemplify a system of discriminatory processes (see also Chapter 8). In simple terms, this means that within the field, being able to claim whiteness and class status as forms of property, a 'set of entitlements' (Skeggs, 2005: 972) that can be displayed and used to individual advantage, is an important factor in how professional hierarchies are constructed.

From this perspective, understanding racialisation and class discrimination in public relations begins with the issue of who or what is *positioned* as a person of colour, or as working class, who or what is *positioned* as middle class or white through public relations work, and how privilege and disadvantage are distributed accordingly. In many cases, this positioning will coincide with physical appearance: as Hall (1996: 11) notes, the body acts as 'the signifier of the condensation of subjectivities in the individual over time', and is inescapable in the sense that one's physical presence itself prompts categorisations and responses in different social contexts (Puwar, 2004; Ahmed, 2006). That said, the 'conceptual promiscuity and lability' (Goldberg, 2015: 10) of race means that its boundaries are fluid, while economic and social change produces shifts in class boundaries and identities (Savage et al., 2013). Consequently there is always space for bodies to surprise, to fit where they are not expected and to be excluded where they should belong (Puwar, 2004; Ahmed, 2007).

The research conducted thus far on race and class in public relations has focused on the experiences of practitioners positioned as 'other' in the field, on the specific characteristics of campaigns directed at particular ethnic groups, and on the experience of marginalised communities as audiences for public relations campaigns. It has also focused on countries and practitioners based in the global North and West – there is no critical research on the nature of race and class in industries in the global South, and very little on non-white practitioners outside the United States and United Kingdom. These patterns indicate that the academic field is itself contributing to the normativity of whiteness and middle-class identities associated with the occupation. Nonetheless, the research that has been conducted is important, and below I outline in more detail the findings relating to race and class within the fields (in its structures, discourses and practitioners' lived experiences) as well as in the other fields and contexts that public relations acts for and upon.

RACE AND CLASS WITHIN THE INDUSTRY

STRUCTURES

Research on the structures of public relations reveals the occupational field to be a hierarchical system of relations that has its own dynamic, driven by the impetus towards professionalisation (see Chapter 8); racialisation and class discrimination are put to work within this system in order to realise professional outcomes. They appear not only as sources of domination, but also as an impetus for resistance and reconfiguration (Edwards, 2014b). Industry surveys[4] have repeatedly demonstrated that minority ethnic practitioners are both under-represented across the profession and are particularly scarce in senior management and leadership positions (Chartered Institute of Public Relations, 2015; Ford and Brown, 2015; Wolf, 2016). Findings from qualitative studies have also regularly shown that organisations seek practitioners who 'fit' with their own (white) identity, rather than people who differ from the norm (Pompper, 2004). The 'white leader prototype' (Logan, 2011) is likely to play a role here, where identities stereotypically associated with leadership are linked to whiteness, and the subjectivities associated with people of colour do not prompt the same perceptions. This puts them at a disadvantage when it comes to recruitment or promotion for senior positions, and can also limit their visibility with clients and in high-profile positions as spokespeople (Len-Rios, 1998; Edwards, 2014b).

CASE STUDY 9.1
DIVERSITY IN THE PROFESSION: THE US CASE

In the USA, the legacy of slavery, a long history of discrimination against black Americans, and a strong civil rights movement have all helped put racial equality on the national political agenda. In the public relations profession, the importance of the struggle for equality is evidenced by the presence of the National Black Public Relations Society (see www.nbprs.org) as well as different branches of the association across the country. The society was founded in 1998 and functions as a professional network and an advocate for black professionals working in the communications industries. It runs a range of services for members, delivering both professional training and support services that recognise and mitigate the potential for marginalisation (e.g. peer-to-peer support, mentoring and networking opportunities). In addition, US industry surveys, trade articles and individual company initiatives all reinforce the fact that diversity in the industry is important. The focus on diversity is justified through the business case (the industry needs to serve a more diverse audience), and by the fact that discrimination is still experienced by practitioners from minority groups in the USA – talking about diversity does not automatically make it happen. Nonetheless, the situation is in stark contrast to the situation in the UK, where research has shown that discrimination does exist, but the industry does little more than name diversity as an important issue and attempt to raise awareness of it, without implementing practical measures to address it. The 'hands-off' approach means that measures to increase diversity lie with individual companies and are correspondingly fragile, since they are not systemically embedded into professional discourse or practice. For more information on the approach to diversity in UK professional associations, see www.cipr.co.uk and www.prca.org.uk.

The specific forms of class stratification in public relations will differ depending on the importance and manifestation of class in different countries. In the UK, for example, class bias is revealed by a recent survey by the Chartered Institute of Public Relations (2015), showing that most practitioners are university educated. The numbers of practitioners attending private, fee-paying schools is double the national average, and the numbers who attended grammar schools (where an entrance exam is usually required and fees are paid) is triple the national average. Ten per cent of practitioners had been schooled abroad, and over half had attended one of the UK's elite universities or received their degree from an overseas university. These elite professionals are over-represented at senior management levels (Bolton, 2015). The stratification of practitioners is echoed in the hierarchies of practice that also mark the industry, where financial and corporate public relations attract the highest salaries, while consumer public relations (more heavily associated with female identities and practitioners) is both less prestigious and less lucrative (Griggs, 2015; The Works Search, 2016).

Class stratification can also affect the public relations function in organisations in ways that disempower practitioners more generally. For example, in the heavily class-based context of Indian society, Sriramesh (1992) found that senior managers in organisations came from higher classes and this status gave them the authority to determine how public relations was practised (if at all) and to know what should be communicated to the public (usually publicity). These patterns of authority may have changed somewhat as the neoliberalisation and opening of the Indian economy to international trade has increased the importance of reputation, audience perceptions and a growing body of middle-class consumers with money to spend. However, class and race (alongside the very specific Indian caste structures) are likely to remain important modes of stratification within the industry (Newsom, 1996).

DISCOURSES

Most research on the racialising and classed nature of public relations discourse is focused on internal, industry discourses about the practices and people involved in public relations and the way they generate a normative identity for the 'ideal' practitioner characterised by assumptions of middle-class identities and whiteness. For example, in the UK the normative practitioner is framed as sociable, able to mix with a wide range of people, in touch with the latest social and cultural trends, technologically savvy, committed to the industry and willing to work long hours for the benefit of the client. A successful practitioner is someone who can deliver excellent client service, in part by building strong client relationships, anticipating and meeting their needs, and acting as a genuine partner rather than a paid consultant (Edwards, 2014b). These attributes are unsurprising in professional contexts; the client (whether internal or external) provides legitimacy and financial support for public relations and so has to take priority, in terms of both the practitioner's work ethic and their personality (a practitioner must not only work effectively, but also socialise effectively).

Often, the potential to do this is assessed based on homology – the degree of similarity between client and consultant (Hanlon, 2004) – which produces bias because most clients are managers, white and middle class (as well as male) and so practitioners who differ from this norm present more of a risk to the client relationship (Atewologun and Singh, 2010; Laurison and Friedman, 2015). The bias is perpetuated in industry publications, where visual depictions of practitioners show the majority are white, young and female, performing a respectable, understated middle-class identity (Skeggs, 1997). Rarely is brash jewellery shown, clothing suggests rather than reveals physical attributes, and practitioners smile, betraying the happiness of those who 'fit' comfortably in the field (Edwards and Pieczka, 2013). In other words, the images suggest that the kind of person most likely to be successful in public relations, and most appropriate in terms of meeting the needs of the field and its clients, is white, middle class, female and young.

Industry discourses also imply the possession of certain forms of capital. Most obviously, working long hours, socialising out of hours and being in touch with the latest technology and trends requires an independent lifestyle, time to spend on non-work activities (such as reading about or experiencing trends, or going out for drinks with work colleagues and clients), limited non-work commitments and the financial wherewithal to fund social events. All these things are usually less available to working-class individuals, who may have more family commitments and less time and money to spend as they choose (Bourdieu, 1984). In addition, the requirement to socialise with a wide range of people suggests the need to be a cultural 'omnivore', a characteristic more usually associated with middle-class than working-class groups (Peterson and Kern, 1996).

LIVED EXPERIENCES

The positioning of racialised and classed individuals in public relations through the field's structures and discourses is viscerally experienced in their day-to-day lives. In the case of racialised practitioners, research has shown they have to work harder and longer than other colleagues before they are recognised with a promotion, increased responsibility or higher salary, suggesting that they are perceived as less trustworthy and/or less capable than their colleagues (Len-Rios, 1998; Edwards, 2013; Pompper, 2013; Ford and Brown, 2015). The practice of pigeonholing and stereotyping can worsen the situation: for example, when practitioners are asked to work on campaigns specifically focused on ethnic groups, or in specialist areas such as the non-profit or public sector because of their race, ethnicity or class (Sha and Ford, 2007; Appelbaum et al., 2015). Such opportunities may allow them to use their knowledge of particular communities in their professional role, but it also potentially limits the breadth of their professional experience and puts them at a further disadvantage compared to their colleagues, who may be more readily offered challenges in higher-status areas of practice (Pompper, 2004; Edwards, 2014b). Moreover, the assumption that a practitioner will automatically identify with a particular community because of their own ethnicity may be misplaced and put them in an awkward or difficult position (Len-Rios, 1998).

Overt racially motivated bullying and professional exclusion have also been noted in some research (Pompper, 2012), while assumptions grounded in stereotyping and discrimination based on the intersections of race and class (for example, that people of colour are less educated and less able to communicate than white people) have also led to practitioners having to deal regularly with micro-aggressions that further contribute to their 'othering' within the field. Micro-aggressions are 'everyday verbal, nonverbal and environmental slights, snubs, or insults, whether intentional or unintentional, that communicate hostile, derogatory, or negative messages to target persons based solely upon their marginalized group membership' (Sue, 2010: 3), and are particularly difficult to resist because they are woven into everyday interactions and are often unconsciously communicated. Examples include situations where practitioners are assumed to be service personnel rather than professionals, where senior practitioners find their status ignored or dismissed in discussions during which their leadership should be recognised, or where practitioners are assumed to be less educated or in need of training in order that they embody the desirable professional (Len-Rios, 1998; Pompper, 2004; Edwards, 2014b).

The regularity of micro-aggressions has the effect of repeatedly defining marginalised practitioners as 'other', prioritising their racialisation and class ascription over their professional identity and producing the need for them to continually reassert their right to belong to the field based on their skill sets and aptitude. Even if they manage to overcome discrimination in one context, the systemic nature of race and class as structuring processes means that new situations bring the same challenges and the same need to justify their presence (Edwards, 2014b). The networking and sociability required in public relations may also pose problems for marginalised practitioners because out-of-office networking frequently takes place in locations such as private executive clubs, golf clubs, or after hours in 'trending' bars and restaurants. These locations have historically been gathering places for members of white, elite groups, where minority ethnic and working-class individuals are less readily welcomed. Practitioners have reported the sense of feeling out of place and being a 'spectacle' in such locations, someone those who 'belong' look over – or overlook – as their right to be in the space is assessed (Puwar, 2004; Edwards, 2013, 2014b).

Practitioners facing discrimination do not simply accept their fate, and it is important to note that these forms of discrimination are not universal or constant; the salience of race and class to their professional circumstances is always a potential, rather than a permanent reality, which gives them the flexibility to anticipate and manage its effects. They use their professional identity, experience and liminal understanding of both whiteness and class to find opportunities to reframe the ways they are perceived, manage others' orientations towards them, and use their race or class identities as a form of communicative expertise. They cultivate formal and informal networking opportunities and seek out mentors who can help them progress (Pompper, 2012). While they work harder and longer to achieve their goals, they also consciously strategise about their position and career development and may use their identity as an asset, changing the way organisations communicate to different groups. They may take advantage of opportunities presented on the basis of their knowledge of the 'other', and use the experience they have gained to set up their own public relations companies (Pompper, 2004; Edwards, 2014b). These actions mean that, while race and class processes clearly produce patterns of disadvantage, there is still space for practitioners to counter discrimination both psychologically and in practice, to exert their own agency and to shape their own careers. They can insist on being visible, demonstrating their belonging and refusing marginal status, achieving senior positions and being recognised as senior strategists (Kern-Foxworth et al., 1994; Len-Rios, 1998; Pompper, 2004; Edwards, 2014b). This dialectic between the imposition of power and resistance to domination is part of the fabric of public relations, always present even if not always readily observed.

RACE AND CLASS BEYOND THE INDUSTRY

The effects of public relations work on constructions of race and class are also filtered through the structures and priorities of the organisations and industries it serves (Sriramesh, 1992; Pompper, 2012). Chameleon-like, and in line with its professional role, it adapts itself to the requirements of industries and clients in order to help them achieve their objectives. In many cases, the effect is to embed ideologies more heavily in social, economic and political arrangements so that alternatives are harder to both articulate and realise (Edwards, 2012b). The specialism of consumer public relations – incorporating a wide range of campaigns from fast-moving consumer goods and retail to fashion and beauty – must cater to the classed and racialised hierarchies that consumption itself promotes (Davis, 2013). Priority targets are those who have the means to participate in consumption; those who do not have the resources to be a lucrative customer are ignored. Consumption is framed as a socially desirable act, merging with other forms of sociality to become embedded in community life, which makes exclusion from it all the more damaging (Trigg, 2001; Voyce, 2006; Miles, 2010; Üstüner and Holt, 2010). The long-standing bias towards whiteness in promotional imagery is one obvious and high-profile example of racialised exclusion in promotional industries (Seiter, 1990; McClintock, 1995).

CASE STUDY 9.2

PROMOTING ETHNIC DIVERSITY: ALCHEMY FESTIVAL, LONDON SOUTH BANK

The Alchemy festival is held every year at London's Southbank centre, the UK's largest celebration of the cultural and artistic output that comes out of the long-standing relationship between the UK and the Indian subcontinent (see http://www.southbankcentre.co.uk/whatson/festivals-series/alchemy). The language used in the promotional material echoes themes of collaboration, relationship, celebration and vibrancy, all of

> which throw a positive light on the idea of mixing cultural communities and traditions. Individual acts are described in terms of their ground-breaking history and potential to challenge boundaries, traditions and start new movements. The images associated with the festival are striking in the frequency of non-white individuals depicted either as performers or in audiences. These narratives generate a sense of inclusion and belonging, particularly for younger, creative communities that regularly mix cultural traditions in their daily lives. Public relations practitioners, as creators of the narratives, use their talents here to promote different ethnic groups and their different identities, as well as to overcome racial discrimination by demonstrating how mixing traditions can create new ways of experiencing, understanding and presenting the world around us. At the same time, however, the promotional narrative positions South Asian culture as 'other', something 'new' that audiences can 'experience': 'A space for the innovative and curious … for those looking to try something new.' The images also include well-known Asian tropes – food, colourful costumes, and dance spectaculars. While these narratives make sense as promotional text, they also have an uncomfortably Orientalist tone, creating a spectacle that objectifies culture for (Western) audiences to observe. Even though the festival emphasises the positive hybridity of global culture, these stereotypes help make the 'other' recognisable and marketable, and fit readily into the promotional narratives.

In government communication, framing policies in particular ways has been shown to influence media coverage (Froehlich and Rüdiger, 2006). It can reinforce the political and economic priorities of governing institutions and, more often than not, hegemonic neoliberal ideologies that marginalise the (racialised) poor, who are constructed as chaotic, uncontrolled, potentially criminal, and therefore presenting a higher risk to capital. Binary oppositions in contested debates are common: innocent asylum-seekers and refugees are juxtaposed with self-serving economic migrants in debates about immigration, while the 'deserving' and 'undeserving' poor are dominant tropes in welfare policy debates. Waymer (2012) illustrates how the idea of 'regeneration' consistently disenfranchises welfare-dependent communities by removing them from neighbourhoods that require 'redevelopment' in order to make space for capital-friendly creative industries and their wealthier, professional and semi-professional workers (Oakley, 2004, 2006; Peck, 2005). In contrast, poorer communities, where ethnic minority groups are often over-represented, receive less investment in their community infrastructure and are more likely to be situated closer to environmentally damaging sites, such as waste dumps or industrial sites. Their objections to corporate infringements on their quality of life, and to the lack of political attention paid to their citizenship, receive less attention from policymakers and corporates (Lipsitz, 1995; Coates, 2008; Kim and Dutta, 2009).

CASE STUDY 9.3

ERASING CONTEXT, INDIVIDUALISING INEQUALITY: GO RED FOR WOMEN

The American Heart Association was set up to promote healthy living in order to prevent heart disease among the US population, and its campaign to help women improve their health, *Go Red for Women*, has a global reach. In the USA, African-American women are at higher risk of heart disease and stroke than Caucasian Americans. The Go Red for Women campaign has focused on the African-American audience, and to this extent it incorporates ethnicity into its overall approach. However, the reasons why African-American women suffer more from these diseases are framed in terms of diet, weight, a lack of knowledge and genetic disorder (see https://www.goredforwomen.org/about-heart-disease/facts_about_heart_disease_in_women-sub-category/african-american-women/). They overlook the fact that African-American women are over-represented in poorer communities in the USA, and live with particular cultural traditions relating to food, hospitality and their own roles within the wider family. Because these contextual factors are ignored, reducing risk becomes an individualised problem, separated from the opportunities that are denied them because of the material impact of their class and/or race (for example, limited access to fresh fruit and vegetables, limited spare time to do exercise, maternal obligations to family members). This implicit erasure of race in public relations discourse ultimately reinforces systemic inequities and makes equality a matter of individual choice.

Even for organisations that ostensibly cater to subordinate groups, class and race discrimination can result in the least privileged groups being overlooked in communication campaigns. Keating's (2013) exploration of the experiences of migrant women workers in Australia, for example, shows how casualised labour and migrant status resulted in some workers becoming forgotten in the mainstream struggle for women's rights and equity. When even well-meaning campaigns like these recognise some aspects of identity but ignore others, they contribute to the erasure of class- and race-based discrimination in particular spheres of activity. They also limit the effectiveness of public relations work. Analyses of health communication (Vardeman-Winter and Tindall, 2010; Vardeman-Winter, 2011; Vardeman-Winter et al., 2013) provide examples of how ignoring normative roles and priorities for women in different ethnic groups can lead to them understanding health messages, but failing to implement any behavioural change because of cultural and class barriers. Even when campaigns are inclusive, they can construct audiences in ways that reinforce or challenge normative class and race hierarchies in specific situations by picking up on and reinforcing the dominant identities linked to their target audiences. For example, a global travel company may construct international travellers as white, Western middle-class professionals, while charities may construct their volunteers as older, time-rich and retired professionals.

Class and race have also been shown to mark the ways in which public relations discourses create corporate identities. Boyd (2012) illustrates how corporate social responsibility (CSR), a major area of public relations work, constructs the corporation as a middle-class 'person', with attributes that parallel well-documented characteristics of the benevolent middle-class devoting spare time and money to deserving groups of less fortunate citizens. Just as middle-class individuals devote resources only after their own well-being is secured, CSR is a luxury that is only undertaken once a corporate's primary objectives of profit and survival are guaranteed. The analogy is a powerful critique that suggests new avenues for exploring the ways in which processes of class and race influence other public relations practices (e.g. reputation management or crisis management) to frame organisations in particular ways and align them with desirable, privileged identities.

CONCLUSION

Race and class processes form part of the structuring logics of what Bourdieu has called the overarching field of power that governs relations in a wide range of fields (Jenkins, 1992). As this chapter has shown, public relations is both embedded within these structuring logics and emerges from them (Bourdieu, 1990), and there is a need to embrace histories of race and class relations as part of the overall story of the field's development. They are not 'special cases' of practice, practitioners or audiences.

An honest examination of race and class in public relations demands *reflexivity* from researchers and practitioners (Pompper, 2005a). We must ask how our research and practice is structured by and structures race and class categories. Given that contemporary forms of racialisation and class discrimination have their roots in historical patterns of exclusion, examining the history of communication in, for and by marginalised communities could reconfigure our understanding of public relations today. The communicative traditions of diasporic communities, for example, or of labour movements, have played a significant role in the successful mobilisation of their interests and generated social change. As such, they have a place in the history of public relations, in the changing socio-cultural context for its work, and, correspondingly, as a potential source of industry development. By placing their traditions at the centre, rather than the margins, of public relations, we might begin to understand their influence on the formal public relations industry – for example, in tactics that have become integrated into contemporary practices, or in prompting changes in campaign discourse that respond to normative social and cultural change.

Reflexivity is also essential if we are to effectively interrogate the continuity between historical and present-day forms of segregation, discrimination and resistance in communication practices. As (mostly) white, middle-class academics we also have a responsibility for perpetuating the normativity of whiteness and middle-class identities in public relations research; we need to scrutinise constructions of race and class in public relations as objects of research in and of themselves, regarding their normative status with a deep suspicion, interrogating how and why they emerge as a 'product of human agency' (Taylor, 2016: 7), and considering whether we want to accept the structures and practices of public relations that they help to produce.

Many people writing on race and class in public relations have suggested new directions for research, but most of those suggestions remain unexplored. There is still scope for extending the inclusion of critical race theory and a critical race 'mentality' in public relations work (Pompper, 2005a), for increasing our attention to intersectionality (Vardeman-Winter et al., 2013) and for adopting a dialectical approach to race in public relations (Munshi and Edwards, 2011). Class remains a significantly understudied but vitally important area for public relations research since it is a crucial locus of inequality and is so central to public relations' own identity and structure. There is also a dire need for more empirical research in different contexts, in order to internationalise and further illuminate race and class processes in different cultural and geographical contexts (Sriramesh and Verčič, 2012).

The fact that research on race and class in public relations is so limited suggests we need to engage in a fundamental shift in the place we allocate to these two categorisations in our scholarship field. Here we can learn from other fields. Taylor (2016), for example, provides a useful overview of the development of black aesthetics, tracking how new questions in research and practice have emerged. Among other things, the study of black aesthetics has reclaimed the creative and cultural activities of pre-modern communities; explored the impact of modernity on the construction and positioning of black aesthetics and its consequences for identity; analysed the reassertion of black consciousness and personhood; engaged with the impact of decolonisation on black aesthetic practice; and considered blackness itself as an object of research. These kinds of developments were only made possible through a process that put black identities and creative acts at the centre of aesthetics, and one might ask what kinds of new insights could emerge if the same exercise were pursued for race and class in public relations. Certainly the theoretical and empirical boundaries of the field would expand, and the universalisation of white, middle-class identities in practice and discourse would be challenged.

In the field of the cultural industries, to which public relations is closely linked, Saha (2016) also provides inspiration for the field with an interrogation of the ways in which cultural production processes reproduce racism on a global scale. He identifies 'the 'rationalizing/racializing logic of capital ... where ideas about race (themselves formed through political, regulatory, and representational discourses of European/white racism in the West) are allowed to manifest insidiously through what appear as neutral, common sense, commercial rationales' (Saha, 2016: 5). The result is that creators and their products are increasingly required to conform to marketable identities that reinforce racialising tropes of the exotic (but commercially desirable) 'other'. One can draw important parallels here between the commercial imperatives in the publishing and media industries that Saha investigates, and the commercial aspects of public relations, where messages that 'sell' are designed to appeal to existing normative identities and discourses and draw on stereotypes – or simply ignore 'other' identities – in the process. Much more research could be conducted to examine how national and transnational public relations agencies, digital communication channels and networks of public relations agencies and clients perpetuate (or sometimes challenge) the race and class divisions that underpin promotional messages. Certainly, the small amount of postcolonial work in public relations has illustrated its tendency to sustain global divisions that have their roots in colonial logic, complicated by neoliberal imperatives, and marginalise communities in the global South as a result (Munshi and Kurian, 2005; Munshi et al., 2011; Edwards and Ramamurthy, 2017).

Finally, resistance to race and class discrimination needs to be incorporated into mainstream analyses of public relations *and* into systems of practice. Resistance is evident in the work done by activist organisations focused on changing the status quo and communicating alternative ways of organising society (Demetrious, 2013; Stokes, 2013), but is also enacted when audiences resist categorisation and assert their identity in response to public relations campaigns, ignoring campaign messages and pursuing their own interpretations of values, attitudes and behaviours in different fields of activity (Gabriel and Lang, 2006; Davila, 2010). These voices can be a vital impetus for change, if given the space to be heard.

NOTES

1. As noted in Chapter 1, I use scare quotes around the word 'race' for this first use to indicate that it is a fluid, socially constructed category, rather than an objective term or an absolute reality.
2. It is important to note that the category 'whiteness', like any racialising category, is not grounded in the colour of one's skin, but in the socially constructed nature of the categorisation process itself. Owen (2007: 211) defines it as 'a social structure that normalizes the interests, needs and values of those *racialized as white*' (my emphasis) and a 'structuring property of the socio-cultural lifeworld' (2007: 212).
3. Race, class and other identity categories intersect such that their effects can be identified but not separated from each other. This intersectionality (see also Chapter 10) means that while each one has identifiable and specific effects that must be investigated, they also interact to produce disadvantage as a *general* systemic outcome (McCall, 2005; Acker, 2006). Their relevance to an individual's social position changes depending on the context, while the articulation between categories shapes the nature of disadvantage and will differ in different situations (Gunaratnam, 2003).
4. Unfortunately most research on diversity has been carried out in Western, developed countries and the research cited here necessarily reflects this bias.

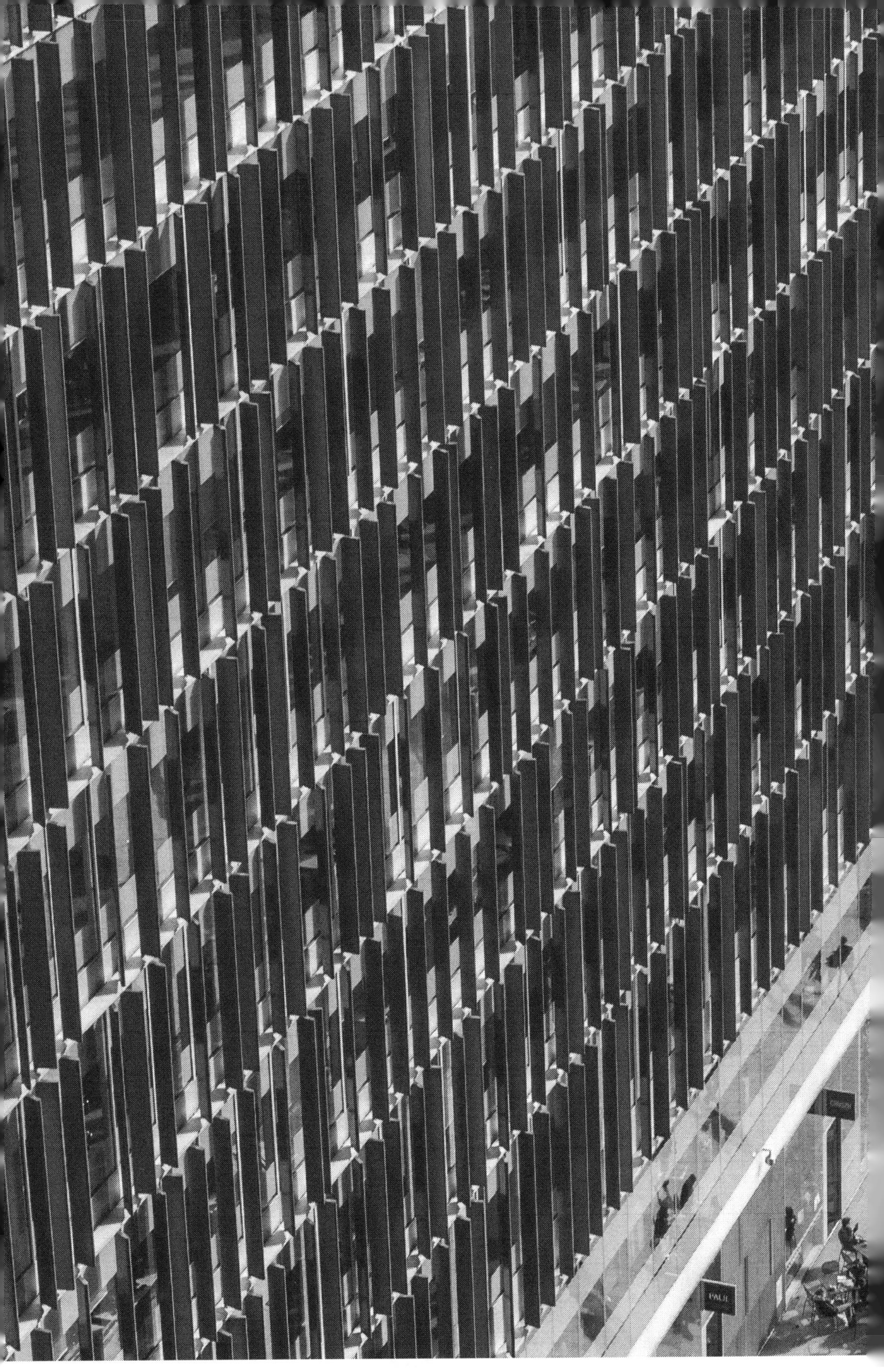
PAUL

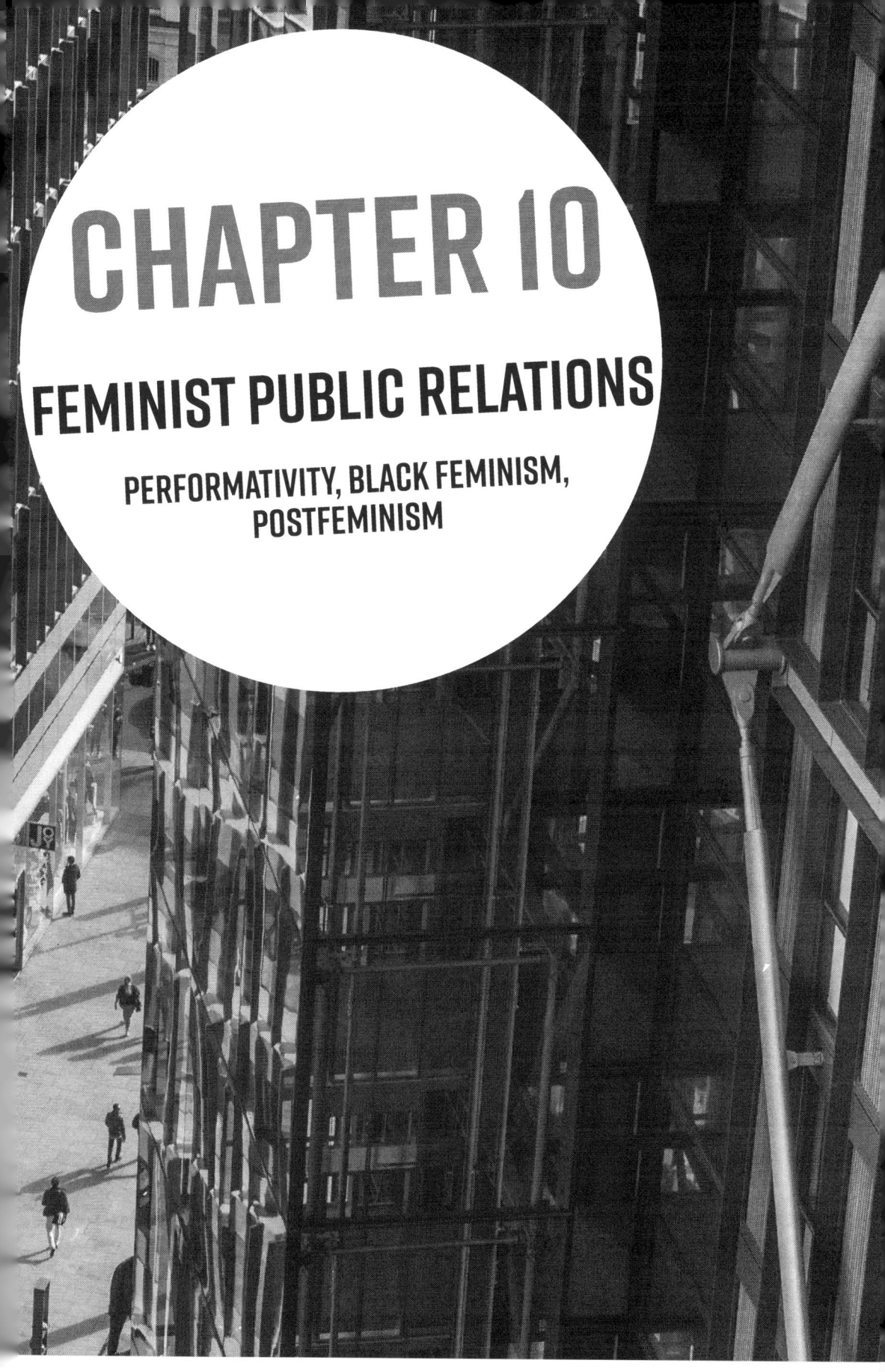

CHAPTER 10
FEMINIST PUBLIC RELATIONS
PERFORMATIVITY, BLACK FEMINISM, POSTFEMINISM

Gender is one of the major axes of structural inequality and has structured the field of public relations work since its inception (Daymon and Demetrious, 2013; Yaxley, 2013; L'Etang, 2015), even though women have historically been some of the most active users of public relations techniques (Lamme and Miller-Russell, 2010). Research has shown that women face significant disadvantages compared to men across almost all aspects of their lives, including employment, pay, physical and emotional abuse, and social freedoms. Historically, gender differences in status and resources were justified by the argument that inferiority was an inevitable outcome of biological differences. However, feminists have long contested these norms, and today gender discrimination is widely accepted as socially constructed, based on assumptions about what women are (not) capable of, rather than being grounded in any kind of physical reality.[1]

Some social change has come about as a result of these struggles: equality laws now forbid discrimination on the basis of gender and sexuality, for example, and in developed countries many workplaces have equal opportunity policies. However, gender inequality takes many different forms and structural changes do not always change practice. Women are still much more likely to be subjected to sexual and domestic violence, women's pay is persistently lower than men's for the same work, they are over-represented in part-time and low-earning sectors, and in many countries their social freedoms are severely curtailed. Women of colour and working-class, Latina, disabled and lesbian women face complex forms of discrimination as a result of the intersection between their gender and other aspects of their identity, and these are difficult to address adequately through universalised structural 'remedies' such as laws or government policy (see, for example, Krizsán et al., 2012). As a result, gender remains implicated in a range of ways as a structuring force that privileges male identities in a wide range of political, economic, social and cultural locations.

Research on gender in public relations generally starts from the fact that it is a socially constructed concept with effects on women's experiences of public relations as practitioners, subjects of public relations discourse and audience members. Golombisky (2015) and Fitch (2016) have provided excellent recent reviews of feminist scholarship in public relations, and I do not propose to duplicate their work here. Rather, in this chapter I respond to Golombisky's (2015) call to expand the scope of feminist research in public relations and incorporate more diverse, performative perspectives of the gendered nature of public relations. I first offer a very brief summary of the two main perspectives on gender in public relations research, to put the subsequent discussion in context. I then engage in more detail with ideas of performativity and gender, drawing on the work of Judith Butler in particular. I problematise and extend the notion of performativity by exploring how it might articulate with two other avenues of feminist scholarship that are underused in public relations: black feminist theory and postfeminism. Finally, I conclude with a reflection on how these and other alternative approaches to gender might expand the socio-cultural approach to public relations.

GENDER IN PUBLIC RELATIONS: DOMINANT APPROACHES

The two main approaches to gender in public relations have been driven by liberal and radical feminism (Golombisky, 2015). Liberal feminism has its origins in the critique of liberal thought and its construction of characteristics such as rationality, logic and intellect as a male domain. Liberal feminists contest the exclusion of women from public arenas that privilege 'male' characteristics, and focus on the importance of equal rights and equal access for women to forms of structural and institutional power. In general, liberal feminists argue that once changes in rights are established, then the individual can be the locus of social change, making the most of the new opportunities available to her (for example by pursuing a career, or a higher level of education) (Whelehan, 1995). This tradition is exemplified in a good deal of early feminist public relations scholarship. For example, the first studies of women's experiences in US industry in the 1980s identified clear structural disadvantages for women, particularly with respect to salary, role, networking opportunities and progression to management, and reflected the liberal approach by arguing for equality of opportunity and pay for women (Broom and Dozier, 1986; Cline et al., 1986; Toth, 1988; Toth and Cline, 1989; Toth and Grunig, 1993). Grunig et al.'s (2000) suggestion that public relations should embrace its 'feminist values' and feminine traits was also an attempt to revalue women's skills and abilities in the profession, based on an alignment between the needs of the occupation and the abilities of women to deliver empathy, to communicate well and to multi-task (Grunig et al., 2008). Hon (1995) proposed a range of liberal solutions to gender inequality in public relations, focused on changes that women could make in their working lives to enhance their opportunities to progress (for example, build social capital, access organisational forms of power, improve social capital and self-esteem).

In contrast to the liberal approach, radical feminists argue that gender discrimination is built into the systems of privilege that men tend to enjoy across all walks of life. Rather than focusing on individual action, they argue for systemic and structural changes that could overturn the assumptions underpinning the attitudes, beliefs, systems and processes that affect women's lives in the public and private sphere (Whelehan, 1995). In public relations, the radical approach has been reflected in arguments for systemic change, including Creedon's (1993) call for a radical critique of systems theory[2] as a means of perpetuating the patriarchal 'infrasystem' that governs organisations, producing gender bias by failing to challenge rational, masculinist views of organisational life. This left it incapable of addressing gender, race and class inequities within the public relations industry, but also in the organisations where public relations practitioners operated. Creedon argued for more critical work to interrogate this theoretical bias, because 'the infrasystem must be explicitly acknowledged, analysed and voiced to be known' (1993: 160). Toth and Grunig

(1993) as well as Creedon (1991) also exercised a radical feminist critique of role theory as a gendered and discriminatory model of public relations work. They argued that the subordination of the technician role (most often carried out by women) to the managerial role (most often carried out by men) ignores the complexity of women's work in public relations and perpetuates gender bias through the reification of male-oriented constructions of leadership and expertise. Aldoory's (2005) agenda for feminist research called for gender to be recognised as a learned social system and adopted more holistically by public relations scholars as a lens through which to examine the experiences of women and men in public relations, as well as the construction of the field itself. Hon (1995) also proposed strategies for changing organisational and social structures in society that would help level the playing field for women in public relations (for example, pushing back against gendered norms within and outwith the industry, changing curriculum content).

While these approaches have provided an important starting point for feminist work in public relations, they have some shortcomings. Liberal approaches fail to address the root cause of systemic discrimination, while the radical approach addresses the system but does not acknowledge the complicated reality that we often play a part in perpetuating gender hierarchies ourselves, even if they leave us disadvantaged. In addition, liberal and radical approaches homogenise the experiences of women, so that the professional lives of women whose identities are marginalised in public relations are subsumed into the majority experience. Explaining these realities can be addressed by drawing on alternative feminist perspectives, and in the next section I examine three – gender and performativity, black feminist theory and postfeminism – which have received relatively little attention in the field, but provide valuable extensions to mainstream feminist work in public relations that better reflect the complex lives of many practitioners.

GENDER AND PERFORMATIVITY

The idea of performativity emphasises action over states of being – one 'does' gender based on (or in contravention of) its normative construction in different contexts (Rakow, 1989), rather than 'being' a particular gender or 'having' a particular sexual orientation. As Rakow (1986: 21) notes, 'Gender is both something we do and something we think with, both a set of social practices and a system of cultural meanings'. As a culturally constructed system of meaning grounded in the intertwining of biology and social norms, she suggests that gender prompts action in particular ways for men and women. Judith Butler's work developed the notion of gender performativity with the idea of the 'regulatory matrix' through which the binary constructs of gender (male–female) and sexuality (hetero–homo) are continually reinforced (Butler, 1990). We 'perform' gender through repeated acts that correspond to our socially constructed male/female identity and, as a collective, we thereby reinforce and sustain gender as an organising principle for society.

Gender performativity does not equate to choosing one's gender; on the contrary, and by definition, 'performed' gender cannot be stable, but constantly shifts. As Butler (1988: 519) notes, 'gender is … an identity tenuously constituted in time – an identity instituted through a stylized repetition of acts. Further, gender … must be understood as the mundane way in which bodily gestures, movements, and enactments of various kinds constitute the illusion of an abiding gendered self'. This performative accomplishment of gender persuades not only the audience, but also the actor, of their identity. The 'acts' that Butler refers to are not only embodied gestures and self-presentations, but also include a crucial role for discourse (Butler, 1993). She argues that language is a form of 'doing', an act in itself with enormous normative regulatory power, and describes the performative production of gender as 'the reiterative and citational practice by which discourse produces the effects that it names' (Butler, 1993: 2). Rakow also reinforces the importance of communication as being at the heart of gender performativity: '[g]ender has meaning, is organized and structured, and takes place as interaction and social practice, all of which are communication processes. That is, communication creates genders who create communication' (Rakow, 1986: 23).

Even though performativity is 'compelled' through norms that pre-exist the individual and are therefore inescapable, the fact that it is constituted of repeated acts incorporates the potential for resistance: there is always 'the possibility of a different sort of repeating, in the breaking or subversive repetition of that style' (Butler, 1988: 592). If we choose not to conform in our performances of gender, we open up the possibility of playing with binary structures, undermining normalised attributions of meaning, power and centrality to different identities, redefining which carry greater worth and which ones are worth less. Moreover, binaries themselves contain the seeds of their own destruction: because privileged identities are always relational (you can only be privileged in relation to someone who is less privileged), Butler (1990) argues that the binary breaks down because privileged and marginalised identities are inseparable. Correspondingly, performances based on binary gendered logic (for example, women should take on the majority of housework because the home is a female domain) can be problematised and challenged. This has crucial consequences for resistance, because it means that groups whose identities are positioned *outside* normative discourse and practice (for example, non-binary or transgender individuals) are never fully marginalised. The constitutive link to majority groups as their 'other' necessarily creates space for them *within* the regulatory matrix, allowing them to assert their right to recognition. Moreover, any rationale for privilege is undermined once the 'other' becomes incorporated into the majority.

Golombisky (2015: 402) argues that adopting gender performativity as a theoretical lens 'enables one to document the communication of gender as-if-ness by which people act as if binary gender is real and important', and can be applied not only to individuals, but also to the industry's systems, structures and processes – its 'infrasystem', in Creedon's (1993) terms. Yet despite its potential for a field where gender permeates structures, practices and professional identities, performativity has not been widely used in public relations research. The studies that do draw on it certainly illustrate its power as a critical approach. For example, Krider and Ross (1997) conducted a phenomenological study of women's lives in public relations, which illustrated the role of gender as a performative infrastructure. They highlighted the ways in which the 'scripts' of womanhood, daughterhood and female professional combine to generate an experience of working in public relations marked by gender inequality and conflicting performative obligations. They concluded that the 'role definition struggle emerging from this study was that of societal expectations, family expectations, and work expectations combining together to create internal conflict' (1997: 450). Yeomans (2010, 2013) highlights the centrality of emotional labour as a performative requirement pervading public relations that manifests differently for men and women, where female skills emphasise a caring, nurturing, supportive role while men are more readily associated with leadership, competitiveness and aggression. In order to meet the expectations of clients and journalists, practitioners must manage both their own and others' emotions, as well as perform their roles in an emotionally appropriate, empathetic way (Yeomans, 2016). Similar results were found by Tindall and Waters (2012) in their study of gay male practitioners, who described the need to perform in line with gay stereotypes (being creative, 'on trend'), masculine norms (being 'strategic') and heterosexual norms in discussions of private lives (limiting the amount they shared about their own experiences).

From a historical perspective, Fitch and Third (2013) outline the ways in which normative gendered identities in the Australian public relations industry in the 1980s not only disciplined women to put up with sexist language and behaviour, but also supported industry structures where women and men tended to work in areas that aligned with gendered constructions of the public (male) and private (female) spheres. In contemporary public relations workplaces, Place (2015a) shows how practitioners' experiences and interpretations of gender betray the continuing power of essentialist, binary male–female identities, and in practice privilege white male heterosexuality. This small but important body of research emphasises that the need to perform gender 'appropriately' in public relations is alive and well, a complex balancing act and potentially double-edged skill that is developed and used in different ways as careers progress (Pompper, 2013; Yeomans, 2016).

As noted above, the need to repeatedly perform gender creates space for resistance, and Weaver (2013) provides a fascinating account of the ways in which women's activism has frequently been performed by using women's bodies as communicative vehicles – sometimes literally, as a surface to write on or to (un)dress in a way that sparks media attention. In many cases, these performances transgress gendered norms about where, when, how and how much of the body should be shown in public spaces. In campaign analyses, research has revealed the variability of gender and the ways in which it can be discursively (re)constructed through content that frames women's roles, identities and experiences in ways that shift male–female binaries and allow women's lives to be understood differently by target audiences (Somerville and Aroussi, 2013; Weaver, 2013). However, the regulatory power of discourse is also illustrated in Sison's (2013) analysis of the communications activity by actors focused on the Reproductive Health Bill in the Philippines, where the gendered, heteronormative regulatory matrix is (re)asserted under conditions where women are marginalised on multiple fronts (in this case, through religion, politics, family structures and the economy).

Gender performativity connects directly with the interests of socio-cultural research in public relations because it focuses on the connections between power, structure and identity. Gendered identities are framed as disciplinary norms reflected in structural forms of privilege, and public relations is implicated as an industry that both produces discourses capable of reinforcing or contesting those identities, and that prompts other, non-discursive acts in response to its discourses. There are many avenues for pursuing performative approaches in feminist scholarship. The current emphasis on practitioner experiences within the industry should continue, since existing work has only scratched the surface of what is possible. How and why practitioners respond to gendered industry discourses by conforming to them, and at what cost, remains a critical question, as does the issue of where and how the gender binary collapses (for example, in the context of campaign teams where 'male' leadership is dependent on 'female' technician skills) and where spaces for resistance are created.

Performativity also opens doors to exploring in more detail how campaigns 'perform' gender and prompt gender performances (for example, in the context of campaigns targeted at women or gay audiences), as well as how the industry itself is enacted in gendered terms through the discourses that it promotes about public relations work. For example, when consultancies promote a 'strategic counsel' role, the emphasis on rationality and logic draws on masculine norms and reinforces the male stereotypes associated with business leadership. A 'partner' or 'trusted advisor' role, on the other hand, calls on concepts of friendship and emotional commitment, characteristics more readily associated with female stereotypes. Both types of discourse circulate and interact across the field of public relations,[3] reflecting the inevitable connection between the two sides of the gender binary and begging the question of where and how other performative acts (e.g. award ceremonies, campaign reports, client pitches) reinforce or challenge the status quo.

Butler's work has plenty of critics and is particularly vulnerable to accusations of inconsistent theorisation of her arguments, as well as being grounded too heavily in discourse and individualism, while not paying enough attention to the material conditions within which discourse has to be understood and deprioritising any kind of pre-constituted subject as an agent for change (see, for example, Nussbaum, 1999; Boucher, 2006). Certainly, as a mechanism for explaining the politics of resistance, the reliance on discourse and individualism is problematic precisely because of the neglect of institutionalised conditions of oppression and a robust notion of subjective agency. Nonetheless, for an occupation in which the production of discourse is central to its existence, Butler prompts important questions about what, exactly, that discourse is 'doing' – not only as a force of institutionalised power (see Chapter 3), but also as a gendered act that prompts other gendered acts.

Golombisky (2015) notes that performativity does create space for the complexity of women's experiences to be taken into account (perhaps because performative acts must be context-dependent, created and received in particular circumstances), and this also allows for the variability of gendered experiences in public relations (for example, between women of colour, middle-class, lesbian and disabled women) to be accommodated. In the next section, I explore how gender performativity can articulate with two other bodies of feminist theory with very different starting points. First, I respond to Golombisky's (2015) call to take better account of intersectional theories of gender by considering how black feminisms and gender performativity might articulate together in the context of public relations. I then consider how performativity and postfeminist theory may be combined to create new insights into public relations as an iconic, postfeminist occupation.

BLACK FEMINISM AND PERFORMATIVITY

At first glance, the combination of black feminist theories and performativity may not seem logical, because their origins lie at opposing ends of the theoretical spectrum. Black feminists argue for the fundamental importance of institutionalised structures of domination and histories of material oppression in shaping the experiences of women of colour. These experiences are very different from those of the white, middle-class women that mainstream liberal and radical feminist theories tend to address (Whelehan, 1995), and need to be taken into account not only because they shape the pre-existing conditions for women's presence in social, economic and political space, but also because they provide resources that women draw on to resist oppression in its different forms. Three important principles of black feminism are particularly relevant to the discussion here.

First, black feminist theory[4] emphasises the importance of 'interlocking' or intersectional forms of oppression, which are the legacy of histories of marginalisation and dehumanisation. Limiting analysis of discrimination to gender cannot capture the full spectrum of disadvantage for black women, because it neglects the racism to which they are simultaneously subjected, and which derive from their status as a desirable and dangerous 'other' that poses a threat to the status quo if it is not controlled (Collins, 1986). Intersectionality treats discrimination as a systemic problem, but with context-specific forms prompted by the interactions between different subjectivities: race and gender, but also class, sexuality and other stigmatised aspects of identity (McCall, 2005; Acker, 2006). Importantly, intersectionality avoids additive models of disadvantage, because they cannot reflect either the complexity of social life or the notion of a unified, if multifaceted, self. As Jordan-Zachery (2007: 261) argues, 'my blackness cannot be separated from my womanness'.

Second, black women occupy a liminal space as 'outsiders within' majority white environments, spaces created by situations of structural inequality. Collins (1999: 86) emphasises that 'Outsider-within identities are situational identities that are attached to specific histories of social injustice – they are not a decontextualized identity category divorced from historical social inequalities that can be assumed by anyone at will'. The liminal position occupied by outsiders-within gives them the ability to understand the unspoken assumptions that underpin (gendered) white privilege, and challenge them either internally, by choosing not to accept the narrative of inferiority imposed on them, or overtly, by explicitly challenging white superiority (Collins, 1990; Jordan-Zachery, 2007; Ladson-Billings, 2009). Thus, outsiders-within are both epistemologically powerful and flexible. In their eyes, discourses that communicate privilege and support material advantage become transparent, their underlying assumptions revealed by, and readily contrasted with, the 'other' worldview to which outsiders-within have access. Thus, they have at their disposal valuable tools for resisting hegemonic power, because their knowledge of the 'other' allows them to continually challenge marginalisation (Rollock, 2012).

The third important pillar of black feminist theory relates to the importance of claiming black cultural life and narratives as important ontological realities, central to black women's experiences and a counter-narrative to hegemonic discourse that can also facilitate resistance (Collins, 1986). The stories that black women told and tell viscerally locate 'other' forms of knowledge and provide a channel through which contemporary black feminists can find self-value and self-affirmation, and a source of wisdom to draw on in the ongoing struggles that constitute black women's lives. Thus, they are a means through which new avenues for liberation can be found (Soyini Madison, 1993). Soyini Madison's (1993) retelling of sharecropper Alma Kapper's life history illustrates powerfully that not only should black narratives be recognised as a valid form of discourse, but that the nature of their performance is crucial. Performance alludes not to Butler's performativity, but to the rhythmical patterns of speech and tonality that reflect the emotional lives of those who deliver the stories. This 'telling' is a public act, a claim to space for personal experiences in public discourses and an exercise in agency (Langellier, 1999).

Black feminist theory, and intersectionality in particular, has inspired an important body of work in public relations. Early research on the experiences of African-American and Latina practitioners (Kern-Foxworth, 1989, 1990; Kern-Foxworth et al., 1994; Len-Rios, 1998; Pompper, 2004, 2005a, 2005b) revealed the ways in which they created successful careers despite ongoing discrimination. Pompper's long-standing research into the experiences of minority ethnic practitioners adopts an intersectional approach incorporating age alongside ethnicity and gender, and demonstrates how these factors interact to systematically and negatively affect the lives of minority and older practitioners (Pompper, 2004, 2005a, 2013). My own extensive study into diversity in the UK industry (Edwards, 2014b) also draws on intersectionality and the history of black British communities to inform an analysis of minority ethnic practitioners' working lives. All these studies have shown that women facing the 'double jeopardy' (Beal, 1970) of gender and race discrimination in public relations face significant obstacles. Their work is assessed differently than that of their colleagues, they are subjected to stereotyping and pigeonholing, they are deprived of formal and informal networking opportunities, they face significant barriers to progression and they must deal regularly with micro-aggressions that remind them of their 'other' status (see Chapter 9).

Beyond the occupational field, Vardeman-Winter and Tindall (2010) used an intersectional approach in their analysis of women-oriented health campaigns, and found that they privilege whiteness and class status over identities of women from marginalised groups. Audience responses to the campaigns illustrate the importance of multiple social roles for their understanding of campaign messages and speak to the relevance of ethnicity, family context, community position and culture as factors that affect the interpretation and uptake of campaigns in a variety of ways (Vardeman-Winter, 2011; Vardeman-Winter et al., 2013). From a theoretical perspective, Creedon (1993) suggested accepting or pursuing 'dissymmetry' in organisations rather than symmetry, as a means of recognising and facilitating different worldviews and valuing differences, and Aldoory (2005) advocated the integration of diversity and intersectionality into feminist analyses of public relations in order to produce better understandings of the patterns, characteristics and meanings of discrimination in different contexts.

Overlaying performativity onto the black feminist analytical lens reveals important alignments that have not yet been explored. The importance of narrative in black feminist theory has not been fully exploited by public relations scholars, and gender performativity offers an important impetus for new work in this area. Most analyses have focused on structural, institutionalised discrimination and on women's descriptions of their experiences in such contexts. However, performativity refocuses attention towards understanding how gendered and racialised discourses *precede* their presence in professional spaces, constructing their identities before they 'exist' and creating the conditions for performing an identity that can 'fit' with occupational norms (Puwar, 2004; Carbado and Gulati, 2013; Edwards, 2014a). Understanding the power that practitioners derive from 'other' gendered narratives, carried with them but originating in a different 'regulatory matrix' specific to their own cultural communities, and how those narratives might facilitate resistance, is also crucial to better explanations of what inspires them to persist in a difficult career. Moreover, if public relations discourses are understood as performative acts, then their performativity should not be limited to an analysis of gender, but should be understood as intersectional in so far as gender and 'race' are always connected. Who 'performs' gender in response to public relations campaigns, how those campaigns define identities that matter through their performativity, and how they leave spaces for resistance (for example, from women whose liminal position defies any kind of categorisation as 'majority' or 'other') would add richness and depth to our current understandings of public relations' place in society and culture.

POSTFEMINISM AND PERFORMATIVITY

In contrast to black feminist theory, to which activism and overt acknowledgement of oppression are crucial, postfeminism has recently emerged as a way of analysing the complex discourses and representations related to women that circulate in contemporary media and popular culture. They are marked by a repudiation of the second-wave feminist focus on institutionalised inequalities as outdated and no longer relevant, and the adoption of feminist narratives of empowerment and self-determination (McRobbie, 2008). They reinvoke a naturalised gender binary and combine this with a strong emphasis on individualism and self-control that justifies the requirement for women to continuously self-monitor and self-discipline (Gill, 2007).

Postfeminist narratives also re-establish the private sphere as an appropriate space for women to occupy, undermining feminist challenges to their exclusion from public life and leading to a problematic relationship with professional working lives. In postfeminist discourse, professional women are frequently cast as outsiders; committed to work, they violate the notion that work is a 'lifestyle choice', sacrifice family and marriage (Negra, 2004; Leonard, 2007) and, in the case of older professional women, are too distant from the girlhood privileged in postfeminist subjectivities as well as too closely associated with the censorious feminist 'past' that postfeminism rejects (Projansky, 2007; Wearing, 2007).

The objects of postfeminist self-surveillance are the tools through which gender and sexuality are performed: the body (particularly the presentation of heterosexuality and sexual availability), accessories, clothing and the home environment. Individual taste, choice and decision-making become the basis for asserting appropriate, heterosexualised forms of feminine power. By linking self-objectification with power, postfeminism 'sutures' feminist discourses of liberation with discipline that works against empowerment, producing strategies for self-management that are 're-presented not as something done to women by some men, but as the freely chosen wish of active, confident, assertive female subjects' (Gill, 2007: 153). This 'conformity through choice' is difficult to challenge because of its alignment with widely circulating neoliberal discourses of individualism, market freedom and consumption, which encourage the dismissal of social and political concerns in favour of market principles (Couldry, 2010). In the process, feminist discourses have been reshaped in the service of decontextualised, depoliticised and deracinated market-friendly subjectivities, where the construction and performance of an appropriate self is the (internalised) responsibility of the individual woman rather than any state or institution (Gill and Scharff, 2011).

Postfeminism intersects with public relations in a number of ways. Pompper (2013), for example, shows how privilege tends to be allocated to white, middle-class and younger women – identities that fit comfortably with postfeminist ideology and support the idea of public relations as a space where postfeminist discourses may find a home. The desirable feminist values for public relations presented by Grunig et al. (2000) include highly gendered attributes (e.g. forgiveness, altruism, nurturing and cherishing children) that arguably reinforce the postfeminist reductionist positioning of women in the private sphere. Yeomans' (2010, 2013) analyses of the requirement for female professional identities to be centred around emotional labour are also reminiscent of postfeminism's problematic acceptance of conformity-through-choice as a route to success.

In popular culture, representations of public relations practitioners reinforce the industry's postfeminist identity. Bridget Jones, Edina from the TV series *Absolutely Fabulous* and Samantha from *Sex and the City* work as public relations professionals (Johnston, 2010), apparently requiring no formal skill set other than the ability to look good and socialise. Fitch (2015) reveals the multiple and contradictory gendered portrayals of both the occupation and its practitioners in the US television series *True Blood*. Reflecting on the dependence of postfeminism on promotional culture, she also notes the importance of intertextuality in the series, which blurs the boundaries between reality and fiction by incorporating normative promotional discourses and practices into the public relations work that takes place as part of the series narrative. The long hours and hard work that public relations actually requires are overlooked in these representations (Bowen, 2003), and instead public relations offers an appropriate, pseudo-professional space in which young, female practitioners can perform the exclusive, aspirational aspects of identity privileged by postfeminism, including financial independence, education, whiteness and membership of the middle and/or upper classes (Tasker and Negra, 2007), while remaining unthreatening in terms of economic or political power.

CASE STUDY 10.1

ETSY.COM: POSTFEMINIST PROMOTION

Etsy.com provides an interesting example of postfeminist discourse in action. The site hosts online shops for women craftworkers who want to sell their work, usually from home or a private studio. Etsy promotes craft to consumers who are interested in finding 'different' and 'unique' products, and is part of a movement to reclaim women's home-based creative work , and small-scale production more generally, as an authentic and valuable mode of working in contrast to the mass production and globalisation of commerce that mark contemporary modernity (Luckman, 2013). In principle, the site empowers women by providing them with a space where they can showcase a wide range of craft work and earn money for their efforts. However, politics is subsumed by commerce in the advice that sellers are given in order to successfully promote their products. Empowerment comes through commercial success rather than more complicated challenges such as managing work–life balance, using a business as a way to assert authority in the home, or earning extra income as a way of securing better choices in other areas of life. Sellers are advised that success comes from customers – most commonly, middle-class consumers who can afford to pay for uniqueness and difference – 'loving' the products they see. Love is realised through the promotional use of photography and narratives that represent middle-class whiteness as *both* the normative craftworker and craft consumer identity. Studios are represented as modern, tidy, bright, spacious places devoted only to creative work; the challenges common to many women's lives – of managing complex family lives or juggling multiple jobs, for example – do not intrude on creative space. Photography is used to help sellers 'shine bright', and show carefully manicured images of the creative process, personalised through pets, cups of tea and favourite tools, and demonstrating the 'love and care' that go into products and packaging. By telling their 'story' about where the 'beloved products' have come from, sellers can add additional emotional appeal. Thus, the claim that Etsy embraces difference and uniqueness extends to products rather than craftworkers themselves, who are encouraged to promote themselves in terms of commercially viable identities that attract the right kind of consumer. At the same time, Etsy's approach to promotion illustrates how the apparent advantage of the internet for commercialising craft and microproduction simultaneously obscures the political history associated with craft, its gendered nature (most craftwork is done by women) and the many ways that women can and do use craft to address the political, social and personal challenges they face (Luckman, 2013). (See Etsy's Seller Handbook for more examples of their approach to promotion.)

The link between postfeminism and performativity is obvious on one level, given that there is an emphasis in both theories on the importance of performing a discursively constructed identity in order to 'fit' with normative ideals. Postfeminism also privileges individual subjectivities, just as performativity places individual responses to gendered discourse at its heart. However, performativity enables us to identify the fatal flaw in postfeminism, grounded as it is in an unsustainable gender binary that is inevitably open to contestation. As a result, even if postfeminist discourses and representations are taken up uncritically by younger women who have grown up in a neoliberal world where the individualisation of inequality may seem inevitable, the principle of conformity-through-choice is likely to face important caveats, and possible reversal (non-conformity-through-choice) in the context of challenging professional lives where structural inequalities can be all too obvious. Resistance to postfeminism may then make the most of the fictitious binary structures on which it depends. For example, female public relations practitioners frequently distance themselves from gendered roles, and especially from postfeminist stereotypes of a non-professional (or *un*professional) identity. Instead, they assert their reliability and expertise by demonstrating the 'objective professional' and 'trusted advisor' status common to consultancy professions (Froehlich and Peters, 2007; Yeomans, 2013). In so doing, they co-opt their 'other' – the masculine side of the gender binary – and reassert their right to 'belong' in public, professional life.

CASE STUDY 10.2

CONTESTING GENDERED NORMS? POSTFEMINIST 'LIBERATION' IN FASHION PUBLIC RELATIONS

Fashion public relations is an obvious public relations specialism where gendered norms play a significant role in structuring practice. The primary role of a fashion public relations practitioner is to secure brand and product exposure and coverage, usually via photo opportunities, celebrity sponsorship, distributing sample products, and managing events. Nominally, clothing and accessories are the object of promotional work, but in the process of promoting them, fashion public relations practitioners cannot avoid presenting specific body types and identities as more desirable than others. Models tend to be Caucasian, slim and tall, while celebrities are wealthy, live exclusive lifestyles and are also usually slim. Associating 'fashion' with these ideal bodies and identities inevitably excludes the majority of the female population that does not or cannot conform, yet simultaneously reifies them as ideals towards which all women should strive. Given this, fashion public relations could take some responsibility for the promotion of unrealistic and unhealthy body types, which some argue are a factor in the rise in eating disorders among young women. On the other hand, some fashion public relations campaigns have countered such gendered stereotypes – perhaps the best-known being the 'Real Beauty' campaign, run by cosmetics company Dove, where the models were everyday women of average size, rather than professionals, and the campaign was specifically designed to challenge the modelling industry's idealised body types. Nonetheless, even here the notion of 'beauty' remains positioned as a desirable attribute, defining womanhood and underpinned by discourses of deficiency: we do not 'love' ourselves enough, we should be satisfied with ourselves as we are, we must not aspire to unattainable goals. These postfeminist narratives of self-discipline and self-management erase the systemic roots of discrimination, while simultaneously reinscribing them by sustaining gender binaries and obscuring 'other' identities (the campaigns rarely show gay women or women with disabilities, and women of colour remain in the minority). The intransigent reality of gender as a structured and systemic form of inequity – embedded as Butler's heteronormative, gendered matrix – is thus visible even when campaigns try to work against gendered norms.

For more analyses of fashion, beauty campaigns and Dove, see, for example, Gill and Elias (2014) and Banet-Weiser (2012).

CONCLUSION: NEW DIRECTIONS

Fitch et al. (2016) have argued for the importance of 'talking back' to normative public relations thinking in order to transgress existing boundaries and transform the gendered distribution of power in theory and practice. In part, this requires the integration of a much wider range of theoretical approaches to addressing gender and sexuality issues in public relations. The use of public relations theory to frame many studies of gender and sexuality leaves its gender and heteronormative bias relatively intact, and in the few studies where other theories have been used, the inherent theoretical challenge to normative scholarship is often left unexplored. Performativity, black feminist theory and postfeminism all illustrate how approaches to gender and feminist theory that depart from the dominant liberal and radical models can open up the theoretical and analytical landscape, enabling stronger critique of the patriarchal infrasystem; the diversity of women's experiences and the situated meaning of gendered hierarchies; the complex effects of intersectionality, including bias towards age, whiteness and homophily; as well as queer and LGBT perspectives (Creedon, 1993; Aldoory, 2005; Daymon and Demetrious, 2013; Pompper, 2013; Tindall and Waters, 2013).

Black feminism, for example, requires that the universalisation of whiteness in empirical studies of practitioners (which, unless specifically focused on diversity, usually assume that all practitioners are white and heterosexual) be interrogated and challenged, and that 'other' narratives are more extensively integrated into the full picture of public relations as an industry and a socio-cultural phenomenon. Postfeminism prompts questions about the alignment of neoliberalism and postfeminist discourses in public relations industry narratives, and the ways in which public relations materials prompt the performance of postfeminist identities among audiences. How postfeminism affects the ongoing constitution of gender and heterosexuality within the field is under-researched, yet knowing how practitioners react to deprofessionalised, sexualised representations of public relations practitioners, and how those representations affect the way they are received by colleagues, clients and journalists, is as important as pointing out that such representations exist. Clarifying how both black feminist narratives and postfeminism produce opportunities for discipline, self-governance and resistance for the diverse body of practitioners that make up the field is crucial to recognising the complicated performative demands of intersectional identities in today's public relations workplaces.

Golombisky (2015) notes the potential for a more robust embedding of performativity, intersectionality and standpoint theory as a means of paying greater attention to the political and social dynamics of gender in public relations, as well as developing reflexivity among scholars and research participants. She also argues for the introduction of transnational, third space and womanist feminisms that 'critique, theorize, and practice feminisms differently in a world that has become communicatively global, corporately neocolonial, and culturally diasporic' (Golombisky, 2015: 408). Alongside performativity, intersectionality and standpoint theory, they support a movement towards a more politicised feminist scholarship in public relations. Queer theory could also provide a vital interruption to gendered and heteronormative bias in public relations (Tindall and Waters, 2013). Its roots are in social constructivism and poststructuralist principles of fragmentation and fluidity, particularly in relation to the links between biological sex, sexuality and gender. Queer theorists explore how political, economic and socio-cultural exigencies lead to continually evolving identities and subjectivities, and 'queering' – deconstructing taken-for-granted identity categories to explore their unstable, fragmented nature (Jagose, 1996; Gamson, 2000) – has provided rich opportunities for thinking differently about both theory and empirical work in a range of academic fields. Queering public relations would prompt greater reflexivity about how Butler's 'regulatory matrix' shapes the research questions we ask and those we ignore; the assumptions we make about audience and practitioner identities, their immutability and longevity; the methods we perceive to be 'appropriate' for public relations research; and the knowledge we obscure as a result of all these choices (Edwards and L'Etang, 2013).

Important research questions also come from cognate fields. Feminist media scholars, for example, have explored a wide range of issues relating to the representation, reception and production of gendered identities as well as how women journalists engage politically with issues of representation, identity and gender inequality through their work (Byerly and Ross, 2006). In public relations, more critical work on the construction and representation of gender in and through public relations campaigns is needed, while questions about how, when and where women in public relations choose or are able to work as feminists and activists – 'performing' feminism – would align with womanist and third space feminist approaches, and could address transnational feminist interests by incorporating the global landscape of public relations into research designs, so that the breadth of women's experiences is properly reflected (Shome and Hegde, 2002; Dutta and Pal, 2011).

Elsewhere, feminists have highlighted the gendered dimensions of technology and representation (Thumim, 2012; Bassett, 2013; Haraway, 2013; Thornham, 2013), and work in queer studies has shown how digital technologies allow LGBT individuals to manage and construct their identity in online and offline spaces (Pullen and Cooper, 2010). Given that public relations is a field dominated by women and by digital technologies, interesting questions could be raised about how gender and sexuality play into the use, deployment and status of technology in public relations workplaces and campaigns, as well as among practitioners. Quantitative research could also offer a valuable complement to the more traditional qualitative methods that have dominated feminist public relations work. Quantitative analyses, while they come with their own ontological and epistemological challenges, can help to illustrate large-scale patterns of discrimination and reinforce the significance of the individual experiences and cases reported in qualitative work (see, for example, Davidson and Burke, 2004; Byerly and Ross, 2006).

There is a danger of postfeminist attitudes inserting themselves into the assumptions and priorities that shape research on public relations. The occupation is a site where many women enjoy very successful careers, earn good salaries and are respected for their work. Women may not seem particularly disadvantaged, and perhaps this is one reason why relatively few scholars in the field (and almost no men at all) engage in feminist research. Yet numerous research studies and industry surveys show unequivocally that gender discrimination is alive and well, reinforced through task hierarchies, salary differentials and gendered expectations of labour. These structural inequalities limit the agency and choices of practitioners as well as audiences, but are also part of the professional 'game' that practitioners buy into and through which their behaviour is regulated (see Chapter 8). They are particularly difficult to eliminate, because they are embedded within the 'infrasystem' of public relations itself as well as being reinforced by the wider regulatory matrix identified by Butler.

We might therefore approach gender discrimination as one of public relations' 'wicked' problems: it has multiple manifestations, it is linked systemically to other forms of positive and negative discrimination (see Chapter 9), and there is no clear solution that can be universally applied (Rittel and Webber, 1973). As Rittel and Webber (1973) note, wicked problems must be repeatedly *re*-solved, and in a networked world, where digital communication facilitates connections beyond the located experiences of discrimination, new opportunities for resolving gender discrimination will continually emerge. Taking feminist research in public relations beyond its current comfort zone, to places that both challenge us and recognise 'others', is one way of finding out what those opportunities are as the struggle for equality continues.

NOTES

1. New gender categories have also emerged and now include transgender, non-binary, third gender and others.
2. Systems theory is an approach to public relations that is grounded in the idea of organisations as a set of subsystems that interact with each other and the external environment. Public relations is one of the organisational subsystems (Gregory, 2009: 26).
3. For a detailed investigation of industry discourses, see Edwards (2014a).
4. Black feminist theory does not speak for all women whose histories and present create intersectional oppressions, but the principles of accounting for intersectionality, liminal space and narrative do stand as important tools for investigating other cultural, social and political economic contexts. They facilitate recognition of the important fact that it is impossible to talk about a singular 'woman's experience'; rather, the diversity of women's experiences must be taken into account (King, 1988; Mohanty, 1988; Spivak, 1988; Brah, 1994; Puwar, 2004).

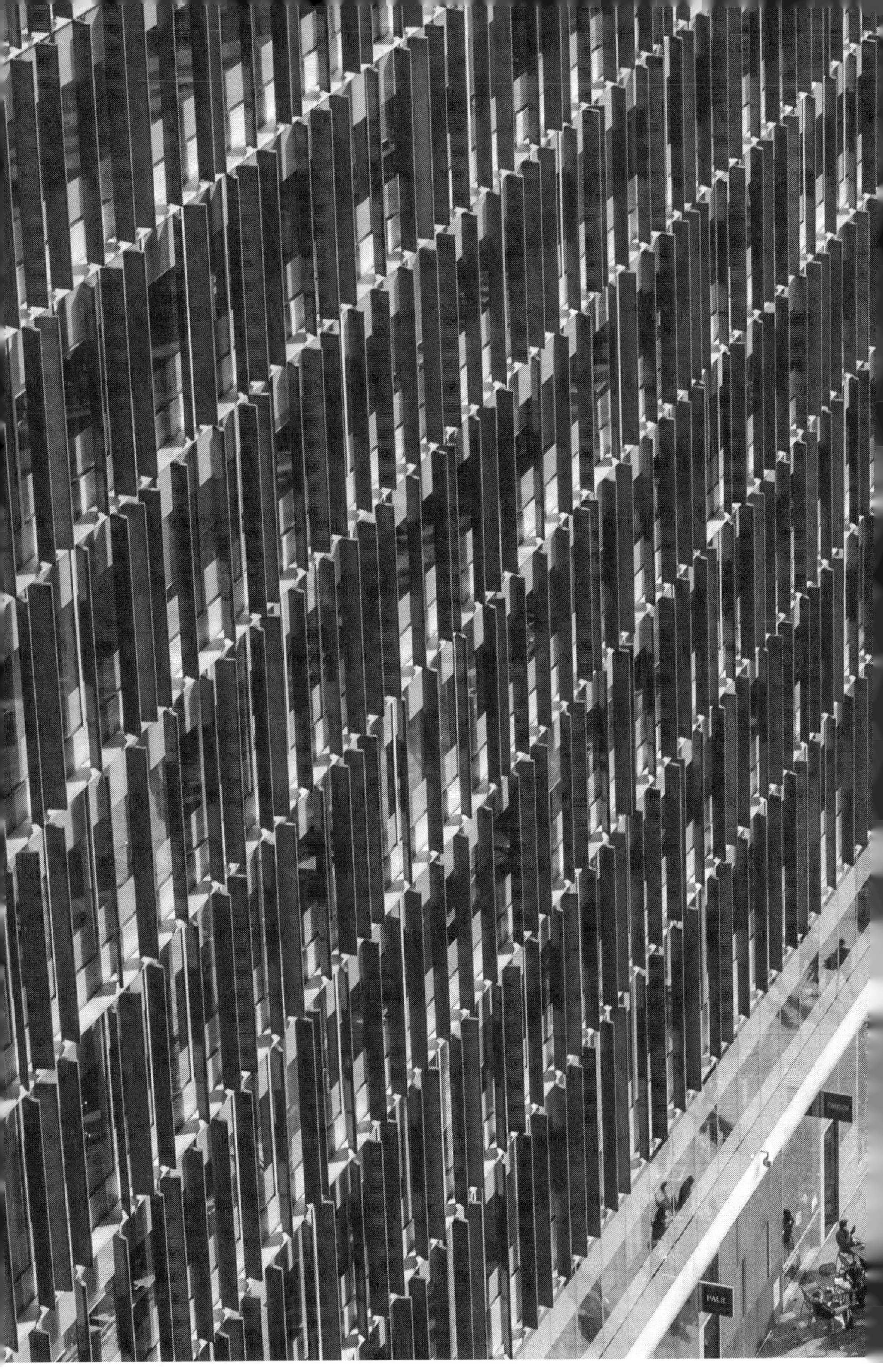
PAUL

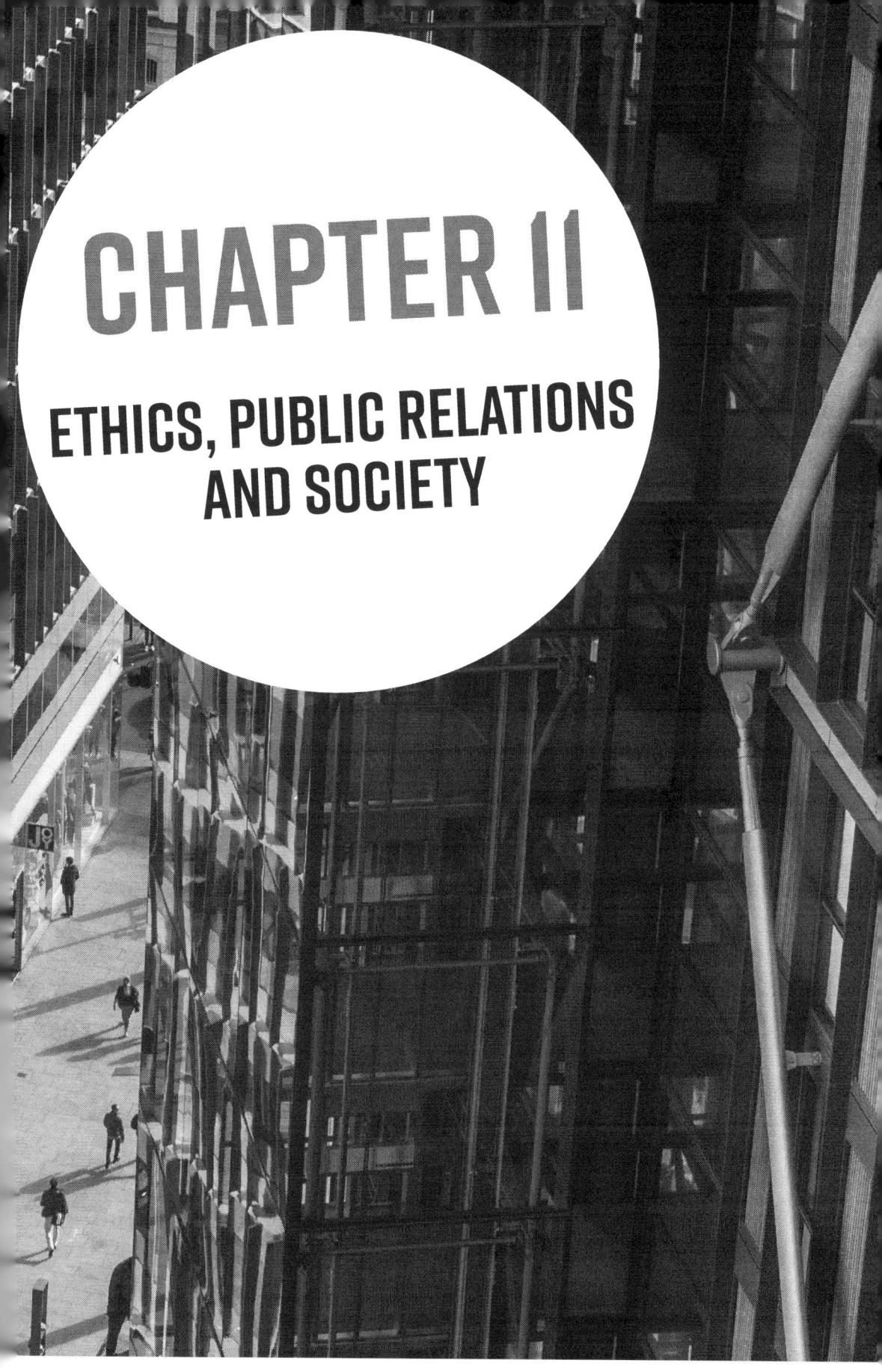

CHAPTER 11
ETHICS, PUBLIC RELATIONS AND SOCIETY

INTRODUCTION

Public relations practitioners and scholars have engaged in discussions of ethics and ethical practice to explain how public relations can (or cannot) result in a positive contribution to society, in part as a response to the industry's reputational problem. Ethical claims are also tightly linked to the occupation's legitimacy as a profession (Merkelsen, 2011; see also Chapter 8 earlier). However, despite industry claims to take its social obligations seriously, in practice public interest issues tend to take second place to client and contractual considerations in ethical discussions (L'Etang, 2006a; Kim and Ki, 2014). Industry codes are rarely enforced, ethical training in public relations remains scarce, and ethical management – the systematic embedding of ethical thinking in organisations – is fragmented at best (Bowen, 2008; Lee and Cheng, 2012; Tilley, 2015). As Harrison and Galloway (2005: 3) note, '[t]here is no consensus as to how practitioners are to weave their way through the minefield of competing ethical imperatives', and the label 'spin doctor' persists as a moniker of unethical practice.

To some extent, the vagueness of ethical principles in public relations is due to the fact that the context for practitioner decision-making is increasingly complex and there are many different ways of approaching ethics in public relations, none of which has a clear advantage over the others (Fitzpatrick and Bronstein, 2006; Gregory, 2009). One of the most common theories of ethics used in public relations scholarship is utilitarianism (also known as consequentialism), which focuses on the outcomes of decisions and is aimed at maximising benefits by doing good for the highest possible number of people. In contrast, situationist ethical approaches analyse the characteristics of particular circumstances and weigh up possible options to come to a decision about what counts as ethical (Fawkes, 2014a). Deontological perspectives, on the other hand, follow the principle that all individuals should follow the same principles of ethical behaviour, and that those principles, rather the specifics of individual situations, should govern decision-making (L'Etang, 1992). Discourse ethics applies Habermasian principles of dialogue to the ways that practitioners and organisations engage with audiences, and stipulates specific parameters for what counts as ethical discourse (Leeper, 1996). Finally, virtue ethics positions the individual as the locus of ethics and morality, rather than societal expectations or discourse, such that virtuous characters will inevitably apply ethics responsibly to their decision-making (Harrison and Galloway, 2005).

For socio-cultural analyses, ethics is an important aspect of public relations practice because it relates to how power and influence are understood and used by practitioners, as well as to how practitioners themselves are subjected to power in their working lives. Ethics, then, has both externally-facing and internally-facing dimensions for the profession. More generally, discussions about ethics relate directly to how we decide our engagement with others should be normatively regulated, what is acceptable behaviour and what should be sanctioned. As a promotional industry, public relations should regularly be asking questions about whether the ends it works towards (e.g. promotional success) justify the means used in campaigns (e.g. intrusion into our private spheres, co-optation of 'free labour', escalation of promotional communication), and to what extent negative effects might be mitigated or eliminated.

In this chapter I begin by considering what challenges exist to public relations' claims of acting ethically. Such claims are frequently made as a means of demonstrating professional status, but are extremely difficult to evidence. I then draw on the dialectical approach set out by Cheney et al. (2011) to discuss alternative ways of thinking about ethics in public relations. I propose a socio-cultural 'turn' in ethical thinking that draws on insights from the dialectical approach and permits the integration of ethical perspectives from outwith the public relations field. I conclude by arguing that a more in-depth and complex engagement with ethics as a constitutive element of communication would help us better understand public relations' role in society.

PUBLIC RELATIONS' ETHICAL CHALLENGES: PERSUASION, SELF-INTEREST, CONFLICTING PRIORITIES AND ORGANISATIONS

For any profession, engaging with ethics is an ontological necessity, essential for shoring up claims of professional morality. While the claim to be a profession brings status and financial rewards, it also imposes an obligation to take seriously responsibilities to society (Fitzpatrick and Gauthier, 2001; L'Etang, 2011; Fawkes, 2014b; see also Chapter 8). Industry debates about ethical behaviour respond to this obligation and are often linked to professional standards and societal expectations, while codes of practice provide guidance for practitioners in an effort to ensure compliance (Theaker, 2012; Kim and Ki, 2014). Being seen to act ethically also helps to secure trust, which has become an established part of public relations discourse. Practitioners are self-described 'trust strategists' (Bourne, 2013, 2015) and encourage trust in their clients as part of their efforts to build strong stakeholder relationships; acting unethically undermines the industry's claim to this important territory. Nonetheless, some aspects of practice are particularly challenging because they inevitably undermine ethical behaviour. These include persuasion, self-interest, the inevitability of conflicting priorities, and the fact that most public relations work is carried out for already powerful institutions.

PERSUASION

Fawkes (2010) has noted the reluctance of scholars to acknowledge persuasion as part of public relations, because it highlights the ways in which practitioners can help to perpetuate potential power asymmetries between organisations and their audiences. Persuasion is also closely associated with propaganda and manipulation, which suggests the desire to have power 'over' audiences rather than power 'with' them (Berger, 2005; Weaver et al., 2006). L'Etang (2006b) points out that in definitional terms, there is little to distinguish between public relations and propaganda, and the fact that meaning is co-created between organisations and audiences means that 'one person's public relations may be another person's propaganda' (2006b: 28). While practitioners may not be particularly worried by the fact that they persuade people every day through the language they use (Morris and Goldsworthy 2008), normative theoretical models of public relations idealise more equal distributions of power and leave little space for persuasion (Grunig, 2000, 2009; Fawkes, 2010; L'Etang, 2011).

SELF-INTEREST

Self-interest is central to public relations and clashes with claims to act in the public interest (L'Etang, 2006a). Most obviously, client self-interest is the reason why public relations services are employed in the first place. This does not mean that practitioners must only ever do what clients want them to do; their role as advisors and boundary spanners may allow them to persuade clients of alternative paths to realising their interests. However, it does require practitioners to retain an instrumental approach to communication – it is impossible for them to be completely altruistic. Self-interest also applies to the motivations of practitioners, who are encouraged to actively plan and manage their careers from an early stage – for example, through the integration of placements, networking opportunities and mentoring into public relations degree courses. Choices about what organisations to work for and what area of practice to specialise in are likely to be made – to a greater or lesser extent – with an eye to how that work might contribute to professional recognition and future success.

CONFLICTING PRIORITIES

Ethical challenges also arise from the fact that public relations practitioners must balance their own interests, client interests, the needs of the profession, the needs of audiences and the wider public, and the needs of non-human actors such as the environment, in the decisions they make about how, when and what to communicate (Parsons, 2004). These conflicts are exacerbated by the fact that public relations is a global industry, and the interests of global audiences divided by power asymmetries may be diametrically opposed (Munshi et al., 2011). There is no formula for choosing between these different priorities; in reality, outcomes are dependent on how individual practitioners interpret their situation, and some interests will have to be prioritised while others are ignored.

POWERFUL CLIENTS

Ironically, the links to powerful sectors on which public relations depends for its survival also threaten its credibility as an altruistic and ethically sound occupation. It is an activity most frequently deployed by corporate and government organisations, where socio-economic and political power are concentrated, and stands accused of shoring up their structural and discursive hegemony at the expense of other interests. Its role in the non-profit sector notwithstanding, this means it contributes to existing imbalances of communicative and material power (Moloney, 2006; Davis, 2013; Edwards, 2016b). More broadly, because public relations is inextricably linked to organisations, practitioners are embedded in organisational systems and processes and are implicated when organisations behave unethically (Jackall, 2010).[1]

These challenges are difficult to surmount because they are an inevitable aspect of doing public relations. They co-exist and interact to make ethical dilemmas in practice particularly complex. Perhaps because of this, practitioners and scholars have tended to view ethics as an adjunct to public relations practice, framing the topic objectively and deconstructing the occupational context into a series of characteristics that can be analysed for ethical purposes. Ethics then becomes a matter of practitioners making the right choices in certain situations (Baker and Martinson, 2001; Parsons, 2004; Meisenbach, 2006), or of 'owning' and mitigating the impact of less than desirable characteristics of their work (Messina, 2007; Fawkes, 2015). However, if we take a different starting point and accept that communication is 'a defining – rather than peripheral – feature of the human condition' (Mumby, 2011: 84), then communication is reframed *as action* (rather than a means to action) – and always has ethical dimensions. Consequently, because 'it is impossible to step outside the context of ethical considerations in our uses of symbols with one another' (Cheney et al., 2011: 1), ethics can be understood as intrinsic to *all* public relations work, and engaging with ethical questions is an integral part of research and practice.

ETHICAL DIALECTICS IN PUBLIC RELATIONS

Cheney et al. (2011) identify a number of dialectics that structure communication ethics. The theoretical–practical dialectic describes the ongoing disconnect between idealised theories and actual experience; relatedly, the academic–lay dialectic reflects the contrast between abstract conceptualisations and pragmatic implementations of ethics. Universal–particular and global–local dialectics engage with the potentially productive tension between universalising Western and masculine discourses about ethics, and resistance/reinterpretation of those discourses and assumptions in different contexts. Finally, the rational–emotional dialectic recognises the influence of the pervasive opposition between rationality and emotion on ethical thinking. As outlined below, theories of ethics and models of ethical decision-making dominate public relations and tend to promote academic, universalising and rational ways of thinking, while studies of ethics in practice (which are much less common) reveal the ways in which context, emotion and situated forms of knowledge combine with rationality to shape individuals' day-to-day choices.

THEORETICAL-PRACTICAL/ACADEMIC-LAY

The first two dialectics dominate discussions of ethics in public relations. Theoretical/academic dimensions are reflected in the presentation of ethics as a form of ideal behaviour described in abstract theories and models, and are implemented through the application of principles and rules. For example, consequentialist or teleological models of ethics underpin theories of public relations' advocacy role, justifying actions based on the principles that the ends (organisational benefits) justify the means, and that delivering benefits to the greatest number of people is the top priority (Fitzpatrick and Gauthier, 2001; Gregory, 2009). Non-consequentialist or deontological models of ethics focus on the duty to act in line with universal ethical principles and depend on rational analysis of the options available by autonomous individuals. This theory underlines the boundary spanner, relationship management and 'ethical conscience' theories of public relations, where practitioners facilitate a balanced, two-way conversation between organisations and their audiences and take on the role of corporate conscience (Bowen, 2008; Fawkes, 2012a; St. John and Pearson, 2016: 22). Both rhetorical and dialogic theories of communication have been presented as inherently ethical forms of public relations because of their emphasis on a genuine commitment to reasoned argumentation, shared communication power, mutual recognition and respect, a willingness to engage in dialogue and consultation, empathy, and a willingness to take risks as a result of the commitment to the relationship (Heath, 2001a; Kent and Taylor, 2002; Meisenbach and Feldner, 2009; Porter, 2010; Hyde, 2011).

Models developed to guide practitioner decision-making also reflect the theoretical and academic side of these two dialectics. For example, the Potter Box (Parsons, 2004) requires practitioners to ask a series of questions to identify an ethical issue and then adopt a planned approach to resolving it, incorporating problem definition, analysis of personal and professional values relevant to the situation, application of moral principles, and determination of where their loyalties should be placed. The TARES model is similar: practitioners arrive at an ethical decision by asking questions that assess truthfulness, authenticity, respect, equity and social responsibility (Baker and Martinson, 2001).

These theories and models of ethics stand in opposition to the practice/lay dimensions of the dialectics, which take a more pragmatic perspective of the problems and complexities at the public relations coalface. One important difference between the two schools of thought is that the inherently persuasive nature of public relations is recognised and accepted in practice/lay-driven discussions (Seib and Fitzpatrick, 1995; Gregory, 2009; Berg, 2012). Morris and Goldsworthy (2008: 185), for example, go so far as to argue that public relations 'should not claim to be anything other than partial' and to suggest otherwise would be a false claim to morality. Acknowledging the importance of persuasion introduces complex questions of how competing priorities and interests are balanced in day-to-day practice, and on what basis choices should be (and are) made (Fitzpatrick and Gauthier, 2001; Richards, 2004; Saldaña et al., 2016).

Fawkes (2010, 2014b) argues that practitioners and scholars must accept the 'shadow' of persuasion in public relations and actively engage with it as a valid aspect of public relations' professional identity, rather than designating it as bad practice. She advocates a professional journey characterised by self-examination, reflexivity and openness in order to arrive at a place where public relations' self-understanding and professional identity is more robust, based on 'wholeness' rather than denial (Fawkes, 2012b). In fact, qualitative studies engaging with practitioners' lived experience of doing public relations show that they already actively reflect on ethics. Practitioners and scholars raise uncomfortable issues about personal ethics, attitudes to power over media and audiences, the role of organisational hierarchies in public relations workplaces, and relationships with internal or external clients. They try to deal pragmatically with the difficulties and inconsistencies in applying ethical thinking as part of their normal practice, taking individual, organisational and societal considerations into account when evaluating their behaviour (Bowen, 2008; Place, 2015b; Tilley, 2015).

UNIVERSAL-PARTICULAR/GLOBAL-LOCAL

The theoretical models described above universalise specific ethical perspectives, and particularly those rooted in the Aristotelian and Platonic traditions. They break ethics down into different elements such as 'truth', 'authenticity' and 'respect' that are presumed to be universally understood, accepted and applicable in all circumstances (Parsons, 2004; Messina, 2007; Stoker and Stoker, 2012). They largely ignore the structural realities of the industry that create complexity in practice, including its global power, gendered hierarchies, competitive, profit-driven identity and the domination of corporate and government clients. Consequently, they fail to acknowledge difference and diversity either within the industry, as factors that affect practice, or outwith it, as factors that affect its impact on society and culture. While models of situational ethics are more pragmatic than the theories outlined above, prompting practitioners to consider personal, professional and client interests and values when considering different courses of action (Fitzpatrick and Gauthier, 2001; Parsons, 2004), they remain limited because the range of factors that practitioners consider are still driven by client and profession, rather than by public relations' role and influence in the wider world.

The particular/local dimensions of these dialectics are reflected in studies of practitioners' actual experiences of ethical decision-making, where universals are seen to break down because they can never be unequivocally defined. Such studies reveal the importance of tacit knowledge based on experience, rather than ethical formulae, to resolving ethical dilemmas (Bowen, 2004, 2008; Eschenfelder, 2011; Berg, 2012). They also show that not all public relations practitioners buy into the idea that ethics should be part of public relations' remit, or guide their actions (Morris and Goldsworthy, 2008). In Bowen's (2008) qualitative study of practitioners' attitudes towards the idea of being an 'ethical conscience', for example, some argued that doing the job they are contractually employed to do is the priority, while others regarded ethical counsel as essential to achieving a strong reputation and long-term stability. Managers may be more optimistic about their behaviour than less senior staff and espouse a more idealistic view, overlooking the 'grey' areas of practice that other colleagues recognise (Tilley, 2015). In the final analysis, whether practitioners have any power to influence the organisations and clients they work with is a permanently open question (Bowen, 2008).

These studies of ethics in context reveal the complicated logics of practice that give rise to local decision-making. However, they tend to focus on Western contexts and organisations, ignoring structures of geography, gender and client that shape the experiences they describe (but see Tilley, 2015). The almost complete lack of discussion of such structures in public relations' ethical scholarship means that, to find a counterpoint to the universalisation of Western perspectives, one has to consider work that is more broadly critical of public relations, highlighting the ways in which it marginalises audiences and interests from the global South, the gendered nature of public relations work, and its role as part of a broader neoliberal political economic system that increases, rather than shrinks, the gap between dominant and dominated groups (Dutta and Pal, 2005; Munshi and Kurian, 2005; Dutta and Pal, 2011; Waymer, 2012; Tindall and Waters, 2013; Vardeman-Winter et al., 2013). This work, which I discuss in more detail below, raises questions about the ethics of public relations' impact in different spaces and lives, and can also introduce new perspectives and 'readings' of public relations that inform a more open approach to ethical thinking (Ward and Wasserman, 2010).

RATIONAL-EMOTIONAL

Rationality saturates ethical thinking in public relations. The classic teleological and deontological approaches both depend on rational decision-making based on a set of criteria (a particular outcome, a measure of benefit, or the application of universal norms to a situation). Models such as TARES and the Potter Box are equally dependent on practitioners following a series of steps in a logical fashion, in order to reach the 'right' ethical outcome. Even when scholars try to bridge the distance between ideal models and actual practice, rationality tends to dominate. Messina (2007), for example, argues that ethical persuasion should be based on respect for the audience's capacity to reason and facilitate well-crafted decisions, while Fawkes's exhortation to actively reflect on the role of persuasion in practice suggests that rationality can be used to overcome the emotionally difficult association of persuasion with propaganda and bad practice. Applications of Habermasian discourse ethics also privilege rationality: Burkart (2007), for example, proposes a consensus-oriented model of public relations based on Habermas's Theory of Communicative Action, focused on developing rational consensus between organisations and audiences through a dialogic process of claim and counter-claim about the validity (intelligibility, truth, trustworthiness, legitimacy) of organisational statements. From a slightly different perspective, Meisenbach (2006) uses Habermas's Principle of Universalisation to propose a five-step process that can be used by organisations to develop normative validity for their claims in dialogue with audiences.

The emotional side of this dialectic does make an appearance in the form of virtue ethics, focused on the individual's ability to find intrinsic motivation in acting in the interests of others rather than themselves, and the ways in which individual virtue might scale up to a business-led form of morality (Harrison and Galloway, 2005; Wang et al., 2015). The desire to act virtuously develops through training and practice, but is not only rational; it is also driven by the pleasure derived from an emotional commitment to doing good. Ethical behaviour follows automatically, since a virtuous individual will always focus on the good of others when faced with a decision. Virtue ethics is, to a certain extent, reflective and reflexive: a virtuous person is open to learning from others, taking risks, discovering and acknowledging their own limitations. A related – albeit more rational – approach is moral reasoning, where the focus is on how practitioner decisions are shaped by their understanding of the moral dimensions of situations and decisions, as well as their commitment to moral actions (Cabot, 2005; Place, 2015b; Saldaña et al., 2016).

Seen through the lens of these dialectics, favouring theoretical/academic, universalising/global and rational approaches creates a very narrow arena for thinking about ethics in public relations, obscuring relational, emotional and communicative dimensions. Nor are the discussions particularly helpful for practitioners trying to navigate the ethical challenges noted above. They offer no guidance for dealing with a public lack of trust in the occupation, or for the fact that societal interests are regularly undermined by persuasion and self-interest, despite the latter being prominent features of practice.[2] They offer limited help to practitioners trying to navigate and prioritise conflicting interests, even though such conflicts are often precisely the reason why ethical dilemmas arise. They do not reflect the reality that organisational culture, professional codes, and societal norms, values and expectations all influence ethical decision-making alongside a practitioner's personal desires and demands, nor that fast-moving environments and crises invariably leave little time for ethical debates or recourse to ethical models (Bowen, 2008; St. John and Pearson, 2016). Finally, public relations' dependence on organisations and their behaviour means that at least some of its ethical reputation is out of its control, but models of ethics that depend on individual autonomy are unable to mitigate the impact of external parties, since they assume that the individual is fully empowered to decide the best course of action. The dialectical approach reveals these shortcomings and provides a valuable starting point for adopting an approach to ethics that is more socio-culturally informed.

A SOCIO-CULTURAL 'TURN' IN PUBLIC RELATIONS ETHICS: EXPANDING THE TERRAIN FOR DISCUSSION

The complexity of ethics in public relations notwithstanding, there is scope for addressing the shortcomings of existing ethical approaches by engaging with language, the currency of public relations, as a socio-cultural intervention. Language 'shapes discursive practices that, in turn, shape the form, content, and ways of knowing, feeling and valuing what happens' in the world (Buzzanell, 2011: 70). The socio-cultural approach to public relations acknowledges this constitutive role for language and also understands communication as integral to the construction of relations between different groups. Correspondingly, ethics must concern itself with 'how particular forms of subjectivity and agency are communicatively constructed and privileged over other forms' (Mumby, 2011: 88), and with the corresponding implications for the distribution of power between and within groups. This starting point means that ethics is always relevant to public relations, because all communication influences the production and circulation of power (McKie and Xifra, 2016) and public relations therefore has ethics imbricated in all its activities.

The changing shape of the industry is a second important starting point. Ward and Wasserman (2010) point out that, in the case of journalism, the advent of new media means that professional territory is increasingly blurred, and journalists themselves come under scrutiny more often, challenged to be more transparent about their identity and position (Singer, 2010). In public relations, similar dynamics apply: the contemporary division between 'audience' and 'practitioner' is fluid, with plenty of individuals instigating their own campaigns for causes they care about, while the integration of digital media into campaigns often leads to collaboration rather than separation (particularly in the case of viral or social media campaigns). This expands the theoretical arena for public relations ethics to include not only individual-, industry- and organisational-level practices, but also systemic issues that shape public relations' impact on society at a local, national and transnational level (Tilley, 2015).

CASE STUDY II.I

LEGITIMISING THE OLYMPICS: DEFENDING RIO 2016

In 2016, the build-up to the Olympic Games in Rio de Janeiro was marred by stories about the dangers of being bitten by mosquitoes carrying the Zika virus, the unstable

> political situation in Brazil, and the level of preparedness of the Olympic facilities. The International Olympic Committee's (IOC) decision to give the games to Rio was challenged by many, but the Communications Director, Mark Adams, said in response, 'What people really need to remember is that we are in a country in the middle of a serious political economic and political crisis but it's been worth it', and 'If the Olympic Games are about one thing it's about spreading these values around the world. It's worked in South America, so why not Africa next?' (Davies, 2016).
>
> The challenges to the IOC can be understand as an ethical dilemma for Mr Adams, namely, should he agree with the obvious fact that Rio had struggled to put on the games as it coped with its internal crises and that the IOC may have been hoping for too much when it gave the games to Rio, or should he remain loyal to the organisation and defend its identity and legitimacy? Mr Adams chose the latter – and in doing so, new ethical issues arise. To take the IOC's 'side' in the debate means minimising the real problems that the city was facing, and the fact that the games had necessarily diverted funds away from support for disenfranchised groups in Rio and elsewhere in the country. By arguing that the Olympics disseminate desirable 'values' and claiming this had 'worked' in South America, Mr Adams also maintains the subordinated position of developing nations (in South America and Africa) as being in need of development, cultural improvement or education from the West in order to do well. Thus, while Mr Adams may not have intended to reinforce the image of Rio and Brazil as a struggling developing nation, the way he interprets his communicative role inevitably leads to these ethically undesirable outcomes.

Habermasian and Foucauldian discourse ethics provide one route to engaging with a socio-cultural 'turn'. As noted above, from a pure Habermasian perspective, private interests will always distort public interests, and strategies such as those advocated by Burkart (2007) and Meisenbach (2006) are a way of shoring up, not sharing, power (Mumby, 2011). However, Habermas also emphasises the importance of dialogue and debate in communication, prompting an outward-looking, societal frame of reference for public relations that makes room for genuine engagement with audiences and causes located beyond the organisation (Habermas, 1984; Leeper, 1996).

A Foucauldian approach to discourse ethics is more critical, providing tools for exploring how public relations produces regimes of truth through the use of discourse, thereby reinforcing forms of structural and material power through the hegemonic dominance of certain ideologies, such as the ideology of the market (Motion and Leitch, 2007; Bourne, 2013). It also opens the way to exploring how practitioners themselves are governed by certain hegemonies to conform to the requirements of the occupational field (Place and Vardeman-Winter, 2013; Edwards, 2014a). At the same time, Foucault's understanding of power as both fluid and productive means that such regimes are always contested and open to change. Thus, 'public relations becomes a tool of social power and change for utilization by not only those who hold hegemonic power, but also those who seek to challenge and transform that power and reconfigure dominant perceptions of the public interest' (Weaver et al., 2006: 21).

Alongside these two frameworks, perspectives from outside public relations scholarship also have the capacity to expand the territory of ethical scholarship in the field, and rehabilitate some of the neglected areas of practice revealed by the dialectical approach. Below I briefly illustrate four options as starting points for future research.

COMMUNITARIAN ETHICS

Christians (2007) suggests in the context of journalism that communitarian approaches to ethics are an appropriate way of engaging with complex ethical questions, because they focus on the socially embedded and relational nature of ethical decision-making. Communitarian interpretations of public relations are well established, framing the industry in terms of its contribution to community cohesion and civil society through its ability to connect groups, organisations and individuals, building trust and social capital (Kruckeberg and Starck, 1988; Leeper, 2001; Sommerfeldt, 2013), and communitarian ethics fits well within this tradition. Stoker and Stoker (2012: 42), for example, position public relations practitioners as 'members of a human community in which communication in all its forms plays a critical role in human inquiry and development'. By framing practitioner identity in terms of communication beyond client or professional group, they extend the idea of how practitioners might be able to act ethically *in society* through communication, serving the public interest. Public relations that serves the public interest, they argue, will 'promote democratic processes of debate, discussion, and persuasion and encourage public inquiry through the truthful dissemination of facts and research' (2012: 40). Empirically, the suggestion of an absolute form of 'truth' is problematic, given that public relations can be used both for and against the interests of a wide range of publics and truth is therefore a matter of standpoint. However, the link to democracy is important and can be made more powerfully by asking how the deployment of public relations discourses in different contexts, as part of the 'process of human inquiry and development', might shape the quality and content of its contribution to democracy and public discussion (Edwards, 2016b).

FEMINIST ETHICS

Feminist ethics is another route to understanding public relations ethics in the context of human relationships, allowing for reflection on how public relations promotes or limits conditions for living a full and flourishing life. Koehn (1998: 5–9) outlines six principles for feminist ethics: recognition of the relational self; benevolent concern for the vulnerable;

the publicness of the private; the importance and value of difference; an emphasis on imaginative (rather than rational) discourse; and a focus on making a difference by changing the world (see also Buzzanell, 2011). This takes the discussion of public relations ethics into new terrain, where '[r]eciprocal care and understanding – rooted in human experience and not in formal consensus – are the basis on which moral discourse is possible' (Christians, 2007: 124). The inclusion of diverse voices means that ethical norms and values are constantly being (re)constructed, changing depending on the standpoint of people located in different times, spaces and places. The iterative reframing permits an ongoing contestation of power and means that, when perspectives converge to unseat normalised practices that privilege male identities, the focus on individual experience and voice can lead to interventions delivering structural change (Buzzanell, 2011).

Feminist ethics is applied rather than abstract: in public relations, pertinent issues include its contribution to the lives of women and other marginalised groups, as well as the ways in which those groups facilitate the power of dominant groups (including the public relations industry itself) through their presence or absence in public relations work (see, for example, Vardeman-Winter, 2011; Vardeman-Winter et al., 2013). The objective would be not simply to observe and analyse the 'other's' problems, but to engage actively and reflectively with interactions where public relations is implicated in both 'othering' and resistance (Lugones, 1991). Feminist ethics also prompts a turn towards a critical examination of norms and behaviours within the profession. Surma and Daymon (2013), for example, emphasise the need to reclaim an ethics of care as central to public relations practice, particularly for practitioners whose work lives are driven by neoliberal norms of market, competition and consumption. The imposition of a split between private and public lives, they argue, can create conflict between different ways of being and limit the ability of practitioners to live a full and satisfying life. An ethics of care would permit more reflection on the pressures that public relations work imposes, whether those pressures are justified and how they might be changed.

The challenges of ethical dilemmas in practice also come under scrutiny through a feminist lens: walking an ethical tightrope on a daily basis and facing situations where ethical advice is ignored can result in cynicism, self-limiting approaches to ethics (such as displacement of responsibility, or limiting the scope of ethical practice) and resignation to the sometimes impossible situations that result from multiple dependencies (Tilley, 2015). Rather than accepting these feelings as inevitable, an ethics of care would prompt a focus on how practitioners might be supported through such situations, so that 'the gap between happens and what is desired is lessened' (Buzzanell, 2011: 74). Thus, while the fundamental basis of feminist ethics is to address and eliminate gender hierarchies (Buzzanell, 2011), the incorporation of marginalised experiences and voices into ethical questions means that the approach can go beyond gendered issues (Jaggar, 1991), extending the range and depth of ethical challenges.

CASE STUDY II.2

BREWING UP A STORM? BREWDOG AND ITS 'TRANSGENDER' BEER

In 2015, Brewdog, a small international craft beer brewery based in Scotland, launched a crowdfunding campaign that featured humorous depictions of homeless and transgender people. The brewery was accused of making light of the situations of these marginalised groups and faced a lot of public anger from gay and transgender groups in the UK, expressed and circulated via social media. In response, Brewdog developed and launched 'No Label', the 'world's first transgender beer', made from a more diverse range of hops than is usually the case in brewing. All profits from the new beer were donated to charities supporting the LGBT community. The launch was designed to demonstrate that Brewdog had not intended to behave unethically and was committed to supporting diversity. However, while in some quarters it was received very positively, it was challenged by others. Some members of the transgender community objected to their identity being used as a brand, while others argued that the idea of 'no label' ignored the fact that binary representations of gender still structured the world – simply launching a new beer did not address this fundamental issue (and perhaps did more to support Brewdog's 'punk' identity than anything else). The case shows how the complex and difficult realities of life experienced by marginalised groups inevitably affect the way communication about and with them is interpreted – even when that communication is well-meaning. The diversity of experience and opinion within the transgender community and its supporters meant that Brewdog's beer was never going to receive a straightforward reception.

GLOBALISED ETHICS

Globalisation can also provide an impetus for more innovative ethical thinking in public relations. Ward (2005) argues that the global nature of the media today requires a different approach to ethical principles for journalism, a cosmopolitan approach that recognises the global dimensions of its professional responsibilities, values and social role. Journalists are understood to be part of the global human community, with corresponding obligations to humanity rather than only to their particular profession, culture or territory. Applied to public relations, Ward's perspective is a reminder that the networked, digital context for public relations work creates a constantly shifting environment, where the reach of campaigns can extend across the world and audiences come into contact with public relations work in many different public and private spaces. As a result, expectations of its contributions to public life will constantly evolve and ongoing discussions of public relations ethics are an inevitable, 'never-ending task of inventing and reinterpreting its moral framework' (Ward, 2005: 8).

From a critical postcolonial perspective, globalisation raises important and difficult questions about public relations' support for the exploitation and 'othering' of subaltern populations, through its role in generating the global discourses that support neocolonial structures of power that privilege the global West and North over the global South and East. Dealing adequately with the uncomfortable reality that public relations work has always contributed to the exploitation of marginalised and disenfranchised groups requires the industry to take responsibility for its historical and current lack of care in relation to these groups, and question its moral identity in the process. Engaging in discussion about the ethics of this 'shadow' of public relations (Fawkes, 2009) would have the important consequence of making some of the most invidious but ignored forms of the 'unseen power' of public relations visible (Cutlip, 1994). It would show how the unreflexive implementation of public relations can lead to the exploitation of hidden and silenced audiences (for example, by helping Union Carbide to avoid the human consequences of the fatal gas leak at its Bhopal subsidiary in 1984).[3] It could also help practitioners avoid the wrath of audiences when campaigns work against the public interest, as happened to global agency Bell Pottinger in 2017 when it was accused of running a social media campaign that stoked racial tensions in South Africa and distracted attention from corruption among the country's elites (see Cox, 2017).

A global postcolonial ethics would also recognise the importance of resistance, and challenge public relations to consider how its work facilitates resistance to power on the part of subaltern populations and activist groups (Dutta, 2011). Given that communication is constitutive of the human condition, public relations work should not be understood as playing a supporting role in the production of hegemonic power *and* resistance, but must instead be seen as fundamental to both, because of its ability to control both the construction and flow of knowledge, information, voice and discourse (Dutta-Bergman, 2005; Dutta and Pal, 2011; Munshi et al., 2011; Johnston, 2016). This opens up the possibility of imagining alternative, more equitable global futures that incorporate indigenous and marginalised voices into communication structures – as well as imagining how public relations work might enable such futures as part of its ethical practice (McKie and Munshi, 2007; Munshi and Kurian, 2016).

THE ETHICS OF PROMOTION

The socio-cultural turn also invites consideration of public relations' macro-level position as one of a number of promotional industries that shape markets and consumption (see Chapter 2). Paying attention to the promotional culture in which public relations thrives prompts ethical questions about the kind of world that we want to live in and public relations' role in constructing (or obstructing) it. Critics argue that the increasing 'personalisation' of marketing and the growth of promotional industries have created a world of 'promotional excess' (Moloney, 2006). Promotional logic has permeated public and private spaces to an unprecedented extent (Moor, 2007; Davis, 2013; Cronin, 2016), and public relations has played a significant role in the extension of this logic by constructing itself as a locus of (variously) reputation management, risk management, trust and engagement. The extensive use of digital, networked communication channels by practitioners means that we can no longer escape public relations campaigns. We are subjected to them in personal, as well as public, spaces (via mobile devices, tablets and pay TV, for example), and ethical thinking should address the consequences of this reality. In part, this means recognising that the technology underpinning digital channels itself plays a role in defining the power that public relations exerts, (re)shaping meaning through automated algorithms and platform architectures, and monopolising human and financial resources at the expense of other modes of communication (van Dijck, 2013; Collister, 2016). Fundamental questions can be posed about the desirability of promotional logic. Are we entitled to market-free spaces in our lives, and should or could the public relations industry work towards that reality? Should the industry worry at all about the degree to which it adds to – and profits from – the information and promotional saturation that we face, or the impact it has on our daily lives? And to what extent do unseen but sometimes uncontrollable digital architectures compromise the ability of public relations practitioners to promise ethical behaviour?

Focusing on public relations as promotion also invites questions about its role in the reproduction of inequalities in promotional cultures. Moloney (2006) points out that not all participants in markets have the same ability to use public relations, so information flows are inevitably distorted. This prompts important questions about how public relations resources are accessed, and whether the industry might promote a more equitable distribution of its tools in order to alleviate communicative inequality. Questions can be asked about what the overall balance should be between different public relations objectives (working towards a generalisable social good, or towards the enhancement of private interests, or both) and about the desirability of the public relations strategies used to achieve those objectives (puffery, exaggeration and deception, or evidence-based arguments and an openness to dialogue). Finally, a promotional perspective also raises questions about the production of subjectivities through public relations (see Chapter 1) and the resources available to consumers to navigate promotional work. Whether and how consumers choose to engage with public relations, the impact it has on their sense of identity, self-esteem and vision of possible futures, and how their responses in turn affect the ways in which public relations is – and could be – practised, could open the way to empowering audiences in discussions of public relations' ethical norms and values.

CONCLUSION

Mumby (2011: 94) notes that 'ethical questions arise precisely from exposure to the other – from the call of the other that affects me despite myself'. This openness is inherent to a socio-cultural 'turn' in thinking about public relations ethics, and would counter the closed and overly rational approach that currently dominates theory and practice. Ward and Wasserman (2010: 277) define closed ethics as a 'form of ethics discourse where the guidelines are primarily (or only) intended for a relative[ly] small group of people, and places substantial limits on meaningful nonmember participation in discussing, critiquing, and changing the guidelines'. In contrast, open ethics 'encourages a more open and participatory approach to the ethics discourse in question'. Adopting ethical thinking in order to demonstrate professionalism in public relations will inevitably prompt a closed approach to ethics because of its instrumental value to professional status. However, the increasingly permeable boundaries between audiences and organisations suggest that public relations ethics is no longer a matter only for formally recognised practitioners, but should be a focus for negotiation with those who are co-opted into or otherwise affected by public relations work.

Within the industry, this kind of socio-cultural 'turn' in ethical thinking in public relations would build on emerging research that recognises practitioners not only as loci of moral behaviour or influence, but also as individuals struggling with social and professional circumstances that have a visceral impact on their lives. Tilley (2015) shows how practitioners resist representations of public relations as unethical, but also feel trapped and frustrated by the constant struggle to demonstrate ethical responsibility as well as by the profession's denial of questionable practices. Because the system of global capitalism is so fundamental to public relations' survival, the parameters for ethical practice may seem non-negotiable and taken as given, with no arena for discussion or debate. These 'invisible-yet-material obstacles and limitations' to ethical practice are not insignificant, but are largely ignored by current ethical models in public relations, even those that take power into account. As Tilley (2015: 95) notes,

> we need to develop a far better and deeper understanding of the barriers and challenges that practitioners face ... including to what they are allowed to discuss. We need to more accurately diagnose the nature and sources of the feelings of anger and frustration before we can presume to offer a 'cure'.

Open, proactive and wide-ranging debates about the substance of ethics in public relations is more than justifiable and could be a transformative exercise. They are unlikely to eliminate bad practice, or to 'clean' up public relations so that its outcomes are always ethically sound. As noted in the introduction to this chapter, it may be impossible to arrive at a definitive version of 'public relations ethics', because there are so many ways to engage with ethics and all have a part to play in how public relations practices are assessed in different contexts. Nonetheless, if the ethics of public relations can be based on discussions that adopt a more inclusive approach to audiences, context, practice and lived experiences of public relations, it may result in a more widely accepted articulation of ethics to guide practice in complex local, national and transnational environments. By facilitating the integration of neglected realities of public relations into ethical discussions, a sociocultural 'turn' could also help practitioners navigate their way towards a more sustainable and personally satisfying balance between self-interest and social justice.

NOTES

1. From this perspective, the boundary spanner role for public relations (often held up as its most ethical role) is also its Achilles heel: because practitioners are supposed to be the communicative bridge between organisations and the outside world, if they do not reveal or combat unethical activities, then by definition they must either be incompetent (because they were unable to fulfil their communicative function effectively) or complicit (because they actively chose not to fulfil their communicative function). In either case, claims to ethical practice are compromised.
2. Harrison and Galloway (2005) point out that even a virtuous practitioner may make unethical decisions because of a passionate loyalty to their client.
3. The Bhopal disaster continues to be a fraught issue over 30 years after it happened. At least 15,000 people have died as a result of the gas leak in 1984 and the site remains toxic because it has never been fully cleaned up. Union Carbide's responsibility is contested (see http://www.bhopal.com/Bhopal-Plant-History-and-Ownership), and activists continue to demand that the site be cleaned up to stop the ongoing toxic effects of the gas leak damaging the health and lives of local communities (see https://www.bhopal.net).

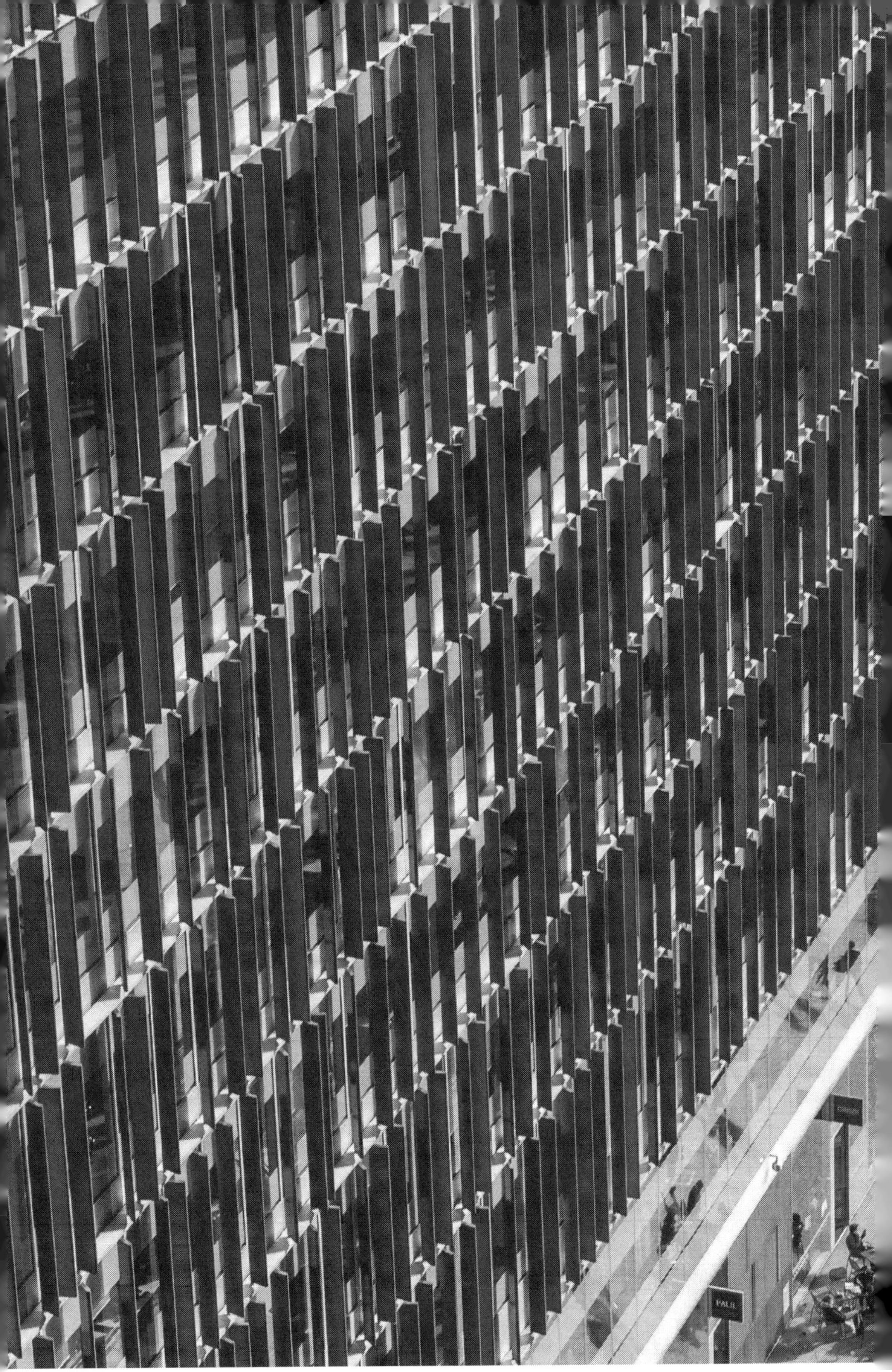
PAUL

CHAPTER 12

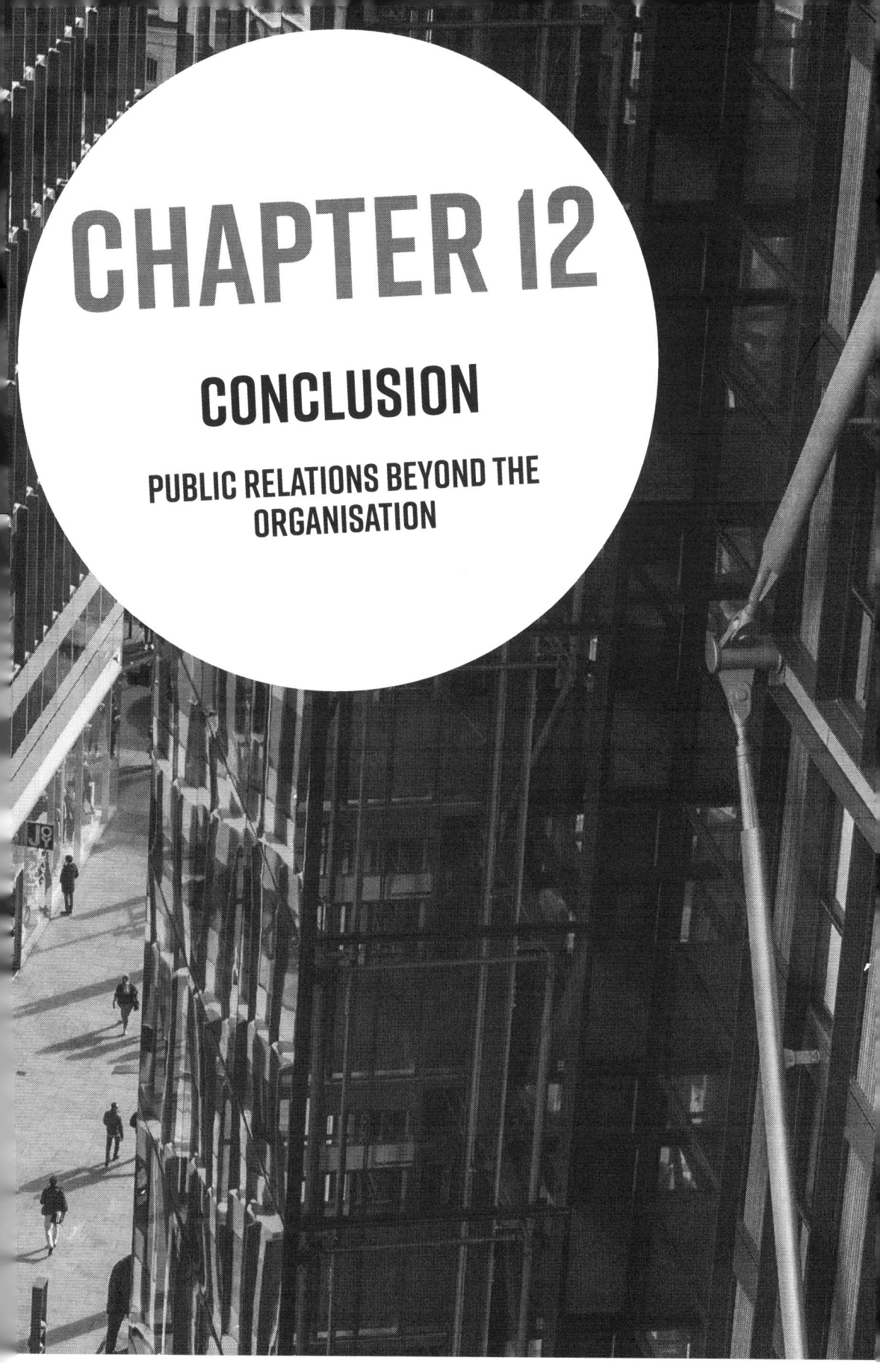

CONCLUSION

PUBLIC RELATIONS BEYOND THE ORGANISATION

Each of the previous chapters has illustrated how a socio-cultural approach to public relations might be implemented in relation to a range of topics. None of them provides an exhaustive prescription of how research should be conducted, but each throws light on alternative ways of thinking about public relations beyond the organisational context. To conclude, I return to the broader topic of the socio-cultural 'turn' in public relations to consider the opportunities and challenges for extending the approach. I begin by reflecting again on the characteristics of socio-cultural research as outlined in Chapter 1, and pointing out those areas where more work could be done to enhance the ways we think about public relations in society and culture. I then consider some of the global problems we could and perhaps should be addressing, before reflecting on the challenges we face if we try to engage with these problems through a sustainable socio-cultural agenda for scholarship.

MIND THE GAP...

Some of the characteristics of socio-cultural research in public relations that I outlined in Chapter 1 are more prevalent than others in current scholarship. To some extent, this reflects the 'habits of mind' we absorb as scholars, which orient us to research problems in particular ways (Edwards, 2012a). To break out of these patterns, we need to reflect on how our instinctive orientation has created an imbalance in focus, and what gaps exist as a result.

First, socio-cultural research is designed to reveal complexity and to question received knowledge about what public relations is and does. Foucauldian scholars have engaged very effectively in this way with public relations, for example by revealing how the discourses of practitioners and organisations are deeply ideological (see Chapter 3). Scholars arguing in favour of public relations' place as part of a 'fully functioning', healthy civil society also contribute to the picture of how public relations does not simply produce communication for organisations, but also intervenes in societal arrangements. In general, research in this area focuses on the visible parts of public relations work: what is said, the relationships that are built, the campaign materials that are distributed. It can also favour theory over practice, so that empirical studies applying the theoretical approaches being advocated remain relatively few.

However, complexity necessarily demands that we interrogate not only what is visible, but also what is hidden; in public relations practice, a good deal of work goes on out of sight of the public eye, and these activities merit investigation (Bourne, 2016; Demetrious, 2016). Public relations outputs are the tip of an iceberg of training, preparation and implicit and explicit knowledge, all of which can help reveal the ways in which public relations draws on and intentionally or unintentionally influences society and culture. At the same time, the questions we ask in our research projects can themselves hide aspects of public relations work by simply diverting attention away from them. Audience responses to campaigns are sorely under-researched, for example, despite the fact that their consumption of public relations work is fundamental to the ways that campaign meanings are constructed and circulate (see Chapter 2). The ideologically loaded use of data and digital platforms is also neglected, but has significant implications for the effects of public relations on our public and private lives (Collister, 2016).

Our sampling and methods can contribute to the invisibility of 'other' practitioners and their experiences (Pompper, 2012), as well as 'other' audiences who are subsumed in the notion of a standardised, categorised 'target' audience, or excluded from that privileged location yet still affected by public relations activities (Munshi, 2005; Vardeman-Winter et al., 2013; Place and Vardeman-Winter, 2016). Research sites tend to emphasise large, already influential corporate and government organisations, which can obscure the scale of public relations work that takes place elsewhere and the ways in which other kinds of organisations also shape the world in fundamental ways (Moloney and McKie, 2016). For example, alongside activist organisations and NGOs, transnational governance bodies such as the World Trade Organization, the International Monetary Fund, the United Nations, the European Union, the Asia-Pacific Economic Cooperation forum, and the Arab League all have enormous influence on global flows of capital, resources, communication and culture. Religious organisations such as the Catholic and Anglican Churches and national and international Muslim and Sikh councils communicate explicitly to intervene in moral issues and norms circulating in society and culture (see, for example, Tilson, 2006), while terrorist organisations are adept at using communication to shape people's thinking and adjusting their communication to achieve spectacular recognition, with horrific consequences (Somerville and Purcell, 2011). These kinds of organisations have received precious little attention from public relations scholars, despite their historical and contemporary influence.

The second characteristic noted in the introduction was that socio-cultural research recognises the mutual transformation of society, culture and public relations. Plenty of work has addressed one side of this equation by showing the impact of public relations on the ways we think about and engage with each other, as well as on resource flows and inequalities. However, much less scholarship has been published on the topic of public relations practitioners as reflexive subjects of their own work. Like other cultural intermediaries, they will either consciously take up or reject the meanings and norms that they communicate through campaigns, or simply absorb and respond to them as part of the naturally understood 'way of the world' (Hodges, 2011; see also Chapter 2). The ways in which these changes result in the profession as a whole adjusting to contemporary circumstances are also part of this reflexivity (Demetrious, 2016). While some work has focused on practitioners' experiences as professionals, the transformational dimension of their working lives has yet to be fully explored. Understanding it better would shed light on the differences between public relations in cultural contexts beyond

Western, developed countries. It could also illustrate more effectively the important role that individual practitioners play in shaping the final outcomes of practice, countering the scholarly tendency to subsume their day-to-day agency into the motivations and outputs of the organisations they work for.

The third characteristic of socio-cultural research relates to the focus on public relations as an agent of symbolic and material change in society and culture. The emphasis on discourse in socio-cultural research and the cultural-economic model of public relations have contributed to our understanding of symbolic change, but there is still a gap in empirical work examining the mechanisms through which these symbolic interventions alter the availability of material resources for different social groups at local, national and international levels. Critical approaches to globalisation and public relations, including postcolonial work, have begun to address the area (see, for example, Bardhan and Weaver, 2011b; Dutta, 2011), but they are often theoretical or text-based rather than empirical. The issue here is not to demonstrate a causal link between public relations and the allocation of resources, but to understand how the ways of thinking prompted by public relations work have concrete effects on the ways that resources circulate. How, for example, do beauty bloggers make young girls think about their identities and what decisions do they make about how to use their time, income and influence as a result of their exposure to the blogs? How do decisions about commissioning beauty bloggers in fashion campaigns take resources away from other outlets for communicating identity norms, and what effect might this have on the construction of those norms? And how do campaigns that normalise the notion of beauty as a parameter for self-realisation circulate across global networks to drive resource allocation on a transnational basis? Going beyond the texts of public relations to understand the material implications of meaning production is crucial if socio-cultural research on public relations is to speak to audiences beyond the academy.

The fourth and fifth characteristics noted in the introduction are intimately connected to each other and to the above discussion. Engaging with power is central to socio-cultural scholarship in public relations, and is most often realised by interrogating the role of dominant institutions in struggles over social, cultural and political transformations. However, research could address complex and varied forms of resistance to hegemony more consistently, by engaging with the intense and impactful communicative work done by non-profit organisations, community activists, subaltern populations, and sometimes practitioners themselves (Moloney and McKie, 2016). This work is as important in shaping dominance as the efforts of elites to influence us from 'above'. Yet hegemonic and activist campaigns are rarely analysed as *connected* campaigns or communication strategies; too often, they are situated in separate worlds (and separate studies), their interactions and mutually transformative effects overlooked. One remedy could be to make the emphasis on activist voices in postmodern, postcolonial and activist scholarship more central to research (Holtzhausen, 2012; Demetrious, 2013; Dutta, 2016), while the fluidity emphasised in studies of networked communication structures would highlight the relational aspect of communication and force an examination of interactions rather than unilateral activities (Schölzel and Nothhaft, 2016).

Finally, the methodological imperatives of socio-cultural research drive us to qualitative methods, but even in these contexts our standpoint too often remains that of the dispassionate academic observer or the embedded practitioner. Standpoint theory demands that we move, psychologically and sometimes physically, in order to truly understand the experiences of our participants. Displacing ourselves is essential, since to be displaced is to be *out of* place, which necessarily removes one from one's comfort zone and introduces uncertainty. This is no bad thing for researchers, who must guard against the constant threat of comfortable isolation and complacency in their work. Being out of place means we find ourselves in new spaces, where other people reside. We must find ways to share their lives, even if only for a short time, so that we can also share their standpoint and are able to hear, see and tell the experiences of our participants from their perspectives, not only our own (Mohanty, 1988; Munshi and Kurian, 2016).

With this in mind, there is room to pay more attention to the position of audiences and the lived experience of being subject to public relations work. We can also ask many more questions about the organisational actors who work with public relations practitioners and are subject to its effects through the prism of organisational practice. Senior managers who are coached to speak, engage, create relationships and adjust their behaviour in line with promotional imperatives are often assumed to be happy collaborators, but the lack of truly dialogic and collaborative approaches in public relations (Kent, 2013) suggests that giving up their power to the vagaries of communication may be more difficult than we think. Introducing greater reflexivity about how the questions we ask and the methods we choose actively *produce* the knowledge we publicise and circulate (Skeggs et al., 2008) would also make visible how our work constructs the lives of those we speak about and with. These are vitally important ethical considerations for researchers in the contemporary context, where there is an increasingly urgent need to actively engage with the world outside academia in order to meet global challenges (McKie and Munshi, 2007; McKie and Xifra, 2016).

SITES OF ENGAGEMENT

In Chapter 1, I outlined the kinds of topics that socio-cultural research engages with: questions of structural power, agency and identity, collective agreement and change. Each of the subsequent chapters has focused on a broad area that we can draw on to understand the relationship between society and culture. There are, of course, much more specific, urgent problems that socio-cultural research on public relations could, and perhaps should, address. A list of potential research areas would extend beyond the pages of this book, but here I briefly discuss three that have received relatively little attention in public relations research, yet constitute some of the most pressing issues in the contemporary conjuncture: the global refugee crisis, climate change and post-truth information ecologies.

The global refugee crisis is a human rights crisis of epidemic proportions (United Nations Refugee Agency, 2017). Refugees are often particularly visible when they come from a major event such as the war in Syria, or large-scale climate events such as drought leading to famine. However, a large proportion of forced movement is also within-country and much of this receives far less public attention. Regardless of the reason, millions of displaced persons and refugees often end up in camps for years rather than months or weeks, while those who are able to move face unimaginable risks before they get to safety. The burden of housing refugees has been left to low- and middle-income countries, while the developed world concentrates on maintaining borders and increasing security (Shetty, 2016). In developed countries, discourses about migration, disseminated by the different actors involved (NGOs, national governments, global governance bodies), help to construct the refugee crisis for Western eyes. They highlight the humanitarian problem but also frame refugees as an implicit threat to national security and integrity; issues of acceptance or refusal of refugees are often the main topic of public discussions, while human rights and the legal and humanitarian responsibilities of host countries are rarely front and centre of debates (Philo et al., 2013; Johnston, 2016). Moreover, public discourse can privilege some refugees (often from high-profile conflicts rather than within-country, or climate refugees) over others (Georgetown University, 2015), potentially generating better public knowledge and acceptance about the plight of some groups and making it harder for others to argue their case for acceptance.

Public relations practitioners are at the heart of this discourse production, creating and contributing to the flow of the discussion through their organisational roles. As yet, however, the role of public relations in constructing these discourses has received little attention (but see Johnston, 2016; Surma, 2016) and there is an urgent need to explore how public relations work helps to frame the crisis, how it contributes to the social and cultural climate in which migrant individuals and families are welcomed (or not), how it affects the erasure of some populations and issues in favour of others, and what the material consequences are for the distribution of resources, access to safety and provision of human rights for those most in need.

Climate change, too, is an urgent global problem that has long received attention but on which action has been remarkably slow. It constitutes an immediate existential threat to populations in the global South, while it demands significant changes to the ways that people in developed (and generally safer) countries live and work. It represents fertile ground for public relations practitioners to help change attitudes and behaviour in ways that will improve the situation, and many organisations have used communication to do just that. However, while the science of climate change is unequivocal, debates about causes and effects continue, partly as a result of powerful corporates intent on protecting their investment in technologies and industries that damage the planet, and on using communication to undermine arguments in favour of change (Dunlap and McCright, 2011). The scale of their interference is significant and there is room for much more research in the area focused on how the public relations industries are complicit in the production of doubt and delay in the debate (Roper et al., 2016).

Given that public relations is not only the province of the powerful (Moloney and McKie, 2016), we also need to pay attention to the workings of communication by activists, scientists, NGOs and governments, to avoid further reifying the position of dominant groups by devoting our attention only to critiquing their actions. Moreover, while discursive analyses are essential, the importance to our survival of material changes in the ways we manage and use resources is self-evident. It is vital to understand the consequences of climate change debates for resource allocation, not only for populations in developed countries, but also for those in the global South whose lives are already disrupted and sometimes destroyed by climate events (Munshi and Kurian, 2005). Research should therefore also attend to the conditions under which discourses and climate change information produced by public relations campaigns can prompt agency and change at institutional, organisational and individual levels.

Finally, the advent of a post-truth information environment is particularly challenging for public relations because it has the potential to undermine the positive impact that the profession could have on society and culture. In a fragmented information ecology, if sources can no longer be relied upon for their integrity, the danger exists that audiences become eternal sceptics, and persuading them of anything becomes a fragile endeavour. Critics of public relations might argue that this is a good thing, but in fact without the capacity to communicate effectively, our ability to reach agreement about collective living, our capacity to make decisions about our lives and minimise the risks associated with those decisions, and our ability to challenge the limitations imposed on us by others, all become impossible. That said, in the context of a promotional industry the notion of truth is problematic; audiences are there to be persuaded, public relations has long been in the business of producing fake news on behalf of organisations, and as such it is complicit in the creation of a post-truth environment.

A post-truth research agenda might interrogate the impact of the idea of post-truth on current public relations practice, including how practitioners engage with the idea of truth, where their own boundaries lie in terms of full truths, half truths or partial truths, and what ethical considerations arise when considering how 'truthful' one should be. Reflexivity is also required, through historical analyses of how the notion of truth has been adjusted and adapted for the purposes of promotion, how the production of fake news at scale has contributed to public relations' success as an industry and supported the global expansion of some agencies, and how individual practitioners have dealt with the ethical implications of being 'truthful' or not in relation to different audiences, as compared to how they operate now.

PRACTICAL CHALLENGES

While some 'habits of mind' have no doubt dictated our research topics and contributed to the gaps that currently exist, we also face real challenges to expanding and developing our work. Perhaps the most obvious factor to those of us working in this area is that there are relatively few critical and socio-cultural scholars in the field – certainly less than 100 at the time of writing – and doctoral candidates also remain thin on the ground. While the group is growing slowly, there is only so much that this number of scholars can achieve. More generally, the demands of socio-cultural research and writing are significant because they require us to be interdisciplinary, to reach across scholarly boundaries to inform our work and engage deeply with other disciplines in order to think differently about public relations. This requires time and effort that can be in scarce supply. It also has personal consequences: we are likely to publish less, what we do publish may be harder to place, and we may end up marginalised in departments where functional work dominates.

A second significant challenge relates to the methodologies required to complete the picture we are trying to build, which are difficult to pursue. More often than not they require us to go onsite, conduct ethnographic work and spend time trying to understand practice 'at the coalface'. We need to engage with audiences, spending time unpicking their experience of public relations in the context of their daily lives. In the current academic environment, the time and money required to conduct such studies is necessarily limited. Moreover, if we are to have any hope of de-Westernising public relations, the sites of our research have to go beyond our own locales, to where subaltern populations live, experience and create communication (Dutta, 2016). This may mean visiting another part of our city, but it should also involve travelling to other countries and experiencing other cultures, so that we are able to see the world of public relations and promotional discourse through eyes other than our own (Mohanty, 1988). Just as urgent is the fact that methods appropriate to the changing social and cultural context require us to upskill. We need to at least understand digital methods, network analyses and algorithmic logic, and preferably know how to apply analytical tools, because these infrastructures are now fundamental to practice (Collister, 2016).

These challenges notwithstanding, continuing to change the way we work in order to improve the scope and strength of this area of public relations research remains essential. Borrowing from Munshi and Kurian (2015), we might think of ourselves as being in pursuit of sustainable citizenship within the academy, where we demonstrate 'an ethical commitment to long-term holistic sustainability grounded in social justice that explicitly recognises and addresses power differentials and marginality' (Munshi and Kurian, 2015: 154). This requires that we take a political stance towards our own research, but also recognise research itself as a political endeavour, with the capacity to empower some (including ourselves) and marginalise others. Socio-cultural research in public relations can then be thought of as resistance, voice and empowerment. Focused in the right way, it has the capacity to change the world around us, as well as altering the foundations of the field in which we work.

REFERENCES

Abbott, A. (1988) *The System of Professions: An Essay on the Division of Expert Labor*. Chicago, IL: University of Chicago Press.

Acker, J. (2006) Inequality regimes: Gender, class and race in organizations. *Gender & Society*, 20, 441–64.

Ackroyd, S. (1996) Organization contra organizations: Professions and organizational change in the United Kingdom. *Organization Studies*, 17, 599–621.

Adams, T. (2015) Sociology of professions: International divergences and research directions. *Work, Employment and Society*, 29, 154–65.

Adbrands (2016) The top marketing groups worldwide. http://www.adbrands.net/agencies_index.htm [accessed 26 September 2016].

AFAQS (2017) How Procter & Gamble India touched the pickle, hearts and lives. Mumbai: AFAQS! http://www.afaqs.com/news/story/44803_How-Procter--Gamble-India-touched-the-pickle-hearts-and-lives [accessed 16 June 2017].

Ahmed, S. (2000) *Strange Encounters: Embodied Others in Postcoloniality*. London: Routledge.

Ahmed, S. (2006) *Queer Phenomenology: Orientations, Objects, Others*. Durham, NC: Duke University Press.

Ahmed, S. (2007) A phenomenology of whiteness. *Feminist Theory*, 8, 149–68.

Aldoory, L. (2003) The empowerment of feminist scholarship in public relations and the building of a feminist paradigm. *Communication Yearbook*, 27, 221–55.

Aldoory, L. (2005) A (re)conceived feminist paradigm for public relations: A case for substantial improvement. *Journal of Communication*, 55, 668–84.

Aldoory, L. and Toth, E. (2002) Gender discrepancies in a gendered profession: A developing theory for public relations. *Journal of Public Relations Research*, 14, 103–26.

Aldridge, M. and Evetts, J. (2003) Rethinking the concept of professionalism: The case of journalism. *British Journal of Sociology*, 54, 547–64.

Allcott, H. and Gentzkow, M. (2017) Social media and fake news in the 2016 election. *Journal of Economic Perspectives*, 31, 211–36.

Alvesson, M. (1994) Talking in organizations: Managing identity and impressions in an advertising agency. *Organization Studies*, 15, 535–63.

References

Alvesson, M. and Johansson, A.W. (2002) Professionalism and politics in management consultancy work. In T. Clark and R. Fincham (eds), *Critical Consulting: New Perspectives on the Management Advice Industry*. Oxford: Blackwell.

Amoore, L. (2009) Algorithmic war: Everyday geographies of the war on terror. *Antipode*, 41, 49–69.

Anderson-Gough, F., Grey, C. and Robson, K. (1998) Work hard, play hard: An analysis of organizational cliche in two accountancy practices. *Organization*, 5, 565–92.

Anderson-Gough, F., Grey, C. and Robson, K. (2000) In the name of the client: The service ethic in two professional services firms. *Human Relations*, 53, 1151–74.

Anderson-Gough, F., Grey, C. and Robson, K. (2006) Professionals, networking and the networked professional. *Research in the Sociology of Organizations*, 24, 231–56.

Andrejevic, M. (2002) The work of being watched. *Critical Studies in Media Communication*, 19, 230–48.

Andrejevic, M. (2009) The work of being watched: Interactive media and the exploitation of self-disclosure. In J. Turow and M.P. McAllister (eds), *The Advertising and Consumer Culture Reader*. New York: Routledge.

Andrews, M., Van Leeuwen, M. and Van Baaren, R. (2013) *Hidden Persuasion: 33 Psychological Influence Techniques in Advertising*. Amsterdam: BIS Publishers.

Anduiza, E., Cristancho, C. and Sabucedo, J. (2014) Mobilization through online social networks: The political protest of the indignados in Spain. *Information, Communication & Society*, 17, 750–64.

Anthias, F. (2001) The concept of 'social division' and theorising social stratification: Looking at ethnicity and class. *Sociology*, 35, 835–54.

Anthias, F. (2013) Intersectional what? Social divisions, intersectionality and levels of analysis. *Ethnicities*, 13, 3–19.

Anthony, S. (2012) *Public Relations and the Making of Modern Britain: Stephen Tallents and the Birth of a Progressive Media Profession*. Manchester: Manchester University Press.

Appadurai, A. (1990) Disjuncture and difference in the global cultural economy. *Theory, Culture & Society*, 7, 295–310.

Appadurai, A. (1996) *Modernity at Large: Cultural Dimensions of Globalization*. Minneapolis, MN: University of Minnesota Press.

Appelbaum, L., Walton, F. and Southerland, E. (2015) An examination of factors affecting the success of under-represented groups in the public relations profession. http://www.prsafoundation.org/wp-content/uploads/2015/10/CCNY-Diversity-Study-FINAL.pdf [accessed 16 October 2017].

Aronczyk, M. (2013a) Market(ing) activism: Lush cosmetics, ethical oil, and the self-mediation of protest. *JOMEC Journal*, 4, 1–21.

Aronczyk, M. (2013b). The transnational promotional class and the circulation of value(s). In M.P. McAllister and E. West (eds), *The Routledge Companion to Advertising and Promotional Culture*. New York: Routledge.

Aronczyk, M. (2015) Understanding the impact of the transnational promotional class on political communication. *International Journal of Communication*, 9, 2007–26.

Aronczyk, M., Edwards, L. and Kantola, A. (2017) Apprehending public relations as a promotional industry. *Public Relations Inquiry*, 6, 139–55.

Arthur W. Page Society (2007) *The authentic enterprise: Relationships, values and the evolution of corporate communications*. New York: Arthur W. Page Society.

Arvidsson, A. (2005) Brands: A critical perspective. *Journal of Consumer Culture*, 5, 235–58.

Arvidsson, A. (2006) *Brands: Meaning and Value in Media Culture*. London: Routledge.

Asen, R. and Brouwer, D. (eds) (2001) *Counterpublics and the State*. New York: SUNY Press.

Ashcraft, K. (2007) Appreciating the 'work' of discourse: Occupational identity and difference as organizing mechanisms in the case of commercial airline pilots. *Discourse & Communication*, 1, 9–36.

Ashcraft, K., Muhr, S., Rennstam, J. and Sullivan, K. (2012) Professionalization as a branding activity: Occupational identity and the dialectic of inclusivity-exclusivity. *Gender, Work and Organization*, 19, 467–88.

Ashra, N. (2014) Non-government organisations and pressure groups. In R. Tench and L. Yeomans (eds), *Exploring Public Relations*. Harlow: Pearson Education.

Asia-Pacific Association of Communication Directors (2016) Who we are. Hong Kong: Asia-Pacific Association of Communication Directors. http://www.apacd.com/who-we-are [accessed 9 September 2016].

Atewologun, D. and Singh, V. (2010) Challenging ethnic and gender identities: An exploration of UK black professionals' identity construction. *Equality, Diversity and Inclusion: An International Journal*, 29, 332–47.

Atkinson, P. (1983) The reproduction of professional community. In R. Dingwall and P. Lewis (eds), *The Sociology of the Professions*. London: Macmillan.

Auger, G. (2013) Fostering democracy through social media. *Public Relations Review*, 39, 369–76.

Bächtiger, A., Niemeyer, S., Neblo, M., Steiner, J. and Marco, R.S. (2010) Disentangling diversity in deliberative democracy: Competing theories, their blind-spots, and complementarities. *Journal of Political Philosophy*, 18, 32–63.

Baker, S. and Martinson, D.L. (2001) The TARES test: Five principles for ethical persuasion. *Journal of Mass Media Ethics*, 16, 148–75.

Banet-Weiser, S. (2012) 'Free self-esteem tools?' Brand culture, gender and the Dove Real Beauty campaign. In R. Mukherjee and S. Banet-Weiser (eds), *Commodity Activism*. New York: New York University Press.

Barber, B. (2007) *Consumed: How Markets Corrupt Children, Infantilize Adults and Swallow Citizens Whole*. New York: Norton.

Barberá, P., Jost, J., Nagler, J., Tucker, J. and Bonneau, R. (2015) Tweeting from left to right: Is online political communication more than an echo chamber? *Psychological Science*, 26, 1531–42.

Bardhan, N. (2003) Rupturing public relations metanarratives: The example of India. *Journal of Public Relations Research*, 15, 225–48.

Bardhan, N. (2011) Culture, communication and third culture building in public relations within global flux. In N. Bardhan and C.K. Weaver (eds), *Public Relations in Global Cultural Contexts: Multi-paradigmatic Perspectives*. New York: Routledge.

Bardhan, N. and Weaver, C. K. (eds) (2011a) Introduction: Public relations in global cultural contexts. In N. Bardhan and C.K. Weaver (eds), *Public Relations in Global Cultural Contexts: Multi-paradigmatic Perspectives*. New York: Routledge.

Bardhan, N. and Weaver, C. K. (eds) (2011b) *Public Relations in Global Cultural Contexts: Multi-paradigmatic Perspectives*. New York: Routledge.

Barnes, S.J. and Scornavacca, E. (2004) Mobile marketing: The role of permission and acceptance. *International Journal of Mobile Communications*, 2(2), 128–39.

Bassett, C. (2013) Feminism, expertise and the computational turn. In H. Thornham and E. Weissman (eds), *Renewing Feminisms: Radical Narratives, Fantasies and Futures in Media Studies*. London: IB Tauris.

Bauman, Z. (1998) *Globalization: The Human Consequences*. Cambridge: Polity Press.

Beal, F. (1970) Double jeopardy: To be Black and female. In R. Morgan (ed.), *Sisterhood is Powerful: An Anthology of Writings from the Women's Liberation Movement*. New York: Random House.

Beck, U., Giddens, A. and Lash, S. (1994) *Reflexive Modernisation: Politics, Tradition and Aesthetics in the Modern Social Order*. Cambridge: Polity Press.

Beck, U., Bonns, W. and Lau, C. (2003) The theory of reflexive modernization: Problematic, hypotheses and research programme. *Theory, Culture & Society*, 20, 1–33.

Becker, L., Lauf, E. and Lowrey, W. (1999) Differential employment rates in the journalism and mass communication labor force based on gender, race and ethnicity: Exploring the impact of affirmative action. *Journalism & Mass Communication Quarterly*, 76, 631–45.

Benería, L., Berik, G. and Floro, M. (eds) (2016) *Gender, Development, and Globalization: Economics as if All People Mattered*. New York: Routledge.

Benhabib, S. (2004) *The Rights of Others: Aliens, Residents and Citizens*. Cambridge: Cambridge University Press.

Benkler, Y. (2006) *The Wealth of Networks: How Social Production Transforms Markets and Freedom*. New Haven, CT: Yale University Press.

Bennett, W.L. and Manheim, J. (2006) The one step flow of communication. *The Annals of the American Academy of Political and Social Science*, 608, 213–32.

Bentele, G. and Wehmeier, S. (2003) From literary bureaus to a modern profession: The development and current structure of public relations in Germany. In K. Sriramesh and D. Verčič (eds), *The Global Public Relations Handbook: Theory, Research and Practice*. Mahwah, NJ: Lawrence Erlbaum.

Berg, K. (2012) The ethics of lobbying: Testing an ethical framework for advocacy in public relations. *Journal of Mass Media Ethics*, 27, 97–114.

Berger, B.K. (2005) Power over, power with, and power to relations: Critical reflections on public relations, the dominant coalition, and activism. *Journal of Public Relations Research*, 17, 5–28.

Bernays, E. (2005 [1928]) *Propaganda*. New York: Ig Publishing.

Berryman, R. and Kavka, M. (2017) 'I guess a lot of people see me as a big sister or a friend': The role of intimacy in the celebrification of beauty vloggers. *Journal of Gender Studies*, 26, 307–20.

Bévort, F. and Suddaby, R. (2016) Scripting professional identities: How individuals make sense of contradictory institutional logics. *Journal of Professions and Organization*, 3, 17–38.

Binkley, S. (2008) Liquid consumption: Anti-consumerism and the fetishized de-fetishization of commodities. *Cultural Studies*, 22, 599–623.

Birchall, C. and Coleman, S. (2015) Creating spaces for online deliberation. In S. Coleman and D. Freelon (eds), *Handbook of Digital Politics*. Cheltenham: Edward Elgar.

Blumler, J. and Gurevitch, M. (1995) *The Crisis of Civic Communication*. Abingdon: Routledge.

Blum-Ross, A. and Livingstone, S. (2017) 'Sharenting,' parent blogging, and the boundaries of the digital self. *Popular Communication: The International Journal of Media and Culture*, 15, 110–25.

Bohman, J. (2000) The division of labor in democratic discourse: Media, experts, and deliberative democracy. In S. Chambers and A. Costain (eds), *Deliberation, Democracy and the Media*. Lanham, MD: Rowman & Littlefield.

Bohman, J. (2004) Expanding dialogue: The Internet, the public sphere and prospects for transnational democracy. *Sociological Review*, 52, 131–55.

Bohman, J. (2012) Representation in the deliberative system. In J. Parkinson and J. Mansbridge (eds), *Deliberative Systems: Deliberative Democracy at the Large Scale*. Cambridge: Cambridge University Press.

Boltanski, L. and Chiapello, E. (2005) *The New Spirit of Capitalism*. London: Verso.

Boltanski, L. and Thévenot, L. (2006 [1991]) *On Justification: Economies of Worth*. Princeton, NJ: Princeton University Press.

Bolton, P. (2015) Grammar school statistics. Briefing paper number 1398. London: House of Commons Library.

Bolton, S. and Muzio, D. (2007) Can't live with 'em; can't live without 'em: Gendered segmentation in the legal profession. *Sociology*, 41, 47–64.

Bonilla-Silva, E. (2010) *Racism without Racists: Color-blind Racism and Racial Inequality in Contemporary America*. Lanham, MD: Rowman & Littlefield.

Boucher, G. (2006) The politics of performativity: A critique of Judith Butler. *Parrhesia*, 1, 112–41.

Bourdieu, P. (1984) *Distinction: A Social Critique of the Judgement of Taste*. London: Routledge & Kegan Paul.

Bourdieu, P. (1990) *The Logic of Practice*. Cambridge: Polity Press.

Bourdieu, P. (1991) *Language and Symbolic Power*. Cambridge: Polity Press.

Bourdieu, P. (1992) *The Field of Cultural Production: Essays in Art and Literature*. Cambridge: Polity Press.

Bourdieu, P. (2000). *Pascalian Meditations*. Stanford, CA: Stanford University Press/ Polity Press.

Bourdieu, P. (2005) *The Social Structures of the Economy*. Cambridge: Polity Press.

Bourne, C. (2013) Reframing trust, power and public relations in global financial discourses: Experts and the production of mistrust in life insurance. *Public Relations Inquiry*, 2, 51–77.

Bourne, C. (2015) Thought leadership as a trust strategy in global markets: Goldman Sachs' promotion of the 'BRICs' in the marketplace of ideas. *Journal of Public Relations Research*, 27, 322–36.

Bourne, C. (2016) Extending PR's critical conversations with advertising and marketing. In J. L'Etang, D. McKie, N. Snow and J. Xifra (eds), *The Routledge Handbook of Critical Public Relations*. London: Routledge.

Bourne, C. (2017). *Trust, Power and Public Relations in Financial Markets*. Abingdon: Routledge.

Bourne, C. and Edwards, L. (2012) Producing trust, knowledge and expertise in financial markets: The global hedge fund industry 're-presents' itself. *Culture and Organisation*, 18, 107–22.

Bowen, S. (2003) 'I thought it would be more glamorous': Preconceptions and misconceptions among students in the public relations principles course. *Public Relations Review*, 29, 199–214.

Bowen, S. (2004) Expansion of ethics as the tenth generic principle of public relations excellence: A Kantian theory and model for managing ethical issues. *Journal of Public Relations Research*, 16, 65–92.

Bowen, S. (2008) A state of neglect: Public relations as 'corporate conscience' or ethics counsel. *Journal of Public Relations Research*, 20, 271–96.

Boyd, J. (2012) The corporation-as-middle-class-person: Corporate social responsibility and class. In D. Waymer (ed.), *Culture, Social Class, and Race in Public Relations: Perspectives and Applications*. Lanham, MD: Lexington.

Brah, A. (1994) 'Race' and 'culture' in the gendering of labour markets: South Asian young Muslim women and the labour market. In H. Afshar and M. Maynard (eds), *The Dynamics of Race and Gender: Some Feminist Interventions*. London: Taylor & Francis.

Breese, E.B. (2011) Mapping the variety of public spheres. *Communication Theory*, 21, 130–49.

Brock, D. and Saks, M. (2016) Professions and organizations: A European perspective. *European Management Journal*, 34, 1–6.

Brogan, P. (1992) *The Torturer's Lobby: How Human Rights-abusing Nations Are Represented in Washington*. Washington, DC: Center for Public Integrity.

Broom, G.M. and Dozier, D.M. (1986) Advancement for public relations role models. *Public Relations Review*, 12, 37–56.

Brown, A. (2015) *The changing categories the U.S. has used to measure race*. Washington, DC: Pew Research Center.

Bruce, S. (2017) PR professionals' skills and competencies not fit for modern future proof public relations. *Influence*, 8 March. London: Chartered Institute of Public Relations. www.influence.cipr.co.uk/2017/03/08 [accessed 19 July 2017].

Bull, A. (2010) *Multimedia Journalism: A Practical Guide*. Abingdon: Routledge.

Burkart, R. (2007) On Jürgen Habermas and public relations. *Public Relations Review*, 33, 249–54.

Butler, J. (1988) Performative acts and gender constitution: An essay in phenomenology and feminist theory. *Theatre Journal*, 40, 519–31.

Butler, J. (1990) *Gender Trouble: Feminism and the Subversion of Identity*. New York: Routledge.

Butler, J. (1993) *Bodies that Matter: On the Discursive Limits of Sex*. New York: Routledge.

Buzzanell, P. (2011) Feminist discursive ethics. In G. Cheney, S. May and D. Munshi (eds), *The Handbook of Communication Ethics*. New York: Routledge.

Byerly, C. and Ross, K. (2006) *Women & Media: A Critical Introduction*. Malden, MA: Blackwell.

Cabot, M. (2005) Moral development and PR ethics. *Journal of Mass Media Ethics*, 20, 321–32.

Calhoun, C. (1992) Introduction: Habermas and the public sphere. In C. Calhoun (ed.), *Habermas and the Public Sphere*. Cambridge, MA: MIT Press.

Callon, M. (1986) Some elements of a sociology of translation: Domestication of the scallops and the fishermen of St. Brieuc Bay. In J. Law (ed.), *Power, Action and Belief. A New Sociology of Knowledge?* London: Routledge & Kegan Paul.

Cammaerts, B. and Van Audenhove, L. (2005) Online political debate, unbounded citizenship, and the problematic nature of a transnational public sphere. *Political Communication*, 22, 147–62.

Carastathis, A. (2008) The invisibility of privilege: A critique of intersectional models of identity. *Les Ateliers de l'Ethique*, 3, 23–38.

Carbado, D. and Gulati, M. (2013) *Acting White: Rethinking Race in Post-racial America*. New York: Oxford University Press.

Carroll, A.B. (2008) A history of corporate social responsibility: Concepts and practices. In A. Crane, D. Matten, A. McWilliams, J. Moon and D. Siegel (eds), *The Oxford Handbook of Corporate Social Responsibility*. New York: Oxford University Press.

Carruthers, S. (1995) *Winning Hearts and Minds: British Governments, the Media and Colonial Counter-insurgency 1944–1960*. London: Leicester University Press.

Castells, M. (2000) *The Rise of the Networked Society*. Oxford: Blackwell.

Castells, M. (2009) *Communication Power*. Oxford: Oxford University Press.

Castells, M. (2012) *Networks of Outrage and Hope: Social Movements in the Internet Age*. Cambridge: Polity Press.

Castilla, E. (2008) Gender, race, and meritocracy in organizational careers. *American Journal of Sociology* 113, 1479–1526.

Chambers, S. (2009) Rhetoric and the public sphere: Has deliberative democracy abandoned mass democracy? *Political Theory*, 37, 323–50.

Chambers, S. (2012) Deliberation and mass democracy. In J. Parkinson and J. Mansbridge (eds), *Deliberative Systems: Deliberative Democracy at the Large Scale*. Cambridge: Cambridge University Press.

Channel 4 (2016) C4 launches major campaign for Rio Paralympics: We're The Superhumans. News release, 14 July. London: Channel 4 Television Corporation. http://www.channel4.com/info/press/news/c4-launches-major-campaign-for-rio-paralympics-were-the-superhumans [accessed 16 June 2017].

Chartered Institute of Public Relations (2015) State of the profession 2015. London: Chartered Institute of Public Relations. https://www.cipr.co.uk/sites/default/files/SOPR15_ResearchReport_FINAL_UPDATE.pdf [accessed 28 November 2017]

Chartered Institute of Public Relations (2017) State of the profession 2017. London: Chartered Institute of Public Relations. https://www.cipr.co.uk/sites/default/files/10911_State%20of%20PR%202017_f1.pdf [accessed 28 November 2017]

Chartered Institute of Public Relations/Public Relations Consultants Association (2013) Careers in public relations. London: Chartered Institute of Public Relations. https://www.cipr.co.uk/sites/default/files/Public_Relations_Careers_Pack_201314.pdf [accessed 28 November 2017]

Cheney, G., Munshi, D., May, S. and Ortiz, E. (2011) Encountering communication ethics in the contemporary world: Principles, people and contexts. In G. Cheney, S. May and D. Munshi (eds), *The Handbook of Communication Ethics*. New York: Routledge.

Chiapello, E. (2003) Reconciling the two principal meanings of the notion of ideology: The example of the concept of the 'Spirit of Capitalism'. *European Journal of Social Theory*, 6, 155–71.

Chiapello, E. and Fairclough, N. (2002) Understanding the new management ideology: A transdisciplinary contribution from critical discourse analysis and new sociology of capitalism. *Discourse & Society*, 13, 185–208.

China International Public Relations Association (2016) Welcome. Beijing: China International Public Relations Association. http://www.cipra.org.cn/templates/T_Content/index.aspx?nodeid=53 [accessed 22 September 2016].

Chouliaraki, L. (2006) *The Spectatorship of Suffering*. London: Sage.

Christensen, L.T. and Langer, R. (2009) Public relations and the strategic use of transparency: Consistency, hypocrisy, and corporate change. In R. Heath, E. Toth and D. Waymer (eds), *Rhetorical and Critical Approaches to Public Relations II*. New York: Routledge.

Christensen, L.T., Morsing, M. and Cheney, G. (2008) *Corporate Communications: Convention, Complexity, Critique*. London: Sage.

Christiano, T. (2012) Rational deliberation among experts and citizens. In J. Parkinson and J. Mansbridge (eds), *Deliberative Systems: Deliberative Democracy at the Large Scale*. Cambridge: Cambridge University Press.

Christians, C. (2007) Utilitarianism in media ethics and its discontents. *Journal of Mass Media Ethics*, 27, 113–31.

Chung, C., Nam, Y. and Stefanone, M. (2012) Exploring online news credibility: The relative influence of traditional and technological factors. *Journal of Computer-Mediated Communication*, 17, 171–86.

Clean Clothes Campaign (2017) Statement of the Bangladesh Accord's Witness Signatories on the three-year renewal of the agreement. Amsterdam: The Clean Clothes Campaign. https://cleanclothes.org/news/2017/06/29/statement-of-the-bangladesh-accord-witness-signatories-on-the-agreement2019s-3-year-renewal [accessed 3 July 2017].

Cline, C., Toth, E., Turk, J., Walters, L., Johnson, N. and Smith, H. (1986) *The Velvet Ghetto: The Impact of the Increasing Percentage of Women in Public Relations and Business Communication*. San Francisco, CA: IABC Foundation.

Coates, R. (2008) Covert racism in the USA and globally. *Sociology Compass*, 2, 208–31.

Cohen, J. (1989) Deliberation and democratic legitimacy. In A. Hamlin and P. Pettit (eds), *The Good Polity: Normative Analysis of the State*. Oxford: Blackwell.

Cohen, L., Wilkinson, A., Arnold, J. and Finn, R. (2005) 'Remember I'm the bloody architect!': Architects, organizations and discourses of profession. *Work, Employment and Society*, 19, 775–96.

Cohen, N. (2013) Commodifying free labour online: Social media, audiences, and advertising. In M.P. McAllister and E. West (eds), *The Routledge Companion to Advertising and Promotional Culture*. New York: Routledge.

Cole, M. (2004) 'Brutal and stinking' and 'difficult to handle': The historical and contemporary manifestations of racialisation, institutional racism, and schooling in Britain. *Race, Ethnicity and Education*, 7, 35–56.

Coleman, S. and Blumler, J. (2009) *The Internet and Democratic Citizenship*. Cambridge: Cambridge University Press.

Coleman, S. and Price, V. (2012) Democracy, distance and reach: The new media landscape. In S. Coleman and P. Shane (eds), *Connecting Democracy: Online Consultation and the Flow of Political Communication*. Cambridge, MA: MIT Press.

Collins, P.H. (1986) Learning from the outsider within: The sociological significance of Black feminist thought. *Social Problems*, 33, 14–32.

Collins, P.H. (1990) *Black Feminist Thought: Knowledge, Consciousness and the Politics of Empowerment*. London, Harper-Collins.

Collins, P.H. (1999) Reflections on the outsider within. *Journal of Career Development*, 26, 85–8.

Collister, S. (2016) Algorithmic public relations: Materiality, technology and power in a post-hegemonic world. In J. L'Etang, D. McKie, N. Snow and J. Xifra (eds), *The Routledge Handbook of Critical Public Relations*. London: Routledge.

Coombs, W.T. and Holladay, S. (2007) *It's Not Just PR: Public Relations in Society*. Malden, MA: Blackwell.

Coombs, W.T. and Holladay, S. (2010) *PR Strategy and Application: Managing Influence*. Malden, MA: Wiley-Blackwell.

Coombs, W.T. and Holladay, S. (2012) Privileging an activist vs. a corporate view of public relations history in the U.S. *Public Relations Review*, 38, 347–53.

Cornelissen, J., Van Bekkum, T. and Van Ruler, B. (2006) Corporate communications: A practice-based theoretical conceptualization. *Corporate Reputation Review*, 9, 114–33.

Corner, J. and Pels, D. (2003) *Media and the Restyling of Politics*, Thousand Oaks, CA: Sage.

Cottle, S. (2003) *News, Public Relations and Power*. London: Sage.

Couldry, N. (2010) *Why Voice Matters: Culture and Politics after Neoliberalism*. London: Sage.

Couldry, N. (2012) *Media, Society, World*. Cambridge: Polity Press.

Couldry, N. (2014) What and where is the transnationalized public sphere? In K. Nash (ed.), *Transnationalizing the Public Sphere*. Cambridge: Polity Press.

Cox, J. (2017) UK PR giant Bell Pottinger sacks partner and apologises for South African campaign accused of fuelling racism. *The Independent*, 7 July.

Creedon, P. (1991) Public relations and 'women's work': Toward a feminist analysis of public relations roles. *Public Relations Research Annual*, 3, 67–84.

Creedon, P. (1993) Acknowledging the infrasystem: A critical feminist analysis of systems theory. *Public Relations Review*, 19, 157–66.

Cronin, A. (2004) Currencies of commercial exchange: Advertising agencies and the promotional imperative. *Journal of Consumer Culture*, 4, 339–60.

Cronin, A. (2008) Mobility and market research: Outdoor advertising and the commercial ontology of the city. *Mobilities*, 3, 95–115.

Cronin, A. (2016) Reputational capital in 'the PR University': Public relations and market rationalities. *Journal of Cultural Economy*, 9, 396–409.

Cronin, D. (2013) *Corporate Europe: How Big Business Sets Policies on Food, Climate and War*. London: Pluto Press.

Curran, J. (2002) *Media and Power*. London: Routledge.

Curtin, P.A. (2011) Discourses of American Indian racial identity in the public relations materials of the Fred Harvey company, 1902–1936. *Journal of Public Relations Research*, 23, 368–96.

Curtin, P.A. (2016) Exploring articulation in internal activism and public relations theory: A case study. *Journal of Public Relations Research*, 28, 19–34.

Curtin, P.A. and Gaither, T.K. (2007) *International Public Relations: Negotiating Culture, Identity and Power*. Thousand Oaks, CA: Sage.

Curtin, P.A., Gaither, T.K. and Ciszek, E. (2016) Articulating public relations practice and critical/cultural theory through a cultural-economic lens. In J. L'Etang, D. McKie, N. Snow and J. Xifra (eds), *The Routledge Handbook of Critical Public Relations*. London: Routledge.

Cutlip, S.M. (1994) *Public Relations: The Unseen Power. A History*. Hillsdale, NJ: Lawrence Erlbaum Associates.

Dahlberg, L. (2001) The internet and democratic discourse: Exploring the prospects of online deliberative forums extending the public sphere. *Information, Communication & Society*, 4, 615–33.

Dahlberg, L. (2007) The internet, deliberative democracy and power: Radicalizing the public sphere. *International Journal of Media and Cultural Politics*, 3, 47–64.

Dahlgren, P. (2005) The internet, public spheres, and political communication: Dispersion and deliberation. *Political Communication*, 22, 147–62.

Davenport, T. and Beck, J. (2002) *The Attention Economy: Understanding the New Currency of Business*. Boston, MA: Harvard Business Press.

Davidson, M.J. and Burke, R.J. (2004) Women in management worldwide: Facts, figures and analysis – An overview. In M.J. Davidson and R.J. Burke (eds), *Women in Management Worldwide: Facts, Figures and Analysis*. Aldershot: Ashgate.

Davies, N. (2008) *Flat Earth News: An Award-Winning Reporter Exposes Falsehood, Distortion and Propaganda in the Global Media*. London: Chatto & Windus.

Davies, W. (2016) Has the Olympics been a success for Brazil? BBC News, 20 August. http://www.bbc.co.uk/news/world-latin-america-37133278

Davila, A. (2010) A nation of 'shop 'til you drop' consumers? On the overspent Puerto Rican consumer and the business of shopping malls. In M. Aronczyk and D. Powers (eds), *Blowing Up the Brand: Critical Perspectives on Promotional Culture*. New York: Peter Lang.

Davis, A. (2002) *Public Relations Democracy: Public Relations, Politics and the Mass Media in Britain*. Manchester: Manchester University Press.

Davis, A. (2003) Whither mass media and power? Evidence for a critical elite theory alternative. *Media, Culture & Society*, 25, 669–90.

Davis, A. (2007) *The Mediation of Power*. London: Routledge.

Davis, A. (2009) Journalist–source relations, mediated reflexivity and the politics of politics. *Journalism Studies*, 10, 204–19.

Davis, A. (2013) *Promotional Cultures: The Rise and Spread of Advertising, Public Relations, Marketing and Branding*. Cambridge: Polity Press.

Daymon, C. and Demetrious, K. (2010) Gender and public relations: Perspectives, applications and questions. *PRism*, 7.

Daymon, C. and Demetrious, K. (eds) (2013) *Gender and Public Relations: Critical Perspectives on Voice, Image, and Identity*. Abingdon: Routledge.

De Brooks, K. and Waymer, D. (2009) Public relations and strategic issues management challenges in Venezuela: A discourse analysis of Crystallex International Corporation in Las Cristinas. *Public Relations Review*, 35, 31–9.

De Sousa Santos, B. and Rodríguez-Garavito, C. (eds) (2005) *Law and Globalization from Below: Towards a Cosmopolitan Legality*. Cambridge: Cambridge University Press.

Dean, J. (2005) Communicative capitalism: Circulation and the foreclosure of politics. *Cultural Politics*, 1, 51–74.

Delgado, R. and Stefancic, J. (2001) *Critical Race Theory: An Introduction*. New York: New York University Press.

Demetrious, K. (2013) *Public Relations, Activism and Social Change: Speaking Up*. New York: Routledge.

Demetrious, K. (2016) Sanitising or reforming PR? Exploring 'trust' and the emergence of critical public relations. In J. L'Etang, D. McKie, N. Snow and J. Xifra (eds), *The Routledge Handbook of Critical Public Relations*. London: Routledge.

Department for Culture, Media and Sport (2001) *The Creative Industries Mapping Document 2001*. London: DCMS.

Deuze, M. (2004) What is multimedia journalism? *Journalism Studies*, 5, 139–52.

Dimitrov, R. (2015) Silence and invisibility in public relations. *Public Relations Review*, 41, 636–51.

Dirlik, A. (2003) Global modernity? Modernity in an age of global capitalism. *European Journal of Social Theory*, 6, 275–92.

Doerfel, M. and Taylor, M. (2004) Network dynamics of interorganizational cooperation: The Croatian civil society movement. *Communication Monographs*, 71, 373–94.

Downey, J. and Fenton, N. (2003) New media, counter publicity and the public sphere. *New Media & Society*, 5, 185–202.

Dozier, D.M. and Lauzen, M.M. (2000) Liberating the intellectual domain from the practice: Public relations, activism and the role of the scholar. *Journal of Public Relations Research*, 12, 3–22.

Dryzek, J. (1990) *Discursive Democracy: Politics, Policy and Political Science*. Cambridge: Cambridge University Press.

Dryzek, J. (2000) *Deliberative Democracy and Beyond: Liberals, Critics, Contestations*. Oxford: Oxford University Press.

Dryzek, J. (2002) *Deliberative Democracy and Beyond: Liberals, Critics, Contestations*. Oxford: Oxford University Press.

Dryzek, J. (2009) Democratization as deliberative capacity building. *Comparative Political Studies*, 42, 1379–1402.

Dryzek, J. (ed.) (2010a) *Foundations and Frontiers of Deliberative Governance*. Oxford: Oxford University Press.

Dryzek, J. (2010b) Deliberative turns. In J. Dryzek (ed.), *Foundations and Frontiers of Deliberative Governance*. Oxford: Oxford University Press.

Dryzek, J. (2010c) Communication and rhetoric. In J. Dryzek (ed.), *Foundations and Frontiers of Deliberative Governance*. Oxford: Oxford University Press.

Dryzek, J. (2010d) Governance networks. In J. Dryzek (ed.), *Foundations and Frontiers of Deliberative Governance*. Oxford: Oxford University Press.

Du Bois, W.E.B. (1989[1903]) *The Souls of Black Folk*. New York: Bantam Classics.

Du Gay, P. and Salaman, G. (1992) *The cult[ure] of the customer*, 29, 615–33.

Du Gay, P., Hall, S., Janes, L., Mackay, H. and Negus, K. (1997) *Doing Cultural Studies: The Story of the Sony Walkman*. London: Sage/Open University.

Duhe, S., and Sriramesh, K. (2009). Political economy and public relations. In K. Sriramesh and D. Verčič (eds), *The Global Public Relations Handbook: Theory, Research and Practice*. New York: Routledge.

Dunlap, R. and McCright, A. (2011) Organized climate change denial. In J. Dryzek, R. Norgaard and D. Schlosberg (eds), *The Oxford Handbook of Climate Change and Society*. Oxford: Oxford University Press.

Dutta, M.J. (2011) *Communicating Social Change: Structure, Culture and Agency*. New York: Routledge.

Dutta, M.J. (2015) Decolonizing communication for social change: A culture-centered approach. *Communication Theory*, 25, 123–43.

Dutta, M.J. (2016) A postcolonial critique of public relations. In J. L'Etang, D. McKie, N. Snow and J. Xifra (eds), *The Routledge Handbook of Critical Public Relations*. London: Routledge.

Dutta, M.J. and Pal, M. (2011) Public relations and marginalization in a global context: A postcolonial critique. In N. Bardhan and C.K. Weaver (eds), *Public Relations in Global Cultural Contexts: Multi-paradigmatic Perspectives*. New York: Routledge.

Dutta, M.J., Ban, Z. and Pal, M. (2012) Engaging worldviews, cultures, and structures through dialogue: The culture-centred approach to public relations. *PRism*, 9.

Dutta-Bergman, M. (2005) Civil society and public relations: Not so civil after all? *Journal of Public Relations Research*, 17, 267–89.

Dutton, W.H. (2009) The fifth estate emerging through the network of networks. *Prometheus: Critical Studies in Innovation*, 27, 1–15.

Edelman (2017) What we do. http://www.edelman.com/what-we-do/ [accessed 8 December 2017].

Edwards, L. (2009) Symbolic power and public relations practice: Locating individual practitioners in their social context. *Journal of Public Relations Research*, 21, 251–72.

Edwards, L. (2011) Critical perspectives in global public relations: Theorizing power. In N. Bardhan and C.K. Weaver (eds), *Public Relations in Global Cultural Contexts: Multi-paradigmatic Perspectives*. New York: Routledge.

Edwards, L. (2012a) Defining the 'object' of public relations research: A new starting point. *Public Relations Inquiry*, 1, 7–30.

Edwards, L. (2012b) Exploring the role of public relations as a cultural intermediary. *Cultural Sociology*, 6, 438–54.

Edwards, L. (2013) Institutional racism in cultural production: The case of public relations. *Popular Communication: The International Journal of Media and Culture*, 11, 242–56.

Edwards, L. (2014a) Discourse, credentialism and occupational closure in the communications industries: The case of public relations in the UK. *European Journal of Communication*, 29, 319–34.

Edwards, L. (2014b) *Power, Diversity and Public Relations*. London: Routledge.

Edwards, L. (2015) Understanding public relations as a cultural industry. In K. Oakley and J. O'Connor (eds), *The Routledge Companion to Cultural Industries*. London: Routledge.

Edwards, L. (2016a) An historical overview of the emergence of critical thinking in PR. In J. L'Etang, D. McKie, N. Snow and J. Xifra (eds), *The Routledge Handbook of Critical Public Relations*. London: Routledge.

Edwards, L. (2016b) The role of public relations in deliberative systems. *Journal of Communication*, 66, 60–81.

Edwards, L. (2018) Luc Boltanski, the sociology of critique, and public relations. In Ø. Ihlen and M. Fredriksson (eds), *Public Relations and Social Theory II*. Sage.

Edwards, L. and Hodges, C.E.M. (2011) Introduction: Implications of a radical sociocultural 'turn' in public relations scholarship. In L. Edwards and C.E.M. Hodges (eds), *Public Relations, Society and Culture: Theoretical and Empirical Explorations*. London: Routledge.

Edwards, L. and L'Etang, J. (2013) Invisible and visible identities and sexualities in public relations. In N. Tindall and R. Waters (eds), *Coming Out of the Closet: Exploring LGBT Issues in Strategic Communication with Theory and Practice*. New York: Peter Lang.

Edwards, L. and Pieczka, M. (2013) Public relations and 'its' media: Exploring the role of trade media in the enactment of public relations' professional project. *Public Relations Inquiry*, 2, 5–25.

Edwards, L. and Ramamurthy, A. (2017) (In)credible India? A critical analysis of India's nation branding. *Communication, Culture and Critique*, 10, 322–43.

Einstein, M. (2016) *Black Ops Advertising: Native Ads, Content Marketing and the Covert World of the Digital Sell*. New York: OR Books.

Elliott, R. and Wattanasuwan, K. (1998) Brands as symbolic resources for the construction of identity. *International Journal of Advertising*, 17, 131–44.

Elmer, P. (2007) Unmanaging public relations: Reclaiming complex practice in pursuit of global consent. *Public Relations Review*, 33, 360–7.

Emirbayer, M. and Mische, A. (1998) What is agency? *American Journal of Sociology*, 103, 962–1023.

Equality Now (2017) End FGM. London: Equality Now. https://www.equalitynow.org/issues/end-female-genital-mutilation [accessed 2 August 2017].

Erjavec, K. (2005) Hybrid public relations news discourse. *European Journal of Communication*, 20, 155–79.

Eschenfelder, B. (2011) The role of narrative in public relations pedagogy. *Public Relations Review*, 37, 450–5.

Escobar, A. (2001) Culture sits in places: Reflections on globalism and subaltern strategies of localization. *Political Geography*, 20, 139–74.

Esser, F. and Strömbäck, J. (eds) (2014) *Mediatization of Politics: Understanding the Transformation of Western Democracies*. Basingstoke: Palgrave Macmillan.

European Association of Communication Directors (2016) About us: Idea and aims. Brussels: European Association of Communication Directors. https://www.eacd-online.eu/about-us/idea-and-aims [accessed 9 September 2016].

European Communication Monitor (2016) About the European Communication Monitor. http://www.communicationmonitor.eu [accessed 9 September 2016].

Evetts, J. (2003) The sociological analysis of professionalism: Occupational change in the modern world. *International Sociology*, 18, 395–415.

Evetts, J. (2006) The sociology of professional groups: New directions. *Current Sociology*, 54, 133–43.

Evetts, J. (2011) A new professionalism? Challenges and opportunities. *Current Sociology*, 59, 406–22.

Evetts, J. (2013) Professionalism: Value and ideology. *Current Sociology*, 61, 778–796.

Ewen, S. (1976) *Captains of Consciousness: Advertising and the Social Roots of the Consumer Culture*. New York: McGraw-Hill.

Ewen, S. (1996) *PR! A Social History of Spin*. New York: Basic Books.

Fairclough, N. (2003) *Analysing Discourse: Textual Analysis for Social Research*. London: Routledge.

Fairclough, N. (2006) *Language and Globalization*. London: Routledge.

Fanon, F. (2008 [1952]) *Black Skin, White Masks*. London: Pluto Press.

Faulconbridge, J. and Muzio, D. (2008) Organisational professionalism in globalising law firms. *Work, Employment and Society*, 22, 7–25.

Fawkes, J. (2009) Integrating the shadow: A Jungian approach to professional ethics in public relations. *Ethical Space*, 6, 30–9.

Fawkes, J. (2010) The shadow of excellence: A Jungian approach to public relations ethics. *Review of Communication*, 10, 211–27.

Fawkes, J. (2012a) Interpreting ethics: Public relations and strong hermeneutics. *Public Relations Inquiry*, 1, 117–40.

Fawkes, J. (2012b) Saints and sinners: Competing identities in public relations ethics. *Public Relations Review*, 38, 865–72.

Fawkes, J. (2014a) Public relations' professionalism and ethics. In R. Tench and L. Yeomans (eds), *Exploring Public Relations*. Harlow: Pearson Education.

Fawkes, J. (2014b) *Public Relations Ethics and Professionalism: The Shadow of Excellence*. London: Routledge.

Fawkes, J. (2015) A Jungian conscience: Self-awareness for public relations practice. *Public Relations Review*, 41, 726–33.

Fenton, N. and Downey, J. (2003). Counter public spheres and global modernity. *Javnost – The Public*, 10, 15–32.

Fitch, K. (2014) Professionalisation and public relations education: Industry accreditation of Australian university courses in the early 1990s. *Public Relations Review*, 40, 623–31.

Fitch, K. (2015) Promoting the Vampire Rights Amendment: Public relations, postfeminism and True Blood. *Public Relations Review*, 41, 607–14.

Fitch, K. (2016) Feminism and public relations. In J. L'Etang, D. McKie, N. Snow and J. Xifra (eds), *The Routledge Handbook of Critical Public Relations*. London: Routledge.

Fitch, K. and Third, A. (2010) Working girls: Revisiting the gendering of public relations. *PRism*, 7.

Fitch, K. and Third, A. (2013) Ex-journos and promo girls: Feminization and professionalization in the Australian public relations industry. In C. Daymon and K. Demetrious (eds), *Gender and Public Relations: Critical Perspectives on Voice, Image and Identity*. Abingdon: Routledge.

Fitch, K., James, M. and Motion, J. (2016) 'Talking back: Reflecting on feminism, public relations and research', *Public Relations Review*, 42, 279–87.

Fitzpatrick, K. and Bronstein, C. (eds) (2006) *Ethics in Public Relations*. Thousand Oaks, CA: Sage.

Fitzpatrick, K. and Gauthier, C. (2001) Toward a professional responsibility theory of public relations ethics. *Journal of Mass Media Ethics*, 16, 193–212.

Fletcher, W. (2008) *Powers of Persuasion: The Inside Story of British Advertising: 1951–2000*. Oxford: Oxford University Press.

Ford, R. and Brown, C. (2015) State of the PR industry: Defining and delivering on the promise of diversity. White Paper. Van Nuys, CA: National Black Public Relations Society.

Foucault, M. (ed.) (1980) *Power/Knowledge: Selected Interviews and Other Writings*. New York: Pantheon.

Foucault, M. (1981) The order of discourse. In R. Young (ed.), *Untying the Text: A Poststructuralist Reader*. Boston: Routledge & Kegan Paul.

Foucault, M. (1982) The subject and power. In H.L. Dreyfus and P. Rabinow (eds), *Michel Foucault: Beyond Structuralism and Hermeneutics*. Brighton: Harvester.

Foucault, M. (1991) Governmentality. In G. Burchell, C. Gordon and P. Miller (eds), *The Foucault Effect: Studies in Governmentality*. Chicago, IL: Chicago University Press.

Fournier, V. (1999) The appeal to 'professionalism' as a disciplinary mechanism. *Sociological Review*, 47, 280–307.

Fraga, L., Martinez-Ebers, V., Lopez, L. and Ramirez, R. (2006) *Strategic intersectionality: Gender, ethnicity, and political incorporation*. Berkeley, CA: Institute of Governmental Studies.

Frank, T. (1997) *The Conquest of Cool: Business Culture, Counterculture and the Rise of Hip Consumerism*. Chicago, IL: University of Chicago Press.

Franklin, B. (1994) *Packaging Politics: Political Communications in Britain's Media Democracy*. London: Arnold.

Franklin, R., Lewis, J. and Williams, A. (2012) Journalism, news sources and public relations. In S. Allan (ed.), *The Routledge Companion to News and Journalism*. Abingdon: Routledge.

Fraser, N. (1990) Rethinking the public sphere: A contribution to the critique of actually existing democracy. *Social Text*, 25/26, 56–80.

Fraser, N. (2007) Transnationalizing the public sphere: On the legitimacy and efficacy of public opinion in a post-Westphalian world. *Theory, Culture & Society*, 24, 7–30.

Freedman, D. (2008) *The Politics of Media Policy*. Cambridge: Polity Press.

Friedson, E. (2001) *Professionalism: The Third Logic*. Cambridge: Polity Press.

Froehlich, R. and Peters, S. (2007) PR bunnies caught in the agency ghetto? Gender stereotypes, organizational factors and women's careers in PR agencies. *Journal of Public Relations Research*, 19, 229–54.

Froehlich, R. and Rüdiger, B. (2006) Framing political public relations: Measuring success of political communication strategies in Germany. *Public Relations Review*, 32, 18–25.

Fuchs, C. (2014) Social media and the public sphere. *TripleC*, 12, 57–101.

Gabriel, D. (2015) Challenging the Whiteness of Britishness: Co-creating British social history in the blogosphere. *Online Journal of Media and Communication Technologies*, 6.

Gabriel, D. (2016) Race, racism and resistance in British academia. In K. Fereidooni and M. El (eds), *A Critical Study of (Trans) National Racism: Interdependence of Racist Phenomenon and Resistance Forms*. Wiesbaden: Springer VS.

Gabriel, Y. and Lang, T. (2006) *The Unmanageable Consumer*. London: Sage.

Gamson, J. (2000) Sexualities, queer theory, and qualitative research. In N.K. Denzin and Y.S. Lincoln (eds), *Handbook of Qualitative Research* (2nd edn). Thousand Oaks, CA: Sage.

Gandy, O. (1982) *Beyond Agenda Setting: Information Subsidies and Public Policy*. Norwood, NJ: Ablex.

Ganesh, S., Zoller, H. and Cheney, G. (2005) Transforming resistance, broadening our boundaries: Critical organizational communication meets globalization from below. *Communication Monographs*, 72, 169–91.

Gaonkar, D.P. and Povinelli, E. (2003) Technologies of public forms: Circulation, transfiguration, recognition. *Public Culture*, 15, 385–97.

Garnham, N. (1992) The media and the public sphere. In C. Calhoun (ed.), *Habermas and the Public Sphere*. Cambridge, MA: MIT Press.

Georgetown University (2015) Look beyond Syrian crisis, head of UN refugee agency says. Washington, DC: Georgetown University. https://www.georgetown.edu/un-high-commissioner-guterres [accessed 8 August 2017].

Gerbaudo, P. (2012) *Tweets and the Streets: Social Media and Contemporary Activism*. London: Pluto Press.

Giddens, A. (1979) *Central Problems in Social Theory: Action, Structure and Contradiction in Social Analysis*. Berkeley, CA: University of California Press.

Giddens, A. (1984) *The Constitution of Society: Outline of the Theory of Structuration*. Cambridge: Polity Press.

Giddens, A. (1990) *The Consequences of Modernity*. Cambridge: Polity Press.

Giddens, A. (1991) *Modernity and Self-Identity: Self and Society in the Late Modern Age*. Stanford, CA: Stanford University Press.

Giddens, A. (1999) *Runaway World: How Globalisation Is Shaping our Lives*. London: Profile.

Giddens, A. (2006) *Sociology*. Cambridge: Polity Press.

Gill, R. (2007) Postfeminist media culture: Elements of a sensibility. *European Journal of Cultural Studies*, 10, 147–66.

Gill, R. and Elias, A.S. (2014) 'Awaken your incredible': Love your body discourses and postfeminist contradictions. *International Journal of Media and Cultural Politics*, 10, 179–88.

Gill, R. and Scharff, C. (2011) Introduction. In R. Gill and C. Scharff (eds), *New Femininities: Postfeminism, Neoliberalism and Subjectivity*. Basingstoke: Palgrave Macmillan.

Gillborn, D. (2012) The white working class, racism and respectability: Victims, degenerates and interest convergence. In K. Bhopal and J. Preston (eds), *Intersectionality and 'Race' in Education*. New York: Routledge.

Giroux, H. (2015) Flipping the script: Rethinking working class resistance. Sacramento, CA: Truthout. http://www.truth-out.org/news/item/31238-flipping-the-script-rethinking-working-class-resistance [accessed 5 August 2017].

Global Alliance for Public Relations (2016) Who we are. Lugano: Global Alliance for Public Relations. http://www.globalalliancepr.org/who-we-are/ [accessed 9 September 2016].

Goldberg, D.T. (2015) *Are We All Postracial Yet? Debating Race*. Cambridge: Polity Press.

Goldman, R. and Papson, S. (1996) *Sign Wars: The Cluttered Landscape of Advertising*. New York: Guilford Press.

Golombisky, K. (2015) Renewing the commitments of feminist public relations theory: From velvet ghetto to social justice. *Journal of Public Relations Research*, 27, 389–415.

Goodin, R. (2005) Sequencing deliberative moments. *Acta Politica*, 40, 182–96.

Goodin, R. and Dryzek, J. (2006) Deliberative impacts: The macro-political uptake of mini-publics. *Politics & Society*, 34, 219–244.

Gregory, A. (2008) Competencies of senior practitioners in the UK: An initial study. *Public Relations Review*, 34, 215–23.

Gregory, A. (2009) Ethics and professionalism in public relations. In R. Tench and L. Yeomans (eds), *Exploring Public Relations*. Harlow: Pearson Education.

Gregory, A. (2015) *Planning and Managing Public Relations Campaigns: A Strategic Approach*. London: Kogan Page.

Grey, C. (1998) On being a professional in a 'Big Six' firm. *Accounting, Organizations and Society*, 23, 569–87.

Griggs, I. (2015) Show me the money: Salary survey shows how financial PR is bringing home the bacon. *PR Week*, 28 May.

Grunig, J.E. (1992) *Excellence in Public Relations and Communication Management*. Hillsdale, NJ: Lawrence Erlbaum.

Grunig, J.E. (2000) Collectivism, collaboration, and societal corporatism as core professional values in public relations. *Journal of Public Relations Research*, 12, 23–48.

Grunig, J.E. (2009) Paradigms of global public relations in an age of digitalisation. *PRism*, 6.

Grunig, J.E., Grunig, L., Sriramesh, K., Huang, Y.H. and Lyra, A. (1995) Models of public relations in an international setting. *Journal of Public Relations Research*, 7, 163–86.

Grunig, L., Toth, E. and Hon, L. C. (2000) Feminist values in public relations. *Journal of Public Relations Research*, 12, 49–68.

Grunig, L., Toth, E. and Hon, L. C. (eds) (2008) *Women in Public Relations: How Gender Influences Practice*. New York: Routledge.

Guidry, J., Kennedy, M. and Zald, M. (eds) (2000) *Globalizations and Social Movements: Culture, Power and the Transnational Public Sphere*, Ann Arbor, MI: University of Michigan Press.

Gunaratnam, Y. (2003) *Researching 'Race' and Ethnicity: Methods, Knowledge and Power*. London: Sage.

Gunnarsson, B.-L. (2009) *Professional Discourse*. London: Continuum.

Gutmann, A. and Thompson, D. (1996) *Democracy and Disagreement: Why Moral Conflict Cannot Be Avoided in Politics, and What Should Be Done about It*. Cambridge, MA: Harvard University Press.

Habermas, J. (1984) *The Theory of Communicative Action. Vol. 1: Reason and the Rationalization of Society*. London: Heinemann Educational.

Habermas, J. (1989) *The Structural Transformation of the Public Sphere: An Inquiry into a Category of Bourgeois Society*. Cambridge: Polity Press.

Habermas, J. (1996) *Between Facts and Norms*. Cambridge: Polity Press.

Hall, S. (1981) Notes on deconstructing 'the popular'. In R. Samuel (ed.), *People's History and Socialist Theory*. London: Routledge & Kegan Paul.

Hall, S. (1988a) *The Hard Road to Renewal: Thatcherism and the Crisis of the Left*. London: Verso.

Hall, S. (1988b) New ethnicities. In K. Mercer (ed.), *Black Film/British Cinema*. London: Institute of Contemporary Arts.

Hall, S. (1990) Cultural identity and diaspora. In J. Rutherford (ed.), *Identity: Community, Culture, Difference*. London: Lawrence and Wishart.

Hall, S. (1996) Who needs 'identity'? In S. Hall and P. Du Gay (eds), *Questions of Cultural Identity*. London: Sage.

Hall, S. (1997a) *Representation: Cultural Representations and Signifying Practices*. London: Sage/Open University.

Hall, S. (1997b) The spectacle of the 'other'. In S. Hall (ed.), *Representation: Cultural Representations and Signifying Practices*. London: Sage/Open University.

Hall, S. (2000) Conclusion: The multi-cultural question. In B. Hesse (ed.), *Un/settled Multiculturalisms*. London: Zed Books.

Hall, S., Critcher, C., Jefferson, T., Clarke, J. and Roberts, B. (2013) *Policing the Crisis: Mugging, the State and Law and Order* (2nd edn). Basingstoke, Palgrave Macmillan.

Hallahan, K. (2000) Inactive publics: The forgotten publics in public relations. *Public Relations Review*, 26, 499–515.

Hampton, M. (2012) The Fourth Estate ideal in journalism history. In S. Allan (ed.) *The Routledge Companion to News and Journalism*. Abingdon: Routledge.

Hanchey, J. (2016) Agency beyond agents: Aid campaigns in sub-Saharan Africa and collective representations of agency. *Communication, Culture & Critique*, 9, 11–29.

Hang, G. and Zhang, A. (2009) Starbucks is forbidden in the Forbidden City: Blog, circuit of culture and informal public relations campaign in China. *Public Relations Review*, 35, 395–401.

Hanlon, G. (1999a) *Lawyers, the State and the Market: Professionalism Revisited*. London: Macmillan.

Hanlon, G. (1999b) Professionalism as enterprise – Service class politics and the redefinition of professionalism. *Sociology*, 32, 43–63.

Hanlon, G. (2004) Institutional forms and organizational structures: Homology, trust and reputational capital in professional service firms. *Organization*, 11, 187–210.

Haraway, D. (2013) *Simians, Cyborgs, and Women: The Reinvention of Nature*. New York: Routledge.

Harlow, S. and Guo, L. (2014) Will the revolution be Tweeted or Facebooked? Using digital communication tools in immigrant activism. *Journal of Computer-Mediated Communication*, 19, 463–78.

Harrington, B. (2015) Going global: Professionals and the micro-foundations of institutional change. *Journal of Professions and Organization*, 2, 103–21.

Harris, C. (1993) Whiteness as property. *Harvard Law Review*, 106, 1707–91.

Harrison, K. and Galloway, C. (2005) Public relations ethics: A simpler (but not simplistic) approach to the complexities. *PRism*, 3.

Harrison, R., Newholme, T. and Shaw, D. (eds) (2005) *The Ethical Consumer*. London: Sage.

Harvey, D. (2001) Globalization and the 'spatial fix'. *Geographische Revue*, 2, 23–30.

Harvey, D. (2003) *The New Imperialism*. Oxford: Oxford University Press.

Harvey, D. (2005) *A Brief History of Neoliberalism*. New York: Oxford University Press.

Haugaard, M. (2002) *Power: A Reader*. Manchester: Manchester University Press.

Hearn, A. (2008) Meat, mask, burden: Probing the contours of the 'branded self'. *Journal of Consumer Culture*, 8, 197–217.

Hearn, A. (2012) Brand me 'activist'. In R. Mukherjee and S. Banet-Weiser (eds), *Commodity Activism: Cultural Resistance in Neoliberal Times*. New York: New York University Press.

Hearn, A. (2015) The politics of branding in the new university of circulation. *International Studies of Management & Organization*, 45, 114–20.

Hearn, A. (2017) Verified: Self-presentation, identity management, and selfhood in the age of big data. *Popular Communication*, 15, 62–77.

Heath, R. (2001a) A rhetorical enactment rationale for public relations: The good organization communicating well. In R. Heath (ed.), *The Handbook of Public Relations*. Thousand Oaks, CA: Sage.

Heath, R. (2001b) Shifting foundations: Public relations as relationship building. In R. Heath (ed.), *The Handbook of Public Relations*. Thousand Oaks, CA: Sage.

Heath, R. (2006) Onward into more fog: Thoughts on public relations' research directions. *Journal of Public Relations Research*, 18, 93–114.

Heath, R., and Waymer, D. (2009). Activist public relations and the paradox of the positive: A case study of Frederick Douglass' Fourth of July Address. In R. Heath, E. Toth and D. Waymer (eds), *Rhetorical and Critical Approaches to Public Relations II*. New York: Routledge.

Heath, R., Waymer, D. and Palenchar, M. (2013) Is the universe of democracy, rhetoric and public relations whole cloth or three separate galaxies? *Public Relations Review*, 39, 271–9.

Held, D. and McGrew, A. (2007a) *Globalization/Anti-globalization: Beyond the Great Divide*. Cambridge: Polity Press.

Held, D. and McGrew, A. (2007b) Introduction: Globalization at risk? In D. Held and A. McGrew (eds), *Globalization Theory: Approaches and Controversies*. Cambridge: Polity Press.

Henderson, A. (2005) Activism in 'paradise': Identity management in a public relations campaign against genetic engineering. *Journal of Public Relations Research*, 17, 117–37.

Hendriks, C. (2002) Institutions of deliberative democratic processes and interest groups: Roles, tensions and incentives. *Australian Journal of Public Administration*, 61, 64–75.

Hendriks, C. (2006a) Integrated deliberation: Reconciling civil society's dual role in deliberative democracy. *Political Studies*, 54, 486–508.

Hendriks, C. (2006b) When the forum meets interest politics: Strategic uses of public deliberation. *Politics & Society*, 34, 571–602.

Hesmondhalgh, D. (2010). User-generated content, free labour and the cultural industries. *Ephemera: Theory and Politics in Organisation*, 10(3/4), 267–84.

Hesmondhalgh, D. (2013) *The Cultural Industries* (3rd edn). London: Sage.

Hickerson, C. and Thompson, S. (2009) Dialogue through wikis: A pilot exploration of dialogic public relations and wiki websites. *PRism*, 6.

Hickman, C. (1997) The devil and the one drop rule: Racial categories, African Americans and the US census. *Michigan Law Review*, 95, 1161–1265.

Hiebert, R. (2005) Commentary: New technologies, public relations and democracy. *Public Relations Review*, 31, 1–9.

Hill+Knowlton (2016) Our philosophy. London: Hill+Knowlton. http://www.hillandknowlton.co.uk/hk/our-philosophy/ [accessed 22 September 2016].

Hodges, C. (2006) 'PRP culture': A framework for exploring public relations practitioners as cultural intermediaries. *Journal of Communication Management*, 10, 80–93.

Hodges, C. (2011) Public relations in the postmodern city: An ethnographic account of PR occupational culture in Mexico City. In L. Edwards and C.E.M. Hodges (eds), *Public Relations, Society and Culture: Theoretical and Empirical Explorations*. London: Routledge.

Hodges, C. and Edwards, L. (2014) Public Relations practitioners. In J. Smith Maguire and J. Matthews (eds), *The Cultural Intermediaries Reader*. London: Sage.

Hodgson, D. (2002) Disciplining the professional: The case of project management. *Journal of Management Studies*, 39, 803–21.

Hodgson, D. (2007) The new professionals: Professionalisation and the struggle for occupational control in the field of project management. In D. Muzio, S. Ackroyd and J. Chanlat (eds), *Redirections in the Study of Expert Labour: Medicine, Law and Management Consultancy*. Basingstoke: Palgrave Macmillan.

Holmes Group (2016) Global top 250 PR agency ranking 2016. New York: Holmes Group. http://www.holmesreport.com/ranking-and-data/global-communications-report/2016-pr-agency-rankings/top-250 [accessed 2 September 2016].

Holmes Report and International Communications Consultancy Organisation (2013) World PR report. New York/London.

Holtzhausen, D. (2011) The need for a postmodern turn in global public relations. In N. Bardhan and C.K. Weaver (eds), *Public Relations in Global Cultural Contexts: Multi-paradigmatic Perspectives*. New York: Routledge.

Holtzhausen, D. (2012) *Public Relations as Activism: Postmodern Approaches to Theory and Practice*. New York: Routledge.

Hon, L.C. (1995) Toward a feminist theory of public relations. *Journal of Public Relations Research*, 7, 27–88.

Hon, L.C. (1997) To redeem the soul of America: Public relations and the civil rights movement. *Journal of Public Relations Research*, 9, 163–212.

Honneth, A. (1996) *The Struggle for Recognition: The Moral Grammar of Social Conflicts*. Cambridge: Polity Press.

Hook, D. (2001) Discourse, knowledge, materiality, history: Foucault and discourse analysis. *Theory & Psychology*, 11, 521–47.

Horkheimer, M. and Adorno, T. (2002) *Dialectic of Enlightenment: Philosophical Fragments*. Stanford, CA: Stanford University Press.

Htun, M. (2004) From 'racial democracy' to affirmative action: Changing state policy on race in Brazil. *Latin American Research Review*, 39, 60–89.

Hulko, W. (2009) The time- and context-contingent nature of intersectionality and interlocking oppressions. *Affilia*, 24, 44–55.

Hutton, J.G. (1999) The definition, dimensions and domain of public relations. *Public Relations Review*, 25, 199–214.

Hutton, J.G. (2010) Defining the relationship between public relations and marketing: Public relations' most important challenge. In R. Heath (ed.) *The SAGE Handbook of Public Relations*. Thousand Oaks, CA: Sage.

Hyde, M. (2011) Ethics, rhetoric and discourse. In G. Cheney, S. May and D. Munshi (eds), *The Handbook of Communication Ethics*. New York: Routledge.

Ice, R. (1991) Corporate publics and rhetorical strategies: The case of Union Carbide's Bhopal crisis. *Management Communication Quarterly*, 4, 341–62.

Ihlen, Ø. (2011) On barnyard scrambles: Towards a rhetoric of public relations. *Management Communication Quarterly*, 25, 423–41.

Ihlen, Ø. and Van Ruler, B. (2009) Introduction: Applying social theory to public relations. In Ø. Ihlen and B. Van Ruler (eds), *Public Relations and Social Theory: Key Figures and Concepts*. New York: Routledge.

Ilmonen, K. (2004) The use of and commitment to goods. *Journal of Consumer Culture*, 4, 27–50.

Institute of Education Sciences (2009) Fast Facts: What is the percentage of degrees conferred by sex and race? Washington, DC: US Department of Education. http://nces.ed.gov/fastfacts/display.asp?id=72 [accessed 1 October 2009].

Jackall, R. (2010) *Moral Mazes: The World of Corporate Managers*. New York: Oxford University Press.

Jackall, R. and Hirota, J. (2000) *Image Makers: Advertising, Public Relations and the Ethos of Advocacy*. Chicago, IL: University of Chicago Press.

Jacobs, L., Cook, F. and Delli Carpini, M. (2010) *Talking Together: Public Deliberation and Political Participation in America*. Chicago, IL: University of Chicago Press.

Jaggar, A. (1991) Feminist ethics: Projects, problems, prospects. In C. Card (ed.) *Feminist Ethics*. Lawrence, KS: University of Kansas Press.

Jagose, A. (1996) *Queer Theory: An Introduction*. New York: New York University Press.

Jenkins, H. (2006) *Convergence Culture: Where Old and New Media Collide*. New York: New York University Press.

Jenkins, R. (1992) *Pierre Bourdieu*. London: Routledge.

Jensen, I. (2001) Public relations and emerging functions of the public sphere: An analytical framework. *Journal of Communication Management*, 6, 133–47.

Jhally, S. (1990) *The Codes of Advertising: Fetishism and the Political Economy of Meaning in the Consumer Society*. New York: Routledge.

Jin, B. and Lee, S. (2013) Enhancing community capacity: Roles of perceived bonding and bridging social capital and public relations in community building. *Public Relations Review*, 39, 290–2.

Jobber, D. (2010) *Principles and Practices of Marketing*, Maidenhead: McGraw-Hill.

Johnson, T. J. (1972) *Professions and Power*. London: Macmillan.

Johnston, J. (2010) Girls on screen: How film and television depict women in public relations. *PRism*, 7, 1–16.

Johnston, J. (2016) Public relations, the postcolonial *other* and the issue of asylum seekers. In J. L'Etang, D. McKie, N. Snow and J. Xifra (eds), *The Routledge Handbook of Critical Public Relations*. London: Routledge.

Jordan-Zachery, J. (2007) Am I a Black woman or a woman who is Black? A few thoughts on the meaning of intersectionality. *Politics and Gender*, 3, 254–63.

Josephs, J. (2013) Jamaica's water sector not a runaway success. *Water & Wastewater International*, 28(5). Available at: http://www.waterworld.com/articles/wwi/print/volume-28/issue-5/regional-spotlight-us-caribbean/jamaica-s-water-sector-not-a-runaway-success.html [accessed 28 November 2017].

Juris, J. (2005). The new digital media and activist networking within anti-corporate globalization movements. *Annals of the American Academy of Political and Social Science*, 597, 189–208.

Kantola, A. (2014). Mediatization of power: Corporate CEOs in soft capitalism. *Nordicom Review*, 35(2), 29–41.

Kaur, R. (2012) Nation's two bodies: Rethinking the idea of 'new' India and its other. *Third World Quarterly*, 33, 603–21.

Keating, M. (2013) Rethinking women's resistance and agency: The case of retrenched textile workers. *Labour and Industry: A Journal of the Social and Economic Relations of Work*, 23, 137–49.

Kebede, R. (2015) The high costs of Jamaica's crumbling water infrastructure. *Citylab*, 10 December.

Keller, K. (2013) *Strategic Brand Management: Building, Measuring, and Managing Brand Equity*. Harlow: Pearson Education.

Kennedy, H. (2016) *Post, Mine, Repeat: Social Media Data Mining Becomes Ordinary*. Basingstoke: Palgrave Macmillan.

Kent, M.L. (2013) Using social media dialogically: Public relations role in reviving democracy. *Public Relations Review*, 39, 337–45.

Kent, M.L. and Taylor, M. (2002) Toward a dialogic theory of public relations. *Public Relations Review*, 28, 21–37.

Kern-Foxworth, M. (1989) Status and roles of minority PR practitioners. *Public Relations Review*, 15, 39–47.

Kern-Foxworth, M. (1990) Ethnic inclusiveness in public relations textbooks and reference books. *Howard Journal of Communications*, 2, 226–37.

Kern-Foxworth, M., Gandy, O., Hines, B. and Miller, D. (1994) Assessing the managerial roles of black female public relations practitioners using individual and organizational discriminants. *Journal of Black Studies*, 24, 416–34.

Kim, I. and Dutta, M.J. (2009) Studying crisis communication from the subaltern studies framework: Grassroots activism in the wake of Hurricane Katrina. *Journal of Public Relations Research*, 21, 142–64.

Kim, K.K. and Cheng, H. (2013) Globalization, penetration, and transformation: A critical analysis of transnational advertising agencies in Asia. In M.P. McAllister and E. West (eds), *The Routledge Companion to Advertising and Promotional Culture*. New York: Routledge.

Kim, S.-Y. and Ki, E.-J. (2014) An exploratory study of ethics codes of professional public relations associations: Proposing modified universal codes of ethics in public relations. *Journal of Mass Media Ethics*, 29, 238–57.

King, D. (1988) Multiple jeopardy, multiple consciousness: The context of a Black feminist ideology. *Signs: Journal of Women in Culture & Society*, 14, 42–72.

Kipping, M. (2011) Professionals and field-level change: Institutional work and the professional project. *Current Sociology* 59, 423–42.

Kipping, M., Kirkpatrick, I. and Muzio, D. (2006) Overly controlled or out of control? Management consultants and the new corporate professionalism. In J. Craig (ed.), *Production Values: Futures for Professionalism*. London: Demos.

Klein, N. (2000) *No Logo*. London: Flamingo.

Koehn, D. (1998) *Rethinking Feminist Ethics: Care, Trust and Empathy*. London: Routledge.

Kotler, P. and Keller, K. (2009) *Marketing Management*. Upper Saddle River, NJ: Pearson/Prentice Hall.

Kotler, P., Hessekiel, D. and Lee, N. (2012) *Good Works! Marketing and Corporate Initiatives that Build a Better World . . . and the Bottom Line*, Hoboken, NJ: Wiley.

Kozinets, R.V. and Handelman, J.M. (2004) Adversaries of consumption: Consumer movements, activism and ideology. *Journal of Consumer Research*, 31, 691–704.

Krause, S. (2008) *Civil Passions: Moral Sentiment and Democratic Deliberation*. Princeton, NJ: Princeton University Press.

Krider, D. and Ross, P. (1997) The experiences of women in a public relations firm: A phenomenological explication. *International Journal of Business Communication*, 34, 437–53.

Krishnaswamy, R. (2008) Postcolonial and globalization studies: Connections, conflicts, complicities. In R. Krishnaswamy and J. Hawley (eds), *The Postcolonial and the Global*. Minneapolis, MN: University of Minnesota Press.

References

Krizsán, A., Skjeie, H. and Squires, J. (2012) *Institutionalizing Intersectionality: The Changing Nature of European Equality Regimes*. Basingstoke: Palgrave Macmillan.

Kruckeberg, D. and Starck, K. (1988) *Public Relations and Community: A Reconstructed Theory*. New York: Praeger.

Kuhn, T. (2009) Positioning lawyers: Discursive resources, professional ethics and identification. *Organization*, 16, 681–704.

Kurian, P., Munshi, D. and Bartlett, R. (2014) Sustainable citizenship for a technological world: Negotiating deliberative dialectics. *Citizenship Studies*, 18, 393–409.

Kwami, J. (2016) Development from the margins? Mobile technologies, transnational mobilities, and livelihood practices among Ghanaian women traders. *Communication, Culture & Critique*, 9, 148–68.

Ladson-Billings, G. (2000) Racialized discourses and ethnic epistemologies. In N.K. Denzin and Y.S. Lincoln (eds), *The Handbook of Qualitative Research*. Thousand Oaks, CA: Sage.

Ladson-Billings, G. (2009) 'Who you callin' nappy-headed?' A critical race theory look at the construction of Black women. *Race, Ethnicity and Education*, 12, 87–99.

Lages, C. and Simkin, L. (2003) The dynamics of public relations: Key constructs and the drive for professionalism at the practitioner, consultancy and industry levels. *European Journal of Marketing*, 37, 298–328.

Lair, D., Sullivan, K. and Cheney, G. (2005) Marketization and the recasting of the professional self: The rhetoric and ethics of personal branding. *Management Communication Quarterly*, 18, 307–43.

Lamme, M. and Miller-Russell, K. (2010) Removing the spin: Toward a new theory of public relations history. *Communication Monographs*, 11, 280–362.

Langellier, K. M. (1999) Personal narrative, performance, performativity: Two or three things I know for sure. *Text and Performance Quarterly*, 19, 125–44.

Larson, M. (1977) *The Rise of Professionalism: A Sociological Analysis*. Berkeley, CA: University of California Press.

Latour, B. (2005) *Reassembling the Social: An Introduction to Actor-Network Theory*. Oxford: Oxford University Press.

Laurison, D. and Friedman, S. (2015) Introducing the class ceiling: Social mobility and Britain's elite occupations. LSE Sociology Department Working Paper Series. London: London School of Economics.

Leach, R. (2009) Public relations and democracy. In R. Tench and L. Yeomans (eds), *Exploring Public Relations*. Harlow: Pearson Education.

Lears, T. and Jackson, J. (1994) *Fables of Abundance: A Cultural History of Advertising in America*. New York: Basic Books.

Lee, B. and LiPuma, E. (2002) Cultures of circulation: The imaginations of modernity. *Public Culture*, 14, 191–213.

Lee, S.-T. and Cheng, I.-H. (2012) Ethics management in public relations: Practitioner conceptualizations of ethical leadership, knowledge, training and compliance. *Journal of Mass Media Ethics*, 27, 80–96.

Leeper, R.V. (1996) Moral objectivity, Jurgen Habermas's discourse ethics and public relations. *Public Relations Review*, 22, 133–50.

Leeper, R.V. (2001) Argument for communitarianism. In R. Heath (ed.), *The Handbook of Public Relations*. Thousand Oaks, CA: Sage.

Lees-Marshment, J. (2001) The product, sales and market-oriented party: How Labour learnt to market the product, not just the presentation. *European Journal of Marketing*, 35, 1074–84.

Leichty, G. and Springston, J. (1996) Elaborating public relations roles. *Journalism and Mass Communications Quarterly*, 73, 467–77.

Leitch, S. and Davenport, S. (2009) Strategic ambiguity as a discourse practice: The role of keywords in the discourse on sustainable biotechnology. *Discourse Studies*, 9, 43–61.

Leitch, S. and Motion, J. (2010) Publics and public relations: Effecting change. In R. Heath (ed.), *The SAGE Handbook of Public Relations*. Thousand Oaks, CA: Sage.

Leitch, S. and Neilson, D. (2001) Bringing publics into public relations: New theoretical frameworks for practice. In R. Heath (ed.), *The Handbook of Public Relations*. Thousand Oaks, CA: Sage.

Len-Rios, M. (1998) Minority public relations practitioner perceptions. *Public Relations Review*, 24, 535–55.

Leonard, P. (2003) 'Playing' doctors and nurses? Competing discourses of gender, power and identity in the British National Health Service. *Sociological Review*, 51, 218–37.

Leonard, S. (2007) 'I hate my job, I hate everybody here': Adultery, boredom and the 'working girl' in twenty-first century American cinema. In Y. Tasker and D. Negra (eds), *Interrogating Postfeminism: Gender and the Politics of Popular Culture*. Durham, NC: Duke University Press.

L'Etang, J. (1992) A Kantian approach to codes of ethics. *Journal of Business Ethics*, 11, 737–44.

L'Etang, J. (2004) *Public Relations in Britain: A History of Professional Practice in the 20th Century*. Mahwah, NJ: Lawrence Erlbaum Associates.

L'Etang, J. (2005) Critical public relations: Some reflections. *Public Relations Review*, 31, 521–6.

L'Etang, J. (2006a) Corporate responsibility and PR ethics. In J. L'Etang and M. Pieczka (eds), *Public Relations: Critical Debates and Contemporary Practice*. Mahwah, NJ: Lawrence Erlbaum Associates.

L'Etang, J. (2006b) Public relations and propaganda: Conceptual issues, methodological problems and public relations discourse. In J. L'Etang and M. Pieczka (eds), *Public*

Relations: Critical Debates and Contemporary Practice. Mahwah, NJ: Lawrence Erlbaum Associates.

L'Etang, J. (2008) *Public Relations: Concepts, Practice, Critique.* London: Sage.

L'Etang, J. (2011) Public relations and marketing: Ethical issues and professional practice in society. In G. Cheney, S. May and D. Munshi (eds), *The Handbook of Communication Ethics.* New York: Routledge.

L'Etang, J. (2015) 'It's always been a sexless trade'; 'It's clean work'; 'There's very little velvet curtain': Gender and public relations in post-Second World War Britain. *Journal of Communication Management*, 198, 354–70.

L'Etang, J. and Piezcka, M. (1996) *Critical Perspectives in Public Relations.* London: International Thomson Business Press.

Leveson, B. (2012) *An Inquiry into the Culture, Practices and Ethics of the Press: Report.* London: The Stationery Office.

Levin, S. (2017) Pay to sway: Report reveals how easy it is to manipulate elections with fake news. *The Guardian*, 13 June.

Lewis, J., Wren, M., Williams, A. and Franklin, R. (2008) A compromised Fourth Estate? UK news journalism, public relations and news sources. *Journalism Studies*, 9, 1–20.

Lilleker, D. and Scullion, R. (2008) *Voters or Consumers: Imagining the Contemporary Electorate.* Cambridge: Cambridge Scholarly Publishing.

Lipsitz, G. (1995) The possessive investment in Whiteness: Racialized social democracy and the 'White' problem in American Studies. *American Quarterly*, 47, 369–87.

Liu, B., Levenshus, A. and Horsley, S. (2012) Communication practices of US elected and non-elected officials. *Journal of Communication Management*, 16, 220–43.

Livesey, S.M. and Kearns, K. (2002) Transparent and caring corporations? A study of sustainability reports by the Body Shop and Royal Dutch/Shell. *Organizational Environment*, 15, 233–58.

Logan, N. (2011) The White Leader prototype: A critical analysis of Race in public relations. *Journal of Public Relations Research*, 23, 442–57.

Luckman, S. (2013) The aura of the analogue in a digital age: Women's crafts, creative markets and home-based labour after Etsy. *Cultural Studies Review*, 19, 249–70.

Lüders, M. (2008) Conceptualizing personal media. *New Media & Society*, 10, 683–702.

Lugones, M. C. (1991) On the logic of pluralist feminism. In C. Card (ed.), *Feminist Ethics.* Lawrence, KS: University of Kansas Press.

Lunt, P. and Livingstone, S. (2013) Media studies' fascination with the concept of the public sphere: Critical reflections and emerging debates. *Media, Culture & Society*, 35, 87–96.

Lunt, P. and Stenner, K. (2005) The Jerry Springer Show as an emotional public sphere. *Media, Culture & Society*, 27, 59–81.

Lury, C. (2004) *Brands: The Logos of Global Economy.* London: Routledge.

MacLeod, M. and Park, J. (2011) Financial activism and global climate change: The rise of investor-driven governance networks. *Global Environmental Politics*, 11, 54–74.

Macnamara, J. (2005) *Jim Macnamara's Public Relations Handbook*. Sydney: Archipelago Press.

Macnamara, J. (2013) Beyond voice: Audience-making and the work and architecture of listening as new media literacies. *Continuum: Journal of Media and Cultural Studies*, 27, 160–75.

Macnamara, J. (2014a) Journalism–PR relations revisited: The good news, the bad news, and insights into tomorrow's news. *Public Relations Review*, 40, 739–50.

Macnamara, J. (2014b) *Journalism and PR: Unpacking 'Spin', Stereotypes and Media Myths*. New York: Peter Lang.

Manning, P. (2001) *News and News Sources: A Critical Introduction*. London: Sage.

Mansbridge, J. (1999) Everyday talk in the deliberative system. In S. Macedo (ed.), *Deliberative Politics: Essays on Democracy and Disagreement*. Oxford: Oxford University Press.

Mansbridge, J. (2003) Rethinking representation. *American Political Science Review*, 97, 515–27.

Mansbridge, J., Bohman, J., Chambers, S., Estlund, D., Follesdal, A., Fung, A., Lafont, C., Manin, B. and Martí, J.-L. (2010) The place of self-interest and the role of power in deliberative democracy. *Journal of Political Philosophy*, 18, 64–100.

Mansbridge, J., Bohman, J., Chambers, S., Christiano, T., Fung, A., Parkinson, J., Thompson, D. and Warren, M. (2012) A systemic approach to deliberative democracy. In J. Parkinson and J. Mansbridge (eds), *Deliberative Systems: Deliberative Democracy at the Large Scale*. Cambridge: Cambridge University Press.

Marchand, R. (1998) *Creating the Corporate Soul: The Rise of Public Relations and Corporate Imagery in American Big Business*. Berkeley, CA: University of California Press.

Margolis, H. (1993) *Paradigms and Barriers: How Habits of Mind Govern Scientific Beliefs*. Chicago, IL: Chicago University Press.

Marques, A. and Maia, R. (2010) Everyday conversation in the deliberative process: An analysis of communicative exchanges in discussion groups and their contributions to civic and political socialization. *Journal of Communication*, 60, 611–35.

Martin, J. and Nakayama, T. (1999) Thinking dialectically about culture and communication. *Communication Theory*, 9, 1–25.

Martin, J. and Nakayama, T. (2010) Intercultural communication and dialectics revisited. In T. Nakayama and R. Halualani (eds), *The Handbook of Critical Intercultural Communication*. Malden, MA: Wiley-Blackwell.

Mattelart, A. (2003) *The Information Society*. Thousand Oaks, CA: Sage.

McAllister-Spooner, S. (2009) Fulfilling the dialogic promise: A ten-year reflective survey on dialogic internet principles. *Public Relations Review*, 5, 320–2.

McCall, L. (2005) The complexity of intersectionality. *Signs: Journal of Women in Culture & Society*, 30, 1771–1800.

McClintock, A. (1995) *Imperial Leather: Race, Gender and Sexuality in the Colonial Conquest*. New York: Routledge.

McFall, L. (2007) Which half? Accounting for ideology in advertising. In M. Saren, P. Maclaren, C. Goulding, R. Elliot, A. Shankar and M. Catterall (eds), *Critical Marketing: Defining the Field*. Oxford: Butterworth-Heinemann.

McIntosh, P. (1997) White privilege and male privilege: A personal account of coming to correspondences through work in Women's Studies. In R. Delgado and J. Stefancic (eds), *Critical White Studies: Looking behind the Mirror*. Philadelphia, PA: Temple University Press.

McKie, D. and Munshi, D. (2007) *Reconfiguring Public Relations: Ecology, Equity and Enterprise*. Abingdon: Routledge.

McKie, D. and Xifra, J. (2016) Expanding critical space: Public intellectuals, public relations and an 'outsider' contribution. In J. L'Etang, D. McKie, N. Snow and J. Xifra (eds), *The Routledge Handbook of Critical Public Relations*. London: Routledge.

McKinney, K.D. (2005) *Being White: Stories of Race and Racism*. New York: Routledge.

McNair, B. (2004) PR must die: Spin, anti-spin and political public relations in the UK, 1997–2004. *Journalism Studies*, 5, 325–38.

McRobbie, A. (2008) *The Aftermath of Feminism*. London: Sage.

Mead, G.H. (1934) *Mind, Self, and Society*. Chicago, IL: University of Chicago Press.

Meijer, I.C. (1998) Advertising citizenship: An essay on the performative power of consumer culture. *Media, Culture & Society*, 20, 235–49.

Meisenbach, R.J. (2006) Habermas's discourse ethics and Principle of Universalization as a moral framework for organizational communication. *Management Communication Quarterly*, 20, 39–62.

Meisenbach, R.J. and Feldner, S.B. (2009) Dialogue, discourse ethics and Disney. In R. Heath, E. Toth and D. Waymer (eds), *Rhetorical and Critical Approaches to Public Relations II*. New York: Routledge.

Melanin Millennials (2017) Melanin Millennials. London: Soundcloud.

Mellese, M.A. and Müller, M.G. (2012) Mapping text–visual frames of sub-Saharan Africa in the news: A comparison of online news reports from Al Jazeera and British Broadcasting Corporation websites. *Communication, Culture & Critique*, 5, 191–229.

Merkelsen, H. (2011) The double-edged sword of legitimacy in public relations. *Journal of Communication Management*, 15, 125–43.

Messina, A. (2007) Public relations, the public interest and persuasion: An ethical approach. *Journal of Communication Management*, 11, 29–52.

Metzger, M., Flanagin, A. and Medders, R. (2010) Social and heuristic approaches to credibility evaluation online. *Journal of Communication*, 60, 413–39.

Michie, D. (1998) *The Invisible Persuaders*. London: Bantam.

Mickey, T. J. (2002) *Deconstructing Public Relations: Public Relations Criticism*. Mahwah, NJ: Lawrence Erlbaum Associates.

Miège, B. (1987). The logics at work in the new cultural industries. *Media, Culture & Society*, 9, 273–89.

Miège, B. and Garnham, N. (1979) The cultural commodity. *Media, Culture & Society*, 1, 297–311.

Miles, S. (2010) *Spaces for Consumption*. Thousand Oaks, CA: Sage.

Miller, D. (2005) Corporate public relations in British and multinational corporations. Swindon: Economic and Social Research Council.

Miller, D. and Dinan, W. (2000) The rise of the PR industry in Britain 1979–98. *European Journal of Communication*, 15, 5–35.

Miller, D. and Dinan, W. (2007) *A Century of Spin: How Public Relations Became the Cutting Edge of Corporate Power*. London: Pluto Press.

Miller, D., and Harkin, C. (2010) Corporate strategy, corporate capture: Food and alcohol industry lobbying and public health. *Critical Social Policy*, 30, 564–89.

Ministry of Women and Child Development (2016) National Policy for Women 2016: Articulating a vision for empowerment of women. New Delhi: Government of India. http://www.wcd.nic.in/sites/default/files/draft%20national%20policy%20for%20women%202016_0.pdf

Mohanty, C. (1988) Under Western eyes: Feminist scholarship and colonial discourses. *Feminist Review*, 30, 61–88.

Moloney, K. (2004) Democracy and public relations. *Journal of Communication Management*, 9, 89–97.

Moloney, K. (2006) *Rethinking Public Relations: PR Propaganda and Democracy*. Abingdon: Routledge.

Moloney, K. and McKie, D. (2016) Changes to be encouraged: Radical turns in PR theorisation and small-step evolutions to PR practice. In J. L'Etang, D. McKie, N. Snow and J. Xifra (eds), *The Routledge Handbook of Critical Public Relations*. London: Routledge.

Moor, L. (2007) *The Rise of Brands*. London: Berg.

Moran, G., Muzellec, L. and Nolan, E. (2014) Consumer moments of truth in the digital context: How 'search' and 'e-word of mouth' can fuel consumer decision-making. *Journal of Advertising Research*, 54, 200–4.

Morris, T. and Goldsworthy, S. (2008) *PR – A Persuasive Industry? Spin, Public Relations and the Shaping of the Modern Media*. Basingstoke: Palgrave Macmillan.

Mosco, V. (2009) *The Political Economy of Communication*. Thousand Oaks, CA: Sage.

Motion, J. and Leitch, S. (1996) A discursive perspective from New Zealand: Another world view. *Public Relations Review*, 22, 297–310.

Motion, J. and Leitch, S. (2002) The technologies of corporate identity. *International Studies of Management & Organization*, 32, 45–64.

Motion, J. and Leitch, S. (2007) A toolbox for public relations: The oeuvre of Michel Foucault. *Public Relations Review*, 33, 263–8.
Motion, J. and Leitch, S. (2016) Critical discourse analysis: A search for meaning and power. In J. L'Etang, D. McKie, N. Snow and J. Xifra (eds), *The Routledge Handbook of Critical Public Relations*. London: Routledge.
Motion, J. and Weaver, C.K. (2005) A discourse perspective for critical public relations research: Life Sciences Network and the battle for truth. *Journal of Public Relations Research*, 17, 49–67.
Mouffe, C. (1999) Deliberative democracy or agonistic pluralism? *Social Research*, 66, 745–58.
Mukherjee, R. and Banet-Weiser, S. (eds) (2012) *Commodity Activism: Cultural Resistance in Neoliberal Times*. New York: New York University Press.
Mumby, D.K. (1988) *Communication and Power in Organizations: Discourse, Ideology, and Domination*. Norwood, NJ: Ablex.
Mumby, D.K. (2005) Theorizing resistance in organizational studies: A dialectical approach. *Management Communication Quarterly*, 19, 19–44.
Mumby, D.K. (2011) Power and ethics. In G. Cheney, S. May and D. Munshi (eds), *The Handbook of Communication Ethics*. New York: Routledge.
Mumby, D.K. and Stohl, C. (1991) Power and discourse in organization studies: Absence and the dialectic of control. *Discourse & Society*, 2, 313–332.
Munshi, D. (2005). Through the subject's eye: Situating the other in discourses of diversity. In G. Cheney and G. Barnett (eds), *International and Multicultural Organizational Communication*. Creskill, NJ: Hampton Press.
Munshi, D. and Edwards, L. (2011) Understanding 'race' in/and public relations: Where do we start and where should we go? *Journal of Public Relations Research*, 23, 349–67.
Munshi, D. and Kurian, P. (2005) Imperializing spin cycles: A postcolonial look at public relations, greenwashing, and the separation of publics. *Public Relations Review*, 31, 513–20.
Munshi, D. and Kurian, P. (2015) Imagining organizational communication as sustainable citizenship. *Management Communication Quarterly*, 29, 153–9.
Munshi, D. and Kurian, P. (2016) Public relations and sustainable citizenship: Towards a goal of representing the unrepresented. In J. L'Etang, D. McKie, N. Snow and J. Xifra (eds), *The Routledge Handbook of Critical Public Relations*. London: Routledge.
Munshi, D., Broadfoot, K. and Smith, L. T. (2011) Decolonizing communication ethics: A framework for communicating Otherwise. In G. Cheney, S. May and D. Munshi (eds), *The Handbook of Communication Ethics*. New York: Routledge.
Munshi, D., Kurian, P., Morrison, T. and Morrison, S. (2014) Redesigning the architecture of policy-making: Engaging with Māori on nanotechnology in New Zealand. *Public Understanding of Science*, 25, 287–302.
Muzi Falconi, T. (2006) *How big is public relations (and why does it matter)? The economic impact of our profession*. Gainesville, FL: Institute for Public Relations.

Muzio, D. and Kirkpatrick, I. (2011) Introduction: Professions and organizations: A conceptual framework. *Current Sociology*, 59, 389–405.

Muzio, D., Hodgson, D., Faulconbridge, J., Beaverstock, J. and Hall, S. (2011) Towards corporate professionalization: The case of project management, management consultancy and executive search: *Current Sociology*, 59, 443–64.

Mynster, A. and Edwards, L. (2014) Building blocks of individual biography? Non-governmental organizational communication in reflexive modernity. *Management Communication Quarterly*, 28, 319–46.

Nash, K. (ed.) (2014) *Transnationalizing the Public Sphere*. Cambridge: Polity Press.

Negra, D. (2004) Quality postfeminism: Sex and the single girl on HBO. *Genders Online Journal*, 39.

Negus, K. (2002) The work of cultural intermediaries and the enduring distance between production and consumption. *Cultural Studies*, 16, 501–15.

Newsom, D. (1996) Gender issues in public relations practice. In H. Culbertson and N. Chen (eds), *International Public Relations: A Comparative Analysis*. New York: Routledge.

Nixon, S. and Du Gay, P. (2002) Who needs cultural intermediaries? *Cultural Studies*, 16, 495–500.

Noordegraaf, M. (2007) From 'pure' to 'hybrid' professionalism: Present-day professionalism in ambiguous public domains. *Administration & Society*, 39, 761–85.

Noordegraaf, M. (2015) Hybrid professionalism and beyond: (New) forms of public professionalism in changing organizational and societal contexts. *Journal of Professions and Organization*, 2, 187–206.

Nussbaum, M. (1999) The professor of parody. *New Review*, 22, 37–45.

Oakley, K. (2004) Not so cool Britannia: The role of the creative industries in economic development. *International Journal of Cultural Studies*, 7, 67–77.

Oakley, K. (2006) Include us out: Economic development and social policy in the creative industries. *Cultural Trends*, 15, 255–73.

Oesch, D. (2006) Coming to grips with a changing class structure: An analysis of employment stratification in Britain, Germany, Sweden and Switzerland. *International Sociology*, 21, 263–88.

O'Neill, J. (2002) The rhetoric of deliberation: Some problems in the Kantian theory of deliberative democracy. *Res Publica*, 8, 249–68.

Owen, D. (2007) Towards a critical theory of whiteness. *Philosophy & Social Criticism*, 33, 203–22.

Page, T. and Adams, E. (2014) Public relations tactics and methods in early 1800s America: An examination of an American anti-slavery movement. *Public Relations Review*, 40, 684–91.

Pal, M. and Dutta, M.J. (2008) Public relations in a global context: The relevance of critical modernism as a theoretical lens. *Journal of Public Relations Research*, 20, 159–79.

Papacharissi, Z. (2002) The virtual sphere: The internet as a public sphere. *New Media & Society*, 4, 9–27.

Papadopoulos, Y. (2012) On the embeddedness of deliberative systems: Why elitist innovations matter more. In J. Parkinson and J. Mansbridge (eds), *Deliberative Systems: Deliberative Democracy at the Large Scale*. Cambridge: Cambridge University Press.

Parameswaran, R. (2008) The other sides of globalization: Communication, culture and postcolonial critique. *Communication, Culture and Critique*, 1, 116–25.

Parkinson, J. (2004) Why deliberate? The encounter between deliberation and new public managers. *Public Administration*, 82, 377–95.

Parkinson, J. (2006) Rickety bridges: Using the media in deliberative democracy. *British Journal of Political Science*, 36, 175–83.

Parkinson, J. (2012) Democratizing deliberative systems. In J. Parkinson and J. Mansbridge (eds), *Deliberative Systems: Deliberative Democracy at the Large Scale*. Cambridge: Cambridge University Press.

Parsons, P. (2004) *Ethics in Public Relations: A Guide to Best Practice*. London: Kogan Page.

Patriotta, G., Gond, J. and Schultz, F. (2011) Maintaining legitimacy: Controversies, orders of worth, and public justifications. *Journal of Management Studies*, 48, 1804–36.

Peck, J. (2005) Struggling with the creative class. *International Journal of Urban and Regional Research*, 29, 740–70.

Peruzzo, C. (2009) Organizational communication in the third sector: An alternative perspective. *Management Communication Quarterly*, 22, 663–70.

Peters, C. and Witschge, T. (2015) From grand narratives of democracy to small expectations of participation: Audiences, citizenship and interactive tools in digital journalism. *Journalism Practice*, 9(1), 19–34.

Peterson, R. and Kern, R. M. (1996) From snob to omnivore. *American Sociological Review*, 61, 900–7.

Philo, G., Bryant, F. and Donald, P. (2013) *Bad News for Refugees*. London: Pluto Press.

Pieczka, M. (2000) Objectives and evaluation in public relations work: What do they tell us about expertise and professionalism? *Journal of Public Relations Research*, 12, 211–33.

Pieczka, M. (2006) Public relations expertise in practice. In J. L'Etang and M. Pieczka (eds), *Public Relations: Critical Debates and Contemporary Practice*. Mahwah, NJ: Lawrence Erlbaum Associates.

Pieczka, M. (2008) The disappearing act: Public relations consultancy in research and theory. Paper presented at the 58th Annual Conference of the International Communications Association, Montreal.

Pieczka, M. and L'Etang, J. (2006) Public relations and the question of professionalism. In J. L'Etang and M. Pieczka (eds), *Public Relations: Critical Debates and Contemporary Practice*. Mahwah, NJ: Lawrence Erlbaum Associates.

Place, K. (2015a) Binaries, continuums, and intersections: Women public relations professionals' understandings of gender. *Public Relations Inquiry*, 4, 61–78.

Place, K. (2015b) More than just a gut check: Evaluating ethical decision making in public relations. *Journal of Media Ethics*, 30, 252–67.

Place, K. and Vardeman-Winter, J. (2013) Hegemonic discourse and self-discipline: Exploring Foucault's concept of bio-power among public relations professionals. *Public Relations Inquiry*, 2, 305–25.

Place, K. and Vardeman-Winter, J. (2016) Science, medicine and the body: How public relations blurs lines across individual and public health. In J. L'Etang, D. McKie, N. Snow and J. Xifra (eds), *The Routledge Handbook of Critical Public Relations*. London: Routledge.

Pompper, D. (2004) Linking ethnic diversity and two-way symmetry: Modeling female African-American practitioners' roles. *Journal of Public Relations Research*, 16, 269–99.

Pompper, D. (2005a) 'Difference' in public relations research: A case for introducing critical race theory. *Journal of Public Relations Research*, 17, 139–69.

Pompper, D. (2005b) Multiculturalism in the public relations curriculum: Female African-American practitioners' perceptions of effects. *Howard Journal of Communications*, 16, 295–316.

Pompper, D. (2012) On social capital and diversity in a feminized industry: Further developing a theory of internal public relations. *Journal of Public Relations Research*, 24, 86–103.

Pompper, D. (2013) Interrogating inequalities perpetuated in a feminized field: Using critical race theory and the intersectionality lens to render visible that which should not be disaggregated. In C. Daymon and K. Demetrious (eds), *Gender and Public Relations: Critical Perspectives on Voice, Image and Identity*. Abingdon: Routledge.

Poor, N. (2005) Mechanisms of an online public sphere: The website Slashdot. *Journal of Computer-Mediated Communication*, 10(2).

Porter, L. (2010) Communicating for the good of the state: A post-symmetrical polemic on persuasion in ethical public relations. *Public Relations Review*, 36, 127–33.

Powell, H. (2013a) *Promotional Culture and Convergence: Markets, Methods, Media*. London: Routledge.

Powell, H. (2013b) The promotional industries. In H. Powell (ed.), *Promotional Culture and Convergence*. London: Routledge.

Projansky, S. (2007) Mass magazine cover girls: Some reflections on postfeminist girls and postfeminism's daughters. In Y. Tasker and D. Negra (eds), *Interrogating Postfeminism: Gender and the Politics of Popular Culture*. Durham, NC: Duke University Press.

Public Relations and Communications Association (2016) PR census 2016. London: Public Relations Consultants Association.

Public Relations Consultants Association (2009) The FrontLine guide to a career in PR. London: Public Relations Consultants Association.

Public Relations Institute of New Zealand (2014) PRINZ trends survey 2014. Auckland: Public Relations Institute of New Zealand.

Pullen, C. and Cooper, M. (eds) (2010) *LGBT Identity and Online New Media*. New York: Routledge.

Puwar, N. (2004) *Space Invaders: Race, Gender and Bodies out of Place*. Oxford: Berg.

Rakow, L. (1986) Rethinking gender research in communication. *Journal of Communication*, 36, 11–26.

Rakow, L. (1989) From the feminization of public relations to the promise of feminism. In E. Toth and C. Cline (eds), *Beyond the Velvet Ghetto*. San Francisco, CA: IABC Research Foundation.

Rampersad, R. (2014) 'Racialised facilitative capital' and the paving of differential paths to achievement of Afro-Trinidadian boys. *British Journal of Sociology of Education*, 35, 73–93.

Ramsey, P. (2016) The public sphere and PR: Deliberative democracy and agonistic pluralism. In J. L'Etang, D. McKie, N. Snow and J. Xifra (eds), *The Routledge Handbook of Critical Public Relations*. London: Routledge.

Reay, D. (2008) Class, authenticity and the transition to higher education for mature students. *Sociological Review*, 50, 398–418.

Reskin, B. (2012) The race discrimination system. *Annual Review of Sociology*, 38, 17–35.

Richards, I. (2004) Stakeholders versus shareholders: Journalism, business and ethics. *Journal of Mass Media Ethics*, 19, 119–29.

Richey, L. and Ponte, S. (2011) *Brand Aid: Shopping Well to Save the World*. Minneapolis, MN: University of Minnesota Press.

Ridgeway, C. and Correll, S. (2004) Unpacking the gender system: A theoretical perspective on gender beliefs and social relations. *Gender & Society*, 18, 510–31.

Rittel, H. and Webber, M. (1973) Dilemmas in a general theory of planning. *Policy Sciences*, 4, 155–69.

Rollock, N. (2012) The invisibility of race: Intersectional reflections on the liminal space of alterity. *Race, Ethnicity & Education*, 15, 65–84.

Roper, J. (2005) Symmetrical communication: Excellent public relations or a strategy for hegemony? *Journal of Public Relations Research*, 17, 69–86.

Roper, J. (2012) Environmental risk, sustainability discourses, and public relations. *Public Relations Inquiry*, 1, 69–87.

Roper, J., Ganesh, S. and Zorn, T. (2016) Doubt, delay, and discourse: Skeptics' strategies to politicize climate change. *Science Communication*, 38, 776–99.

Rosanvallon, P. (2008) *Counter-democracy: Politics in an Age of Distrust*. Cambridge: Cambridge University Press.

Ruskin, G. and Schor, J. (2009) Every nook and cranny: The dangerous spread of commercialized culture. In J. Turow and M. McAllister (eds), *The Advertising and Consumer Culture Reader*. New York: Routledge.

Saha, A. (2016) The rationalizing/racializing logic of capital in cultural production. *Media Industries*, 3.

Said, E. (1994) *Culture and Imperialism*. London: Vintage.

Saks, M. (2015) Inequalities, marginality and the professions. *Current Sociology Review*, 63, 850–68.

Saks, M. (2016) A review of theories of professions, organizations and society: The case for neo-Weberianism, neo-institutionalism and eclecticism. *Journal of Professions and Organization*, 3, 170–87.

Saldaña, M., Sylvie, G. and McGregor, S.C. (2016) Journalism–business tension in Swedish newsroom decision making. *Journal of Mass Media Ethics*, 31, 100–15.

Sallot, L.M. and Johnson, E. (2006) Investigating relationships between journalists and public relations practitioners: Working together to set, frame and build the public agenda, 1991–2004. *Public Relations Review*, 32, 151–9.

Sanders, L. (2002). Is PR marketing light? Not at conglomerates. *Advertising Age*, 30 September.

Sanders, M. (2012) Theorizing nonprofit organizations as contradictory enterprises: Understanding the inherent tensions of nonprofit marketization. *Management Communication Quarterly*, 26, 179–85.

Savage, M., Devine, F., Cunningham, N., Taylor, M., Li, Y., Hjellbrekke, J., Le Roux, B., Friedman, S. and Miles, A. (2013) A new model of social class? Findings from the BBC's Great British Class Survey experiment. *Sociology*, 47, 219–50.

Saxer, U. (1993) Public relations and symbolic politics. *Journal of Public Relations Research*, 5, 127–51.

Scammell, M. (2006) Political advertising: Why is it so boring? *Media, Culture & Society*, 28, 763–84.

Schlesinger, P. (1990) Rethinking the sociology of journalism: Source strategies and the limits of media-centrism. In M. Ferguson (ed.), *Public Communication: The New Imperative*. London: Sage.

Schölzel, H. and Nothhaft, H. (2016) The establishment of facts in public discourse: Actor-Network-Theory as a methodological approach in PR-research. *Public Relations Inquiry*, 5, 53–69.

Schroeder, R. and Ling, R. (2014) Durkheim and Weber on the social implications of new information and communication technologies. *New Media & Society*, 16, 789–805.

Schudson, M. (1989) The sociology of news production. *Media, Culture & Society*, 11, 263–82.

Schudson, M. (1993) *Advertising, the Uneasy Persuasion: Its Dubious Impact on American Society*. New York: Routledge.

Schultz, E. (2017) After Kendall Jenner ad debacle, what's next for Pepsi? *Advertising Age*, 6 April.

Schwartz-DuPre, R. L. and Scott, S. (2015) Postcolonial globalized communication and rapping the *kufiyya*. *Communication, Culture & Critique*, 8, 335–55.

Schwarz, A. and Fritsch, A. (2014) Communicating on behalf of global civil society: Management and coordination of public relations in international nongovernmental organizations. *Journal of Public Relations Research*, 26, 161–83.

Seib, P. and Fitzpatrick, K. (1995) *Public Relations Ethics*. Fort Worth, TX: Harcourt Brace.

Seiter, E. (1990) Different children, different dreams: Racial representation in advertising. *Journal of Communication Inquiry*, 14, 31–47.

Senft, T. and Baym, N. (2015) What does the selfie say? Investigating a global phenomenon. *International Journal of Communication*, 9, 1588–1606.

Sha, B.L. and Ford, R. (2007) Redefining 'requisite variety': The challenge of multiple diversities for the future of public relations excellence. In E. Toth (ed.), *Future of Excellence in Public Relations and Communication Management*. Mahwah, NJ: Lawrence Erlbaum Associates.

Shetty, S. (2016) Tackling the global refugee crisis: Sharing, not shirking responsibility. Amnesty International. https://www.amnesty.org/en/latest/campaigns/2016/10/tackling-the-global-refugee-crisis-sharing-responsibility/ [accessed 8 August 2017].

Shome, R. and Hegde, R. (2002) Postcolonial approaches to communication: Charting the terrain, engaging the inheritance. *Communication Theory*, 12, 249–70.

Silverstone, R. (2006) *Media and Morality*. Cambridge: Polity Press.

Simon, B. (2011) Not going to Starbucks: Boycotts and the out-sourcing of politics in the branded world. *Journal of Consumer Culture*, 11, 145–67.

Simpson, B. (2009) Pragmatism, Mead and the practice turn. *Organization Studies*, 30(12), 1329–47.

Singer, J. (2010) Journalism ethics amid structural change. *Daedalus*, 139, 89–99.

Sison, M. (2013) Gender, culture and power: Competing discourses on the Philippine Reproductive Health Bill. In C. Daymon and K. Demetrious (eds), *Gender and Public Relations: Critical Perspectives on Voice, Image and Identity*. Abingdon: Routledge.

Skeggs, B. (1994) Refusing to be civilised: 'Race', sexuality and power. In H. Afshar and M. Maynard (eds), *The Dynamics of Race and Gender: Some Feminist Interventions*. London: Taylor & Francis.

Skeggs, B. (1997) *Formations of Class and Gender: Becoming Respectable*. London: Sage.

Skeggs, B. (2005) The making of class and gender through visualizing moral subject formation. *Sociology*, 39, 965–82.

Skeggs, B., Thumim, N. and Wood, H. (2008) 'Oh goodness, I am watching reality TV': How methods make class in audience research. *European Journal of Cultural Studies*, 11, 5–24.

Smith Maguire, J. and Matthews, J. (2014) Introduction: Thinking with cultural intermediaries. In J. Smith Maguire and J. Matthews (eds), *The Cultural Intermediaries Reader*. London: Sage.

Smyth, R. (2001). The genesis of public relations in British colonial practice. *Public Relations Review*, 27(2), 149–61.

Soar, M. (2000) Encoding advertisements: Ideology and meaning in advertising production. *Mass Communication & Society*, 3, 415–37.

Social Mobility Commission (2017) Time for change: An assessment of government policies on social mobility 1997–2017. London: Social Mobility Commission.

Somerville, I. (1999) Agency versus identity: Actor-network theory meets public relations. *Corporate Communications: An International Journal*, 4, 6–13.

Somerville, I. and Aroussi, S. (2013) Campaigning for 'women, peace and security': Transnational advocacy networks at the United Nations Security Council. In C. Daymon and K. Demetrious (eds), *Gender and Public Relations: Critical Perspectives on Voice, Image and Identity*. Abingdon: Routledge.

Somerville, I. and Kirby, S. (2012). Public relations and the Northern Ireland peace process: Dissemination, reconciliation and the 'Good Friday Agreement' referendum campaign. *Journal of Public Relations Inquiry*, 1(3), 231–55.

Somerville, I. and Purcell, A. (2011) A history of Republican public relations in Northern Ireland from 'Bloody Sunday' to the 'Good Friday Agreement'. *Journal of Communication Management*, 15, 192–209.

Sommerfeldt, E. (2013) The civility of social capital: Public relations in the public sphere, civil society, and democracy. *Public Relations Review*, 39, 280–9.

Sommerlad, H. (1995) Managerialism and the legal profession: A new professional paradigm. *International Journal of the Legal Profession*, 2, 159–85.

Sommerlad, H. (2007) Researching and theorizing the processes of professional identity formation. *Journal of Law and Society*, 34, 190–217.

Sommerlad, H. (2008) 'What are you doing here? You should be working in a hair salon or something': Outsider status and professional socialization in the solicitors' profession. *Web Journal of Current Legal Issues*, 2.

Sommerlad, H. (2009) That obscure object of desire: Sex equality and the legal profession. In R. Hunter (ed.), *Rethinking Equality Projects*. Oxford: Hart Publishing.

Soyini Madison, D. (1993) 'That was my occupation': Oral narrative, performance and Black feminist thought. *Text and Performance Quarterly*, 13, 213–32.

Spivak, G.C. (1988) Can the subaltern speak? In C. Nelson and L. Grossberg (eds), *Marxism and the Interpretation of Culture*. Urbana, IL: University of Illinois Press.

Sriramesh, K. (1992) Societal culture and public relations: Ethnographic evidence from India. *Public Relations Review*, 18, 201–11.

Sriramesh, K. (2002) The dire need for multiculturalism in public relations education: An Asian perspective. *Journal of Communication Management*, 7, 54–70.

Sriramesh, K. (2009) Globalisation and public relations: The past, present, and the future. *PRism*, 6.

Sriramesh, K. and Verčič, D. (2007) Introduction to this special section: The impact of globalization on public relations. *Public Relations Review*, 33, 355–9.

Sriramesh, K. and Verčič, D. (eds) (2009) *The Global Public Relations Handbook: Theory, Research and Practice*. New York: Routledge.

References

Sriramesh, K. and Verčič, D. (eds) (2012) *Culture and Public Relations: Links and Implications*. Abingdon: Routledge.

St. John III, B. and Pearson, Y. (2016) Crisis management and ethics: Moving beyond the public-relations-person-as-corporate-conscience construct. *Journal of Media Ethics*, 31, 18–34.

Starck, K. and Kruckeberg, D. (2001) Public relations and community: A reconstructed theory revisited. In R. Heath (ed.), *The Handbook of Public Relations*. Thousand Oaks, CA: Sage.

Stauber, J. and Rampton, S. (1995) *Toxic Sludge Is Good for You: Lies, Damn Lies and the Public Relations Industry*. Monroe, ME: Common Courage.

Steans, J. (2003) Globalization and gendered inequality. In D. Held and A. McGrew (eds), *The Global Transformations Reader*. Cambridge: Polity Press.

Stewart, A. (2001) *Theories of Power and Domination*. London: Sage.

Stoker, K. and Stoker, M. (2012) The paradox of public interest: How serving individual superior interests fulfill public relations' obligation to the public interest. *Journal of Mass Media Ethics*, 27, 31–45.

Stokes, A. (2013) You are what you eat: Slow Food USA's constitutive public relations. *Journal of Public Relations Research*, 25, 68–90.

Stokes, S. (1998) Pathologies of deliberation. In J. Elster (ed.), *Deliberative Democracy*. Cambridge: Cambridge University Press.

Stole, I. (2013) The fight against critics and the discovery of 'spin': American advertising in the 1930s and 1940s. In M.P. McAllister and E. West (eds), *The Routledge Companion to Advertising and Promotional Culture*. New York: Routledge.

Straughan, D.M. (2004) 'Lift every voice and sing': The public relations efforts of the NAACP, 1960–1965. *Public Relations Review*, 30, 49–60.

Strömbäck, J. (2008) Four phases of mediatization: An analysis of the mediatization of politics. *International Journal of Press/Politics*, 13, 228–46.

Strömbäck, J. and Kiousis, S. (eds) (2011) *Political Public Relations: Principles and Applications*. New York: Routledge.

Sue, D.W. (2010) *Microaggressions and Marginality: Manifestations, Dynamics and Impact*. Hoboken, NJ: Wiley.

Sue, D.W., Capodilupo, C.M., Torino, G.C., Bucceri, J.M., Holder, A.M.B., Nadal, K.L. and Esquilin, M. (2007) Racial microaggressions in everyday life: Implications for clinical practice. *American Psychologist*, 62, 271–86.

Surma, A. (2016) Pushing boundaries: A critical cosmopolitan orientation to public relations practice. In J. L'Etang, D. McKie, N. Snow and J. Xifra (eds), *The Routledge Handbook of Critical Public Relations*. London: Routledge.

Surma, A. and Daymon, C. (2013) Caring about public relations and the gendered cultural intermediary role. In C. Daymon and K. Demetrious (eds), *Gender and Public Relations: Critical Perspectives on Voice, Image and Identity*. Abingdon: Routledge.

Swartz, D. (1997) *Culture and Power: The Sociology of Pierre Bourdieu*. Chicago, IL: University of Chicago Press.

Swingewood, A. (2000) *A Short History of Sociological Thought*. Basingstoke: Palgrave Macmillan.

Tackey, N.D., Barnes, H. and Khambhaita, P. (2011) Poverty, ethnicity and education. JRF Programme Paper. York: Institute for Employment Studies.

Tasker, Y. and Negra, D. (2007) Introduction: Feminist politics and postfeminist culture. In Y. Tasker and D. Negra (eds), *Interrogating Postfeminism: Gender and the Politics of Popular Culture*. Durham, NC: Duke University Press.

Taylor, M. (2010) Public relations in the enactment of civil society. In R. Heath (ed.), *The SAGE Handbook of Public Relations*. Thousand Oaks, CA: Sage.

Taylor, M. (2011) Building social capital through rhetoric and public relations. *Management Communication Quarterly*, 25, 436–54.

Taylor, M. and Doerfel, M. (2005) Another dimension to explicating relationships: Measuring inter-organizational linkages. *Public Relations Review*, 31, 121–9.

Taylor, P.C. (2016) *Black is Beautiful: A Philosophy of Black Aesthetics*. Hoboken, NJ: Wiley.

Tench, R. and Yeomans, L. (eds) (2014) *Exploring Public Relations*. Harlow: Pearson Education.

Tench, R., Zerfass, A., Verhoeven, P., Verčič, D., Moreno, A. and Okay, A. (2013) *Communication management competencies for European practitioners*. Leeds: Leeds Metropolitan University.

Terranova, T. (2000) Free labor: Producing culture for the digital economy. *Social Text*, 18, 33–58.

The Works Search (2016) Annual salary survey 2015/16 results for PR and corporate communications professionals. London: The Works.

Theaker, A. (2012) *The Public Relations Handbook*. London: Routledge.

Thévenot, L., Moody, M. and Lafaye, C. (2000) Forms of valuing nature: Arguments and modes of justification in French and American environmental disputes. In M. Lamont and L. Thévenot (eds), *Rethinking Comparative Cultural Sociology: Repertoires of Evaluation in France and the United States*. Cambridge: Cambridge University Press.

Thompson, B. and Weaver, C.K. (2014). The challenges of visually representing poverty for international non-government organisation communication managers in New Zealand. *Public Relations Inquiry*, 3(3), 377–93.

Thompson, C. (2004) Marketplace mythology and discourses of power. *Journal of Consumer Research*, 31, 162–80.

Thompson, D. (2008) Deliberative democratic theory and empirical political science. *Annual Review of Political Science*, 11, 497–520.

Thompson, J.B. (2003) The globalization of communication. In D. Held and A. McGrew (eds), *The Global Transformations Reader*. Cambridge: Polity Press.

Thörn, H. (2007) Social movements, the media and the emergence of a global public sphere: From anti-apartheid to global justice. *Current Sociology*, 55, 896–918.

References

Thornham, H. (2013) Articulating technology and imagining the user: Generating gendered divides across media. In H. Thornham and E. Weissman (eds), *Renewing Feminisms: Radical Narratives, Fantasies and Futures in Media Studies*. London: IB Tauris.

Thornham, H.M. and Gómez Cruz, E. (2018) Not just a number? NEETs, data and datalogical systems. *Information, Communication and Society*, 21, 306–21.

Thumim, N. (2012) *Self-representation and Digital Culture*. Basingstoke: Palgrave Macmillan.

Tilley, E. (2015) The paradoxes of organizational power and public relations ethics: Insights from a feminist discourse analysis. *Public Relations Inquiry*, 4, 79–98.

Tilson, D. (2006) Devotional–promotional communication and Santiago: A thousand-year public relations campaign for Saint James and Spain. In J. L'Etang and M. Pieczka (eds), *Public Relations: Critical Debates and Contemporary Practice*. Mahwah, NJ: Lawrence Erlbaum Associates.

Tindall, N. (2007) Identity, power, and difference: The management of roles and self among public relations practitioners. Unpublished doctoral dissertation, University of Maryland, College Park.

Tindall, N. and Waters, R. (2012) Coming out to tell our stories: Using queer theory to understand the career experiences of gay men in public relations. *Journal of Public Relations Research*, 24, 451–75.

Tindall, N. and Waters, R. (2013) *Coming Out of the Closet: Exploring LGBT Issues in Strategic Communication with Theory and Practice*. New York: Peter Lang.

Titscher, S., Meyer, M., Wodak, R. and Vetter, E. (2000) *Methods of Text and Discourse Analysis*. London: Sage.

Toledano, M. (2010) Professional competition and cooperation in the digital age: A pilot study of New Zealand practitioners. *Public Relations Review*, 36, 230–7.

Tolson, A. (2010) A new authenticity? Communicative practices on YouTube. *Critical Discourse Studies*, 7, 277–89.

Toth, E. (1988) Making peace with gender issues in public relations. *Public Relations Review*, 14, 36–47.

Toth, E. (2006) Building public affairs theory. In C.H. Botan and V. Hazelton (eds), *Public Relations Theory II*. Mahwah, NJ: Lawrence Erlbaum.

Toth, E. and Cline, C. (eds) (1989) *Beyond the Velvet Ghetto*. San Francisco, CA: IABC Research Foundation.

Toth, E. and Grunig, L. A. (1993) The missing story of women in public relations. *Journal of Public Relations Research*, 5, 153–75.

Trenwith, L. (2010) The emergence of public relations in New Zealand from 1945 to 1954: The beginnings of professionalisation. *New Zealand Journal of Applied Business Research*, 8, 51–62.

Trigg, A. (2001) Veblen, Bourdieu, and conspicuous consumption. *Journal of Economic Issues*, 35, 99–115.

Turow, J. (2006) *Niche Envy: Marketing Discrimination in the Digital Age*. Cambridge, MA: MIT Press.

Turow, J. (2011) *The Daily You: How the New Advertising Industry Is Defining Your Identity and Your Worth*. New Haven, CT: Yale University Press.

Tyler, I. (2008) 'Chav mum, chav scum': Class disgust in contemporary Britain. *Feminist Media Studies*, 8, 17–34.

United Nations Refugee Agency (2017) Global response. Geneva: United Nations Refugee Agency. http://refugeesmigrants.un.org/global-response [accessed 8 August 2017].

Urbaniti, N. and Warren, M. (2008) The concept of representation in democratic theory. *Annual Review of Political Science*, 11, 387–412.

USC Annenberg Center for Public Relations (2016) Global communications report 2016. Los Angeles, CA: University of Southern California.

Üstüner, T. and Holt, D. B. (2010) Toward a theory of status consumption in less industrialized countries. *Journal of Consumer Culture*, 37, 37–56.

Van Dijck, J. (2013) *The Culture of Connectivity: A Critical History of Social Media*. Oxford: Oxford University Press.

Van Dijk, T.A. (1977) *Text and Context: Explorations in the Semantics and Pragmatics of Discourse*. Harlow: Longman.

Van Dijk, T.A. (1996) Discourse, power and access. In C. Caldas-Coulthard and M. Coulthard (eds), *Texts and Practices: Readings in Critical Discourse Analysis*. London: Routledge.

Van Leeuwen, T. (2008) *Discourse and Practice: New Tools for Critical Discourse Analysis*. Oxford: Oxford University Press.

Vardeman-Winter, J. (2011) Confronting whiteness in public relations campaigns and research with women. *Journal of Public Relations Research*, 23, 412–41.

Vardeman-Winter, J. and Tindall, N. (2010) 'If it's a woman's issue, I pay attention to it': Gendered and intersectional complications in The Heart Truth media campaign. *PRism*, 7.

Vardeman-Winter, J., Tindall, N. and Jiang, H. (2013) Intersectionality and publics: How exploring publics' multiple identities questions basic public relations concepts. *Public Relations Inquiry*, 2, 279–304.

Verhoeven, P. (2008) Who's in and who's out? Studying the effects of communication management on social cohesion. *Journal of Communication Management*, 12, 124–35.

Victor, D. and Stevens, M. (2017) United Airlines passenger is dragged from an overbooked flight. *New York Times*, 10 April.

Vilanilam, J. (2011) *Public Relations in India: New Tasks and Responsibilities*. New Delhi: Sage.

Vivienne, S. (2017) 'I will not hate myself because you cannot accept me': Problematizing empowerment and gender-diverse selfies. *Popular Communication: The International Journal of Media and Culture*, 15, 126–40.

Voyce, M. (2006) Shopping malls in Australia: The end of public space and the rise of 'consumerist citizenship'? *Journal of Sociology*, 42, 269–86.

Waisbord, S. (2013) *Reinventing Professionalism: Journalism and News in Global Perspective*. Cambridge: Polity Press.

Wang, Y., Cheney, G. and Roper, J. (2015) Virtue ethics and the practice–institution schema: An ethical case of excellent business practices. *Journal of Business Ethics*, 138, 67–77.

Ward, S. (2005) Philosophical foundations for global journalism ethics. *Journal of Mass Media Ethics*, 20, 3–21.

Ward, S. and Wasserman, H. (2010) Towards an open ethics: Implications of new media platforms for global ethics discourse. *Journal of Mass Media Ethics*, 25, 275–92.

Waring, J. (2014) Restratification, hybridity and professional elites: Questions of power, identity and relational contingency at the points of 'professional–organisational intersection'. *Sociology Compass*, 8, 688–704.

Waters, R., Tindall, N. and Morton, T. (2010) Media catching and the journalist-public relations practitioner: How social media are changing the practice of media relations. *Journal of Public Relations Research*, 22, 241–64.

Watson, T. and Noble, G. (2007) *Evaluating Public Relations: A Best Practice Guide to Public Relations Research, Planning and Evaluation*. London: Kogan Page.

Waymer, D. (ed.) (2012) *Culture, Social Class, and Race in Public Relations: Perspectives and Applications*. Lanham, MD: Lexington Books.

Wearing, S. (2007) Subjects of rejuvenation: Ageing in postfeminist culture. In Y. Tasker and D. Negra (eds), *Interrogating Postfeminism: Gender and the Politics of Popular Culture*. Durham, NC: Duke University Press.

Weaver, C.K. (2001) Dressing for battle in the new global economy: Putting power, identity and discourse into public relations theory. *Management Communication Quarterly*, 15, 279–88.

Weaver, C.K. (2011) Public relations, globalization, and culture: Framing methodological debates and future directions. In N. Bardhan and C.K. Weaver (eds), *Public Relations in Global Cultural Contexts: Multi-paradigmatic Perspectives*. New York: Routledge.

Weaver, C.K. (2013) Mothers, bodies and breasts: Organizing strategies and tactics in women's activism. In C. Daymon and K. Demetrious (eds), *Gender and Public Relations: Critical Perspectives on Voice, Image and Identity*. Abingdon: Routledge.

Weaver, C.K. and Motion, J. (2002) Sabotage and subterfuge: Public relations, democracy and genetic engineering in New Zealand. *Media, Culture & Society*, 24, 325–43.

Weaver, C.K., Motion, J. and Roper, J. (2006) From propaganda to discourse (and back again): Truth, power, the public interest and public relations. In J. L'Etang and M. Pieczka (eds), *Public Relations: Critical Debates and Contemporary Practice*. Mahwah, NJ: Lawrence Erlbaum Associates.

Weber, L. (2001) *Understanding Race, Class, Gender and Sexuality: A Conceptual Framework*. New York: McGraw-Hill.

Wernick, A. (1991) *Promotional Culture: Advertising, Ideology and Symbolic Expression*. London: Sage.

Whelehan, I. (1995) *Modern Feminist Thought*. Edinburgh: Edinburgh University Press.

Wilensky, H. (1964) The professionalization of everyone? *American Journal of Sociology*, 70, 137–58.

Williams, R. (1958) *Culture and Society 1780–1950*. London: Chatto and Windus.

Williams, R. (1980) Advertising: The magic system. *Problems in Materialism and Culture*. London: New Left.

Williamson, J. (1978) *Decoding Advertisements*. London: Marion Boyars.

Willis, P. (2012) Engaging communities: Ostrom's economic commons, social capital and public relations. *Public Relations Review*, 38, 116–22.

Willis, P. (2014) Preach wine and serve vinegar: Public relations, relationships and doublethink. *Public Relations Review*, 41, 681–8.

Witz, A. (1992) *Professions and Patriarchy*. London: Routledge.

Wolf, K. (2016) Diversity in Australian public relations: An exploration of practitioner perspectives. *Asia Pacific Public Relations Journal*, 17, 62–77.

Woofitt, R. (2005) *Conversation Analysis and Discourse Analysis: A Comparative and Critical Introduction*. London: Sage.

Wright, D. (2005) Mediating production and consumption: Cultural capital and 'cultural workers'. *British Journal of Sociology*, 56, 105–21.

Wydick, D. (2014). 10 reasons fair trade coffee doesn't work. *The Huffington Post*. https://www.huffingtonpost.com/bruce-wydick/10-reasons-fair-trade-coffee-doesnt-work_b_5651663.html [accessed 10 December 2017].

Yang, A. and Taylor, M. (2013) The relationship between the professionalization of public relations, societal social capital and democracy: Evidence from a cross-national study. *Public Relations Review*, 39, 257–70.

Yaxley, H. (2013) Career experiences of women in British public relations (1970–1989). *Public Relations Review*, 39, 156–65.

Yeomans, L. (2010) Soft sell? Gendered experience of emotional labour in UK public relations firms. *PRism*, 7.

Yeomans, L. (2013) Gendered performance and identity in PR consulting relationships: A UK perspective. In C. Daymon and K. Demetrious (eds), *Gender and Public Relations: Critical Perspectives on Voice, Image and Identity*. Abingdon: Routledge.

Yeomans, L. (2016) Imagining the lives of others: Empathy in public relations. *Public Relations Inquiry*, 5, 71–92.

Yosso, T.J. (2005) Whose culture has capital? A critical race theory discussion of community cultural wealth. *Race, Ethnicity and Education*, 8, 69–91.

Zaharna, R.S. (2001) 'In-awareness' approach to international public relations. *Public Relations Review*, 27, 135–48.

Zerfass, A., Moreno, A., Tench, R., Verčič, D. and Verhoeven, P. (2017) European Communication Monitor 2017. Brussels: EACD/EUPRERA.

References

Zerfass, A., Verčič, D., Verhoeven, P., Moreno, A. and Tench, R. (2012). European Communication Monitor 2012: Challenges and competences for strategic communication. Results of an empirical survey in 42 countries Brussels: EACD/EUPRERA.

Zoller, H. (2004) Dialogue as global issue management: Legitimizing corporate influence in the transatlantic business dialogue. *Management Communication Quarterly*, 18, 204–40.

Zwick, D., Bonsu, S.K. and Darmody, A. (2008) Putting consumers to work. *Journal of Consumer Culture*, 8, 163–96.

INDEX

Abbott, A., 148
aboriginal tribes, 91
Absolutely Fabulous, 190
access, 113–14
accountability, 88–9, 92
activism, 15, 28, 42, 43n, 50, 56–7, 72, 73, 79, 81, 88, 92, 99, 107, 117, 122, 124, 133, 177, 184–5, 219, 220
Adams, Mark, 207
advertising, 24, 25, 26, 29, 30, 31, 74, 82
advertorials, 47
advocacy, 204
Africa, 77
African-American, 174, 187
age, 79–80, 170, 187
agency, human, 8, 9
agonistic pluralism, 112
Akita Inu Tourism, 35–6
Alchemy Festival, 172–3
Aldoory, L., 182, 188
algorithms, 16, 27, 113, 212, 224
American Heart Association, 174
Amnesty International, 55, 115
anti-colonial movements, 73
anti-globalisation movement, 18
anti-racism movements, 73
anti-slavery movements, 73
Appadurai, A., 123, 127–8, 133, 134, 138
Arab League, 219
archives, 40
Aronczyk, M., 27, 32, 136
Ashcraft, K., 156
Asia, 77tab, 122, 173
Asia-Pacific Economic Cooperation forum, 219
associations, industry, 40, 60, 143, 147, 149, 150, 152, 158n
asylum-seekers, 173
attention economy, 4
audiences, 74, 75–6
austerity, 150
Australia, 174, 184

Bauman, Z., 127
beauty blogging/vlogging, 33–4, 220
beer, 210
Bell Pottinger, 211
Benkler, Y., 18
Bhopal, 211, 214n
big data, 14, 16, 27
black aesthetics, 176
black feminism, 165, 186–8, 193, 195n
black-boxed knowledge, 18
blogs, 4, 15, 33–4, 35–6, 70, 117, 151, 220
BlueFocus, 76, 77tab, 131
Boltanski, L., 12, 46–7, 48–9, 53–4, 55, 61
boundary spanner, 202, 214n
Bourdieu, Pierre, 46–7, 48, 58–61, 62, 175
Bourne, C., 50
Bowen, S., 204
branding, 4, 10, 14, 24, 29, 31, 74, 82, 156
Brazil, 164, 206–7
Breese, E.B., 110
Brewdog, 210
Brexit, 135–6
Bridget Jones, 190
bullying, 170
Burkart, R., 205, 207
Butler, Judith, 180, 182–3, 185–6, 187, 192, 194, 195

campaign level, public relations, 97
campaigns, 87, 97, 99–100, 109, 110, 158, 167, 170
Canadian Energy Pipeline Association, 91
capital, 72, 130, 131, 133, 166
capitalism, 2, 74, 124, 213
Castells, M., 93
Centre for Research and Analysis of Migration, 135
centres of calculation, 17–18
Channel 4, 4
charities, 39, 55, 74, 137, 175
Chartered Institute of Public Relations (CIPR), 149, 154, 168

Cheney, G., 199, 201
China, 76, 77tab, 131, 132, 153
China International Public Relations Association, 153
Christiano, T., 93
Christians, C., 208
circuit of culture, 24, 34–41
circulation, 75–6
cisgender, 6, 20n
citizen engagement, 119n
citizen forums, 87
citizen journalists, 15, 145
citizen voices, 117
citizenship, 26
civic world, 54, 56, 57
civic engagement, 42
civil society, 28, 39, 86, 96, 104, 107, 108, 208, 218
class, 6, 9, 58, 79–80, 82, 112, 152, 155–6, 162–77, 180, 186, 188
client sovereignty, 155
climate change, 93, 116, 222–3
Climate Justice Taranaki, 56–7
closed ethics, 213
Coates, R., 164
codes of practice, 143, 198, 199
collective welfare, 56
colonisation, 130, 131, 132, 166
commodification, 66, 67–8, 74–6
common good, 54, 55, 58, 87
common worlds, 54
communication, 66–70, 183, 201, 208
communication ethics, 201
communication networks, 17
communication science, 108
communicative action, 111
communicative capitalism, 43n
communicative reason, 111
communitarianism, 107
conformity-through-choice, 189, 190, 191
conscience, ethical, 202, 204
consequentialism, 198, 202
constructivism, 124, 194
consultancies, 76–9, 82, 122, 146, 148, 149, 150, 152, 154
consumer public relations, 69, 114, 169, 172
consumption, 75–6
consumption, moment of, 35, 38
consumption labour, 29
control, 66
core-periphery relations, 76–9
corporate activism, 28

corporate social responsibility, 39, 54, 133, 175
corporations *see* multinational corporations
Couldry, N., 96
counter-public spheres, 110, 114, 117
craft beer, 210
creative industries, 30, 173
Creedon, P., 181, 182, 183, 188
critical race theory, 176
critical theory, 66, 68, 128
cultural capital, 166
cultural flows, 123, 127–8, 130, 133, 134, 135, 138
  see also flows
cultural industries, 68, 70, 73, 82, 176
cultural intermediaries, 39–41, 43n, 60–1, 219
cultural norms, 4, 5, 24, 26, 30, 37, 41, 42, 123, 124, 134, 156
  see also norms
cultural-economic model, 34
culture, 25–9, 34, 40, 130
Curran, J., 119n
Curtin, P.A., 34
customer loyalty, 74
customer sovereignty, 158

Dahlberg, L., 111–12
Dahlgren, P., 113
damage limitation, 30
data analytics, 16
datafication, 14, 16
Davis, A., 28
Daymon, C., 209
decisiveness, 89
deepening, 123
deficiencies, 165
degrees, 60, 148
deliberation, 86, 89, 94
deliberative capacity, 90
deliberative democracy, 86–8, 89, 104, 112
deliberative quality, 94–7
deliberative systems, 86–7, 88–94, 96–7, 98
Demetrious, K., 73
democracy, 62, 72–3, 86–100, 208
Dentsu Public Relations, 35–6
deontology, 198, 204
deregulation, 13, 142
developed countries, 76, 77, 119n, 130, 180
developing countries, 76–7, 79, 130
dialectic of control, 8
digital age, 9, 12, 13, 14–17, 74, 98
digital channels, 27
digital communication, 27, 124
digital marketing, 82

digital skills, 156
digital technologies, 14–17, 24, 92, 194
　see also digital age
digitisation, 67, 106
Dinan, W., 71
Dirlik, A., 122, 124
disabled people, 4, 80, 97, 155, 180, 192
disagreement, 11–12
discipline, occupational, 150–1
discourse
　Bourdieusian approach to, 58–61, 62
　definition, 100n
　discourse analysis, 47
　discourse ethics, 198, 205, 207–8
　discourse technologists, 51, 63
　Foucauldian discourse theory, 49–52, 61–2, 218
　justificatory discourses, 53–8, 62
　nature of, 46–9
　public relations as profession, 144, 148
　race and class in public relations, 169–70
　as technology of public relations' professional project, 151–4
discrimination, 99, 162, 163–6, 167, 168, 170, 171, 174, 180, 186
discursive democracy, 94–5
disembedding, 123, 128
dissymmetry, 188
distanciation, 14, 123, 128
distributed deliberation, 90
diversity, 168–9, 172–3, 177n, 187, 188
Doerfel, M., 108
domestic violence, 81, 180
domestic world, 54
double jeopardy, 188
Dove, 192
Dryzek, J., 88–9, 90, 94–5, 100n
dual closure, 155

economic status, 163
Edelman, 77tab, 146, 154
electoral-representative democracy, 86
Emirbayer, M., 8
emotion, 90, 99, 111, 112
emotional labour, 184, 190
employment status, 163
empowered spaces, 88, 89, 92, 100
empowerment, 189
energy industry, 91, 96
engagement, 95, 97, 98, 100n, 119n
English language, 113
environment, 70
environmental journalism, 114

environmental protection, 86, 92, 110, 139
environmental sustainability see sustainability
equal opportunities policies, 162, 180
equality, 156, 162, 168, 180, 181
Escobar, A., 127
ethics
　of care, 209
　closed and open, 213
　communication, 201
　communitarian, 208
　conflicting priorities, 200
　discourse, 198, 205, 207–8
　ethical conscience, 202, 204
　ethical dialectics, 201–2
　ethical management, 198
　feminist, 208–9
　globalised, 210–11
　persuasion, 199–200, 202–3, 204–5
　powerful clients, 201
　of promotion, 211–12
　in public relations, 198–9
　rational-emotional dialectic, 201, 204–5
　self-interest, 200
　socio-cultural turn, 206–12
　theoretical-practical/academic-lay dialectics, 201, 202–3
　universal-particular/global-local dialectics, 201, 203–4
ethnicity, 6, 58, 68, 151, 155–6, 167, 170, 172–3, 187
　see also race
ethnoscapes, 127, 135, 136
Etsy.com, 190–1
European Union, 115, 135–6, 219
Evetts, J., 154
Ewen, S., 158n
exchange value, 67, 74, 75
exclusion, 155–7, 162, 170
executive strategy, 76
expert systems, 124, 128
extensity, 123, 124
eye-witness footage, 15

Facebook, 16, 132
fact-checking, 106
fair trade, 129
Fairclough, N., 48
fake news, 15, 25, 223
fashion, 192, 220
Fawkes, J., 199–200, 203, 204
female genital mutilation, 39, 81

273

Index

feminism
  gender discrimination, 180
  liberal and radical, 181–2
  public sphere, 114
  Rape Crisis England and Wales (RCEW), 99–100
  see also women
field of power, 175
fields, 158n
fifth estate, 116
finance, of consultancies, 76, 77tab, 78
financescapes, 127, 130, 131, 133, 135, 136
financial crises, 13, 124
financial journalism, 114
financial markets, 51
Fitch, K., 184, 190, 193
fixity, 126–7, 133, 136
  see also mobility-fixity dialectic
flows, 127–8, 131, 137
Foucault, M., 48, 49–52, 61–2, 143, 144, 207–8, 218
fourth estate, 105
France, 76, 77tab
Frankfurt School, 70
Fraser, N., 109–10
free labour, 27
free market system, 13, 142
Fuchs, C., 113
Fur Out Campaign, 35–6

Gaither, T.K., 34
Galloway, C., 198, 214n
Gandy, O., 71
Gaonkar, D.P, 36
gay, 4, 79, 110, 184, 185, 192, 210
  see also LGBT
gender, 6, 58, 82, 97, 145, 152, 155–6, 170
  discrimination, 79, 180, 181, 186, 187–8, 195
  equality, 52–3, 86, 93, 184
  performativity, 182–6, 188
general public, 109
generalisable interests, 94–5, 96, 98, 100n
generalised other (Mead), 8
genres, 49
genuine engagement, 95, 98, 100n
Giddens, A., 8, 10, 14, 123
global flows, 138, 219
  see also flows
global industry, 122
global modernity, 122, 134
global South, 79, 92, 125, 129, 130, 167, 177, 204, 211, 222, 223
global structures, 130–3

globalisation, 2, 12, 17, 67, 74, 111, 122–4, 125–8, 130–5, 136–7, 211, 220
glocalisation, 124
Go Red for Women campaign, 174
Goldsworthy, S., 202–3
Golombisky, K., 180, 183, 186, 193
Goodin, R., 90
government communication, 173
grassroots organisations, 26–7, 39, 79, 81, 87, 107
green world, 54, 56, 57
Grunig, J.E., 181–2, 189–90

Habermas, J., 11, 104, 105, 108, 109, 111, 198, 205, 207
habitus, 59–60, 150, 151, 152, 154, 155
Hall, S., 10, 164, 167
Harrison, K., 198, 214n
Harvey, D., 124, 126–7
health campaigns, 50, 174–5, 188
heart disease, 174
Heath, R., 108
hegemony-resistance dialectic, 126, 137
Held, D., 124
heterosexuality, 6, 184, 189, 193
Hiebert, R., 107
hierarchy, 149
higher education, 18, 51
Hill+Knowlton Strategies, 77tab, 78, 146, 154
Hodges, Caroline, 5, 20n
Hon, L.C., 181, 182
human rights, 51, 55, 92, 110, 139, 222

I (Mead), 8
ideal speech situation, 111
identity, 9–11
identity, moment of, 35, 37–8, 39
identity scripts, 157
ideoscapes, 127, 128, 131, 133, 135, 136
imaginary worlds, 27
imagination, 128, 134, 136, 138
in-awareness approach, 124
inclusivity, 95, 97, 109, 111
India, 4, 52–3, 169, 172–3
Indignados movement, 18
industrial world, 54, 56, 57
industry associations, 40, 60, 143, 147, 148, 149, 150, 152, 158n
inequality, 7, 13, 71, 94, 125, 127, 133, 138, 149, 162, 165, 180
inequality regimes, 151
influencers, 30
infrasystem, 181, 183, 195

274

in-house public relations, 82
inscribed information, 18
inspired world, 54
Instagram, 4, 16, 38
instrumental reason, 111
intensity, 123, 124
interdiscursivity, 52
interest groups, 93
intermediaries, 30
International Monetary Fund, 13, 132, 219
international non-governmental organisations (INGOs), 27
International Olympic Committee (IOC), 207
internet, 16, 106, 112–13, 124
intersectionality, 176, 177n, 180, 186, 187–8, 193, 195n
intertextuality, 52, 190
issue level, public relations, 97

Jamaica, 131–2
Japan, 35–6
Jensen, I., 107
Jordan-Zachery, J., 186
journalism, 72, 82, 105, 106–7, 114, 116, 118, 206, 208, 210
jurisdiction, 144–8, 151–2, 154, 156
justice, 55, 57, 125, 137, 138, 139, 187, 214, 224
justificatory discourses, 47, 53–8, 62

Kaitiaki, 56
Kapper, Alma, 187
Keating, M., 174
Ketchum, 77tab, 78
knowledge-based occupations, 142
Koehn, D., 208–9
Krider, D., 184
Kruckeberg, D., 107
Kurian, P., 224
Kwami, J., 125

labour movements, 175
language, 58–63, 130, 206
Latina, 180, 187
Lee. B., 32
legitimacy, 53, 55, 56–7, 58, 62, 86, 144–5, 147, 148, 151, 152, 154, 156
legitimation, 55, 57
Leitch, S., 62–3, 107
lesbian, 180, 186
L'Etang, J., 70–1, 158n, 200
LGBT, 6, 193, 194, 210
   see also gay; lesbian; transgender

liberal feminism, 181, 182
lifeworld organisations, 107
liminal space, 195n
linguistic capital, 58
linguistic fields, 58–9
linguistic hierarchy, 59
linguistic markets, 58
LiPuma, E., 32
listening, 109
lived experiences, 170–2
lobbying, 96, 100, 145
local-global dialectic, 126, 137

Macnamara, J., 109
Madison, Soyina, 187
madness, 49
managerial tasks, 149
Manning, P., 67, 72
Mansbridge, J., 90
Maori, 56–7
Marchand, R., 71
marginalised groups, 92–3
market world, 54, 56, 57
marketisation, 14, 16, 26, 68
marketplace mythologies, 30
markets, 13–14
materiality, 52
McGrew, A., 124
McNair, B., 107
me (Mead), 8
Mead, George Herbert, 8
meaning, 24, 31–2, 35, 36, 41–2, 124, 128, 152
media
   hierarchies, 118
   industries, 177
   media relations, 69, 70, 76, 106, 118
   organisations, 105, 106–7, 116–17
   training, 69, 74
mediascapes, 127, 128, 133, 135, 136
mediated sociality, 117
mediation, 138
mediatised capitalist democracy, 28
Meisenbach, R.J., 205, 207
menstruation, 4
Messina, A., 204
micro-aggressions, 171, 188
Miège, B., 68–9, 73, 82
migration, 39, 50, 51, 124, 127, 135–6, 138, 173, 174, 222
Miller, D., 71
Mische, A., 8
mobile media, 80, 117, 124

mobility-fixity dialectic, 126–7, 131, 137
modernity, 2, 10, 53, 122, 124, 126, 133, 134, 176, 190
Mofu Mofu Dogs (Fluffy Dogs), 35–6
Moloney, K., 72–3, 212
moments of fixity, 130
moments of truth, 33
moral reasoning, 205
Morris, T., 202–3
Mosco, V., 66–8, 73
motion, 138
Motion, J., 62–3
Mouffe, C., 111–12
MSL Group, 77tab, 78
multinational corporations, 27, 79, 116, 122
Mumby, D.K., 213
Munshi, D., 224

narrative, 188, 195n
National Black Public Relations Society, 168
National Policy for Women (India), 52–3
National Test of Occupational Qualification of PR Practitioners, 153
National Water Commission (NWC), Jamaica, 131–2
nationalism, 125, 126
nation-states, 111, 125, 126
neoliberalism, 13–14, 26, 42, 67, 71, 72, 74, 82, 98, 125, 142, 149, 151, 169, 173, 177, 189, 191, 193, 209
neo-Weberian analysis, 143, 144
network analytics, 97
network governance, 93, 98
network logic, 93–4
network theories, 17, 32
networked communication, 82, 92, 124, 212, 220
networked societies, 2, 13, 17–18, 93, 109, 111, 112
networked technologies, 75
networking, 151, 171, 188
networks, 74
New Zealand, 51, 56–7
news media, 72, 116, 117, 119n
No Label, 210
non-binary, 183, 195n
non-governmental organisations (NGOs), 27, 86, 92, 115, 116, 117, 130, 219, 222, 223
Noordegraf, M., 147
norms, 4, 7, 8, 24, 30, 39, 41, 67, 89, 97, 124, 133, 156, 157, 209
  see also cultural norms
not-for-profit sector, 149, 220

occupational field, 142, 144, 148–9, 152, 155, 157, 158n
Ogilvy PR, 77tab, 78
oil industry, 91, 96
Olympics (Rio 2016), 206–7
Omnicom, 78
one-drop rule, 164
online activism, 16
online communication, 27, 76, 80, 109, 112–13, 116
online journalism, 116
open ethics, 213
orders of discourse, 49
orders of worth, 54, 55, 56–7, 58
organizing professions, 147
'other,' 9, 16, 24, 97, 125, 137, 156, 163, 165, 167, 171, 173, 177, 188, 209, 211
outsiders-within, 187
Owen, D., 165–6, 177n

Papacharissi, Z., 113
Papadopoulos, Y., 93, 112
Paralympics, 4
performativity
  black feminism and, 186–8
  gender, 182–6
  intersectionality and, 193
  postfeminism and, 188–92
personalisation, 212
Peters, C., 119n
Philippines, 185
Pieczka, M., 148, 158n
pigeonholing, 170, 188
pigmentocracy, 166
pipelines, oil, 91
Place, K., 50, 184
plebiscitary rhetoric, 87
political economy, 66–82
political marketing, 43n
Pompper, D., 187, 189
postcolonial theory, 125–6, 137, 156, 177, 211
postfeminism, 188–92, 193, 194–5
poststructuralism, 194
post-truth, 223
Potter Box, 202, 204
Povinelli, E., 36
power, 6, 8–9, 17–18, 32, 40, 42, 46–7, 48–52, 53, 54, 55, 58, 59, 61–2, 63, 67, 70, 76, 105, 114, 119n, 125, 126, 144, 152, 157–8, 162, 198, 200, 206, 207–8
  see also symbolic power
press releases, 106

Index

privacy, 42
private sphere, 189, 190
Proctor and Gamble, 4
product launch campaigns, 27
production, 75–6
production, moment of, 34, 38
productive sociality, 81
professional projects, 144–58
professionalisation, 142–3, 144, 152–4, 158n, 167
professionalism, 142, 143, 144, 147, 152–4, 155, 158n, 166
professions, 143–5, 146, 147–8
programmers, 17
promotional industries
   advertising, branding and public relations, 29–31
   histories of, 43n
   promotional intermediaries, 24, 39–41
   society and culture, 25–9
   YouTube, 33–4
propaganda, 200, 205
pseudo-preferences, 87
public engagement, 146, 147
public health campaigns, 50
public interest, 94–5, 208
Public Relations, Society and Culture, 2
public spaces, 88, 89, 112
public sphere
   defending public relations, 107–9
   feminist-oriented, 114
   Jürgen Habermas, 105
   new developments in theory, 109–13
   online, 112–13
   plurality of participants, 109–10, 111–12
   power differentials across, 114
   public relations and, 106–7
   transnationality, 111, 114, 115–16, 125
   variability in access, practice and influence, 113–14
Publicis Groupe, 78
publicity, 87

queer theory, 194

race, 6, 20n, 79–80, 82, 97, 145, 151, 152, 155–6, 162–77, 186, 188
   see also ethnicity
racialisation, 164, 165, 166, 167, 171, 175
racism, 73, 162, 164, 165, 176
radical feminism, 181–2
Rakow, L., 182, 183
Ramsey, P., 112

Rape Crisis England and Wales (RCEW), 99–100
rationality, 111, 112, 113
Real Beauty campaign, 192
recontextualisation, 47
Referendum, on EU membership, 135–6
reflexivity, 8, 9, 10, 95, 97, 175, 203, 219
refugees, 127, 136, 137, 173, 222
regeneration, 173
regimes of truth, 49, 50, 62
regulation, moment of, 34, 38–9
regulatory matrix, 182, 183, 185, 188, 194, 195
relationship management, 146, 148, 202
religious organisations, 219
representation, 35, 36–7, 39, 92
Reproductive Health Bill, 185
reputation, 74, 145, 148, 150, 212
resource allocation, 220
revenues, of consultancies, 76, 77tab, 78
rhetoric, 90, 100, 202
Rio de Janeiro (2016 Olympics), 206–7
risk, 126, 137, 149, 212
Rittel, H., 195
role theory, 182
Roper, J., 51
Ross, P., 184
rural communities, 80
Russia, 115

Saha, A., 176–7
Saks, M., 149
same-sex marriage, 110
sampling, 219
scripts, 184
search engine optimisation, 16, 27
second-wave feminism, 189
self-help, 74
self-interest, 88, 90
self-representations, digital, 15, 16
Sex and the City, 190
sexism, 184
sexual violence, 52–3, 92, 99–100
sexuality, 97, 180, 182
   see also gay; heterosexuality; LGBT
Shell, 56–7
signifiers, 10, 29, 167
Sison, M., 185
situational ethics, 198, 203
Skeggs, B., 8–9, 164
sociability, 151, 169, 170, 171
social capital, 96, 104, 108, 118, 166, 181, 208
social class *see* class

Index

social closure, 144
social cohesion, 108, 208
social commons, 108
social constructivism, 124, 194
social logics, 68–70, 74, 76, 82
social media, 10, 15, 25, 32, 68, 69–70, 75, 80, 81, 97, 109, 123, 206
social mobility, 7, 9, 144, 156
social movements, 15, 18, 28, 87, 88, 97, 107, 112
social structures, 6–7
socialisation, 150
sociality, 8
society, 25–9, 67
socio-cultural research, 2–6, 19, 218–24
socio-cultural turn, 3, 4, 6, 20, 20n, 199, 206, 207, 211, 213, 214, 218
South Africa, 77, 211
South Asia, 172–3
Southbank Centre, 172–3
spatialisation, 66, 67, 68, 74, 76–9
spin, 107, 198
sponsorship, 30, 76
Sriramesh, K., 169
Standing Rock Sioux tribe, 91
standpoint theory, 193, 221
Starck, K., 107
stereotyping, 170, 186, 188
Stoker, K. & M., 208
strategic action, 111
strategic counsel, 185
strategic planning, 74
stratification, 79
structuration, 66, 67, 68, 74, 79–81
styles, 49
subaltern groups, 126, 129, 133, 134–5, 211, 220, 224
Superhumans campaign, 4
Surma, A., 209
surveillance, 15, 16, 25
surveys, industry, 167
sustainability, 51, 55, 56–7, 137
switchers, 17, 18
symbolic capital, 60
symbolic power, 41, 47, 48, 58, 60, 61, 166
see also power
symbolic violence, 59–60
Syrian civil war, 115, 222
systemic level, public relations, 97, 98
systems approach, 89, 90
systems organisations, 107
systems theory, 181, 195n

Taiwan, 35–6
TARES model, 202, 204
tasks, 148–9, 155
Tati (beauty vlogger), 33–4
Taylor, M., 108
Taylor, P.C., 176
technical tasks, 149
technoscapes, 127, 133, 135, 136
teleology, 202, 204
territorialism, 125
terrorism, 117, 124, 219
texts, 152
Thévenot, L., 12, 48–9, 53–4, 61
Third, A., 184
third cultures, 134
third gender, 195n
third space feminism, 193, 194
Thompson, C., 30
Tilley, E., 213
time-space distanciation, 14, 123, 128
Tindall, N., 184, 188
Toth, E., 181–2
Touch the Pickle campaign, 4
tourism, 132
training, 148, 149
traits perspective, 143, 154
transcultural spaces, 134
transgender, 183, 195n, 210
see also LGBT
translation role, 93, 98
transmission, 88
transnational corporations, 124, 125, 126, 128, 131, 150
transnational feminism, 193
transnational promotional class (TPC), 27, 124
transnational public relations associations, 122
transnationality, 111, 113, 114, 115–16, 125
True Blood, 190
Trump, Donald, 91
trust, 51, 199, 205, 208
truth, 49–50, 61–2, 208, 223
Twitter, 4, 16, 75, 132

Union Carbide, 211, 214n
United Kingdom, 71, 135–6, 143, 167, 168–9, 187
United Nations, 115, 125, 132, 137, 219
United States of America, 71, 76, 77tab, 91, 115, 122–3, 130, 164, 168, 174
unmediated communication, 117
Urbaniti, N., 94
use value, 67, 74, 75
utilitarianism, 198

278

Vardeman-Winter, J., 50, 188
velocity, 123
viral campaigns, 27, 30, 42, 75, 81, 206
virtual sphere, 113
virtue ethics, 198, 205
vlogs, 4, 33–4
voice, 52, 95–6, 97, 98, 105

Ward, S., 206, 210–11, 213
Waring, J., 150
Warren, M., 94
Wasserman, H., 206, 213
water, 131–2
Waters, R., 184
Watson, Tom, 43n
Waymer, D., 173
wealth, 67
Weaver, C.K., 184–5
Webber, M., 195
Weber Shandwick, 77tab, 154
websites, consultancy, 146, 148, 149, 150
whiteness, 6, 149, 151, 155, 165–6, 167, 168, 170, 172, 176, 177n, 184, 188, 191
will to power, 50
will to truth, 49, 50
Williamson, J., 26

Willis, P., 108
Witschge, T., 119n
Witz, A., 156
womanist feminism, 193–4
women
 activism, 184–5
 discrimination, 180
 entry into professions, 146
 exclusion from public sphere, 109
 health communication campaigns, 174–5
 in public relations, 151, 155
 rights, 114
 violence against in India, 52–3
 see also feminism
World Bank, 13, 125
world of fame, 54
World Trade Organization, 18, 125, 219
WPP, 78

Yeomans, L., 184, 190
Yosso, T.J., 166
YouTube, 33–4, 70, 132

Zaharna, R.S., 124
Zika virus, 206

Made in the USA
Lexington, KY
21 January 2019